FEUDAL GERMANY

James Westfall Thompson

VOLUME II

FREDERICK UNGAR PUBLISHING CO.
New York

Republished 1962

First published 1928

Second printing, 1966

Printed in the United States of America

Library of Congress Catalog Card No. 62-17093

TABLE OF CONTENTS

VOLUME I. OLD WEST FEUDAL GERMANY

VOLUME II. NEW EAST FRONTIER COLONIAL GERMANY

APPENDIX

INDEX

LIST OF MAPS

VOLUME II

NEW EAST FRONTIER COLONIAL GERMANY

CHAPTER XII

THE GERMAN CHURCH AND THE CONVERSION OF THE SLAVS OF THE ELBE

RELIGION was a highly developed institution among the Slavs, and—at least among the Baltic and Elbean Wends—the priest class was an influential caste.[1] The most striking fact of their belief was the dualism which pervaded it.[2] It was like ancient Manicheism, or like the belief of the Cathari in this respect.[3] They deified the forces of nature like many primitive peoples, and a black horse, sacred to the local god, was an object of great veneration among them, and was used as an instrument of divination.[4]

The Wendish temples[5] were imposing structures, usually built of wood, but that of Triglav in Brandenburg was of stone. The two most famous Slavonic fanes were those of the god Riedegost or Redigast, of which the Redarii were cus-

[1] Upon the religion of the Wends see *Mythology of All Races* (Gray and Moore, ed.; Boston, 1918), III, 2; Lippert, *Socialgesch. Böhmens*, II, 1–11; G. Krek, *Einleitung in die slavische Literatur* (4th ed., 1906), pp. 84 f.; *Cambridge Mediaeval History*, Vol. II, chap. xiv; Hauck, *Kirchengesch, Deutschlands*, III, 69–87; Schulze, *Kolonisierung*, pp. 19–43, 86–116; Lavisse, *La Marche de Brandenbourg*, pp. 10–15; Wendt, *op. cit.*, I, 16–18; Guttmann, *Forschungen zur Preuss. und Brandenb. Gesch.*, IX, 400–403; Bernard, *De Adamo Bremensi Geographo* (1895), pp. 63–71; Fisher, *Mediaeval Empire*, II, 3–6. Adam of Bremen, II, 18; III, 50; IV, 18; Herbordus, II, 31–33, 35; III, 6–7, 22–23, 36; Ebbo, II, 13; III, 1, 3–8; Helmold, I, 6, 52, 69, 83; II, 12; Thietmar, VI, 17–18, 23–25, are the fullest sources.

[2] "Est autem Slavorum mirabilis error; nam in conviviis et compatacionibus suis pateram circumferunt, in quam conferunt, non dicam consecracionis, sed execracionis verba sub nomine deorum, boni scilicet atque mali, omnem prosperam fortunam a bono deo, adversam a malo dirigi profitentes. Unde etiam malum deum lingua sua Diabol sive Zcerneboch, id est nigrum deum, appelant" (Helmold, *Chron. Slav.*, I, 52).

[3] Gieseler, *Ueber den Dualismus der Slaven*, pp. 357 f.; Schmidt, *Histoire des Albigeois*, I, 7–8; II, 271–72.

[4] Herbordus, *Vita Ottonis ep. Babenb.* II, 33.

[5] Hauck, *Kirchengesch.*, III, 84–85, has collected all the references to them.

todians, at Rethra;[1] and that of the god Svantowit at Arkona in the island of Rügen. Rethra was so completely destroyed in 1121 by Lothar, then duke of Saxony, that its exact location was unknown for centuries, but it was supposed to have been upon the Tollensee.[2]

One of the romances of modern archaeology is the discovery and excavation of the site of Rethra. In the year before the late war the Prussian Academy granted a subsidy to Professor C. Schuchardt to make a complete archaeological survey of the remains of the Slavs in the old Wendish territory east of the Elbe. The war interrupted the plan. But in 1918 the survey was begun anew. At this time a young German Assyriologist named Robert Koldewey, whose researches in Mesopotamia were ruined by the war, was associated with Professor Schuchardt. For four summers these two scholars labored. In 1921 their excavations were in Rügen where they discovered and excavated the ruins of the temple of Arkona, disclosing a large square measuring sixty feet each way, with four columns in the interior and traces of the pedestal upon which the figure of the god Svantovit had once stood, exactly as Saxo Grammaticus described it in 1168. Then in the next summer (1922) Rethra was unearthed. The discovery was made through the description of it by Bishop Thietmar of Merseburg. Thietmar, who was of Saxon noble lineage and count of Waldeck, was related to the Saxon imperial house and regularly accompanied Emperor Henry II on his military expeditions against the Slavs. In the course of relating one of these expeditions Thietmar entered into a minute description of Rethra in his *Chronicon*, VI, 23. It is described as a "three-horned castle with three gates." On the east side it sloped toward a lake, and on the west was bor-

[1] It is minutely described by Thietmar, VI, 23. Cf. Adam of Bremen, II, 18, and Helmold, I, 2. According to Schafarik, *Slav. Alterth.*, II, 580, *Rethra* meant "war temple." In Adam of Bremen, III, 21, schol. 71 (77), is an account of how two Bohemian monks penetrated into this sanctuary in 1050 while a *concilium paganorum* was in session, and were discovered and after being tortured were put to death.

[2] Lisch, *Jahrb. d. Ver. f. Mecklenb. Gesch. und Alterthumsk.*, III, 21; *Jahrb. Heinr. II*, I, 260; Schmeidler, *Hamburg-Bremen und Nord-Ost Europa* (1918), pp. 341–60.

dered by a thick belt of virgin forest. Of the three gates, two were on the land side, but the third was a water gate.

The salient point of this description was the *urbs tricornis ac tres in se continens portas*, or "three-horned castle having three gates." The different conjectures of historians as to the meaning of this term explain the long and vain search for the location of Rethra. Both *urbs* and *tricornis* had been misunderstood. The former was erroneously taken to mean "a town," or even "a district," and the latter was thought to signify a three-cornered structure similar to ancient Slavonic triangular forts built by the Slavs upon peninsulas or bends in the rivers, remains of which have been found in the Havel at Ziegenhorn, Schildhorn, and Bestehorn.[1] Thus Thietmar's *urbs tricornis* was erroneously taken to have been an island with three points. Accordingly, previous archaeologists had painfully and for years (1880–1908) explored all the islands in the lakes of Mecklenburg only to find in the end that Rethra was upon no one of them.

Professor Schuchardt, who is both a historian and an archaeologist, knew that in feudal times the word *urbs* meant "a castle," "a fortified place." Accordingly, he assumed that the "horns" of the temple of Rethra must have been vertical not horizontal projections, or, in other words, were towers probably with gates in them, which thus would explain the allusion to the three gates. Hence an *urbs tricornis tres in se continens portas* meant "a castle with three towers," which, seen from a distance, had the appearance of a trident. With this new interpretation in mind the two scholars began a survey of the territory and at last near Feldberg found a physiography which seemed to answer to the requirements. On the east side the site sloped 36 meters toward Lake Lucin. On the west it is to this day girdled for miles by a magnificent forest of beech. Even without digging, remains of a former wall revealed ruins of two gates—one on the north, the other on the south. The third had to be found by excavation, and, as expected, the spade unearthed it in the middle of the west

[1] In each of these cases the suffix "-horn" is a later corruption of Old German *-holm*, meaning "an islet," and has nothing to do with "horn."

side, toward the land. This was not all that was uncovered, however. For later a great outer wall was revealed encircling the three-towered inner *urbs*, which was at once a temple and a castle.

As the whole original structure had been built of wood, towers, gates, and palisades, almost everything had succumbed to the flames when Rethra was destroyed by the German army under Lothar in 1121. But the ends of the timbers which had been set deeply in the ground on blocks of stone and charred débris plainly told the tale. The West Gate was the largest of the three gates. When the East Gate was excavated, striking archaeological evidence confirmatory of Thietmar's description was revealed. For it was the *tercia* [*porta*] *quae orientem respicit et minima est*, *tramitem ad mare*, although nothing was found by this gate to explain Thietmar's *visu nimis horribile*. But it may be conjectured that some imposing figure had once stood in the gate. Unfortunately, not a remnant of evidence remained of the carved idols of the gods and goddesses once worshiped by the Slavs in this temple and portrayed as clad in coats-of-mail, and not a vestige of the gold-and-silver adornment or votive offerings was found which the Bishop of Merseburg describes apparently from the description of an eyewitness.[1] Within the inner compound were found storehouses and magazines like cellars for the storage of supplies, but nothing was in them except a few pieces of shattered pottery. The castle or *urbs* was not large, measuring 115 meters long and 45 wide. But the zone between the *urbs* and the outer ringwall was large enough to accommodate ten thousand people. The whole view of Rethra must have been a striking one—the earliest rays of the rising sun reaching it across the shining

[1] "Hujus parietes variae deorum dearumque imagines mirifice insculptae, ut cernentibus videtur, exterius ornant; interius autem dii stant manu facti, singulis nominibus insculptis, galeis atque loricis terribiliter vestiti." If the statement be a true one that the name of each god and goddess was carved upon the pedestal upon which the sacred figure stood, then the Slavs of the Elbe possessed a written language which, since they were intensely pagan and hostile to Christianity, could have had no relation with the Cyrillian writing of the southern Slavs at this time.

surface of the lake rippled by the morning breeze, while behind the temple loomed the dark beech forest.[1]

Herbordus, in his *Life of Otto of Bamberg* (II, 32),[2] describes the temple of the three-headed god Triglav, one of four temples in Stettin, with some minuteness. "It had sculptures [carved wooden figures?] within and without, and from the walls projected images of men, beasts, birds, the appearance of which was so natural that they might have been thought to be living and breathing." These figures were brightly decorated with colored paints of such quality that

> the colors of the images outside could not be dimmed or washed off either by snow or rain. Into this temple the people brought, in accordance with the ancient custom of their ancestors, the stores and arms of their enemies which they had captured, and whatever spoils they took by land or by sea, as they were directed to do by the law relating to the giving of a tenth.[3] They had also preserved there for the honor and adornment of their gods, horns of wild bulls [the aurochs] covered with gold and set with gems, some for use as drinking horns, and others as musical instruments; swords, too, and knives, and much rich furniture which was rare and beautiful in appearance.

The temple roofs were steep and pointed. The temples often stood in a compound of considerable extent, walled in by a palisade. The right of asylum prevailed within this area, which was also used for public and tribal conferences. As among the druids, the oak seems to have been a sacred tree, and fine specimens of it grew within the temple inclosures. Often the temples were erected within groves of oaks, especially if a spring were there too.

But all this religion, about which we know so little and of which we would know more, was devoted to utter destruction by the bigotry and intolerance of the Christian church.

[1] The first revelation of these discoveries was made by Professor Schuchardt in *Sitzungsber.* of the Berlin Academy for 1921. Since then the complete history of these excavations has been published under the title *Arkona*, *Rethra*, *Vineta* (Berlin: H. Schoetz & Co.). The second edition has recently appeared (1926). A briefer notice of the history is found in *Forschungen und Fortschritte* (Berlin: November 1, 1926), pp. 178–79.

[2] Cf. another description of the temple of Triglav (II, 13, and III, 1). In III, 6, is an account of that of Gerovit (Mars) at Hologast.

[3] Helmold, II, 12, also mentions tithes—*tributa annuatim.*

Commingled with this iconoclastic spirit was also a covetousness on the part of the German clergy which almost baffles belief.

Ever since the conversion of Saxony the temple of Rethra was an object of hatred by Christian Germany. For all opposition to missionary endeavor among the Slavs of the Elbe, every Slavonic rebellion, every lapse to paganism again, emanated from the fanatical priesthood in Rethra. It was the greatest sanctuary of all the Slavs, and like Delphi among the ancient Greeks. The oracle of Rethra was consulted from far and near, even by Christian Danish kings. Upon its walls hung the colored banners of every Slavonic tribe between the Erzgebirge and the Baltic, and the trophies of victorious wars.[1] The priests of Rethra cast omens before every campaign. With them lay final determination of war and peace.

Neither the German church nor the German nobles were willing to let time work out the problem of race contact between the German and the Slav, and permit the gradual transfusion of blood between them and the slow transforming influences of civilization to resolve the issues. There can be little doubt that this might have been possible.[2]

[1] "Vexilla quoque eorum nisi ad expeditionem necessaria et tunc per pedites, hinc nullatenus moventur" (Thietmar, VI, 23 *ad fin.*).

[2] The chronicles have preserved a number of examples of cross-marriages between the aristocracy of both races. About the year 1000 a certain Wendish nobleman named Pribislav eloped with Matilda, the sister of Dietrich of the Nordmark, who was a nun in a convent in Magdeburg. Pribislav was assassinated by two Saxons who were hired by the angry Margrave; whereupon his brother, who had forsaken paganism and become a priest under the German name Liudolf, abandoned his cowl and set forth to avenge his brother's murder, but was apprehended and returned to the church by Henry II. (See the account in Thietmar, IV, 64.) Matilda afterward fell into the hands of a Slav adventurer named Boliliut, an ex-companion of a Saxon outlaw named Kiza, who took her to wife. Helmold, I, 13, cites the case of an Abodrite chieftain named Billug who married the sister of Wago, bishop of Oldenburg. The border was the home of the German outlaw, who fraternized with the Wends (Helmold, I, 19). The most notorious instance of this is the case of the two nephews of Hermann Billung, Wicmann and Ecbert, who quarreled with their uncle and fled to the protection of two Abodrite chieftains, Nako and Stoinef (Widukind, III, 50–51; *Annals of Quedlinburg; Annals of Hildesheim* (955); Thietmar, II, 6, 12–13). In this connection the observation of the Polish historian Dlugoss as to the same process in Poland is interesting ". . . . Prefecti castrorum et munitionum civitatum cis Albim sitarum ab obedientia deditioneque Miecslai regis regnique sui Poloniae deficere ceperunt ignavia desidiaque regis et Almanorum affinitate, qua invicem dando accipiendoque uxores junxerant eis defectionis materiam" (*Hist. Polon.* [ed. Lips, 1711], I, Book II, 184).

The missionary zeal of the medieval German church was hardened with an alloy of worldly self-interest which gave a harsh edge to its pious professions, and the cure of souls was prevailingly subordinated to its hunger for land and its appetite for rich endowments. As early as 591 the synod of Aquileia, representing the Bavarian church, had complained of the tyranny of the Frankish church.[1] Through the efforts of Boniface, the organizer of four Bavarian bishoprics, the Bavarian law of the eighth century "encouraged" donations to the church to the point of compulsion, and punished the murder of a bishop with an impossibly huge fine, or slavery. In the same century, in Ober-Franken, again through Boniface's zeal, and that of Sturm his disciple, the see of Würzburg (741) and the monasteries of Fulda (744) and Hersfeld (769) were founded and heavily endowed with manors and tithes.[2]

The avarice of the medieval church had early been manifested. A synodical letter of the second Council of Tours (566 or 567) exhorted all faithful to imitate the example of Abraham and to pay tithes. But this exhortation failed to produce the desired effect, and in 585 the Council of Macon, after having enjoined all to offer a tithe of their substance at the altar every Sunday, "in order to effectuate the removal of their sins and to have a lot in the merits of Abel" (canon 4), ordained the payment of altar tithes under penalty of excommunication (canon 5). This Council audaciously declared that the tithe was of apostolic foundation and professed the desire to "restore." Yet the formulas of Marculf (*ca.* 650) contain no allusion to the tithe.

Toward the end of the seventh century, however, the practice of the church of exacting a tithe of the price of land transfers seems to have become general. By menace of excommunication, by intimidation, by preying upon the minds of the ignorant and superstitious through attributing natural calamities like droughts and floods to failure to pay tithes, the clergy worked upon the people. In 742 Pepin con-

[1] Riezler, *Geschichte Bayerns*, I, 90.

[2] For Würzburg see Kretschmer, sec. 176; for Fulda and Hersfeld, sec. 103. Tangl has studied the privilege of Fulda in *Mitth. d. Inst. f. oesterr. Gesch.*, Band XX, Heft 2 (1899).

ferred the right to collect tithes upon Fulda. Under Charlemagne in 779 a capitulary converted into positive law, civil and perpetual, what had hitherto been only pious not ecclesiastical obligation, and made permanent what had been merely occasional and voluntary practice. In 794 another capitulary imposed excommunication on those who refused to pay tithes.[1] In 813 the Council of Arles extended the tithe from agricultural produce to industry and commerce. In 909 the synod of Trosly in France imposed the tithe upon servile as well as free craftsmen. In the twelfth century we find the same thing in Germany—a tithe upon agriculture, trade, and industry.

The missionary propaganda of the German church in the Middle Ages was largely a money-making proposition.[2] Christians had to pay tithes, so the "saving of souls" became a lucrative commercial interest. The border peoples, if conquered but unconverted, were subject only to tribute, and the wealth thus acquired went into secular coffers. But evangelization offered spiritual rewards and declared substantial dividends of a material nature for the benefit of the church.[3] Alcuin, in the time of Charlemagne, rebuked Bishop Arno of Salzburg for inhuman treatment of the Slavs in Styria and Carinthia, upon whom he cruelly imposed the tithe.[4]

[1] *Cap. Wormat.* (794): "Qui decimas, post creberrimas admonitiones et praedicationes sacerdotum, dare neglexerint, excommunicentur."

[2] Adam of Bremen, II, 5; III, 22.

[3] Lavisse, *La Marche de Brandenbourg*, p. 37, caustically remarks: "Charlemagne, en assignant aux sièges épiscopaux qui auraient envoyé des missionaries en pays païen une part des revenus payés par les convertis, avait excité l'avidité en même temps que l'émulation des évêques, et les conflits qui éclataient entre les divers diocèses n'étaient point faits pour persuader aux païens que les prêtres de Jésus-Christ ne voulaient que le salut de leurs âmes."

[4] *Monum. Alcuin.* (ed. Jaffé), VI, 301, Ep. 64. So, too, in 796 Alcuin, after the conquest of the Avars, asked Charlemagne to "consider whether it is a good thing to impose on a rude people like this at the beginning of their faith the yoke of tithes, exacted in full amount and from every house." Alcuin even had the moral courage and the critical acumen to challenge the whole system of imposing tithes. For he goes on: "It is to be considered whether the apostles, who were taught by Christ himself and sent forth by him for the evangelization of the world, ever ordered the exaction of tithes, or demanded that they should be given to them" (Ep. 67). For other letters of Alcuin protesting against exploitation of *rudes populi* see *MGH. Epistolae*, IV, 154, No. 107 (796); No. 110, pp. 157–59 (796); No. 111, pp. 159–62

The sordid motives of the German church, in spite of its smooth language and professions of piety, come out strongly in the correspondence between Boniface and Pope Zacharias in 751. Boniface had propounded the question to the Pope whether the tithe should be imposed upon Slav serfs working the church lands. The reply of the pontiff is luminous for the light which it casts upon the inner motives of the church. "Yes," said Zacharias, "for if they do not pay tribute they will think the land is theirs. But if they are made to pay tithes they will know who is lord of the land."[1]

The German clergy for generations connived with Jewish merchants to promote a traffic in Slavonic slaves with the Mohammedan realms of Spain and Egypt. I subjoin two quotations:

Those who especially enjoyed his [the caliph's] confidence were the body known as "Slavs"; it is from Abd-er-Rahman's reign that their influence dates . . . . .

Originally the name of "Slavs" [Arabic, *Saqâliba*] was applied to prisoners captured by the Germanic nations in their wars against Slavonic tribes, and sold by them to the Saracens of Spain; but in course of time a multitude of men belonging to other races began to be classed as "Slavs," and the name was applied to all foreigners who served in the harem, or in the army, whatever their origin. The Cordovan chroniclers call Otto I "king of the Slavs." An Arab traveller of the tenth century explicitly states that the Slavs who were the retainers of the khalif of Spain comprised Galicians, Franks [French and German], Lombards, Calabrians and natives of the northern coasts of the Black Sea. Some of them had been captured by Andalusian pirates; others had been purchased in Italian ports —for the Jews, trading upon the distress of the people, trafficked in children of both sexes and brought them to the sea-ports whence they were

---

(796); No. 113, p. 164 (796). Cf. Hodgkin, *Italy and Her Invaders*, VIII, 149; Justus Moeser, *Osnabr. Gesch.*, I, 189; Lamprecht, *DWL*, I, 2, 872.

[1] *Epp. Bonifacii* (ed. Jaffé), III, 226, No. 80: *Boniface:* "An census a Slavis Christianorum terras incolentibus recipiendus?" *Zacharias:* ". . . . si enim tributo sederint, ipsam quandoque propriam sibi vindicabunt; si vero tributum dederint, norunt dominatorem ipsam habere terram." See also Schafarik, II, 607. Cf. a similar response in *Monum. Boica*, XXVIII, 1, 268 (996), and see Giesebrecht, *Jahrbücher des deutschen Reiches unter Otto II und Otto III*, p. 29, n. 1. It is no wonder that apologists for Boniface, like Fischer (*Bonifatius*, pp. 204 ff.), endeavor to disprove the genuineness of the letters. Sommerlad, *Die wirtschaftliche Tätigkeit der Kirche in Deutschland*, Vol. I, chap. iv, and Stutz, *Gesch. des kirchlichen Benefizialwesens* (1895), are valuable accounts of the land policy of the church in Germany in the seventh and eighth centuries.

carried in Greek or Venetian vessels to their Saracen purchasers. Another class, namely the eunuchs, destined to be attendants in the harems, were imported from France, where large establishments for the supply of these creatures existed, under the direction of Jews: that of Verdun was far-famed [Liutprand, *Antapodosis*, VI, 6; Richer, IV, 103], and there were others in the south [Reinaud, *Invasions des Sarrasins en France*, pp. 233 f.].[1]

With the fourth caliph El-Mo'izz, the conqueror of Egypt [953–75], the Fatimids entered upon a new phase. . . . . He was highly educated and not only wrote Arabic poetry and delighted in its literature, but studied Greek, mastered Berber and Sudani dialects, and is even said to have taught himself Slavonic in order to converse with his slaves from eastern Europe.[2]

The Saxon clergy, perhaps more hungry for landed possessions than even the lay feudality, was not to be deterred from the lucrative business of evangelizing the Wends across the lower Elbe River, whose "conversion" would pour tithes into their coffers and whose toil could be made to exploit the church's lands. It is charitable to indulge the thought that the missionary tradition of Anskar and the monastery of Corvey inspired the aspirations of the German church at this time. But the facts belie this rosy assumption. Charlemagne's conversion of the Saxons by force of arms had established a precedent fatal to the preservation of the liberties of the Baltic Slavs. The issue of the conversion of the Wends had first been raised by Boniface, and the prospect had haunted the mind of the cultured and gentle Alcuin. Since then a century and a half had elapsed and nothing had been done. It was high time, argued the church. For it was unthinkable that the theory of the royal prerogative could tolerate rule over a pagan people.[3]

[1] Dozy, *Spanish Islam*, p. 430.

[2] Lane Poole, *Egypt in the Middle Ages*, pp. 99–101.

[3] This idea comes out clearly in the coronation of Otto I. "Accipe hunc gladium," said the Archbishop of Mainz, "quo eicias omnes Christi adversarios, barbaros et malos Christianos, auctoritate divina tibi tradita omni potestate totius imperii Francorum, ad firmissimam pacem omnium Christianorum" (Widukind, II, 1). For comment see Waitz, VI, 163 ff. The same thought is expressed by Frederick I in the *Canonizatio Caroli Magni* in 1166: "In fide quoque Christi dilatanda, et in conversione gentis barbaricae fortis athleta fuit, sicut Saxonia et Fresonia Hispanis quoque testantur et Wandali, quos ad fidem catholicam verbo convertit gladio" (Harz., *Conc.*, III, 399–400). Adam of Bremen, II, 5, thinks the Slavs of the Elbe were ingrates and should have been grateful for the blessings of Christianity and

In the case of Otto I, his religion was politic and his piety "practical" in the most concrete sense of that term. He was indifferent to the conversion of the Wends, but he could not be indifferent to the demands of the bishops. Accordingly, his reign saw a terrible series of military expeditions and missionary forays across the lower Elbe against the Baltic Slavs, by which the land was conquered as far as the Peene River.[1] Precisely as Charlemagne had utilized the administrative system of the church to extirpate the Saxon tribal organization in Saxony,[2] so the apparatus of the German church was now imposed upon the subjugated Wends in order to crush them.[3] "Ex nomine victorum provincias quoque vocabula sortitas." Beyond the Elbe, a swarm of bishoprics arose—half houses of God, half fortresses. Oldenburg was the earliest episcopal erection at an unknown date.[4] It was an ancient Wendish town, so old that it was called Old Town (Starigard).[5] Havelberg was founded in 946, Brandenburg in 948,[6] Merseburg in 967,[7] Meissen and Zeitz (later removed to

---

tribute which the German conquest imposed upon them: "Otto Sclavos tanta virtute constrinxit ut tributum et Christianitatem pro vita simul et patria libenter offerrent victori."

[1] Sommerfeld, *Gesch. der Germanisierung des Herzogtums Pommern*, p. 10.

[2] "Capitulatio de partibus Saxoniae" (Boretius, *MGH*, *Leges*, I, 2, No. 26, p. 68); cf. the spurious charter for Bremen in Sickel, *Acta Karol.*, II, 393–94, and the interesting statement of Adam of Bremen, I, 13: "Huic parrochiae decem pagos subjecimus, quos etiam abjectis eorum antiquis vocabulis et divisionibus in duas redigimus provincias, his nominibus appellantes, Wigmodiam et Lorgoe."

[3] Cf. Widukind, II, 38; Adam of Bremen, II, 24; Thietmar, II, 20, 22; Helmold, I, 14, 17.

[4] Hauck, III, 105, n. 5; Dehio, *Gesch. des Erzbistums Hamburg-Bremen*, Append. XII; Curschmann, *Diözese Brandenburg*, p. 19, n. 3, think the year was 948. For further information see Kretschmar, *Historische Geographie von Mitteleuropa*, sec. 258.

[5] "Ea quae Slavica lingua Starigard, hoc est antiqua civitas," says Helmoldus the Holsteiner antiquarian of the twelfth century (I, 12). The Germans simply transliterated the name. The derivation is obvious. *Stara* means "old" and *gard* is the same as *grad*, a universal Slav suffix for "town." The Serbian today distinguishes a part of his kingdom by the term *Stara Srbiya*—"Old Serbia." On the foundation of Oldenburg see Curschmann, *Hist. Vierteljahrschrift* (1911), No. 1.

[6] Kretschmer, secs. 270–71.

[7] *Ibid.*, sec. 267.

Naumburg) in 968.[1] The Archbishop of Magdeburg was ecclesiastical ruler, "tocius ultra Albiam et Salam." Manors, tithes, tribute, were showered upon the new bishoprics in the Slav lands by the Ottos,[2] and the "New Plantation" for a season enjoyed great peace and prosperity.[3] "Through the mercy of God and the valor of Otto the Great," Helmold piously exclaims, "complete peace prevailed everywhere; the wastes of Wagria and of the province of Schleswig began to be peopled, nor was there any corner left which was not conspicuous for its towns and villages, and also its many monasteries."[4]

Forcible, wholesale conversion of the Abodrites, the Wilzi, etc., and the imposition of tithes and tribute became the order of the day.[5] The synod of Tribur in 1036 resolved "quod omnes Sclavi decimas dent."[6] The synod of Bamberg in 1059 expressly declared that increase of the tithes was a just motive for forcible conversion of the Slavs.[7] These tithes

[1] *Ibid.*, secs. 268–69.

[2] "Munificentia principis Ottonis cumulati essent temporalium rerum affluentia, unde possent copiose largiri et favorem sibi populi consciscere" (Helmold, I, 12).

[3] "Novella Plantacio [Helmold, I, 12, 14] . . . . in summa prosperitate" (*ibid.*, 13).

[4] Helmold, I, 12.

[5] "Ipse [Otto I] tanta virtute deinceps constrinxit, ut tributum et christianitatem pro vita simul et patria libenter offerrent victori, baptizatusque est totus gentilium populus" (Adam of Bremen, II, 5). "Pax continua fuit, Sclavi sub tributo servierunt" (*ibid.*, 24). "Tribut und Christentum, so heisst es in charakteristischer Verbindung, mussten sie bieten, damit man sie bei Land und Leben lasse" (Guttmann, *op. cit.*, p. 433).

[6] "Constitutiones et acta pub. imperatorum et regum" (*MGH*, *Leges*, IV, 89, sec. 6; cf. Bresslau, *Jahrbücher Konrads* II, 529.

[7] Jaffé, V, 497–98. "Decimam tributi quae de partibus orientalium Franchorum, vel de Sclavis ad fiscum dominicum annuatim persolvere solebant quae secundum illorum linguam steora vel ostarstuopha vocant" (Zeuss, *op. cit.*, p. 648). The bishopric of Bamberg was founded by Henry II in 1007, who detached eastern Franconia ecclesiastically from the see of Würzburg, the latter being indemnified by the gift of 153 manors (Migne, CXL, 115). It was richly endowed by the Emperor with the possessions of the banished Babenbergers, whose lands had passed by confiscation to the fisc in the reign of Ludwig the Child (900–911). Otto II gave them to Henry II of Bavaria, through whose accession to the German kingship in 1002 they again became a part of the crown lands. Bamberg was Henry II's favorite place of residence and the cathedral which he built and in which he lies buried is one of the finest examples of early Romanesque architecture in Germany. The see was ex-

were generally collected in corn, honey, flax, hemp, and cattle,[1] data which show the primitive economy of the Slavonic peoples at this time. Helmold[2] describes with particularity the nature of the tithe and the method of collection in the bishopric of Oldenburg: "Dabatur autem pontifici annuum de omni Wagirorum sive Obotritorum terra tributum, quod scilicet pro decima imputabatur, de quolibet aratro mensura grani et XL resticuli lini et XII nummi puri argenti. Ad hoc unus nummus, precium colligentis. Slavicum vero aratrum par boum aut unus conficit equus."[3]

Aside from tithes and tribute, the Wends were not long in discovering that the saints' days and church festivals were a hardship also. What with their primitive agricultural economy and the enormous tracts of waste and water, their margin of living was a narrow one at best, and they could ill spare relaxing their labors in the fields on these occasions in compliance with the church's prohibition of secular pursuits on holy days. Herbordus, III, 22, relates how one of Otto of Bamberg's companions came in conflict with this resentment:

---

pressly founded as a missionary base among the Slavs of the upper Main region. "Ut et paganismus Sclavorum destrueretur et Christiani nominis memoria perpetualiter inibi celebris habetur. . . . . Per quam [ecclesiam] et de inimico humani generis in vicinas Sclavorum gentes Deo opitulante, triumphabit" (Jaffé, V, 27 and 31; Migne, *loc. cit.*, 118). For the founding of the see, see Gebhardt, *Handbuch d. deutschen Gesch.*, I, 277, sec. 4; Stein, *Gesch. Frankens*, p. 85; Loshorn, *Die Begründung des Bistums Bamberg; Jahrbücher Heinrichs II*, II, 28; Bernhardi, *Lothar von Supplinburg*, pp. 152 f. For Slav serfs on church lands see Waitz, *Deutsche Verfassungsgesch.*, V, 157, n. 3; *Jahrbücher Heinrichs II*, II, 28–31.

[1] A tithe in honey in Brandenburg is mentioned in 965: "totam decimam mellis in pagis . . . . Plonim, Nicici, Sprewa ex utraque parte Sprewae" (*MGH*, *Dip. I*, p. 418. So in the reign of Otto II, in 973 a honey tithe is recorded in the same place: "in Ploni . . . . et in toto Morkeni totoque Drenzile et Heveldo" (*ibid.*, II, 40). A tithe in honey or linen from the Slavs of the Main was granted by Arnulf in 889 to the Bishop of Würzburg (Boehmer, *Regesta Imperii* [751–918], p. 745; Dümmler, *Gesch. des ostfränkischen Reiches*, III, 356). On this whole subject see Nitzsch, I, 342–44.

[2] *Chron. Slav.*, I, 12.

[3] Cf. I, 14, 88. He uses the words *resticuli lini* in I, 12, and *restes lini* in I, 14. The terms are interchangeable, the latter (sing. *restis*) being more usual in medieval Latin. It is used in the sense of a bundle of sticks, of a last of fish, of a roll or bale of cloth, of a measure of grain, etc. Cf. Du Cange, *Glossarium*, *s.v.* The use of linen as money was common among the Slavs like the wampum of the Indians.

It happened after this on the feast of St. Lawrence that a certain priest named Bockens, as he was passing by saw some peasants reaping in their fields. He endeavored discreetly to restrain them and said: "Unhappy men, what are you doing? This is the day of the blessed martyr St. Lawrence which is observed with the utmost respect by the whole church, while you presume to profane it." They answered: "We cannot always be keeping your sabbaths. It is just that we should sometimes provide what is necessary for our households." . . . . In a town called Games a certain peasant and his wife had gone out to reap during the festival of Mary the mother of God and perpetual virgin. When he perceived this Bockens, moved by righteous zeal, expressed his disapproval and said: "It is altogether wrong for you to labor on this great festival day of the Blessed Virgin." (It was now the second day of festival.) They replied: "Yesterday we observed Sunday as a holy day. To-day we must needs work."

It is unnecessary to add that compulsion followed upon these admonitions.

What the actual extent of the landed possessions of these bishoprics beyond the Elbe was, or what the amount of their revenues, it is impossible to say. For they were all swept away, as will be seen shortly, in the great Wendish rising of 983. Helmold confesses his inability to tell, save in general terms, the material possessions of the church in the "New Plantation." But judging from his comment, and from what we know to have been the condition in other Wendish territory—for example, in the Sorben land and in upper Franconia, where the bishopric of Bamberg was—regions which the storm of the Slav reaction did not reach, the revenues of the trans-Elbean bishoprics must have been considerable.[1] The church was a hard taskmaster and exacted heavy service from the Wendish peasantry reduced to serfdom or even slavery upon their own once free lands.[2] The cynical aphorism of Ekkehard of St. Gall, "servi qui non timent, tument,"[3] epito-

[1] Helmold, I, 18.

[2] Thietmar several times alludes to this unfree Wendish peasantry: II, 24; V, 6; VI, 37; VII, 15; cf. Jaffé, V, 652, 809; Waitz, V, 157, n. 3, and esp. Schulze, *Kolonisierung*, pp. 98–116, and Koeniger, *Burchard von Worms*, pp. 208–13.

[3] *MGH.* SS. II, 403. Evidently Ekkehard has here formulated in Latin the old German legal maxim later current: "Knechte schlagen wenn sie nicht zagen." The same kind of proverb occurs in France: "Oignez vilain, il vous poindra; poignez vilain il vous oindra" (Loysel, *Inst. cout.*, Liv. I, tit. 1, reg. 31). In 1009 Henry II gave a whole batch of captive Ljutizi as slaves to the Bishop of Metz (Thietmar, VI, 51 [35]). For employment of Slav slaves in the bishopric of Worms see Koeniger, *op.*

mizes the policy of the hard and worldly feudalized clergy of medieval Germany.

As early as the first Saxon kings there are evidences of peasant unrest on church lands.[1] In the reign of Otto III their discontent had become so great that the crown legislated in suppression of any manifestation of it. The document recites that all classes of the feudality frequently complain that the serfs resist the services exacted of them, advancing various kinds of false pretexts for so doing. In the case of serfs of lay nobles certain methods of proof of status and possibility of relief are provided for. But the law is absolute in declaring that "an unfree man belonging to the church may never become free. We strictly forbid the unfree of the churches to be set free, and we order all those who have by any device been freed to be reduced to servitude again."[2] The church,[3] as the greatest landed proprietor in Germany, had little sentiment and few compunctions of conscience in regard to exploitation of its dependents. Serfdom paid, therefore it was justified.[4] The Council of Pavia in the reign of Henry II decreed that the children of serf priests were slaves of the church, incapable of manumission or of owning private property.[5]

Perhaps one must go to Spanish America in the sixteenth century for an adequate parallel to this history of the spolia-

---

cit., p. 49. Burchard of Worms, the canonist, justified slavery in his treatise on canon law. As late as the thirteenth century pagan (Slav?) slaves were still sold in Germany (Caes. Heisterb., X, 44; Lamprecht, *DWL*, I, 2, n. 4 (1195). Contrary to prevalent opinion and Roman Catholic writers, the medieval church, far from opposing slavery or ameliorating serfdom, indorsed both one and the other, and promoted both practices. See Lamprecht, *op. cit.*, I, 1, 462 and notes. Many other authorities might be cited.

[1] Lamprecht, *DG*, III, 63–64, 67.

[2] This important document is in Altmann-Bernheim, *Ausgewählte Urkunden*, No. 61.

[3] For the official attitude of the Saxon church see Burchard of Worms, *Decretum*, *lex familiae*, secs. 2 and 11. Cf. Schroeder, *Rechtsgesch.* (4th ed., 1902), pp. 457–61; Nitzsch, *DG*, I, 360.

[4] Lamprecht, *DWL*, I, 1, 462 cites Regino, *Caus. synod.*, 1, 366, chap. li (cf. *Concil. Agath.* [*anno* 506]): "Mancipia monachis donata ab abbate non licet manumitti; injustum est enim, ut monachis quotidianum rurale opus facientibus, servi eorum libertatis otio potiantur." Cf. *Vita Oudalr.*, chap. ix (SS. IV, 96, l. 22).

[5] Labbé, *Concilia*, IX, 829–30; Hirsch, *Jhb. Hein. II*, III, 221.

tion of a weaker people by an avaricious priest class backed up by the sword of a powerful government.[1] The pious observations of Bernal Diaz on the benefits conferred upon the Peru of the Incas by Spanish civilization and Christianity have their prototype in the adamantine sanctimoniousness of Thietmar of Merseburg when he reflects upon the "mercies" which the German church had brought to the Sorben.[2]

In its greed for land the church was even divided against itself. This comes out clearly in the case of the diocese of Merseburg. The see was founded in 967 or 968.[3] From 971 to 981 Gisiler was the bishop thereof.[4] But when in 981 he was elevated to the archbishopric of Magdeburg, he maneuvered so as to secure the abolition of the see of Merseburg under the pretext that Halberstadt had never given its written consent to Merseburg's erection ("sine consensu atque subscriptione canonica"). The bishops of Zeitz and Meissen sustained him in this course, the motive of which was plain. The three coveted the lands of Merseburg and plotted the spoliation of the diocese to the aggrandizement of their own sees. The upshot of the scheme was that the diocese of Merseburg was abolished and its lands partitioned among the three avaricious bishops. It was not restored until 1004, when Henry II, whose bold policy in the face of the bishops will soon be noticed, revived Merseburg again.[5]

The church in the Wendish lands was inspired by no genuine religious zeal. Like the bishoprics and monasteries in

[1] For development of this parallel see Bourne, *Spain in America*, pp. 195–201, 259–65.

[2] Thietmar, IX, 3: ". . . . Consuetudines . . . . quamvis dirae, tamen interdum laudabiles." See the whole chapter as an example of clerical moralizing and cf. the legislation of the synod of Tribur in the year 1036 (*MGH. Const. I*, 89, No. 6). Helmold, I, 84, points to the German substitution of trial by battle or by hot plowshares for the methods of Slavonic administration of justice as an evidence of "progress." "Sed offerebant criminibus pulsatos sacerdoti ferro vel vomeribus examinandos."

[3] Kretschmer, sec. 267.

[4] Thietmar, I, 37. For his colonizing on the left bank of the Saale see Hauck, III, 431.

[5] For this scandalous affair see Thietmar, III, 16; Gebhardt, I, 273; and Kretschmer, sec. 267, with literature cited.

England along the Scotch and Welsh Marches, the churches were strategically located to guard the frontier and to hold down the conquered country.[1] Its motives were wholly material. The bishops' seats were simply offices of exploitation. Manorial bailiffs and stewards in the service of the bishops were numerous, but there was no thought of priestly ministration.[2] The only actual churches in the land were in the cathedral places, where the bishop's authority was established and where the center of the system was. Elsewhere there were merely a few scattered chapels, with a single priest, and these were not for the conversion of the Slavs, but to minister to the isolated German communities, chiefly composed of soldiers and wandering merchants. Most of the bishops were intriguing Lorrainers and Flemings like Adalbert of Magdeburg.[3] Of all the German bishops who sat in these Wendish sees in the tenth and the early eleventh centuries, there is only one in whom any real spirituality is discernible—Boso of Merseburg, its first incumbent; and even in this case the evidence is somewhat dubious, for it rests on the flattering unction of an official document.[4] However, Thietmar has preserved for us an anecdote which is so ingenuous that it has an authentic ring, and shows that this Bavarian monk had some of the milk of human kindness in him. Thietmar records how Boso composed a little manual in the Slav tongue for the instruction of his flock, and that he taught them to chant the *Kyrie eleison*, at the same time "exponens eis hujus utilitatem." But to his bewilderment these barbarian children of the forest mistook the words *Kyrie eleison*, which they naturally did not understand the meaning of, for their own Slav word for "elderbush" (*kriolosse*), and so sang.[5]

[1] For a remarkable description of the distribution of ecclesiastical foundations in England for this purpose see Bémont, *Revue hist.*, LXX, 383–84.

[2] "Aber von Pfarren ist nicht die Rede" (Guttmann, *op. cit.*, p. 435). See the comments of Nitzsch, II, 16–17.

[3] Hauck, III, 95–97; Krabbe, *Die ostdeutschen Bistümer* (Berlin, 1906).

[4] "Multum jam in eadem Sclavorum gente convertenda sudavit" (Urk. Otto I, *MGH*, *Dip. I*, p. 502.

[5] Thietmar, II, 36–37; Koeniger, *op. cit.*, p. 182 n. 1.

A certain familiarity with the Slavonic tongue must have been not unusual among some classes of the Germans, as military officers, merchants trading across the frontier, and at least some of the priesthood.[1] Otto I spoke Slavonic,[2] and Thietmar, for all his Saxon scorn of the race, must have understood the language. The internal evidence of his *Chronicon* proves it.[3] A few of the Wendish chieftains embraced the Christian religion for self-advantage.[4] But the mass of the Slavs must have accepted Christianity as they accepted German domination, superficially and morosely.[5] To most of them for generations the founder of Christianity was the "Teutonicus Deus,"[6] who, they must surely have thought, had come to bring not peace but a sword. Even as late as the twelfth century the Christianity of the Sorben was very superficial and chiefly inspired by dread of the German power.[7] And yet the armies of Otto I in his Italian

[1] Hauck, III, 136, and n. 1. Some common German words are of Slav origin, as *Dolmetsch*, "interpreter"; *Grenze*, "border"; *Kummet*, "horse collar"; *Peitsche*, "whip lash"; *Petschaft*, "signet ring"; *Schöps*, "wether, mutton." For the modern Sorbisch speech see Tetzner, p. 291. H. Witte, *Wendische Bevölkerungsreste in Mecklenburg* (Stuttgart, 1905), has tried to prove that German colonization did not exterminate, but Germanized, the Slav.

[2] Widukind, II, 36.

[3] Cosmas, I, 23, speaks of "Dethmarus Saxo olim, orationis causa Pragam profectus"; and of "Theadagus Saxo, lingua perfecte imbutus Sclavonica."

[4] A Sorben knight named Zolunta was a member of Otto II's bodyguard in his ill-fated Calabrian expedition in 982 (Thietmar, III, 23; cf. Giesebrecht, *Kaiserzeit*, II, 168), and there is mention of some others like him (*Ann. Altah. mag.* [1041]; Helmold, I, 16 [Schol. 30]; *Gesta episcop. Camerac. Contin.* [*MGH*, SS. VII, p. 518]). Liutprand, *Legatio*, chap. xxiii, alludes to Wendish hostlers and stablemen.

[5] Adam of Bremen, III, 1, distinguishes the Slavs in the archiepiscopal diocese of Bremen-Hamburg into *pagani* and *pseudo-Christiani*. Cf. the comment of Wipo: "Liutici vocantur, qui olim semichristiani, nunc per apostacam nequitiam omnino sunt pagani" (*Vita Chuonradi*, chap. xxiii).

[6] Ebo, *Vita S. Ottonis episcop. Babenb.*, III, 1.

[7] *Vita S. Winthar.* (1062–63), ep. Merseb. (*MGH*, SS. XII, 246): "Sclavorum genti, quorum copiosam multitudinem error adhuc ydolatriae detinebat"; *Mirac. Heinr.* (*MGH*, SS. IV, 816): "vix vel tenuem fidei videntur habere scintillam." The *Miracula* were written at the end of the twelfth century (Wattenbach, *DGQ*, II, 384; cf. Hauck, III, 135, n. 6). A letter written by a clerk of Liège to Udo of Naumburg (d. 1148) is to the same effect: "Ultra non christianam Salam inter agrestem et barbaram Sclavorum nationem" (cited by Hauck, III, 135, n. 7). Thietmar of Merseburg (I, 3) says that the Wends venerated their own temples more than the Christian churches: "Hunc [Glomuzi fons] omnis incola plus quam aec-

campaigns seem to have had among them considerable numbers of Slavs in the capacity of campfollowers, hostlers, etc.[1]

The blame for the inhuman treatment of the Wendish peoples along the German border must be divided between the Saxon clergy and the Saxon nobles, especially the ruling house of the Billunger. The feud between the church and the nobles was a bitter one and lasted for years.[2] The nobles resented the fondness of the Ottos for churchmen. Above all, they resented the policy of converting the Slavs, for the church's tithes reduced the tribute proportionally. They were content to leave the Wends their own religion, their own leaders, their own laws, provided the Wends regularly paid tribute to them.[3] Saxon avarice, both of the nobles and of the clergy, is alleged time and again by Adam of Bremen and Helmold as the cause of German overthrow beyond the Elbe and the arrest of the eastward expansion of German colonization for one hundred and fifty years.[4] Adam of Bremen writes:

> I have heard that the honest king of the Danes said that the Slav peoples would long since have been converted to Christianity if it had not been for the avarice of the Saxons.[5]

and Helmold mournfully records:

---

clesias spe quamvis dubia, veneratur et timet." The whole paragraph is interesting for the light it throws upon the Slavonic religion. The bulk of the population around the confluence of the Ohre and the Elbe so late as 1161 was still Slav. For Slav paganism around Ratzeburg (1177) see Hauck, IV, 589, n. 2. ". . . . quarum incolae adhuc Sclavi erant" (from a deed cited by Zeuss, *op. cit.*, p. 660). See Hauck, pp. 555–63, for the general growth of the church in the Sorben March in the twelfth century.

[1] Otto rex veniente Italico regno, tanta bene multitudo gentis in Italia, que sic impleverunt faciem terre, sicut situle. Habebat autem secum gentes nationes quorum lingue non agnoscebant gentis. Insuper haec habebat gens que Guinula vocabantur sarcinas et carros et machina portantes. Erat enim aspectus eorum orribilis et curbis properantes, carpentes iter et ad prelium ut ferro stantes. *Benedicti S. Andreae monachi Chronicon* (SS. III, 717); cf. Adam of Bremen, II, 42, Schol. 27(30).

[2] Cf. Giesebrecht, *Otto II*, pp. 91 ff.; *Kaiserzeit*, I, 604 ff., 850; L. Giesebrecht, *Wendische Geschichten*, I, 264 ff.; Hirsch, *Jahrbücher Heinrich II*, III, 183–87; Guttmann, *op. cit.*, p. 420.

[3] Sommerfeld, *op. cit.*, p. 6.

[4] See Hauck, III, 250–51; Hirsch, *Jahrb. Heinrich II*, III, 93 ff.; cf. Adam of Bremen, II, 46; III, 22; Helmold, I, 14, 16, 18, 19, 21, 25, 26.

[5] Adam of Bremen, III, 22.

The princes divided the tribute among themselves. But no mention was made of Christianity. From which the insatiable avarice of the Saxons may be appreciated. They excel all other peoples in arms and the art of war; but they care more for tribute than they do for the winning of souls.[1]

As early as 983 the Abodrite prince, Mistivoi, whom the Saxons had greatly offended, aligned himself with the priests of Rethra and thus brought about a general rising of the Slavs of the Elbe against the Christians.

Under Henry II (1002–24) the German border policy initiated a new and striking course. At this time Boleslav of Poland was formidable to Germany, for he aimed to unite the whole group of separate and detached Slavonic tribes into one body, and narrowly missed so doing. The danger was a real one to Germany, for Boleslav had friends at the German court, among them Henry, margrave of the Bavarian Nordgau, Ernest of Austria, and the king's own brother Brun.[2] In this peril Henry II, adroitly taking advantage of the hostility of the Ljutizi and Redarii to the Polish policy of forcible union, promised them the unmolested enjoyment of their pagan religion in return for their support of the German cause against Boleslav.[3] Henry II was not the supine instrument of the church that tradition has represented him to have been, but a resolute, farsighted ruler without illusions.[4] His statesmanship foiled the probable unification of the western Slavs and diverted Polish ambition eastward toward Russia, while at the same time allowing liberty to the slow process of Germanization of the border peoples to work out the solution through natural contact instead of by compulsory means.[5]

[1] Helmold, I, 21; cf. Sommerlad, *Die wirtschaftliche Tätigkeit der Kirche in Deutschland*, II, 209.

[2] Thietmar, V, 32, 35, 36, 38.

[3] Thietmar, V, 21; VI, 23–25, 28 (*Anno* 1003); Pueschl, *Das Anwachsen der Deutschen.*

[4] See on this Hirsch, *Jahrbücher Heinrich II*, I, 257 ff.; III, 364 ff. (by Bresslau); Matthai, *Die Klosterpolitik Kaiser Heinrichs II* (Göttingen, 1877); Nitzsch, *Deutsche Gesch.*, I, 367; Guttmann, *op. cit.*, p. 419.

[5] For a eulogy of Henry II's border policy see Thietmar, V, 21. He was at Merseburg in November, 1014, and liberated Miesko, son of Boleslav of Poland, there (Thietmar, VII, 5–8), who showed his gratitude by burning Meissen in the next year. Thietmar, VII, 25, gives a vivid account of the heroic resistance.

The wisdom of Henry II's course was soon manifested. The bishops of Havelberg and Brandenburg returned to their devastated sees, and they and other former German towns, like Arneburg, were rebuilt. But unfortunately, some of the German bishops learned nothing and forgot nothing. Benno, bishop of Oldenburg, instituted an inquisition into the former possessions of the diocese which so exasperated the Abodrites that they declared that rather than submit again to the heavy exactions of the church they would quit the country.[1] A second Slav rebellion came in 1018, in which Mistislav, the Abodrite chieftain, and his half-Christianized adherents—for there were some Christian Slavs among them—severely suffered, and the trans-Elbean bishops were again driven out.[2]

This second Slav revolt completed what that of 983 had left unfinished. The first blow had fallen upon Brandenburg and the Havelland,[3] but Nordalbingia had escaped. Now it too was devastated with fire and sword. The priests were slaughtered, the inhabitants dragged off to glut the slave marts along the Baltic Coast, especially in the island of Rügen. Bishop Benno, the man primarily responsible for the insurrection, was absent from his post when this second wave of Slav fury swept the land. But sixty priests were captured and with hands tied behind their backs were whipped through

[1] See the detailed account in Helmold, I, 18.

[2] Thietmar, III, 17 [10]; VIII, 5 [4], distinguishes between the reaction of 983 and 1018. The first was against the German Herrschaft, the second against the Fürsten and the church. He names the Wend leaders as Mistui and Mistivoi. The names mean two separate persons, and not the same man as Adam of Bremen, II, 40–41, and Helmold, I, 16, who follows Adam, say. Cf. Hirsch, *Jahrbücher Heinrich II*, I, 478–86 (excursus of Usinger). In the middle of the reign of Henry IV, as the result of the Slav reaction of 1066, 600 Saxon families which were settled in Holstein and Ditmarsch emigrated to Thuringia (Helm., I, 26). They must have settled in their first home after the Slav insurrection of 1018 had subsided. The early Angle colony around Merseburg, often alluded to by German historians, never existed. The oldest manuscript of the text (*MGH*, SS. VII, 285) contains no mention of it. It is an interpolation in later manuscripts. Cf. Lot in *Revue hist.* (May-June, 1915), p. 31, n. 3.

[3] *Vita Henrici II*, Book I, chap. iii (Migne, *PL*, CXL, 110): ". . . . Sedes episcopales Missnam et Merseburch quae barbarica immanitate adjacentium Sclavorum vastatae fuerant, restauravit." In *ibid.*, chap. iv, it is related that the treasures, etc., of Merseburg were transferred to Magdeburg for safekeeping at this time.

the native towns and villages until they died of exhaustion. The work of the church for seventy years past in Nordalbingia went down in a twelvemonth.[1] Gottschalk, the Abodrite chief, who at first had been tolerant of Christianity, and whose son was educated in the cloister school in Lüneburg, became the formidable avenger of the wrongs of his people.[2]

More than a century and a half later, when the labors of Adolph of Holstein and Henry the Lion permanently established German domination across the great river, Helmold, the Holsteiner priest and author of that vivid record of German eastward expansion, the *Chronica Slavorum*, picturesquely described the ruins which still could be seen of churches, monasteries, and tiny German hamlets which were destroyed in these two uprisings of the Slavs.[3]

But neither the violence of this second Slav rebellion nor the imprecations of the clergy frightened Henry II into renouncing the alliance he had made with the Slavs of the Elbe. Unexpected and ferocious as the insurrection of 1018 was, bitter as the blow must have been to his liberal practice, hostile as the resentment of the bishops was—especially of those who had lost their seats—yet the Emperor's confidence in the essential justice and wisdom of his policy was unshaken. He had the justice to perceive that the Wilzi, the Wagri, the Abodrites, etc., had been "driven to the necessity of paganism" by the cruel oppression of the clergy and Duke Bernhard of Saxony.[4]

[1] "Omnes igitur Sclavi qui inter Albiam et Oddaram . . . . absiderunt a corpore Christi" (Adam of Bremen, II, 42–43; cf. Helmold, I, 19; Thietmar, IX [VIII, 4]; Hauck, III, 253).

[2] See the interesting conversation of Gottschalk, reported by Helmold, I, 19, with a Holsatian refugee whom he met unrecognized in the way.

[3] "Adhuc restant antiquae illius habitacionis pleraque indicia, precipue in silva, quae ab urbe Lutilinburg per longissimas tractus Sleswich usque protrahitur, cujus vasta solitudo et vix penetrabilis inter maxima silvarum robora sulcos pretendit, quibus jugera quondam fuerant dispertita. Urbium quoque seu civitatum formam structura vallorum pretendit. In plerisque etiam rivis qui propter molendina stipandis aquis aggeres congesti sunt ostendunt omnem saltum a Saxonibus quondam inhabitatum" (Helmold, I, 12).

[4] Thietmar, VIII, 4; Adam of Bremen, II, 40, 41, 42, 46; Hirsch, *Jahrb. Heinrich II*, III, 93 ff.

Conrad II (1024–39), no friend of churchmen, attempted to adhere to the policy of Henry II. But the prejudice of the clergy and the continual molestation of the Abodrites and the Wilzi by the Saxons jeopardized this statesman-like course more and more.[1] For over thirty years the strong hand of these two rulers sought to restrain both the Saxon clergy and the Saxon nobles. Wipo, the biographer of Conrad, relates an incident which strikingly illustrates the conditions and the difficulties along the frontier. In 1033 the border situation became so tense that the Emperor went thither to investigate. The Wends accused the Saxons of continually breaking the peace. The Saxons blamed the Wends. The latter offered to put the determination of the question to the judgment of God in trial by battle. Conrad at first hesitated, having scruples whether a heathen could participate in a process of law in which the invisible presence of God was supposed to be, but finally consented. Each side chose a champion, and the Slav champion won, to the great elation of his compatriots and the chagrin of the Saxons, especially the clergy, whose prestige as dispensers of the will of the Almighty was somewhat injured.[2]

But the wise plan of the Salian emperors was increasingly imperiled by the ambition of the Billunger dukes of Saxony and the avarice of the Saxon clergy. Up to the death of Duke Benno in 1011 the Billungers had been loyal, though with diminishing fidelity, to the German crown. But with the accession of Bernhard to the dukedom the Billunger breach both with the crown and with the church widened. As we have seen, the Abodrites were the mildest of the Slav tribes of the lower Elbe, and when the first wild flame of rebellion subsided, Christianity began slowly to recover in Wagria under the active policy of Archbishop Unwan of Bremen (d. 1029) and Bishop Benno of Oldenburg, whose tactless inquisi-

[1] *Heiden sollen nicht erben* ("Heathen have no right to inherit") was a popular medieval proverb in North Germany.

[2] Wipo, *Vita Chuonradi*, chap. xxxiii; for a commentary on the legal technicalities see Waitz, VIII, 30; Bresslau, II, 96–97.

tion into the former possessions of the church there precipitated the rebellion of 1018.[1]

The Saxon Duke, jealous of the enrichment of the church, did everything he could to thwart the Bishop, and at the same time attempted to double the tribute exacted of the Abodrites.[2] Four manors, in particular, were a bone of contention between the Duke and the Bishop.[3] The Abodrites, caught between the hammer of the Bishop and the anvil of the Duke, preferred the Bishop's rule as the less of two evils and when the dispute was referred to the Emperor, testified to the previous existence of the episcopal tithe and promised to pay it as before.[4] This was in 1021, and was the immediate ground of the fierce feud which widened into open war between the Billunger dukes and the bishops of Northern Germany, and which reached an acute phase in the war of Duke Ordulf against Adalbert of Bremen in the early years of the reign of Henry IV.

Thus the peace and prosperity of Nordalbingia and Holstein after the second Slav rebellion subsided, of which Adam of Bremen boasts, was actually as precarious as the quarter of a beleagured town beyond the immediate reach of the shells. Billunger hatred of the church's ascendancy left nothing undone to embarrass it.[5] Moreover, the new King of Denmark, whose ambition for Danish expansion on the mainland had been nourished by Canute, coveted a wider dominion. Conrad II, Canute, and Archbishop Unwan of Bremen had amicably arranged their somewhat conflicting interests in the north.[6] But when Canute died in 1035 and Conrad II in 1039,

[1] Helmold, I, 18. Thietmar of Merseburg, when Henry II restored the bishopric and appointed him to it, exhibited the same greed for land and started proceedings to recover possession of the lands which had passed to others in the dismemberment of the diocese. He did not recoil from acts of violence in so doing, and became bitterly involved with Hermann and Eckhard, sons of Margrave Eckhard, as a result (Thietmar, IX, 20–22).

[2] Wendt, I, 69.

[3] Helmold (ed. Schmeidler), I, 18, and nn. 4–6.

[4] *Ibid.;* cf. Giesebrecht, *Kaiserzeit*, II, 619 f.

[5] Adam of Bremen, III, 22.

[6] *Ibid.*, II, 54; Bresslau, *Jahrb. Konrad II*, I, 101–4. In 1019 Canute made a campaign against the Slavs (*Jahrb. Heinrich II*, III, 185).

political conditions in Northern Germany were changed. Duke Bernhard's son Ordulf was married to a daughter of Magnus of Denmark. The alliance boded ill for the interests of either emperor or church in the north. Things became tenser than before. The Danish King coveted possession of the mouths of the rivers flowing into the Baltic in the interest of Danish Baltic trade,[1] while the Saxon Duke wanted to provoke the Abodrites and Wilzi into a new revolt which would destroy the churches again being established in their lands, use the rising as a pretext for Saxon intervention, and so establish his dominion and tribute over them without any competition from the church.

The Saxon-Danish alliance was formed with the object of effecting this double partition. In pursuance of the plan Ordulf and King Magnus, in 1043, fell upon the Wends at Lyrskog Heath, near Hadeby in Schleswig (September 28) a victory which clinched the Danish capture of Wollin, the most important trading town of the Baltic Slavs at the mouth of the Oder River in 960, which the Danes had renamed Jomsburg.[2] The future was to see a bitter strife between the Germans and the Danes for possession of the Pomeranian coast as a result of this intrigue. But of more immediate importance was the effect upon Nordalbingia. Against the double onslaught the Abodrites were powerless. Their capacity to resist was also hampered by their division into a pagan

[1] In the reign of Otto the Great the ambition of the Danes was a greater menace to Germany in the far north than the Slavonic tribes beyond the lower Elbe were (Sommerfeld, *op. cit.*, p. 7).

That propulsive and expansive energy in the Viking spirit which had made Europe ring with the achievements of the Norsemen in the ninth century was hardly abated in the tenth. Denmark, in the time of Henry the Fowler and Otto the Great, cherished dreams of Baltic dominion which the Saxon could not look upon without anxiety. In 934 Henry I had warred with Gorm of Denmark, strengthened the ancient *limes* established by Charlemagne by carrying the frontier beyond the Eider to the river Schlei, and erected the tiny March of Schleswig between the rivers where a Saxon colony was established at Haddeby (Waitz, *Jahrb. Heinrich I*, pp. 277 f., Exkursus 24). King Sweyn Forkbeard of Denmark (985–1013) built the rampart or dike across the peninsula from Haddeby to protect the kingdom from further German expansion. See article by La Cour, *Historisk Tidsskrift* (8th series, 1909–10), Vol. II; cf. Biereye, *Beiträge zur Gesch. Nordalbingiens im 10 Jahrhundert* (Berlin diss. 1909), p. 192; *Ztschft. f. Ethnologie*, XXXV (1904), 688, with map.

[2] Schafarik, II, 383, 575–77.

and a Christian group, the latter under another Gottschalk. Probably nothing but the loyalty of these Christian Wends to the faith, in spite of all the abuse of them by the church, saved Nordalbingia and Holstein from a second eclipse of the church there at this time.[1] Unfortunately for Germany, the Emperor Henry III during this time was warring against the Bohemians and Hungarians, or else in Italy, and could not interfere. Helmold's comment, which echoes Adam of Bremen's doleful observation, is full of depression: "De Christianitate nulla fuit mentio."[2]

Painfully and slowly civilization began to pick up again in Nordalbingia; peasant settlers from Saxony, and not merely land-hungry nobles, began to filter once more into the region. In the middle of the eleventh century Adam of Bremen proudly says: "Per idem tempus in Sclavania res maximae gestae sunt";[3] and the picture of the prosperity which he paints, if perhaps overcolored, is nevertheless significant of the changed order of things along the lower Elbe.[4]

At this critical juncture, when the affairs of the north were full of tension, friction, and peril, Henry III died (October 5, 1056), leaving the crown to Henry IV, who was a little child, and Germany fell upon evil days. The most statesman-like man in the country was the great archbishop of Bremen, Adalbert (1043–72). But he had bitter enemies in the Saxon Duke and his son, and in his rival for the regency, Archbishop Anno of Cologne. Adalbert was of a noble Saxon family and the ambition which, if he had been a layman, would have driven him to strive for the enlargement of his feudal prerogative and the widening of his feudal lands found a broader field of ambition in his ecclesiastical office. His dream was to convert his archdiocese into an immense patriarchate, having ecclesiastical sway over Lower Germany,

[1] For the extensive source references and literature to the battle of Hadeby and its results see Richter, *Annalen*, II, 361–63; cf. K. Gjerset, *History of the Norwegian People*, I (1915), 275.

[2] Adam of Bremen, III, 22; Helmold, I, 21.

[3] Adam of Bremen, III, 21.

[4] *Ibid.*, III, 18–21; cf. Helm., I, 20.

Denmark, Sweden, Norway, Iceland, and even Greenland.[1] For the realization of this dream of creating a gigantic principality covering the whole Christian north of Europe, Adalbert actually declined the papacy in 1044.[2]

The Baltic Slavs were to have formed a vassal state of the German kingdom within this huge orbit,[3] with the Christian Abodrite duke, Gottschalk, as prince, after the manner of the relation of Poland and Bohemia to the German crown.[4] To be sure, the Abodrites were yet half-pagan and the Wilzi wholly so. But Gottschalk's loyalty and organized missionary effort on the part of the church were counted upon to remedy this condition. Adalbert, unlike any former bishop in the north, worked hand in hand with the Christian Abodrites. He divided the bishopric of Oldenburg into three parts, creating two new Slavonic dioceses for them—Mecklenburg and Ratzeburg—and founded cloisters in Oldenburg, Ratzeburg, and Lenzen.[5] Henry III while he had lived had furthered Adalbert's ideas, for their realization would have spread the power of the Empire too. Moreover, the Emperor needed the support of Adalbert in Saxony which was now dangerously alienated and even hostile to the German crown. The absence of Anno of Cologne at the Council of Mantua gave Adalbert his chance to take advantage of the favor of young Henry IV, and for two years (1064–66) he had things much his own way.

But the prospect of the speedy conversion of the Baltic Slavs roused the fury of the Billunger, for they had no mind to see the tribute diminished by the extension of the church's

[1] Cf. Adam of Bremen, *Descriptio Insularum Aquilonis*, 10, 36, 37. For the medieval church in Greenland see K. Gjerset, *op. cit.*, I, 197–204; Major's ed. of *Voyages of the Venetian Brothers N. and A. Zeno* (Hakluyt Soc., 1873), pp. lxxxvii f., Beamish, *Saga of Eric the Red;* and esp. L. M. Larsen, *Catholic Historical Review* (July–October, 1919).

[2] Adam of Bremen, III, 7.

[3] "Sclavos ita perdomuit ut eum [Adalbertum] quasi regem timerent" (Adam of Bremen, III, 18).

[4] "Gottschalk's Plan war die Gründung eines grossen wendischen Einheitstaates auf christlicher Grundlage und im Bunde mit dem Reich" (Otto Bitense, *Mecklenb. Gesch.* [1912], p. 19; cf. Guttmann, *op. cit.*, p. 419; Wendt, I, 73). Gottschalk married a sister of the Danish King (Adam of Bremen, III, 18).

[5] Adam of Bremen, III, 20; Helmold, I, 22; Dehio, *op. cit.*, Exkurs XIX.

tithe.[1] "He shall not rest," said Duke Ordulf of Adalbert, "while I or my house last." Both parties assiduously built castles, and the north country flamed with war.[2]

The German church was divided into two camps. Anno of Cologne was supported by the Archbishop of Magdeburg and the bishops of Halberstadt, Trier, Minden, and Utrecht, as well as by the leading Saxon nobles.[3] At Tribur in January, 1066, Henry IV was forced to dismiss Adalbert, who fled to Bremen. Then followed four terrible years. The Billunger fell upon Bremen with fire and sword and wrecked the land. Adalbert found refuge in the strong imperial fortress of Goslar, whence he sent the proffer of a thousand manors of his diocese as the price of peace, to Magnus Billung, Duke Ordulf's son. In the end the bishopric was deprived of two-thirds of its possessions, half of the spoil going to the Billunger and half to their partisans. The indomitable Adalbert spent three years in his ruined city, still dreaming of the grandeur he had hoped for and laboring for the reconstruction of the dilapidated diocese.[4] At last Henry IV, who had emancipated himself in 1070 from the control of the combined clerical and feudal opposition around him, recalled Adalbert. But in March, 1072, Adalbert died, as tragically as Wolsey, save for the love of his king for him. Adam of Bremen says that in his last hours he reproached himself for having wasted his life in pursuit of earthly power. But the pious historian's moralizing does not disguise the fact that Adalbert was a big and forceful personality who wrought strenuously for the enlargement of the life and the history of Northern Germany. In the same year his great enemy, Duke Ordulf, also died.

Meanwhile, what had been the effect of these events upon the border situation?

The Saxon greed for the Wendish lands, coupled with the

[1] Adam of Bremen, III, 40, 42.

[2] Adam of Bremen, III, 43; cf. 47–48. For the earlier history of the feud see II, 69; III, 21.

[3] Adam of Bremen, III, 34, 46.

[4] See Adam of Bremen's detailed account (III, 48, 54–56).

bitter feud between the church and the Saxon nobles for control of the Wendish tribute, was a perpetual source of disaffection, and continually tended to upset peace on the frontier. The nobles by trespass and exasperation goaded the Wends into reprisal and thus created a pretext for a war of dispossession in order that they might acquire the coveted lands. The leader of this policy of forcible expropriation was Bernard Billung, duke of the Saxons. The Billunger hatred of the clergy was intense because they did not want the Wendish tribute reduced by the imposition of the tithe. The border was the prey of unceasing predatory raids by the Saxons who bled the wretched Abodrites and Ljutizi of tribute.

Moreover, the pro-Christian inclinations of Gottschalk and the Abodrites had slowly provoked the wrath of the other pagan Slavs along the Baltic Coast farther toward the east, especially the Wilzi and the wilder Rugians, the guardians of the great Slavonic fane on the island of Rügen. They perceived what was quite true, that the extension of Christianity would carry with it the subjugation of the free Slav tribes and that they were likely to pass under the onerous domination of the Saxon dukes. "They preferred to die rather than to become Christian," says Helmold, "or to pay tribute to the Saxon dukes."[1] The sight of the newly established bishoprics of Mecklenburg and Ratzeburg infuriated them, and the pagan priests of their temples seem to have fanned the flame, as the Aztec priesthood inspired their people against the Spanish conquerors in Mexico.

In 1066 a third Slavonic rebellion came, the most formidable and effective of them all. The Wilzi, maddened by Saxon abuse and border aggression, rose in fury and decisively defeated the Saxons.[2] The Christian Abodrite chief Gottschalk was killed at Lenzen, but his wife, who was a daughter of the Danish King, escaped naked to Mecklenburg. Ratzeburg was attacked, the Christian priests and many of the people stoned to death. The sack of Mecklenburg soon followed. The furious Wagri and Wilzi stormed one after an-

[1] Helmold, I, 25. [2] *Chron. Wirzib.* (*MGH*, SS. VI, 31); Wendt, I, 75.

other the long line of Burgwärde which extended from Mecklenburg (formerly the Wiligrad or Great Burg of the Abodrites) through Wismar, Ilow, Bukow, Schwerin, and Dobbin. These Burgwärde were interspersed with lesser posts or forts, between which was an earthen and palisaded wall, some remains of which are still visible between Schwerin and Wismar. The key fortress along this frontier, Mikilinburg, gave the name of Mecklenburg to the land.[1] Bishop John of Mecklenburg was dragged off a captive to the pagan temple at Rethra and there immolated to the high Slav god Redigast (November 10, 1066). Squads of Christian priests were whipped through the Slav towns until they died of exhaustion. The Slavonic bishoprics of Mecklenburg and Ratzeburg were obliterated; the cloisters at Oldenburg, Lenzen, and Ratzeburg destroyed. Even the bishopric of Hamburg was overrun.[2] Hundreds of the population were carried off into slavery, the castle demolished, the garrison thereof being derisively crucified by the furious victors. "Omnes Sclavi," says Adam of Bremen, "facta conspiratione generali ad paganismum denuo relapsi sunt."[3] "Thereafter until the end of his life," writes Helmold, "Duke Ordulf vainly fought against the Slavs, but was never able to win a victory. Many times was he beaten by the pagans and was an object of derision unto his own people."

The few Christian Abodrites in the ruined land lapsed to paganism once more. The entire achievement of German civilization and Germanic Christianity, save around Bremen and in Holstein, was wiped out. Both paid dearly for the cruelty, injustice, and avarice with which they had operated. In completeness of destruction this third great Slav rising excelled those of 983 and 1018.[4]

[1] See Otto Vitense, *Mecklenburgische Geschichte* (1912), p. 11; Kretschmar, *Historische Geographie*, p. 357. Cf. Old English *mickle;* Anglo-Saxon, *micel*= "much," or "great."

[2] Hauck, III, 594.

[3] Adam of Bremen, III, 49–50; Helmold, I, 22–24.

[4] For the history in detail of this Wendish reaction see Adam of Bremen, III, 49–50; Helm., I, 22–25; Wendt, I, 75–79; Raumer, *Regesta*, Nos. 550, 585, 592–93; Breska, *Untersuchungen*, pp. 31–41; Meyer von Knonau, *Jahrb. Heinrich IV*, II, 854–56; Lavisse, *La Marche de Brandenbourg*, pp. 33–34.

The Christian hero of the border was the fierce Burckhardt, bishop of Halberstadt, who in the winter of 1067–68 made a successful raid across the frozen marshes, devastated the country of the Wilzi, burned the Wendish temple at Rethra, and triumphantly rode back to Saxony upon the sacred black horse.[1] In the next winter—winter campaigns were the only practicable method of invasion of so swampy a country[2]—young Henry IV repeated this feat.[3] But the Wends more than held their own. In 1072 they twice attacked Hamburg. All Nordalbingia was a solitude.[4] So great was the danger even west of the Elbe that Bishop Benno II of Osnabrück in 1070 built Aschenberg castle and walled the monastery of Iburg.[5]

The Pontiac of this successful rebellion of the Baltic Slavs to throw off the German yoke was a Rugian chief named Kruto, who fixed his capital on the island of Buku at the confluence of the Trave and the Wochnitz rivers, where later in 1143, Adolph of Holstein founded the present city of Lübeck.[6] For years Duke Ordulf or his son warred against Kruto in vain.[7]

In 1074 or 1075 Gottschalk's son Buthue, with the aid of a force of Holsteiners and men of Ditmarsch furnished him by

[1] *MGH*, SS. III, 128; *Ann. Altah. Maj.* (1069). German children in this region still sing an ancient nursery jingle reminiscent of this event:

"Buko von Halberstadt,
Bring doch meinen Kinde wat.
'Wat sall ik em denn bringen?'
'Goldne Schoh mit Ringen.' "

Literally:

"Buko of Halberstadt,
Bring something to my child.
'What shall I bring to him?'
'Golden shoes with buckles.' "

[2] "Terra etenim illa paganorum aquis et paludibus est plena" (*Annal. Altah.* [1069]).

[3] *Annal. Weissemb.* (1069); *Sigeb. Gembl.* (*MGH*, SS. VI, 362).

[4] "Pagani victores totam Nordalbingiam deinceps habuerunt in sua ditione, bellatoribusque [i.e., the vassals of the bishop] occisis aut in captivitatem ductis, provincia in solitudinem redacta est" (Adam of Bremen, III, 63).

[5] *Mitth. d. Ver. f. d. Gesch. von Osnabrück*, Band XXVII (1902).

[6] Helmold, I, 25, 57.

[7] Adam of Bremen, III, 50; *ibid.*, I, 24.

Duke Magnus, who succeeded Ordulf in 1072, seized Kruto's castle of Plön, on an isthmus between the Grosse and the Kleine Plöner-See, north of Kruto's capital at Buku.[1] It had been craftily left without defenders by the wily Rugian, and Buthue was warned by a German woman against the trap. Morning showed a Slav army in boats around the castle. A parley followed at the end of which the Germans in pairs crossed a bridge of boats into Kruto's camp where, when they had surrendered their arms, they were all put to the edge of the sword. Helmold's epilogue on this catastrophe is as follows:

> And Kruto prevailed and the work prospered in his hands. And the strength of the Saxons was worn down and they served Kruto under tribute .... All the territory of the Nordalbingians, which is divided into three peoples, the Holsteiners, the Sturmarians and those who live in Ditmarsch—these bore the heavy yoke of servitude during the whole life of Kruto, and the land was filled with robbers, who visited rapine and death upon the people of God.

From his rise to power in 1066 until his death in 1093 Kruto was lord of the north.[2] Hundreds of the German population which had settled across the Elbe forsook the country. "In those days more than 600 families of the people of Holstein emigrated across the river [Elbe], seeking a better place where they might be free from danger. And they came into the Harz Mountains and there they themselves and their sons and their grandsons have remained unto this time."[3] The memory of Kruto is still preserved in North German legend as a terrible ogre. I have heard children singing jingles

[1] Helmold, I, 25. The line between the Germans and the Slavs, separating Holstein from the Wendish land, was the little river Schwale, near modern Neumünster, west of the Trave River (see Wigger; *Meck. Annalen*, p. 100, n. 7; Bahr, *Studien zur nordalbingischen Gesch. im 12. Jahrh.* [Leipzig, 1895], pp. 1–9).

[2] "Invaluitque Cruto .... obtinuitque dominium in universa terra Slavorum. Et attritae sunt vires Saxonum, et servierunt Crutoni sub tributo, omnis terra videlicet Nordalbingorum quae disterminatur in tres populos: Holzatos, Sturmarios, Thethmarchos [Holstein, Sturmaria, Ditmarsch]. Omnes hii durissimum servitutis jugum protaverunt omni tempore Crutonis" (Helmold, I, 26; cf. Schafarik, II, 537 f., 574; Hauck, IV, 595).

[3] Helm., I, 26. Probably the settlement of Elbingerode, in the Brockengebirge, is here indicated, for it is not mentioned before the twelfth century, and the name indicates that it was founded by some people from the Elbe Valley.

about him in the streets. The border situation was as if here in America Pontiac's conspiracy in 1763 had been successful, and the Indian tribes west of the Alleghanies combined. German colonization toward the northeast was given a serious setback. "The land was almost reduced to a solitude," is the mournful record. "Travel beyond the Elbe was difficult and hazardous."[1]

In defense of their farms and hamlets the peasantry walled and towered churches, and even cemeteries. The interior chapels of the larger churches sometimes were remodeled so as to be like the courts of a medieval castle. In the open country even corncribs were transformed into local points of resistance.[2]

Under other conditions the formation of a powerful pagan Slavonic state on the north and east of the German kingdom would have been regarded with immense anxiety by the Emperor. But at this juncture (1075) Henry IV had just become involved in the dual conflict with Pope Gregory VII and the revolted Saxons. The year before the Saxons had pleaded the border danger from the Wilzi as a pretext more than an excuse to avoid military service against the Poles.[3] Henry IV must have penetrated the real reason of their evasion, and considering that Saxony was on the verge of open rebellion against him regarded the menace hovering upon the edge of Saxony with some satisfaction, if not elation. According to one account, he even offered money to the Wilzi if they would attack the Saxons, but the Saxons outbid him. Another version is to the effect that Henry offered the Wilzi all the territory which they might conquer from the Saxons.[4]

Henry IV, although he had come forth victorious out of

[1] *Sidonis Epist.* (ed. Schmeidler), p. 236.

[2] See the interesting article of Haupt on the fortified churches of the duchies of the lower Elbe, in *Ztschft. d. Gesellschaft f. Schleswig-Holsteinische Gesch.*, Band XXXII (1902). It applies to an epoch later than this, but yet is not without bearing.

[3] Lambert of Hersfeld (ed. Holder-Egger), p. 147.

[4] Raumer, *Regesta*, Nos. 611, 613, 616. For this pro-pagan policy of Henry IV and Henry V see Schmeidler's edition of Helmold, Praef., p. xvi, and references.

the conflict with the papacy and the revolted German baronage, was friendly to them. Saxony had been the storm center of opposition to the Salian house, and the King perceived the strategic value of a border state friendly to him and hostile to the Saxons lying along the edge of Saxony. To the wrath of the Saxon clergy Henry IV not only befriended the Slavs, but even favored the continuance of paganism among them and opposed the church's missionary activity. His son Henry V, save for one isolated campaign against the Wilzi, adhered to the same policy.

Whatever be the real truth, it is at least certain that Kruto was able for years to hold his own against the aggression of Magnus (duke of Saxony), Eric (the Danish king), and the Margrave of the Nordmark. Of these three, Eric of Denmark was the most dangerous, for the ancient bargain which Conrad II had made with Cnut whereby he resigned Schleswig to Denmark in return for Danish support against the Baltic Slavs was bearing bitter fruit for Germany. Charlemagne's policy and that of the Saxon emperors had been to coop up the Danes within their peninsula. The failure of the Salians to adhere to this course and the alliance between the Danish ruling house and the Billunger whetted the appetite of Denmark so that she hungered to extend her domination along the Baltic Coast, where she had already acquired Jomsburg[1] at the mouth of the Oder. Henry IV for years was too involved with the revolted Saxons and the papacy to be able to give attention to this danger of Denmark becoming the possessor of the mouths of the German rivers. Under the circumstances the presence of a strong Slav state on the north and east as a check to both a hostile Denmark and a hostile Saxony was a great advantage to him.

But the realm created by Kruto was outwardly stronger than it actually was within. His power rested on his own personal achievements and prestige. A Rugian himself, the two other pagan tribes, the Wagrians and Ljutizi, still retained chiefs of their own, though in a subordinate capacity,

[1] Schmeidler (ed. Adam of Bremen), p. 79, n. 1, in a note to "nobilissima civitas Jumne" writes: "Nach allgemeiner Ansicht die berühmte Jomsburg mit den Jomsvikingern, auf dem Silberberge nördlich von Wollin bei Divenow."

who were jealous of Kruto, even if not open rivals. A greater source of weakness to Kruto, though, arose from the fact that the Christian wing of the Abodrites and the Low German population under Kruto's sway—in Holstein and Ditmarsch —secretly connived with the Saxons against him, and found a leader in a son of the late Abodrite duke, Gottschalk, named Henry.[1] In 1093 the united Christian forces, aided by some Saxons, won a great victory over the pagan Wends at Schmilow near Ratzeburg, conquered fourteen Wendish towns, and reduced the Wagrians and Ljutizi to tribute once more.[2]

Holstein and Ditmarsch were free again. But the Christian Abodrite Duke was wise enough not to attempt to impose Christianity upon all the people of his tribe, deeming it better to pay tribute to the Saxons for the indulgence of paganism.[3] Of the German population once there, many had emigrated, the rest had maintained a precarious existence under the Wendish and pagan domination, living in the vicinity of a few Burgwärde which seem never to have been taken by the Wends.[4] The people gladly went back to their abandoned farms. German civilization and Germany's ecclesiastical system returned to the land, "and the houses and churches which had been destroyed were rebuilt."

[1] Helm., I, 34, is much confused in his chronology at this point, and the dates and main facts of this paragraph are established from the *Annals of Hildesheim* (*MGH*, SS. III, 106). Schirrin (*op. cit.*, pp. 114 ff.) regards the whole account in Helm., *loc. cit.*, as romance. Contra are Wigger, pp. 44 ff., and Breska, *Untersuchungen*, pp. 41 ff. According to Helmold, Henry treacherously slew Kruto with the connivance of the latter's Wendish wife, whom Henry married.

[2] On this important battle see L. Giesebrecht, *Wend. Geschichten*, II, 167; Meyer v. Knonau, *Jahrb. Heinrichs IV*, IV, 416; Wendt, I, 80.

[3] "Porro in universa Slavia necdum erat ecclesia vel sacerdos, nisi in urbe tantum quae nunc Vetus Lubika [Alt-Lübeck at the confluence of the little river Swartowe with the Trave] dicitur, eo quod Heinricus cum familia sua, saepius illic moraretur" (Helm., I, 34). Breska, *Ztschft. f. Lübeckische Gesch.*, Band IV (1881), argues, against Schirren, for the accuracy of Helmold's assertion that the Christian Abodrite Duke Henry made an expedition in 1100 against the pagan Wends of Brandenburg. On the Abodrite dukes see Schmeidler, *Hamburg-Bremen und Nordost Europa, etc.*, pp. 318–30; Marquart, *Osteuropäische und ostasiatische Streifzüge* (Leipzig, 1903), pp. 305–29; Biereye, *op. cit.*, pp. 169–76.

[4] Helmold does not call them Burgwärde, as Thietmar a century and a half earlier denominated the Saxon strongholds in the Sorben land. Instead he calls them *munitiones* (I, 34) or *praesidia* (I, 19, 25). He gives the name of two of these—Echeco and Bokeldeburg.

The year 1093 may be regarded as a turning-point in the history of the Baltic Slavs. The three great Slavonic revolts of 983, 1018, and 1066, in spite of their success, had depleted the energies of the tribes, and the residue of their power, after victory, was worn down by almost continuous border warfare with the Saxons. The offensive history of Wendish paganism was ended. At the close of the eleventh century the liberty and the religion of the Baltic Slavs stood upon the defensive.[1] Slowly the ring was tightening around the last devotees of the Slavonic gods, in the territory between the lower Elbe and the Oder. Poland menaced them on the east; Germany on the west. The conversion of the Poles at the end of the eleventh century was followed by a crusade of Boleslav III in 1102 against the Pomeranians. In the ensuing years the land lying between the lower Oder and the Peene and Havel rivers, with the important Wendish towns of Stettin and Wollin, was overrun by the Poles. It was the high-water mark of Polish westward expansion.[2] For the coming of Albrecht the Bear into Brandenburg in 1134 and the extension of German domination over the Uckermark were soon effectually to check the ambition of Poland to acquire the Baltic seaboard.

Perhaps a ray of hope came to the hard-pressed Wends when, in 1106, Magnus Billung,[3] the last of his line, and Udo III, the formidable margrave of the Nordmark, died. But it must have vanished at once. The fatal turning-point in the history of the Baltic Slavs is the year 1106 when Magnus Billung, the last of his house, died and was succeeded in the duchy of Saxony by Lothar of Supplinburg. The new Duke was politically as powerful as his predecessor, and by tradition and family ties represented more than the Billunger the real interests of the Saxon people. The Billunger, as we have seen, were hostile to the conversion of the Slavs because the tithes of the church reduced the tribute which they exacted from the conquered Wends. Their interest had been to pre-

[1] In 1100–1101 Margrave Udo III of the Nordmark recovered Brandenburg for a brief moment (Raumer, *Regesta*, No. 667; *Ann. of Hild.* [*MGH*, SS. III, 107]; *Ann. Sax.* [1101]; *Ann. Rosenv.* [SS. XVI, 102]).

[2] Sommerfeld, *op. cit.*, pp. 16–18; Wendt, II, 4–5.

[3] See B. Köster, *Sachsen unter Herzog Magnus* (1881).

vent missions among the Slavs. But Lothar was an ardent supporter of the church. His accession was followed by a renewal of church energy. For the first time church and state in Saxony were united in a common purpose. The sword of the Duke was extended in favor of the clergy, and a series of attacks began upon the Wends which were at once military expeditions and missionary campaigns. It has been truly said that no such formidable person had appeared in the north since the days of Gero.[1] In 1110 Lothar avenged the murder of one of his vassals, Godfrey of Holstein, in the Abodrite country, by conquering nine of their towns.[2]

The seeming strength and security of the Baltic Slavs was illusory. In the first quarter of the twelfth century it is undeniable that Slavonic paganism was upon the defensive. Although it was true that "ultra Albiam illis temporibus rarus inveniebatur Christianus,"[3] nevertheless Christianity was slowly seeping into the trans-Elbean lands, especially in the territory of Brandenburg, where the extension of the church can be obscurely discerned. There is record of a church at Leitzkau in 1114, and the Archbishop of Magdeburg had a Christian Wendish *praefectus* in his service at Loburg in 1115.

It is fair to say, however, that at this time the Rugian Slavs furnished some provocation for these feats of arms, apart from the religious zeal which actuated the Saxons. Like the Vikings of the ninth century, the Rugians, whose capital was situated on the island of Rügen, were a sea-robber folk, adventurous and fiercely pagan.[4] Their depredations along the Baltic Coast, in Mecklenburg, Holstein, and Schleswig, whence they carried off men, women, and children into slavery, and immense booty, were serious. In 1110 their robber bands fell upon Holstein and penetrated nearly to Hamburg. A cry of protest went up from the land.[5] In 1111 (the

[1] Bernhardi, *Jahrbuch*, p. 19.

[2] Helm., I, 35; *Ann. Hild.* (*MGH*, SS. III, 112).

[3] *Annal. Pegav.* (*MGH*, SS. XVI, 252).

[4] L. Giesebrecht, *Wend. Gesch.*, I, 205 f.; Barthold, I, 324 f.

[5] *Annal. Hildesh.*; *Annal. Sax.* (1110); see the anecdote related by Helmold, I, 35, of a peasant (*rusticus*) whose wife and children had been carried off, who met Count Godfrey of Sturm in the way and bitterly upbraided him.

date is not certain) they again invaded Nordalbingia "as if they were going to possess the land," says Helmold. But Henry, the Christian Abodrite duke, was ready for them, and so great a slaughter of the invaders was made that out of the bodies of the slain a huge mound was erected called the Raniberg, which was long pointed out to the curious. This victory raised the prestige of the Abodrite chief to a high pitch both among the Germans of the lower Elbe and among the converted Wends. When, soon afterward, Duke Henry's son was killed by the Rugians, a united Wendish-Saxon host was gathered to the number of sixteen hundred men, it is said. No Saxon or Christian army had been beyond the Peene River since the time of Otto I.

The campaign was purposely undertaken in the winter season in the hope that it might be possible to cross from the mainland to the island of Rügen upon the ice. The plan was as successful, perhaps, as the leaders had dared to hope. After nine days' march the army reached the Baltic, where they burned all the Rugian fishing villages. When nothing but the frozen strait separated the attackers from the island, the priests of Arkona took alarm and sent a humble message through a Rugian priest (Helmold calls him a *flamen*, not the medieval Latin word for "priest," i.e., *sacerdos*)[1] with the proffer of 400 and then 800 marks. But immunity was not to be purchased so cheaply. In the end the Rugians gave hostages for the payment of the astonishing sum of 4,400 marks. The imposition of this huge indemnity stripped their temple and even private persons; messengers had to be sent to the mainland for contributions. The heart of Baltic Slavdom was shaken to the core by this expedition.[2]

In 1114 Hartbert, titular bishop of Brandenburg, then *in partibus paganorum*, invaded his see and returned, boasting

[1] *Sacerdos* and *presbyter* were used interchangeably. In towns one sometimes finds *parochianus* or *rector* or *pastor ecclesiae*, and *plebanus* in the fourteenth century (Koeniger. *op. cit.*, p. 92, n. 3).

[2] Helmold, I, 38; *Annal. Corb.* (*MGH*, SS. III, 8); *Annalista Saxo* (*MGH*, SS. VI, 75). The date of this expedition is put by Wendt, I, 84, in the winter of 1123–24. Schmeidler, the latest editor of Helmold, places it in 1113–14. Personally I incline to the date 1113–14, for such a campaign as this would naturally follow in retaliation for the great piratical raids of 1110–11.

that he had destroyed many idols of the pagan Wends.[1] On February 9, 1115, Count Otto of Ballenstadt won a crushing victory over the Wends at Köthen.[2] In the winter of 1124–25 Lothar, the Saxon duke, in company with a force of Christian Abodrites, destroyed the temple at Rethra,[3] and would probably have destroyed that of Arkona in Rügen if a thaw had not inopportunely broken up the ice and prevented the army from crossing the strait.[4] In that very spring the Christian Abodrite chief, Henry, died (March 22), and in the ensuing August, Lothar, the Saxon duke, succeeded Henry V, the last of the Salian house, as king and emperor.

It is manifest to the student who reads the history of this time that by 1125 the independence and the religion of the Baltic Slavs were clearly doomed to extinguishment. The division of the Abodrites into a Christian and a pagan group, the careers of such Wendish chieftains as Gottschalk and Henry, are evidences of it. Above all, the change of dynasty in Germany in 1125 was a bad omen for the Baltic Slavs. The old Saxon tradition of conquest and expulsion of the Wends was now identified with the power of the German kingship. Moreover, Lothar was a zealous Christian, not of the calculating Salian kind, and warmly espoused the Saxon clergy's program of forcible conversion of the Wends.

The times were propitious for such achievement. History sometimes has a singular way of clustering men and events within a brief space of years—often, too, within a limited geographical area. Such was the case in North Germany at this time, where a remarkable combination of men and events is to be found. The rise of Conrad the Great of Wettin (1124–56), of Adolph of Holstein in 1130, of Albrecht the Bear in 1134, of Henry the Lion in 1139, was destined to revolutionize the history of Lower Germany. Moreover, by the side of these great lay princes lived and labored church-

[1] "Ritum sum persecutus paganorum . . . . multa atque innumerabilia destruximus idola" (Riedel, *Codex Diplom. Brand.* [1114], X, 69).

[2] *Annal. Sax.* (1115).

[3] Helmold fails us of this information, but the fact is attested by Ebbo, III, 5; cf. Wendt, I, 85, n. 14.

[4] Helmold, I, 38 end; *Anselmi Cont. Sigab.* (*anno* 1124) (SS. VI, 379).

men of a new and progressive type, such as Norbert of Magdeburg (1126–34), Vicelin of Oldenburg (d. 1154), and Otto of Bamberg,[1] the apostle to the Pomeranians (d. 1139).

Born in Swabia in 1060 and early left an orphan, Otto's first recognition came in 1087 when he became chaplain to Judith, the sister of Henry IV, who married Wladislaw, duke of Poland in that year. His early career in Poland made an ineffaceable impression upon Otto. After Judith's death he returned to Germany, was for some time administrator of a monastery in Regensburg, and then entered the service of Henry IV, who, perceiving his remarkable ability, intrusted him with the superintendence of the erection of the cathedral of Speyer. A few years later Otto entered the imperial chancellery. He refused appointment to the sees of Augsburg and Halberstadt, but finally in 1102 when Ruprecht of Bamberg died, Otto became bishop of Bamberg, where he remained until his decease in 1139.

His talent for administration found ample opportunity there, for the diocese had been badly neglected by his predecessors. He busied himself in restoration of the cathedral, in building new churches and convents, and founded a school at Bamberg which shortly became the intellectual center of Germany. It was he who appointed the famous historian Ekkehard of Aura to that abbey. He was not always loyal to Henry IV. In September, 1105, he advocated the cause of Prince Henry, afterward Henry V. He labored to reconcile Pope and Emperor, and was sent on an embassy to Pascal II in 1107. His loyalty to Henry V incurred the anathema of Gelasius II in 1118, and his restoration to his see was due to Calixtus II. During the reign of Lothar II we find Otto deeply interested in the issues of that reign, especially in the papal schism between Anacletus II and Innocent II.

It is, however, as apostle to the Pomeranians that Otto of Bamberg[2] is known to history. In 1122 or 1123 Boleslav III

[1] Bossert, *Württemb. Vierteljahrshefte für Landesgesch.*, Band VI, Heft 4 (1884).

[2] Until the appearance of Georg Jüritsch's masterly *Geschichte des Bischofs Otto I von Bamberg, des Pommern-Apostels* (1102-39) (Gotha: Perthes, 1889) there was no other adequate biography of this greatest missionary of the Latin church among the Slavs. The literature is large: Roepell, *Gesch. Polens*, I, 267–85; Zimmermann

of Poland urged the conversion of the Pomeranians upon him.[1]

Astonishing as it seems, at this time even some of the clergy appear for a brief moment to have been actuated by a new and softer spirit. The German church, in some degree reintegrated by the Cluniac reform, and given new ideals of practical humanitarianism and spiritual enterprise by the spread of French monastic foundations like the Cistercians, began to manifest a refreshing missionary zeal and partially to abandon its brutal desire for increase of tithes merely. Vicelin of Oldenburg and especially the saintly Otto of Bamberg represent a new type of bishop practicing gentle methods, learning the Slav tongue, and considerate of the customs and prejudices of the Wends.[2]

Let us first glance at the history of the conversion of Pomerania. Henry II had founded the bishopric of Bamberg in 1007 as a missionary station among the Wends of the upper Main and the Neckar, and something of the pious spirit of Henry and his empress, the gentle Cunigunde, seems to have affected the traditions of the see. A bishop endued with sincere religious zeal, who learned the Slav language and

---

Otto, Bischof von Bamberg (Freiburg, 1875); Looshorn, *Der heilige Bischof Otto* (Munich, 1888); Maskus, *Bischof Otto von Bamberg, Reichsfürst und Missionar* (Breslau, 1889); Giesebrecht, *Kaiserzeit* (5th ed.), III, 987 ff.; Sommerfeld, *Gesch. der Germanisierung des Herzogtums Pommern*, chap. i (in Schmoller's *Forschungen*, Band XIII [Fünftes Heft, 1896]); Hauck, *Kirchengesch.*, III, 564–87; Lehmann, *Pommern zur Zeit Ottos von Bamberg* (1880); Wehrmann, *Monatsbl. von d. Gesellschaft für Pom. Gesch.* (1887) (on the relations between Bamberg and Pomerania after Otto's death. The anniversary day of the old Bishop, October 1, is still widely observed in Pomerania (Wehrmann, *op. cit.*, p. 66). The Russian scholar Kotliarevsky has supplemented these sources by use of Russian hagiographic sources, which are particularly valuable for elucidating Slavonic racial practices and characteristics. A. Kotliarevsky, *Documents Concerning Otto of Bamberg Illustrative of the History and Archaeology of the Slavs; The Antiquities and History of the Maritime Slavs in the Twelfth Century* [Prague, 1874]). See review by A. Maury, *Journal des savants* (September and October, 1877).

[1] Jüritsch, *op. cit.* p. 252.

[2] Helmold's knowledge of the tongue must have been large, for his observations upon the words and the language are too intimate for it to have been otherwise (see I, 1, 12, 20, 25, 50, 52, 84, 88. In I, 84, he lauds the labors of a priest of Oldenburg in the twelfth century, named Bruno, who "sufficienter amministravit verbum Dei, habens sermones conscriptos Slavicis verbis, quos populo pronuntiaret oportune").

mingled with the hated race with the loving-kindness of a father among his children, is a novel and refreshing type of German ecclesiastic.[1]

The conversion of Pomerania by evangelization and not by the sword is Otto of Bamberg's title to fame. He literally created a new Baltic state in the first half of the twelfth century. Pomerania was nominally under the sway of Poland, and it was the initiative of Duke Boleslav III which first interested Otto in the project of converting the Pomeranians. "Durch sein Verdienst wurde die seit einem Jahrhundert unterbrochene Mission im Osten neubelebt und deutscher Sitte und Sprache die Bahn und Ostseeküsten gebrochen."[2]

In 1107 Duke Boleslaw III, the Wrymouthed (1102–39), had overcome and subjugated the heathen Slavic Pomeranians after the death of the Pomeranian chieftain Swantibor, who had left "Slavia" to his eldest son and Pommerellia to the two younger sons, Stettinberg being the capital of the former and Danzig of the latter. This new acquisition extended far across the Oder to the Baltic coast, including the city of Demmin on the Peene River, its southern boundary touching Dobrilugk in Lusatia.

The Pomeranians were a cognate Slavic people, but they were separated from Poland by a primeval forest, of which Herbord says:

> . . . . A terrible, enormous forest divides Pomerania and Poland. This wood had not been traversed before by any mortal, except that the Duke of Poland in earlier years, before he had conquered the whole of Pomerania, had cut a way for himself and his army by felling and marking the trees.[3]

The inhabitants of Pomerania for a long time were able to resist the numerous attempts at their subjugation. Ancient traditions, however, assert that Pomoří (Pomerania) at one time formed an integral part of Poland, as witnessed by the

[1] See the comments of Lavisse, *La Marche de Brandenbourg*, p. 52; Guttmann, in *Forschungen zur Brand. und Preuss. Gesch.*, IX, 439–40.

[2] Richter, *Annalen*, II, 634 n. The text of Boleslav's charter to the first Christian establishment in Pomerania is in Herbordus, *Dialogus*, II, 20 (Jaffé, V, 775–76).

[3] II, 10.

fact that the capitals of Poland, Gnesen and Kruszwice, were placed so far north.[1]

Though attempts at Christianization had been carried on ever since Boleslaw Chrobry ruled the land and Kolberg was set up as the seat of the Pomeranian bishopric, the inhabitants either resisted the attempts or relapsed into heathenism. Boleslaw the Wrymouthed soon after his subjugation of Pomerania set a Spanish monk, Bishop Bernhard, to convert the people, but he soon had to give up his attempt, for he was laughed to scorn for his humble attire and his bare feet. From among the Polish clergy the Duke could not find a man who could undertake the difficult task, so at last he turned to Bishop Otto of Bamberg. He, having been a chaplain at the court of Boleslaw's father, knew the language, and was generally well adapted to the task. Otto was certainly animated by religious motives when he undertook this great work, for, as Schafarik says of him: "He was one of the most noble of the apostles of the Slavs";[2] but this does not preclude the possibility that even political motives entered into his considerations.[3] Otto was no visionary. He saw a possibility of an extension of his diocese, and the consequent increase of the income of his office, and this also entered into his calculations. Although over sixty years old, he could not refuse, in spite of the hardships he knew it would be necessary to endure. Twice he made the long and arduous journey to the far Baltic coast towns of Stettin and Wollin.

Pomerania then was a land of marsh and fen, of sluggish streams and stagnant lakes, inhabited by a pure Slav people who still lived after the primitive manner of their kind and were absolutely untouched by Christo-German civilization. A fisher-folk chiefly, wealth was estimated in lasts of dried fish and in hives of bees, for honey was a staple article of production. Their food was fish and rye and a few vegetables; they drank a mead of cherry and honey. Their textile skill was considerable, but they were poor farmers. The towns at the mouth of the Oder and the Peene had considerable com-

[1] Schafarik, II, 399. [2] *Ibid.*, p. 404.

[3] Cf. Wehrmann, *Gesch. von Pommern*, p. 61.

merce in raw productions like dried fish, furs, tar, rope, etc., but were astonishingly squalid and miry.[1] The only structures of prominence were the temples.[2] Here, too, was a sacred black horse. Amid this population, which was spared the intolerance, the bigotry, and the greed which were so heavily inflicted upon the Slavs of the Elbe, Otto lived and labored, winning the confidence of the Pomeranians by gentle means.[3] Pomerania was the only Slavonic land under the domination of the Latin church in the Middle Ages which made the transition from paganism to Christianity and from barbarism to civilization by transformation and not by force.[4] Among the many canonized but unhallowed saints of the Roman church Otto of Bamberg justly deserved the halo with which Clement III crowned his memory in 1189.

Otto started out on his journey in 1124, being accompanied by two monks of Michelsberg, Ebo and Herbord, about twenty ecclesiastics of Bamberg, and a numerous retinue of servants. They passed through Bohemia, Silesia, and Poland, and were received with a great pomp by Boleslaw at Gnesen. There they were joined by an escort of Polish soldiers, and by three chaplains from the Polish court, one of whom, however, Adalbert, was a German. It is therefore interesting to note how thoroughly German this mission was. Then the whole company set out across the border forest, following the cleared path which the Duke had made on his warlike expedition. Otto and his company were received by the Pomeranian duke, Warcislaw, or, as Herbord calls him, Wratislaw, who was already a Christian. The Duke treated them kindly, but this may have been the result of his fear of the Polish soldiery which accompanied the Bishop. How Otto

[1] Sommerfeld, *op. cit.*, pp. 62–66.

[2] In Herbordus, II, 32, is a remarkable description of the temple at Stettin. It was adorned with carved wooden figures of men and beasts and birds, brilliantly painted and so true to nature "ut spirare putares ac vivere."

[3] See the anecdote in Herbordus, III, 19, of the boys playing in the street whom Otto spoke to in their own language, and who followed him.

[4] Otto sent the three-headed head of the idol Triglav to Pope Honorius II as a proof of the conversion of the Pomeranians (Kanzow, *Pomerania, oder Ursprunck, Altheit und Geschichte der Völker und Lande Pommern, Cassuben, Wenden, Stettin, Rügen* [ed. Kosegarten], p. 107).

was received by the populace we may judge from the following extract from Herbord:

> We have nothing in common with you. The laws which we inherited from our fathers we will not give up; we are content with the religion which we have. Among the Christians there are thieves and robbers, whose feet are cut off and eyes gouged out; the Christian practices all kinds of crime and punishments upon the Christian. Far from us be such a religion. . . . . Among them were no beggars, no locks and keys; they were highly surprised at the fastened chests of the bishops. Their table was always decked with food, and every stranger could enter and satisfy himself.[1]

However, Otto, in his gorgeous vestments and with his splendid retinue, partly intimidated and partly overawed, and, most assuredly, partly won his audiences. We learn that at the very first town, that of Pierzysk (Pyritz), he won a considerable number who submitted to baptism, although the number usually stated (3,585) people is not to be taken as accurate. Unlike the humbler Bernhard, Otto merely put the question before his hearers as to whether or not they wanted to be baptized. Those who then consented to be baptized were instructed in the Christian faith after baptism, and by priests left in the city for that purpose after the Bishop had left.[2]

In Kammin the missionaries found ready listeners, and built there a small wooden church. When they passed on to Wollin,[3] for the first time they met with opposition. This was a city where the heathen party was strong and active, although it would be a mistake to suppose that it was absolutely untouched by Christianity. One of the richest of the inhabitants, Nedamir by name, was a Christian, who had learned Christianity and had been baptized in Saxony.[4] After a prolonged struggle, the people of Wollin agreed that if the people of Stettin should accept the new faith they would then follow the example. But the people of Stettin, who were

[1] II, 10, 25, 40.

[2] Hauck, *Kirchengeschichte Deutschlands*, IV, 575.

[3] Wollin was the first bishopric established in Pomerania. In 1180, however, the see was removed to Kammin (Wiesener, *Ztschft. f. Kirchengesch.*, Band X, Heft 1 [1888]). The monastery of Stolp (founded in 1153) became an important center for evangelization (Schultz, *Baltische Studien*, Band, XXXI [1881]).

[4] Hauck, IV, 568.

strongly under the domination of the priests of the local temple of Triglav, scornfully rejected the offer of the missionaries, and refused to be intimidated by the Polish soldiery under Count Paulicius into the acceptance of Christianity. At last the threat of the vengeance of Duke Boleslaw induced them to promise to accept the new faith, but they exacted the condition that a part of their heavy taxes be remitted them. The Duke promised to do this, but accompanied his promise with a threat that if the people should fail to live up to the conditions he would bring them to submission by force. Therefore, the people finally yielded and allowed their celebrated temple of Triglav to be destroyed.

Otto founded two churches at Stettin, and then returned to Wollin; the people of that city faithfully kept their promise, and thus Otto was able to establish two churches at that city also. In fact, Otto intended to make Wollin the center of the Pomeranian episcopal diocese, and left Adalbert there with the intention of procuring for him the episcopal dignity. Then Otto pursued his way to Kolberg and Belgrad, and after visiting these cities, returned through all the places where he had planted Christian work, and returned home, arriving at Bamberg at Easter, 1125.

Of course, this short ministry could not do much more than open the land to the Christian missionary work, and predispose it to tolerance of that religion. Still even at that, much was accomplished. Hauck states that the number of the baptized ran up to over twenty-two thousand people, and that in nine places there were eleven mission churches established.[1] But what had been accomplished had been done by reason of the fact that in spite of the constant threat of force which was exerted by the soldiers accompanying Bishop Otto, we do not read of any actual bloodshed or great cruelty committed by these rough champions of Christianity. The Pomeranians were won as far as they were won, because Christianity came to them largely in a peaceful manner, although not entirely without coercion. Thus we can at least partially understand why some Slavic nations—like the Moravians, the Bohemians, to some extent the Poles, later

[1] *Ibid.*, IV, p. 578.

the Russians, etc.—accepted Christianity peaceably and retained it ever after, while other Slavic tribes opposed Christianity with furious and agelong struggles. The reason for the stubborn struggle of the Baltic and the Elbe Slavs is to be sought in the circumstance that Christianity came to them with fire and sword, and that its messengers sought to enslave and exploit these nations in such a shameful manner that this chapter of the history of the expansion of Christianity is one of the blackest.[1]

And yet heathen Pomerania could not give up its struggle quite so easily. Although Christianity came into the land more or less peacably, still it represented the hated overlordship of Poland and the threatening might of Germany. Therefore, moved by the stirring appeals of the patriotic heathen priests, Pomerania—especially Wollin and Stettin—rose in reaction against Christianity and the accompanying foreign domination. After Otto's departure the pagan priests endeavored to arouse the people against the "German God" (*Teutonicus Deus*). The Christians resisted, not without peril to themselves, and Otto, in spite of his sixty-eight years, resolved to return to Pomerania in April, 1128. He selected Usedom as his headquarters, convoked an assembly of the nobles of the country, and was successful, with the aid of Wladislaw, in baptizing a great number, so much so that he dreamed of converting the island of Rügen.

Otto's second journey was not conducted under Polish auspices, but with the aid of Emperor Lothar, who now realized the political possibilities of the missionary work of the Bishop of Bamberg. The party, which besides the clerics, consisted of German knights and soldiers, and was accompanied with ample provision packs, went from Halle down the Saale River to the Elbe, and then up the Havel River. It is interesting to note that the practical Bishop bought a load of salt which he intended to sell in the land of the Slavs.[2]

On Pentecost, 1128, the party arrived at the city of

[1] Schafarik, II, 560.

[2] "So verband er mit dem religiösen Zwecke der Fahrt auch die Absicht, dem Lande, das bisher dem deutschen Handel und Verkehr noch wenig erschlossen war, wirtschaftliche Vorteile zu bringen und aus ihm zu gewinnen" (Wehrmann, *Geschichte von Pommern*, p. 69).

Uznoimia (Usedom), where the missionaries had a considerable success, which followed them to Wolgast also. Thence Otto went on to Stettin and to Wollin, at both of which places the reactionary element was subjugated and the Christian work reinstated. In November, 1128, Otto left Pomerania and returned via Gnesen to his home at Bamberg.

From the fact that Boleslaw the Wrymouthed selected Otto for the difficult task of Christianizing Pomerania, and from the general influence which Otto exercised over the Polish Prince, it is not impossible to believe that Otto tried to induce Boleslaw to put the Polish bishoprics again under the jurisdiction of the Magdeburger metropolitan, as they were before the year 1000. But Boleslaw was not the man to commit such a blunder, and it seems that even the papacy did not favor this plan, because Poland paid the "Peter's pence" regularly, while in Germany this was not a fully established custom.[1]

Nordalbingia, too, at this same time had its Otto of Bamberg in the person of a devoted priest named Vicelin. But in his case his gentle labors among the Wagrians were neutralized by the fierce violence of Henry the Lion and the bigotry of St. Bernard. The work of Vicelin of Oldenburg among the unconverted Abodrites and Wagri is closely interwoven with this period of German trans-Elbean expansion. Helmold writes:

> In these days there was neither church nor priest among all the people of the Wilzi, Abodrites and Wagri, except only in the city of [Alt-]Lübeck, because there the court of Henry [the duke of the Abodrites, who personally was Christian] was established (1126). And at this time there came a certain priest named Vicelin who came to the "king" of the Slavs in [Alt-]Lübeck and asked to be given the right to preach the word of God in his land.[2]

Vicelin was born in a little Saxon hamlet near Minden and was educated in the episcopal school at Paderborn under a then-distinguished master named Hartmann; thence he

[1] Grünehagen, *op. cit.*, p. 15.

[2] I, 41. For critical study of Vicelin's life see C. Schirren, *Beitraege zur Kritik aelterer Holsteinischer Geschichtsquellen* (Leipzig, 1876) (originally in *Ztschft. der Gesellschaft für Schleswig-Holstein-Lauenburg Gesch.*, VII, 281 f., and in the *Forschungen zur deutschen Gesch.*, Band XVII).

passed to the instruction of his uncle, a priest of Fuhlen, in the county of Schaumburg,[1] who seems to have had more than local fame as a scholar. When his uncle died Vicelin went back to Paderborn and afterward to the episcopal school in Bremen. Here his winning personality and high moral qualities exercised a great influence over his clerical pupils, who were accustomed, like boys in a boarding-school, to get "out of bounds" and roam the streets at night, or find unlawful pleasure in frequenting taverns. His efficiency drew the praise of his superior, Bishop Fretherícus, who, however, expressed misgivings of the disciplinary value of moral suasion when compared with the time-honored schoolmaster's rod. But Vicelin could not be persuaded to use the whip upon his pupils, saying that many a good student was ruined by cruelty.[2] In the year 1122–23 Vicelin went to France, then the educational center of Europe, and pursued his studies at Laon under the famous masters, the brothers Anselm and Raoul,[3] "qui in explanacione divinae paginae fuerant eo tempore precipui."

But Vicelin had no taste for the "empty subtleties and mere battles of words"[4] which characterized scholastic education at this time. He pined for some more practical interest. In 1126 he returned to Germany and sought out Norbert, the famous Praemonstratensian archbishop of Magdeburg, who in Brandenburg had begun to imitate the enlightened policy which Otto of Bamberg was so successfully employing in the conversion of the Pomeranians. Although Vicelin did not become a Praemonstratensian,[5] he imbibed the generous missionary enthusiasm of the Norbertines. It was from Nor-

[1] See von Mooyer, *Die vormalige Grafschaft Schaumburg*, p. 25.

[2] This paragraph is derived from Helmold, I, 44.

[3] See G. Le Fevre, *De Anselmo Laudunensi scholastico* (Evreux, 1895).

[4] "Quaestiones supervacuas pugnasque verborum."

[5] See Hirsekorn, *Die Slavenchronik Helmolds* (Göttingen, 1873), p. 42. Helmold (I, 47) gives the form of their agreement together: "Hii ergo sacris connexi federibus statuerunt amplecti celibatum vitae, perdurare in oratione et jejunio, exerceri in opera pietatis, visitare infirmos, alere egentes, tam propriam quam proximorum salutem curare." One MS bears the marginal comment that Vicelin was probably an Augustine. But this form does not appear in the rules of that order.

bert himself that Vicelin first learned of Duke Henry, the Christian Abodrite prince, and speedily conceived the idea that the conversion of Wagria was his appointed task. "At once he took the road into the land of the Slavs" with two companions, Rodolph, a presbyter of Hildesheim, and Ludolf, a canon of Verdun.[1]

The Abodrite ruler received them graciously and they joyfully returned to Saxony in order to bring back the vessels and garments and other apparatus of church worship. The new gospel station was established at Neumünster on the boundary line between German Holstein and Slavonic Wagria.[2] It was a rough and uncouth frontier community in which Vicelin undertook to minister, predominantly Wendish, but with a considerable sprinkling of a hardy, lawless pioneer element—Helmold says it was a *gens bruta.* One is reminded of the frontier missionary labors of Peter Cartwright in America, for even in religion, as in many other aspects of the frontier, the medieval German border reminds one of our own West in pioneer times. A wave of crude revivalism stirred these rude border folk which impressed Helmold with its intensity.[3]

But Vicelin's hopes were soon dashed. Duke Henry died shortly after the mission was established; his sons quarreled until both were killed, and the land was rent with dissension, in the midst of which a band of pirates from Rügen descended upon the country. Border ruffianism prevailed. Peace and order were not restored until the rise of those two strong men of lower Saxony, Adolph of Holstein and Henry the Lion.[4]

[1] These were later joined in their labors by four others, "of whom," says Helmold (I, 47, quoting I Cor. 15:6), "the greater part are fallen asleep" (cf. I, 54). Did Helmold derive his account from actual comrades of Vicelin?

[2] Helmold, I, 47.

[3] "Denique incredibili dictu est, quanta plebium caterva in diebus illis ad penetentiae remedium confugerit, insonuitque vox predicacionis ejus in omni Nordalbingorum provincia"(I, 47). ". . . . Jactumque est misercordia Dei . . . . seminarium novellae plantacionis in Slavia" (I, 54).

[4] This account of Vicelin's early life has been drawn from Helmold, I, 42–49. For literature see A. Boehmer, *Vicelin* (Rostock, 1887); Höhlbaum, "Vicelin und seine Biographen," *Forschungen zur deutschen Gesch.*, XVII, 209–29; Schirren, "Über Vicelins Priesterweihe," *ibid.*, pp. 376–89; Bernhardi, *Lothar II;* cf. Dáhlmann-Waitz., *Quellenkunde der deutschen Gesch.* (last ed., 1912), No. 5477.

Yet in spite of these adverse conditions Vicelin's labors managed to prosper, and a half-dozen wilderness missionary stations were founded.[1] But there were few Germans living across the lower Elbe[2] at this time, except in Holstein[3] where some scattered Burgwärde gave greater security.[4] The private chapel of the Abodrite Duke in Alt-Lübeck was the only Christian edifice in the land before Vicelin's coming.[5] The best element in the country was a considerable colony of German merchants[6] settled in the Abodrite capital. But the new Abodrite Duke Pribislav[7] had apprehensions of the political effect upon his people which might arise from the establishment of a church in the capital of the Abodrites[8] and refused permission. Accordingly, the first public church in Alt-Lübeck was set up across the Trave River on a hill outside the city.[9] The precaution was wisely taken, for the irritation of the Abodrites daily increased because of the steady

[1] Helmold, I, 53, says: "sex vel eo amplius oppida." In I, 58, he describes them as "incommoda fori—forensis ecclesia." The names are recorded in some verses commemorative of Vicelin printed in the Appendix to Schmeidler's edition of Helmold, p. 229, vss. 125 ff. They also are mentioned in a diploma of Lothar II, March 17, 1137, and another of Conrad III, dated January 5, 1139 (Boehmer-Mühlbacher, *Regesta*, Nos. 3348, 3384). But there is some doubt of the trustworthiness of the documents. Cf. Bernhardi, *op. cit.*, p. 800, n. 27; Bahr, *Nordalbing. Studien*, pp. 37 ff.; Schultze, *Die Urkunden Lothars II* (Innsbruck, 1905), pp. 129 ff.

[2] This is established from the testimony of Helmold, I, 8, 48, and 56, though he contradicts himself in I, 24, where he falls into error by following Adam of Bremen. See edition of Helmold by Schmeidler, p. 96, n. 1. It is confirmed by the *Ann. Pegav.* (*anno* 1115). "Ultra Albiam illis temporibus rarus inveniebatur Christianus" (*MGH*, SS. XVI, 252).

[3] Helmold, I, 41. "Sed et Slavorum populi agebant ea quae pacis sunt, eo quod Heinricus Slavorum regulus [observe that he is not called *dux*] comitem Adolfum et contiguos Nordalbingorum populos omni benivolentia amplexatus fuerit."

[4] *Ibid.*, I, 34, 56.

[5] *Ibid.*, I, 34, 41.

[6] *Ibid.*, I, 48: "a mercatoribus quorum non parvam coloniam."

[7] Nine coins of Pribislav have been preserved, which perhaps are testimony of the commercial relations between the Germans and the Elbean Slavs. They were found in 1880 at Michendorf near Potsdam (Eckstein, *Mitth. d. Ver. f. Vaterländische Kultur* [1881–82]).

[8] "Protestatus est omnem Slavorum gentem divinae religioni subjugere" (Helmold, I, 53).

[9] *Ibid.*, I, 48; cf. Ohnesorge, *op. cit.*, p. 69.

encroachment of German settlers into their territory, and the feeling was all the more aggravated by the intolerant preaching which Vicelin could not control and the popular hatred with which the religion of the Slavs was regarded by the German incomers, which found vent in attacks upon their sacred groves and their temples.[1]

The Abodrites and Wagri were dangerously aroused and on the verge of open war to protect their liberty. The pagan population still cherished the memory of the pagan hero Kruto, and was sullenly hostile to their ruler and his and their German Christian neighbors on the edge of the country. They were intensely suspicious—and with good reason—of Adolph of Holstein and the Emperor, who seems to have been resolved upon a policy toward the Abodrites of complete subjugation and compulsory conversion. To that end Lothar II energetically began the building of castles in Wagria, in particular that of Sigberg, and summoned the Saxons dwelling along the border to help in the undertaking. The Abodrites grew furious. To make matters worse Cnut of Denmark seized the opportunity to strengthen and extend Danish sway upon the mainland and invaded Wagria, an incursion in which the Holsteiners who hated the Abodrites and Wagri, co-operated with him. In the excess of his pride Cnut even dragged Pribislav and Niklot (next to the Abodrite duke the greatest lord in Wagria) off into captivity in Schleswig, loaded with chains.[2]

On the German mainland, by 1136, the religion and the independence of the Wends—the latter not complete, for they were subject to Saxon tribute—were confined to the ancient territory of the Abodrites and the Wagri, Old Saxon Nordalbingia (modern Mecklenburg), and Brandenburg.

Unfortunately the moderation of such men as Otto of Bamberg, Norbert of Magdeburg, and Vicelin of Oldenburg was out of temper with the spirit of the twelfth century. It was the age of the Crusades—that great manifestation of medieval bigotry. In 1144 Edessa had been captured by the Moham-

[1] "Lucos et omnes ritus sacrilegos destruens" (Helmold, I, 47; cf. I, 52, which is a dissertation on the religion of the Slavs).

[2] Helmold, I, 49.

medans and Jerusalem was in peril. Europe was fired to a new Crusade. St. Bernard of Clairvaux was the archpreacher of the new expedition. Having prevailed upon Louis VII of France to take the cross at Vézelay, Bernard came to Germany, and on December 27, 1146, Conrad III of Germany also espoused it. But the Saxons held aloof from the movement. The fanatical saint sharply reproached the Saxons for their negligence in not having more earnestly propagated the gospel among their neighbors.[1] He upbraided them for ever having compromised with paganism and permitted the Wends to preserve their religion upon condition of paying tribute, condemning Saxon avarice in hard and heated terms.[2] To the exhortations of Bernard, Henry the Lion and other nobles of the north replied that it was senseless for them to expend blood and treasure beyond sea when the pagan Wends were on the border of Germany. The saint yielded the point and released them from service in the east on condition that they forcibly converted the Wends.

So was engendered the Wendish Crusade of 1147, the effect of which was to break the power of the Baltic Slavs and annex their territory to the German kingdom. It was a sinister mixture of bigotry and lust for land. "They agreed to this: either utterly to destroy the pagan race of the Slavs, or to compel them to become Christian," runs a chronicle of the time.[3] While Conrad III went off to the east, Henry the Lion, Conrad of Wettin, Adalbert of Salzwedel, the archbishops of Magdeburg and Bremen, organized a "home crusade" against the Abodrites and the Wagri. The Abodrite Duke was not without warning of the coming storm, and hastily began to erect a *castrum* at Dubin on the isthmus[4] between Lake Schwerin and a lesser lake, for the protection of his people. At the same time he sent messengers to Adolph of Holstein, asking his protection and reminding him of their

[1] Heinemann, *Albrecht der Bär*, pp. 162, 369–70.

[2] See the collection of references illustrating the complaint of the church on this head in Lavisse, *La marche de Brandenbourg*, p. 68, n. 1.

[3] "Conserserunt in hoc ut viciniam sibi Slavorum gentem paganam aut omnino delerent aut Christianos fieri cogerent" (*MGH*, SS. VIII, 392).

[4] Schmeidler, *Neues Archiv*, XXXIV, No. 3.

friendship. But the Count dared not make so overt a move, whatever his sympathy, for fear of offending the Saxon princes.

Adolph of Holstein had vainly hoped that he might avert the Crusade. He is the first German noble who manifested an intelligent, clear appreciation of the nature and the magnitude of the huge Slavonic problem to the expanding German nation. He could speak the Slav language fluently, and he understood the Slav character.[1] Certain of the impending crusade, Niklot resolved to anticipate the attack as far as possible, and secretly prepared a fleet at the mouth of the Trave in order to strike the province of Wagria before the Saxon forces had crossed his frontier. True to his word, he sought to apprise Adolph of his preparations, but the Count was not at Sigeberg where the messenger endeavored to find him. At dawn on June 26, 1147, the day of the passion of John and Paul, the fleet pushed up the river. Lübeck was in a panic. The merchant ships along the water front were burned. More than three hundred of the citizens were slain. Two squadrons of Niklot's horsemen ravaged the country roundabout. The Westphalian and Dutch colonies on the lower course of the Trave were fired and plundered. Adolph's own Holsteiner settlers alone were spared.[2] But the blow was a serious one to Adolph's colonization schemes, for many of the survivors returned to Flanders.[3]

Meanwhile, the news spread through all Saxony and Westphalia of the rising of the Slavs, and hastened the crusade. By August, 1147, two armies were on foot against them: one under Henry the Lion advanced upon Dubin and was accompanied by the Archbishop of Bremen and a host

[1] Helm., I, 49.

[2] *Ibid.*, I, 63. The Slavs did not molest in person or goods the settlers around Bornhöved and between the Schwale and the Plöner-See. It is not certain that the Abodrites were the ones who fired the farmsteads of the Flemish and Dutch settlers in the region. The hatred of the German settlers, particularly the Holsteiners, for these incomers (*odium advenarum* [*loc. cit.*]) was intense and honest. Helmold records that the belief was current that they, and not the Slavs, were responsible for this destruction.

[3] *Ibid.*, I, 64. The whole chapter is interesting for the evidence it affords of the hatred of the Germans for foreigners. "Nulla gens detestabilior Fresis."

of Saxon nobles; the other massed at Magdeburg under the margraves of Meissen and the Nordmark, Albrecht the Bear of Brandenburg and Conrad of Wettin. With it were the bishops of Havelberg and Brandenburg and the Archbishop of Magdeburg.

Niklot's two strongholds, Dubin and Dimin, which he erected to hold the road between Magdeburg and Hamburg,[1] were besieged, a Danish army lending aid to the attack upon the former, though the Germans looked with scant appreciation upon the unsolicited assistance.[2] They were too suspicious of Denmark's ambition to acquire a foothold on the mainland. "The Danes are warlike at home, but not fond of fighting when abroad," said the Germans scornfully.[3] The land was swampy, and the besiegers could not bring their engines of war up to the walls. Dissension broke out in the army. The lesser fighting men complained that the great nobles and the high clergy wanted to deprive them of their just share of the conquered land. "Is not the land which we have devastated our land?" they said. The Slavs fell back into the marshes and could not be captured. But their towns and villages were given to the flames and the land so reduced to desolation that in the next year a terrible famine came.[4] In the end Pribislav and Niklot succumbed. Their people accepted the Christian faith and were baptized at the edge of the sword. Niklot's despondent words to Henry the Lion need no comment: "Let the God who is in heaven be our god and it will suffice. You may worship your God. We will worship you."[5]

[1] Von Boenigk, *Baltische Studien*, Band XXXIII (1883).

[2] Not until after the Danish defeat at Bornhöved in 1227 was Denmark's claim to the Baltic strand extinguished.

[3] Helm., I, 65; cf. I, 51 and 84, for similar judgments.

[4] On this Crusade see Wendt, II, 20; Hauck, IV, 563 ff., 594–608; All the chroniclers and modern historians have noticed it. The point of view of a Christian Slav is given by Vincent, *Prag. Ann.* (*MGH*, SS. XVII, 663).

[5] Helmold, I, 84. The Abodrites agreed to recognize the Christian religion, to pay a yearly tribute to Henry of Saxony, and to release the captives which they had taken. But of the Slavs who had been taken only the old and the "useless" were released. The younger and more robust were reduced to servitude upon the manors of the church and the nobles (Helm., I, 65).

Adolph of Holstein patched up a peace with Niklot, though there must have been heartburning on each side, and began the heavy task of reconstruction of his wasted province, bravely telling his people that some adversity was unavoidable and that border folk must be strong and not afraid of bloodshed. "He did justice unto his people, suppressing turmoils and liberating the oppressed from the hand of the feudality [*potentiorum*]," says Helmold.[1] With splendid honor he ransomed many captives of his people.[2] But his hopes of establishing a *modus vivendi* between the two races were ruined by the crusade. The nascent civilization of the Wends was nearly destroyed. Border strife and predatory thieving by the Wends became a chronic evil.[3] Adolph's policy of firmness and tact, which deserved to succeed, was ruined by his rival in North Germany, Henry the Lion, whose Slavonic policy was the drastic Roman practice—*divide et impera*—and whose avarice was notorious.[4]

Henry and his Saxon vassals were greater gainers from this crusade than the church. The Saxon Duke collected tribute from the conquered Abodrites, divided the conquered lands among his vassals, and left the church in the lurch. As long as Niklot punctually paid the tribute (which he acquired by pirate raids upon the Danish islands)[5] Henry was indifferent to the church's welfare in the Slav land, and even pretended to be Niklot's friend. He used the situation to his own advantage. The "conversion" of the Abodrites had accentuated the difference between them and the other pagan Wendish tribes, and two of these, the Kycini and the Circipani (stems of the Wilzi), rebelled against Niklot, refusing either to become Christian or to contribute to the tribute exacted by the Saxon Duke. The result was that in 1151 a joint expedition was made by Henry the Lion and Niklot and Adolph of Holstein against them. The celebrated fane at Goderak was destroyed and an immense amount of booty

[1] I, 67. [2] *Ibid.*, I, 66.

[3] "Nam latrocinia Slavorum eo tempore solito plus invaluerunt" (*ibid.*, I, 67).

[4] "In variis autem expedicionibus, quas adhuc adolescens in Slaviam profectus exercuit, nulla de Christianitate fuit mentio, sed tantum de pecunia" (*ibid.*, I, 68).

[5] *Ann. Colbaz* (*MGH*, SS. XIX, 715).

in gold and silver taken from the coffers of the Wendish priests.[1]

In the midst of these waves of war Vicelin had labored with a heavy heart. The destruction of its edifices and farms threw a great burden on the church for the care of the destitute. He was joined at this time by one of his former pupils in Bremen who also had studied in France and who now came to Neumünster.[2] Together Vicelin and his companions worked for the feeding of the hungry, for actual famine prevailed.[3] The door of opportunity was opened to the church to extend its power in Nordalbingia and Wagria as never before. For all the area which had once been Christianized and had been lost in 1066 in the great Slav rebellion under Kruto eighty-four years before[4] lay open again. The restoration of the destroyed sees of Oldenburg, Ratzeburg, and Mecklenburg was now possible. In this work Hartwig I, archbishop of Hamburg-Bremen, who strongly reminds one of Adalbert of Bremen, was a prominent figure.[5] In 1149 he consecrated Vicelin as bishop of the revived see of Oldenburg, where he continued to labor until his death in 1154. Already he had been over twenty-two years in Holstein.[6] In the same year Mecklenburg was filled and Ratzeburg was restored in 1152.[7] The establishment of rural churches was also rapidly pushed, as at Bornhöved and Högersdolf (near Sigeberg, called in the Slav tongue Cuzalina). These sanctuaries were all built of wood cut in the nearby forests by the peasantry.

The natives were quiet but sullen, especially around Oldenburg, where a local Slav cult of the god Prove obtained, whose priest (*flamen*) was a descendant of the pagan chieftain

[1] Helmold, I, 71. This temple could not have been the *fanum celeberrimum* at Rethra, though that is often said; for Rethra was south of the Peene in the country of the Redarii and was destroyed by Lothar II in the expedition of 1124–25. See Wendt, *Germanisierung, etc.*, II, 47, and cf. Arnold of Lübeck, *Chron. Slav.*, V, 24.

[2] Helmold, I, 58. [3] *Ibid.*, I, 66. [4] *Ibid.*, I, 24, 69.

[5] Dehio, "Hartwich von Stade, Erzbischof von Hamburg-Bremen," *Bremisches Jahrbuch* (Göttingen, 1872), VI, 35–154, and separately.

[6] Jaffé, *Lothar*, p. 233.

[7] Dehio, p. 147; Hauck, IV, 618, n. 1, disagrees. Cf. *Neues Archiv*, XXXII, 514, n. 19.

Kruto and was "an idolator and a great pirate."[1] Timidly civilization and Christianity crept into the land, for a new native outbreak was always feared, for which reason castles were again built as before.[2]

Under these strained conditions the public, voluntary espousal of the Christian faith by Pribislav must have come as relief. It was in the dead of winter, in January, 1156, that the summons came to Oldenburg that a priest be sent to him to explain the sacred mysteries. Helmold apparently was one of the little company of priests appointed to accompany the Bishop. After wading through snowdrifts (*inter cumulos nivi*), they came to an abandoned castle where was a little ruined chapel which Vicelin had once built. There they met Pribislav. Helmold, in telling of this adventure, says:

> After having expounded the sacred mysteries, Pribislav asked that we would go with him to his own dwelling-place which was a castle farther off. He received us with much readiness and made things very pleasant for us. A table was set which they heaped with twenty kinds of food. There I learned by actual experience what I had heard before in popular talk that there is no people decenter in the graces of hospitality than the Wends.[3]

Having remained with Pribislav for two days and nights, the little band of cross-bearers went on into Farther Slavonia (*in ulteriorem Slaviam*) in response to another summons from a lesser Wendish chief named Thessemar, who lived near Lake Schwerin. Let Helmold again tell the tale:

> We came to a wood which is the only one in that region, for the whole land stretches away in a plain. There among trees hoary with age we saw the sacred oaks which are dedicated to the local god who is named Prove, enclosed in a court having two entrances, and constructed like a palisade of logs. Besides being sacred to the "penates" and the idols which each [Slavonic] town has, this place was the sanctuary of their whole country to the god, to which a "flamen" and sacramental and sacrificial rites are appointed. There every fortnight the people of the land with a judge and a priest are accustomed to convene for justice. It is forbidden unto all to enter this court save only the priest and those wishing to offer sacrifice,

[1] Helmold, I, 69.

[2] "Jam enim circumjacentja oppida incolebantur paulatim a Christicolis, sed cum grandi pavore propter insidias latronum" (*ibid.*, I, 75). Eight years after the Wendish Crusade, the region of the Plöner-See was still a desert (*ibid.*, I, 83).

[3] Helmold, I, 83. Cf. this judgment with I, 1, and II, 12 (*ad fin.*); also with Adam of Bremen, II, 19.

or those in peril of death, for the right of asylum is not denied. The Slavs display so much reverence for their gods that they do not allow even the blood of their enemies to pollute the approach to the temple. . . . . There is a great variety of idolatry among the Slavs, for all do not follow the same superstitions. Some of their gods are represented in the form of idols in temples, as the idol at Plönen, which is named Podaga; others dwell in groves or forests, like Prove, the god at Oldenburg, who has no idol-form. Many have two or three or even more heads. Among the great variety of divinities who preside over fields and forests they do not recognize a single ruling deity above the rest. . . . .

The bishop had strongly enjoined upon us that we should insist upon the destruction of this sacred grove. The bishop himself leaping down from his horse with his staff struck down the emblems at the gates of the temple, and then, having entered the atrium, we piled wood around the sacred trees and fired a huge pyre—not without fear, however, lest we would be stoned by the crowd. But heaven protected us. After these things we were hospitably entertained at a sumptuous banquet by Thessemar. But the liquors of the Slavs were not sweet and pleasant to us.[1]

A long colloquy followed between Pribislav and the Bishop, at the termination of which the Wend chief said:

If it please the lord duke and you that we have the same worship, let our rights be recognized in the manors and the revenues of the Saxons, and then we shall willingly be Christians. We will build churches and we will pay our share of the tithes.

Pribislav had laid his finger on the sorest and the traditional grievance of the Slavs in their long resistance to Christianity—the land-grabbing of the church and its merciless imposition of the tithe.[2] Only in their consent to use the Slavonic tongue in preaching does the Saxon clergy seem to have advanced beyond the time of Thietmar of Merseburg.[3] They were the same hard, ambitious, avaricious priests as before. In the reconquered dioceses, after the crusade of 1147, the surveyors of the church had set busily to work with

[1] Helmold, I, 84.

[2] "Principes enim vestri," said Pribislav, "tanta severitate grassantur in nos, ut propter vectigalia et servitutem durissimam melior sit nobis mors quam vita . . . . cotidie emungimur et premimur usque ad exinanicionem. Quomodo ergo vocabimus huic religioni novae, ut edificemus ecclesias et percipiamus baptisma, quibus cotidiana indicitur fuga? Si tamen locus esset, quo diffugere possemus. Transeuntibus enim Travenam, ecce similis calamitas illic est, venientibus ad Penem fluvium nichilominus adest. Quid igitur restat, quam ut obmissis terris feramur in mare et habitemus cum gurgitibus?" (Helmold, I, 84, p. 161.)

[3] "Habens sermones conscriptos Slavicis verbis" (*ibid.*).

their measuring ropes to retrace the lines of the former ecclesiastical manors and to mark out new ones. The labor was long and tedious and hard, so much so that it was not completed for years. But as the church practiced surveying, the result was lucrative to it; for swamps and even forest land were not included within the measurement, but were "thrown in," to be cleared and drained afterward, so that the aggregate land acquisitions of the church were very great—"fecit maximum agrorum numerum," says honest Helmold.[1]

Fortunately for Brandenburg, the storm of the Wendish Crusade had not driven over it. The raid of Hartbert, the bishop of Brandenburg, in 1114 to recover his see *in partibus paganorum*, though unsuccessful in its main purpose, seems to have been followed by a slight restoration of Christianity, however, in the region.[2] Henceforward, although the great Slavonic gods Gerovit and Triglav were worshiped at Havelberg and Brandenburg, there was, nevertheless, a handful of Christian Wends in the Brandenburg territory, notably a Wendish chief with the German name Widukind, whose seat was in Havelberg, and another named Pribislav (not to be confused with the Abodrite Pribislav), who dwelt at Brandenburg, whose policies were pro-German and pro-Christian. Since the conversion of the Poles the Wends of the Havel and the Spree were fiercely menaced by them, and between the two alternatives preferred German domination. It was for this purpose that Widukind had sought the Emperor at Merseburg in 1128. The half-French archbishop of Magdeburg at this time, Norbert, a man who expressed the new spirit of the church, as we have seen, seized the opportunity to extend the church into Brandenburg. A church was built in Havelberg, and for a few years the protection of Widukind gave it a precarious security. But the natives were sullenly hostile to the policy of their chief, for they feared with good reason the extension of the church's system of taxation over them again. Accordingly, when Widukind died, in 1136, pagan resentment broke out and destroyed the church. The

[1] Helmold, *ibid.* Cf. I, 69, 71, 77.

[2] *Annal Pegav.* (*MGH*, SS. XVI, 252).

permanent re-establishment of Christianity in Brandenburg was not made until Albrecht the Bear got control of Brandenburg.[1]

Albrecht the Bear in an age of religious bigotry was not a bigot. In an age when German hatred of the Wends was rancorous, he was friendly to them. His policy was a rare combination of firmness and tact. He fended off the Wendish Crusade from his country and largely was content to let time work out the solution of things. He was justified of his enlightened resolution. In 1136 when Widukind died and his sons headed a pagan reaction, the new Margrave acted promptly, and by 1144 Anselm of Havelberg returned to the long-abandoned bishopric.[2]

Most of the Wendish population in Brandenburg accepted the *fait accompli*, both in its political and its religious bearing, without opposition. They acknowledged the faith and the authority of the German church and even began to live German law.[3] But vestiges of Slavonic paganism persisted for many years around Spandau in the heart of the marshes of the Havel and in the Spreewald.[4]

Albrecht kept a restraining hand upon the church in his dominions, and would not let the Wends be taxed with a heavier tithe than German subjects.[5] He was neither a bigot nor an iconoclast. While every other Slav temple had been ruthlessly destroyed, to the regret of the student of history as well as of comparative religion, in Brandenburg Albrecht spared the temple of Triglav. It was converted into a Christian church consecrated to the Virgin, and lasted until

[1] Wendt, I, 83; Ebbo, *Vita Ottonis ep. Babenb.*, III, 3; *Annal. Magdeb.* (*MGH*, SS. XVI, 186); *Annal. Hild.* (*ibid.*, SS. III, 116).

[2] Riedel, *Codex diplom. Brand.*, I, 15, p. 6; Sommerfeld, p. 132. Cf. Helmold, I, 88.

[3] Riedel, II, 2–39; Wohlbrück, *Gesch. des Bistums Lebus*, I, 323 ff. Albrecht's successors unfortunately abandoned this policy of toleration and the Wends were wantonly hunted down and out (Hauck, IV, 558 and n. 3; p. 609 and nn. 1 and 2).

[4] See the long and interesting note in Wendt, II, 21.

[5] "Si Slavi vel in foro vel quacumque commutatione sibi contraxerint aliquos mansos Teutonicorum ejusdem villae, eandem decimam sine contradictione persolvent, quam Teutonicus inde persolvit" (*Urk. des Kl. S. Marien in Erfurt*, quoted by Guttmann, p. 448; cf. Tuttle, *History of Prussia*, I, 26).

Frederick the Great, with unforgivable vandalism, pulled it down in order to use the stones for the erection of his palace at Potsdam. The marvel is that this Wendish sanctuary had been built of stone in a country so devoid of stone that even today brick is the almost universal building material. The first building of modern Berlin made of stone and not of brick was the Bourse, erected in 1859. Think of the devoted labor which must have been expended by this simple people in building a massive stone temple in such an early period, and under such adverse physical conditions; for every block of stone must have been freighted from the mountains of Bohemia, down the Elbe, and up the Havel!

By the middle of the twelfth century only a single islet of independent Slavdom west of the Oder River yet survived. This was the pirate state of Rügen, in its island fortress. Protected by its difficult location, environed by rough and stormy waters,[1] and defended by the bold and fanatical priests of the great temple of Arkona, Rügen held out until 1168.[2] In that year Waldemar of Denmark, who cherished ambitions for the expansion of Danish power along the Baltic coast which were destined to be a source of danger to future Germany,[3] and who also hated the Rugians because of their piratical forays upon the Danish coast and in the Danish islands, organized a formidable expedition against them. Even Christian Slavs participated in it, notably Kazamir and Buggeslav, two Pomeranian princes, and Pribislav

[1] See the description of the great storm of February, 1164, in Helmold, II, 1.

[2] "Sola Rugianorum gens durior ceteris in tenebris infidelitatis usque ad nostra tempora perduravit, omnibus inaccessibilis propter maris circumjacentia" (*ibid.*, I, 12). For a graphic account of this sanctuary, which gathered tribute from all Slavonia see Saxo Grammaticus (ed. O. Elton), pp. 393–95.

[3] Cf. Sommerfeld, chap. v. Although the island of Fehmern is said to have been chiefly settled from Ditmarsch around the middle of the fifteenth century, it is much more probable that this island (which was still purely Slav in the twelfth century) before it fell to Denmark was colonized by Holsteiners from conquered Wagria (Waitz, *Schleswig-Holst. Gesch.*, I, 345; Mannhardt, *Der Baumkultus*, pp. 190–91), and the so-called "Lowlanders," partly from Westphalia, partly from Frisia and Holland who in the twelfth and thirteenth centuries flocked into the lands formerly occupied by the Slavs in order to find new homes there (Helmold, I, 57; Waitz, I, 56). In 1242 we find mention of a *platea Flamingorum* (*Schleswig-Holst., Lauenb. Jahrb.*, IX [1866], 12).

the Abodrite—the last reluctantly, "because the duke [of the Saxons] commanded him."[1] Arkona was captured, the famous temple of the god Svantovit destroyed, the statue of the god dragged through the midst of his subjugated votaries and chopped to pieces and burned, the population scattered or else sold into slavery. Twelve churches were established in Rügen in honor of the extinguishment of the last stronghold of Slavonic paganism in Germany.[2] The last vestiges of the religion of the Baltic Slavs in Rügen were stamped out. The temples and sacred groves were destroyed. The native cult ceased to be a national expression. Where it survived at all, it was furtively practiced around some ancient oak, or by a spring or holy stone,[3] and so degenerated to folk-lore and popular superstition, snatches of which still persist among the peasantry, having lost their heathen label.[4]

There is always a certain melancholy attending the death of the gods, and one feels the pathos and romance of this *Götterdämmerung* as he feels the tragedy in the ancient cry, "Pan is dead," or the fall of Wodan. As with the Druids, as it was in Rome in the fourth century, as it was with the Aztec religion in Mexico, when the body of the votaries had become cowed by force, or grown lax and indifferent to the national religion owing to the attrition or the attraction of a new faith, so it was with the religion of the Baltic Slavs. The priests of the high temples at Rethra and Arkona made the final and futile struggle to preserve the tribal faith.

It is a pity that the Slavic side of this story has been lost. It was of the nature of medieval Christianity to be bigoted

[1] Helmold, II, 12.

[2] *Ibid.*, II, 12–13; Wendt, II, 57–60. Schafarik, II, 537–40; Beyersdorf, *Baltische Studien*, Band XXXIII (1883); Leger, "Svantovit et St. Vitus," *Revue d'histoire des religions*, XLI, No. 3 (1900); Jacob, *Baltische Studien*, Band XLIV (1894). The Slav tongue ceased to be understood in Rügen after the sixteenth century. The half-German, half-Wendish law of the island was compiled at that time by a Rugian noble (Frommhold, *Ztschft. der Savigny-Stiftung, für Rechtsgesch.*, Band XVI, Heft 1 [1895], *Germanische Abteilung*).

[3] "Et inhibiti sunt . . . . jurare in arboribus, fontibus et lapidibus."—Helmold, I, 84. Cf. Mannhardt, *Der Baumkultus*, 31 and 57.

[4] Albertus Magnus was sent into Pomerania in the thirteenth century to suppress these vestiges (Ozanam, *Les Germains*, p. 287).

and intolerant; the church in its mistaken zeal destroyed every vestige of the conquered faith. We know this sad history only from the German enemies of the Baltic Slavs. But if one reads the record between the lines and with sympathetic eyes, it is apparent that there surely was another side. One cannot refuse the meed of honor to those pagan priests of the Wends who were loyal with a desperate fidelity to their historic religion. What Sir Gilbert Murray has said of the dying paganism of the fourth century is applicable here: "Like other conquerors these conquerors were often treacherous and brutal; like other vanquished these vanquished have been tried at the bar of history without benefit of counsel. . . . . Only an ignorant man will pronounce a violent or bitter judgment."[1]

[1] *Four Stages of Greek Religion*, p. 180.

Spread of German Settlements to the Eastward, 800—1400

CHAPTER XIII

THE EXPANSION AND COLONIZATION OF THE GERMAN PEOPLE BEYOND THE ELBE; THE CONFLICT OF SAXON AND SLAV[1]

GERMAN eastward expansion, from the time of the first manifestation of the eastward swing in the eighth century to the termination of the great movement when the last energy spent its force in the conquests of the Teutonic Knights in the morasses of Kurland and Esthonia, advanced in a series of waves whose lengths are measured by the distance between the rivers of Northern

[1] A reviewer of von der Goltz's *Geschichte der deutschen Landwirtschaft* in *Journal of Political Economy*, XII (1903–4), 114 said, à propos of the history of German east colonization: "It is but characteristic of the ignorance of this period prevailing in America that a work on colonization issued some years ago and pretending to treat of every phase connected with colonization at all periods contained not a word about this very important movement, to which the present German Empire so largely owes its existence." Historical study of the western Slavs dates from Christian Hennig (1649–1719). See Tetzner's biographical sketch of Hennig in *Ztschft. d. hist. Ver. f. Niedersachsen* (1903), Heft 2. The next important work was by J. C. von Jordan, *De originibus Slavicis, opus chronolog.-geograph.-historicum ab antiquitate literis nota in seculum usque ad Christianum decimum* (2 vols.; Vindob., 1745). Comparative philology opened a new line of attack for Karl Gottlieb Anton (1751–1818) who published at Leipzig in the years 1783–89 two volumes entitled *Erste Linien eines Versuches über der alten Slaven. Ursprung, Sitten, Gebräuche, Meinungen und Kenntnisse.* Anton had been a student at the University of Leipzig where he became intimately acquainted with some fellow-students from Lausitz of Sorb descent. All previous work, however, was superseded in the middle of the nineteenth century by P. J. Schafarik, *Slovanské Starožitnosti* (Prague, 1837); German translation, and the version usually consulted, by Mosig von Aehrenfeld, entitled *Slawische Alterthümer* (2 vols.; Leipzig, 1843–44; 2d ed. Jireček, 1862–63). In the same year with Schafarik's classic volumes also appeared Zeuss's *Die Deutschen und ihre Nachbarstämme*, which is very valuable for the history of the Slavs in Germany. L. Giesebrecht, *Wendische Geschichten*, although an old book, is valuable. At the present time the Czech scholar Lubor Niederlé and the Austrian scholar Peisker, of the University of Graz, are leading authorities upon the history of the Slavs. For a bibliography of their works see *Cambridge Mediaeval History*, II, 775. Leger has translated Niederlé's *Slavonic Mythology* and his *Slav Antiquities* into French, and extensively reviewed his writings in the *Journal des savants* (1907), pp. 70 and 128; *ibid.* (1908), p. 141; and those on Schaffarik, *ibid.* (1910), pp. 115–24, 155–67; *ibid.* (1911), p. 125.

Europe. The time element, however, in this immense expansion was not always or even nearly uniform. The current moved now slow, now fast. Three times the Germans crossed the lower Elbe and three times were thrown back by the Wends—in 983, 1018, 1066. It was over two hundred years before the Saxons utterly broke the power of the Slavonic tribes situated between the Elbe and the Oder, before they acquired a permanent foothold in Mecklenburg and Brandenburg. At the end of the *Völkerwanderung* the Slavonic western edge impinged on the lower Elbe and the Saale rivers. The Slav world between the eighth and the twelfth century was of huge extent. A line drawn from the mouth of the Elbe to the head of the Adriatic would roughly mark its western boundary.[1]

In general, until the conquest of the Saxons by Charlemagne in the last quarter of the eighth century shook Germany and the Slavonic tribes as no force had since the great migration, the relations between the Germans and the Slavs were amicable. Boniface's missionary labors were peacefully pursued among the Slavs of the Main. A Wendish peasantry cleared the lands around Fulda, and Slavonic colonies were established by Boniface in the territory of the future of Bamberg, where they worked the mines and raised cattle. Some such Slav colonists were even settled in Swabia as far over as the Rhine.[2]

The Wendish Slavs were the western edge of the great Slavonic race which, in the fifth century, extended westward to the Elbe and the Saale rivers and bordered the Baltic.

[1] Adam of Bremen (II, 21), in the eleventh century roughly indicated the area tof he western Slavs: "Sclavania igitur . . . . decies major esse fertur quam nostra Saxonia, praesertim si Boemiam et eos trans Oddaram sunt, Polanos, quia nec habitu nec lingua discrepant, in partem adjeceris Sclavaniae. . . . . Ejus latitudo est a meridie usque in boream, hoc est ab Albia fluvio usque ad mare Scythicum. Longitudo autem illa videtur, quae initium habet ab nostra Hammaburgensi parrochia et porrigitur in orientem, infinitis aucta spatiis, usque in Beguariam, Ungriam et Greciam." By "Beguariam" Adam undoubtedly means *Bulgariam*, not *Bavariam*, as Pertz, *Archiv.*, III, 658, thinks. One MS reads "Bulgariam," and the sense so requires.

[2] Lamprecht, *Deutsche Geschichte* (3d rev. ed., 1906), p. 345; Riedel, *Die Mark Brandenburg*, II, 10, nn. 10–11; Lavisse, *La marche de Brandebourg*, p. 7; Werneburg, *Mitt. d. Vereins f. d. Gesch. von Erfurt* (1882), Heft 10.

Today the Slavonic frontier is marked by a line drawn from the head of the Adriatic to Prague and to Danzig, that is to say, roughly the line of the Vistula River and its vertical projection southward. The Poles and Bohemians are the two greatest surviving blocks of the once widely extended Slavonic occupation of Central Europe.

According to the most probable conjectures, the original country of the Slavs was in the marsh land of the Pripet and the basin of the middle Dnieper. This was Polesie, a triangular area less than half as great as England, the angles of which are roughly indicated by the modern towns of Brest-Litovsk, Miholev, and Kiev.[1] The physical features of the great isthmus between the Baltic and the Black Sea, with the Oder and the Vistula flowing into the former, and the Bug, the Pruth, and the Dniester emptying into the latter, profoundly conditioned the mode and the direction of early Slav expansion. From earliest historic times one can discern those differences which later created the distinction between the northern and the southern Slavs. But early Slav history had no center. The Slavs, unlike the early Germans, had no great tradition to grasp, as the Germans adopted the idea of the Roman Empire and perpetuated it.[2]

It formerly was the prevailing belief of historians of the Slavs that the race remained confined to their original home until the fifth and sixth centuries when they began to expand down the valleys of the Dnieper and Vistula rivers. But recently Niederlé[3] has combated this theory and endeavored to demonstrate that the Slavs, not *en masse* but in small groups, little by little quitted their original country and filtered out

[1] For a study of the evidence leading to this conclusion see Peisker, "The Expansion of the Slavs," *Cambridge Med. Hist.*, Vol. II, chap. xiv. For modern literature in English on the Slavs see Bury, *History of the Eastern Roman Empire*, chaps. xi–xii; Beazeley, *Dawn of Modern Geography*, II, 467–574; Gibbon, *Decline and Fall of the Roman Empire* (ed. Bury), VI, 543–44, with valuable bibliography.

[2] See the suggestive memoir by Hoefler, *Sitzungsb. Akad. d. Wiss. zu Wien*, XCVII (1881), on the nature of medieval Slav history. He distinguishes five periods: (*a*) 375–626; (*b*) 626–895; (*c*) 895–1205; (*d*) 1205–1396; (*e*) 1396–1526.

[3] Lubor Niederlé, *Slovanské Starožilnosti* ("Slav Antiquities") (2 vols.; Prague, 1902–10). The first volume is available in French, *Manuel de l'antiquité Slav* (1923), and L. Leger, *La race Slave* (Paris, 1910), a French translation of an earlier work by Niederlé. The "Antiquities" is reviewed in *Journal des savants* (March, 1911).

and among the surrounding peoples at a remoter epoch than usually believed. This infiltration may have begun before the beginning of the Christian Era. According to archaeological evidence, the earliest expansion was into present Eastern Germany and Northern Hungary. Emigration *en masse* into the regions abandoned by the Germans of the *Völkerwanderung* took place between the second and the fourth centuries.

By the end of the fifth century the mighty westward and southward movement of the German race had almost run its course. The dark woodland east of the Rhine for centuries had poured out tribes and nations—Goths, Franks, Vandals, Burgunds—who had overwhelmed the Roman Empire. The Goths settled in Spain and Italy, the Vandals in Africa, the Franks and Burgunds in Gaul. And ever behind the German nations treading westward the Slavonic tribes crowded in, occupying the abandoned territory until the Slavonic western edge rested on the Elbe and the Saale.[1]

A little later than this northern and northwestward expansion of the Slavs, a southward drift also took place. By the sixth century the forerunners of the southern Slavs had

[1] C. Plattner, "Ueber Spuren deutscher Bevölkerung zur Zeit der slavischen Herrschaft in den östlich der Elbe und Saale gelegenen Ländern," *Forschungen zur deutschen Gesch.*, XVII (1877), 409–526. Cf. *ibid.*, XVIII, 629–31; XX, 165–202. O. Montelius, "Die Einwanderung der Slawen in Norddeutschland," *Mitt. d. Anthrop. Gesellschaft in Wien* (Vienna, 1900), Band XXX; Schafarik, II, 1–50. The radical pro-Slav view is represented by Boguslawski, *Dowody Autochtonizmu* (Warsaw, 1912), who contends that the Slavs were autochthonous in Northeast Germany. His strongest evidence is philological, but the book is nevertheless a pamphlet against the Berlin-Austrian School. The author has considerately given a résumé of his contentions in German in an Appendix. See, further, *Revue critique* (1915), No. 29. One may read S. Zaborowski, "L'autochtonisme des Slaves en Europe, *Revue de l'école d'anthropologie* (1905), as a corrective to such extravagant opinion. In Charlemagne's time there were certainly no great masses of Germanic peoples east of the Elbe and Saale. But Plattner has raised the question whether isolated fragments of German stock did not still remain in the east, not participating in the westward migration. His contentions are combated by Wendt, *Ueber die Nationalität der Bevölkerung der deutschen Ostmarken vor dem Beginne der Germanisierung* (Göttingen, 1878). Haag (*Gesellschaft f. pommersche Gesch. u. Alterthumskunde*, 1878) argues that long before the appearance of the Slavs there the Baltic Coast was peopled by Germans; Schwartz, *Markische Forschungen*, Band XX (1878), from a study of local folklore and popular survivals, concludes that Brandenburg and Pomerania were originally populated by German stock, and that fragments of these peoples remained and even preserved their racial institutions to some degree under the Slav superstratum imposed upon them.

reached the middle Danube through Bohemia and Moravia via the Nab and the Theiss rivers, while farther east the Pruth and the Bug had facilitated their spread around the Carpathians and into the lands along the lower Danube. Thus the huge isthmus of Europe between the Baltic and the Black Sea became a great Slavonia.

At this epoch one distinguishes the broad difference between the northern and the southern Slavs,[1] the differentiation being greater among the former than among the latter. For three distinct groups were now to be found north of the Danube: the Poles of the Vistula, the tribes of the Elbe and Baltic seaboard, and finally the Czechs in the mountainous region of Bohemia. Nothing but conjectures can be made with reference to the eastward and northeastward expansion of the Russian group before the seventh century, for the earliest texts, Byzantine and Arab, pertain to the ninth and tenth centuries. It is true that archaeology has supplemented this paucity of evidence, but the ground is nowhere firm.[2]

As with all primitive peoples the observations and criticisms of their manners and customs[3] made by observers

[1] This separation of the northern and southern Slavs was made permanent by the establishment of the Avars and Magyars between the two groups (600–900). "Ce peuple [the Hungarians] qui devait changer si profondement les destinées de la race slave. ... Les Hongrois implantèrent une domination étrangère au cœur des pays slaves. Ils dispersèrent les membres de la grande famille. ... Dès lors, le fait que, sur le Danube, au point de la réunion de toutes les races slaves, existait un état magyar, finno-ouralien, inattaquable au slavisme par l'énergie de son caractère national, fut la pierre d'achoppement de toute grande tentative d'agglomération slave" (Rambaud, *L'empire grec au Xe siècle*, pp. 335–36).

[2] The earliest allusion to the Slavs by any historian seems to be Procopius *De bello Gothico*, III, 14. After that come the *Strategon* or *Ars militaris*, IX, 3; XI, 5, of Emperor Maurice about 600; the *Tactics* of Emperor Leo in the eighth century; the *De administrando imperio*, chaps. xxxvii–xxxviii, of Constantine Porphyrogenitos in the tenth century. It is difficult to know whether the Arabic sources refer to the Russian Slavs or to the Scandinavians in Russia (Schafarik, I, 9–14). For modern literature see Lippert, *Sozial Gesch. Böhmens*, I, 121 f.; Bury, *History of the Eastern Roman Empire*, chaps. xi, xii; *Cambridge Mediaeval History*, Vol. II, chap. xiv; Meitzen, *Siedelung und Agrarwesen*, II, 141–64; Beazeley, *Dawn of Modern Geography*, II, 467–514; Gibbon, *Decline and Fall of the Roman Empire* (ed. J. B. Bury, 1900), VI, 543–44, with valuable bibliography; Peisker, *Camb. Med. Hist.*, Vol. II, chap. xiv, with bibliography (pp. 770–84); Sir H. H. Howorth, in *Journal Anthrop. Inst.*, VII, 329; VIII, 65; IX, 181.

[3] Schafarik, I, 536–43.

of a different or higher culture must be taken with reservation.

We do not know what rites accompanied the birth of a babe among the early Slavs. We know only from the *Vitae* of Otto of Bamberg that infanticide was sometimes practiced among the Baltic Slavs. The first clipping of a child's hair seems to have been a sort of rite. Whether any ceremony accompanied the advent of puberty is not known. Marriage, as nearly as we can discern from the texts and the evidence of folk-lore, was sometimes by capture,[1] sometimes by purchase. The Russian chronicle attributed to Nestor alludes to violent seizure of young girls at natural springs. According to Saxo Grammaticus, the Danish king, Fritho, after vanquishing the Russians compelled them to substitute marriage by purchase for the more barbaric marriage by capture. In the eleventh century the code of Jaroslav Vladimirovitch imposed heavy penalty for seizure of a woman. Yet many texts attest the persistence of this primitive practice, and it still survives among some of the Balkan Slavs. Other evidence indicates that daughters were purchased of their parents, so much so that a blooming family of daughters was regarded as a source of wealth.

Endeavor has been made to reconstitute the primitive Slavonic rite of marriage after observances which still obtain. Early texts throw little light. In the *Chronicle of Kiev* we learn that the newly married wife was compelled to take off her husband's shoes as a sign of obedience. Marriage usually took place in the autumn in order that the woman might have passed the time of pregnancy before the period of spring planting arrived. On the night that she was wedded the young woman was veiled, sprinkled with millet or rye as a symbol of fecundity, and conducted to the house of her husband. Three times she walked around the house, bending her knees to do homage to the tutelary household genii. On the morrow the pair were purified in running water. All these rites were accompanied with dancing and singing. That polygamy existed along with monogamy among the primitive

[1] Marriage by capture prevailed among the Bohemians in early times (Lippert, *Sozial Gesch. Böhmens*, I, 203).

Slavs is attested by Russian and Czech chroniclers, and by the biographers of Otto of Bamberg. Even polyandry and incest occurred. Yet female morality was high. Boniface commended the prevalence of conjugal fidelity among the Slavs in the eighth century, and is confirmed by Thietmar[1] in the early eleventh century.

The ancient Slavs practiced two modes of disposing of the bodies of their dead—cremation and interment. Their cemeteries, in which an enormous amount of archaeological material has been found, are almost innumerable between the Vistula and the Dnieper rivers, a territory essentially *urslawisch.* In 626 the Slavs who attacked Constantinople burned their dead. The same practice is recorded among the Russians by Arab texts, by Leo the Deacon, by Nestor. Place-names derived from the custom of incineration are common in Slavonic lands. Boniface in 734 tells us that Polaben wives voluntarily caused themselves to be burned with the bodies of their husbands. The Polish chronicler Martin Gallus records the use of funeral urns in 1018. In 1218 the Pomezani, the Natangi, and the Varmians, in a treaty with the Teutonic Knights, agreed to abandon the practice of cremating their dead as a heathen rite. The graves were filled with gifts of food and drink, weapons, instruments, and often the wives, men and women servants, horses and dogs, were slain that the deceased might have comfort and company in the tomb. The practice of placing articles of food in the grave lasted until the eighteenth century, according to the philologist Dobrovsky, and it is said still to obtain in remote parts of Poland, and Great and Little Russia. To Swedish influence must be attributed the occasional practice of burying the dead in a boat.[2]

With regard to food, though the Slavs knew meat and milk, their chief flesh nourishment was fish, living as they did in a world of marsh and a network of rivers. "Instead of in towns they live in marshes and forests," wrote Jordanes in the sixth century. The word for "milk" (*melko*) reminds one of the German *Milch*, and the cow may have been intro-

[1] *Chron. Slav.*, VIII, 2.

[2] Schafarik, I, 578.

duced from the Germans. Dlugosz, a Polish chronicler in the fifteenth century, described the Poles as living "frumento, carne, pisce, melle, lacte et olere." The names for the common cereals—rye, wheat, barley, millet, oats—are identical among all Slav peoples. Rye seems to have been originally a Slav grain. The word for "bread" (*chleb*) was borrowed from the German *Laib* (cf. Eng. "loaf"), and probably replaced an ancient word now lost. Of fruits, some were indigenous, some imported. The most familiar were plums and pears. But the harshness of the climate made fruit cultivation difficult, and Byzantine peddlers soon brought fruits and wines from the south to them. When Prince Oleg in 907 returned from a trip to Constantinople he brought back fruits and wine. In 969 Sviatoslav thought of transferring his capital from Kiev to Periaslavets on the Danube "since all manner of riches were to be found there, silver from Greece, silk, fruits and different wines." The spread of the southern Slavs must have been powerfully influenced by the lure of the orchards and vineyards of the balmier southland. The Slavs' favorite drink was hydromel or beer, of which Otto of Bamberg makes glowing eulogy.[1] This statement applies to both branches of the Slavs. Another fermented drink was *kvas*, made of fermented bread with an admixture of malt. Grape culture was unknown among the primitive Slavs, but they were heavy drinkers. Vladimir, prince of Moscow in the tenth century, told an Arabic traveler that the Mohammedan injunction against the use of alcoholic liquors was an insuperable bar to the conversion of the Slavs to Islam.

Except for the few observations to be found in the writings of Boniface[2] and casual allusions in Carolingian sources, we know little[3] of the history of the Elbean Slavs until the time of Bishop Thietmar of Merseburg, about 1000 A.D. The first

[1] Herbordus, II, 1.

[2] Notably the saint's uncharitable characterization of the "Winedi, quod est foedissimum et deterrimum genus hominum . . . ." (Schafarik, II, 515).

[3] The earliest mention of the Slavs of the Elbe is in Vibius Sequester, *De fluminibus*, in the sixth century, in which he says: "Albis Suevos a Cervatiis dividit," i.e., from the Sorben. Cervetii, Ciervisti, Zerbisti, Kirvisti of Saxon charters are all one and mean Zerbst (Niederlé, p. 131).

attempt of a western writer to describe the western Slavs, i.e., those of the basin of the Elbe and the south coast of the Baltic Sea, was made by Adam of Bremen in the latter half of the eleventh century.[1]

[1] *Gesta Hammaburgensis ecclesia pontificum:* Inestimably valuable as Adam of Bremen is, yet he is often vague and obscure, and his account of the Slavonic tribes between the Elbe and the Oder rivers, especially their geographical distribution, has given rise to extended controversy. According to Giesebrecht (*Nordlandskunde*, pp. 157–66; *Baltische Studien*, VI, 192) Adam was well informed. But the text of Adam of Bremen is notoriously corrupt, and Giesebrecht accuses the scholiast of many blunders and alterations. After the great revolt of the Slavs of the lower Elbe in 983, he argues, the land between the Elbe and the Oder was shut off from Christian knowledge and commercial intercourse, so that ignorance and erroneous ideas of Slavonia naturally came to prevail among the Germans. Lappenberg (*Archiv*, VI, 864), on the other hand, finds the chief source of Adam's limitations in popular German prejudice against the Slavs and contempt for their language, which prevented any intimate knowledge of them from being acquired. Slavonic tribal names and the places occupied by them might interest a diocesan historian of Hamburg, but the Saxons were too indifferent to the promotion of Christianity among the Slavs and too contemptuous of them to be interested.

Giesebrecht has endeavored to control Adam's account by Helmold's *Chronica Slavorum*, written in the last half of the twelfth century by one who dwelt long among the Slavs and knew them more intimately than any other German writer of the Middle Ages. He accepts Adam's testimony when the two agree, provided Helmold has not—as he sometimes has done, especially in the early chapters—slavishly copied his predecessor. The difficulty of clearly distinguishing the tribal names of the Slavs between the Elbe and the Oder and of accurately locating them is very great. Helmold is of better use in amplifying than in emending Adam.

However, it is to be observed that Adam's description of Slavonia falls into two parts: one dealing with the region west of the Peene River, the other with that beyond and eastward of the Peene. The former, which Adam calls Hither Slavonia (*In Sclavania citeriori*, III, 18), was comprehended within the diocese of Hamburg. He is diffuse concerning the first, but brief and obscure about things across the river. He knows a great deal about things which happen around Magdeburg, but is hazy about things *ultra Panim* (III, 21). Beyond the Oder, Adam's ideas are very nebulous, as the use of words implying indirect knowledge, like *comperimus*, *dicunt*, etc., indicates (e.g., IV, 11).

Adam uses the words Sclavi and Winuli interchangeably to denominate the Slavonic peoples between the Elbe and the Oder. (The latter proper name is a variant of the earlier word Winedi used by Einhard. See Pertz, I, 658, where the examples are cited.) The territory he calls Sclavania, but he is loose in application of the term, sometimes using it in a broad sense, sometimes in a narrow sense (e.g., II, 13, 19; IV, 13, for the former usage; II, 40, 46, 69, for the latter usage. In II, 24, "ecclesiae in Sclavania ubique erectae sunt" and "Sclavaniam in duodeviginti pagos dispertitam" undoubtedly refer to Slavonia in the strict sense of the term). The hardness of heart and lack of sympathetic imagination for any culture save their own of tenth-century German historians is a striking and depressing fact. It is glaring in Widukind and Thietmar of Merseburg (e.g., IV, 31 [22]; VI, 46; VII, 4), to whom, for example, Boleslav Chrobry, who is really a heroic figure, appears

The Baltic Slavs lay in modern east Holstein and Mecklenburg-Schwerin.[1] The Wilzi and kindred tribes extended over modern Mecklenburg-Strelitz, Brandenburg, Mittelmark and Uckermark, in the moor and marsh land of the Spree, the Havel, and the Peene rivers; the Pomeranians were in what is today known as Pomerania along the seaboard; the Sorben were in the triangle included between the upper Elbe, the Erzgebirge, and the Saale. They reached eastward to the Bober, and westward to the Werra, Fulda, and upper Main.[2] The blood affinity between the Wilzi and the Poles was close; on the other hand, the Sorben were akin to the Czechs, or

---

only contemptible ("cujus nomen et conversacio .... sacius lateret" [IX, 2]). Even Adam of Bremen, although in the eleventh century a greater objectivity of treatment and stronger disposition to record history truthfully is discernible, is greatly tinctured with this contempt for things other than German and Christian (e.g., I, 63; II, 17, 20). A unique source for our knowledge of the Elbean Slavs is the *Relation* of Ibraham Ibn Jakub, a Jew of North Africa who probably was a member of the Mohammedan embassy sent to Otto I in 973. It is of considerable value. The Arabic text has been established by the Dutch orientalist Goeje. For studies upon it consult Haag, *Baltische Studien*, Band XXXI (1881); Wigger, *Jahrbücher und Jahresbericht des Vereins f. Mecklenburgische Gesch.* (1880), and Westburg's commentary in *Mem. de l'Acad. des sciences de St. Petersbourg, Hist.-Phil.-Kl.*, VIII, 32 f. A German translation may be found in *Geschichtschreiber d. deutschen Vorzeit*, Band XXXII. Ibrahim's important observations are given by Lippert, *op. cit.*, 5, 64, 69, 83 f., 125, 229, 432. Peisker has an excellent article on "The Relations of the Slavs with the Turco-Tartars and the Germans," in the *Vierteljahrschrift f. soz.-wirt. Gesch.*, III, Nos. 2, 3, 4 (1905).

[1] Witte, "Wendische Bevölkerungsreste in Mecklenburg," *Forschungen zur deutschen Landes- und Volkskunde*, XVI (1905), 1–124. The line is indicated by modern Kiel, Neumünster, Alster, and Hamburg (Adam Brem., II, 15; *Visio Godeschalci;* Helmold, II, 14; *Annal. St. Bertin* [*anno* 845] [Prudentius the author]). The Alt Mark perhaps once was Slav, but from 822 one finds names of German villages. In Thuringia between the Elbe, Ohre, Bode, and Saale was a thin sprinkling of Slavs. East of the Saale everything was Slav. Even west of the Saale were certain scattered Slav settlements. Thus villages are mentioned in a charter of Dagobert III of 706 (if the act is not spurious), and some inventories of Fulda and Hersfeld confirm this of the eighth century. In the eleventh century, the region around Saalfeld was still Slav.

[2] Cf. E. Muka, "Die Grenzen des serb. Sprachgebietes in alter Zeit," *Archiv. f. slav. Phil.*, XXVI, 543; Guttmann, "Die Germanisierung der Slawen in der Mark," *Forschungen zur Brand. u. Preuss. Gesch.*, IX (1897), 396–97; Wendt, I, 10–16. "Sorabi Sclavi qui campos inter Albim et Salam interjacentes incolunt" (Einhard, *Annales Lauresh.* [*anno* 782]).

Bohemians.[1] Of these four grand groups of the Baltic Slavs, the confederacy of the Wilzi was most formidable.[2]

The Wilzi were sworn foes of the Franks and allied with the Saxons during the period of Charlemagne's Saxon wars, while, on the other hand, the Abodrites sometimes co-operated with the Franks against both Wilzi and Saxons.[3] The Abodrites appear to have been late comers into the Elbean lands, and seem to have been driven from the region of the Danube, perhaps by the Hun invasion of the fifth century, or possibly by the Avars in the sixth. In the time of Pepin, before he became king, when his half-brother Grifo made trouble and fled to the Saxons, the Sorben offered their aid to Pepin. During the Saxon wars Charlemagne looked with friendly eyes upon the Sorben and the Abodrites. The former fought in the Frank armies, and the latter, in 804, when the Saxons living north of the Elbe were deported into Franconia, were colonized in their room in order to prevent the Saxons from forming an alliance with the warlike Wilzi.[4]

Unfortunately, throughout the Middle Ages the Baltic Slavs produced no historian who wrote in their idiom or in Latin. Their whole history has to be sought in German annals, notably in the chronicles of Helmold and Arnold of

[1] Guttmann, p. 397, n. 1. The formidability of the Sorben is attested by Charlemagne's military legislation (*Capitulare* 807, sec. 5; Baluze, I, 459).

[2] Adam of Bremen, III, 21.

[3] "Sclavi nostri qui dicuntur Abotridi" (*Annales Lauresh.* [*anno* 798]). The military assistance given by the Abodrites to Charlemagne during the last stages of the war with the Saxons [797] was not forgotten by Charlemagne. They were rewarded by being permitted to move into and settle Wagria (East Holstein), which was totally bereft of its Saxon inhabitants (799) and utilized as a buffer people between the Saxons and the Danes. But the latter were too formidable, and in 805 the Emperor annexed Nordalbingia to the Empire, and established the Danemark in the valley of the little river Eyder. With the entry of the Slavs into Wagria, the German world of the Middle Ages shrank to its narrowest area. "Das Deutschtum am Ausgang des 8. Jahrhundert auf die schmalste Basis beschränkt die es je vorher und nachher gehabt hat" (Pueschl, *Das Answachsen der deutschen Städte*, p. 1).

[4] Stein, *Gesch. Frankens*, II, 258; *Ann. Lauresh:* "Imperator . . . . omnes qui trans Albiam et in Wihmuodi habitabant Saxones, cum mulieribus et infantibus, transtulit in Franciam, et pagos transalbianos Abodritis dedit" (804); *Annales Altah.* (803); cf. Wendt, *Germanisierung d. Länder östlich d. Elbe*, I, 19; Guttmann, *op. cit.*, p. 403. The warlike character of the Wilzi is noticed by Einhard both in the *Annales* (789) and the *Vita Karoli*, chap. xii.

Lübeck, the latter being his thirteenth-century continuator. A *corpus* made of all these texts, a French historian has remarked, might take for its epigraph the words of the Saxon chronicler Widukind: "Transeunt sane dies plurimi Saxonibus, his pro gloria et pro magna latoque imperio, illis pro libertate ac ultima servitute varie certantibus."[1]

The Baltic or Wendish Slavs[2] formed a separate group, distinct from the Poles and Bohemians as well as the Litu-Slav stems extending around the bight of the Baltic from the mouth of the Oder to the mouth of the Düna in modern East Prussia and Kurland. They were loosely known as Polaben or Elbslaven,[3] and were divided into four grand divisions—the Abodrites, the Ljutizi (Ger.: Welataben or Wilzi), the Pomeranians, and the Sorben, each of these major groups in turn being subdivided into lesser stem-groups.[4]

[1] Leger, "Les Slaves Baltiques," *Journal des savants* (Jan., 1916). Widukind was more generous in appreciation of the Slavs than later German historians: "Illi vero nichilominus bellum quam pacem elegerunt, omnem miseriam carae libertati postponentes. Est namque hujuscemodi genus hominum durum et laboris patiens, victu levissimo assuetum, et quod nostris gravi oneri esse solet, Slavi pro quadam voluptate ducunt. Transeunt sane dies plurimi, his pro gloria et pro magno latoque imperio, illis pro libertate et ultima servitute varie certantibus" (II, 20).

[2] The only account in English of the Baltic Slavs is the memoir by Sir H. H. Howorth, *Journal Anthrop. Inst.*, IX, 181–232. Since it was written in 1879 some of his conclusions must now be regarded as antiquated or amended.

[3] From the word *po*, meaning "by," and *Labe*, meaning "Elbe" (Wendt, *Die Germanisierung der Länder östlich der Elbe*, II, 11). See Meitzen, *Siedelung und Agrarwesen*, II, 475–93. For a dissertation upon the Polabish language see Morfill, *Trans. Philol. Soc.* (London), XXV, 74 f.

[4] Kindred to the Abodrites were the Wagri, or Waarii of Widukind and Adam of Bremen, III, 68, in east Holstein, the Lingones on the Elbe (*ibid.*, III, 19), the Warnabi on the Warnow (*ibid.;* Helmold, I, 87), and the Dravani west of the Elbe in the Hanoverian Wendland around Lüchow, Gartow, and Wustrow (Wendt, I, 11; Brückner, *Die slavischen Ansiedelungen in der Altmark*, p. 8; *Mecklenburg. Jahrbücher*, VII, 156). The Ljutizi were bitter foes of the Abodrites (Schafarik, II, 576, 587). Akin to the Wilzi were the Redarii and the Uckri (Widukind, III, 54, "Uchri"), whence the name Ucker-Mark; the Lini or Lingones (Helmold, I, 2); the Hevelli (Thietmar, IV, 20; *Annal. Qued.; Annal. Magdbg.; Annal. Palid.;* Helmold, I, 88). Offshoots of the Sorben were the Lusizi (Thietmar, I, 9; VI, 39, 48), the Milzi, the Glomuzani or Daleminzi, the Siusli, the Plisni (Andree, *Wendische Wanderstudien*, pp. 29–38). Ljutizi was the Slav term; Wilzi the German. Adam of Bremen fantastically derives Wilzi from German *wild* and Ljutizi from German *Löwe!* His philology is at least a tribute to their warlike character. Widukind (III, 54) is the first author to indicate the territory occupied by the Wilzi. This German nomenclature first appears in the tenth century (cf. *Annal. Sangall. maj.*, 955). The earlier German

Little by little, conquered and dispossessed or else absorbed by the German race, today the Wends and their language have almost disappeared, the clearest traces of the wide empire they once ruled being afforded by the mutilated and distorted Germanic form of hundreds of place-names upon the map of Germany, especially in Mecklenburg, Pomerania, Saxony, and Brandenburg-Prussia, although Württemberg, Bavaria, and Austria also show traces of former Slav occupation in the names of places, as the Regnitz River by Bamberg and the Pegnitz by Nürnberg.[1]

---

name for the Wilzi was Welatabi (see Einhard, *Vita Caroli*, chap. xv). Adam (II, 18, schol. 17) professes to have learned the early history of the warfare between the Saxons and the Redarii from an old Nordalbingian noble. The word Wend is technically not of racial significance, though it came to be used as such by the Germans, and always to signify the Slavonic peoples of the eastern border, whatever their tribal names. Various forms of spelling of the word Wend are met with in the chronicles (Guinidini, *Chron. Moissac.* [809]; Windei, *Einhardi Annales* [798, 804]; Winuli, *Adam of Bremen*, II, 18; IV, 13; cf. II, 13 and 19, where he uses Sclavi in the sense of Winuli). The earliest western mention of the Slavs as Wends which I know is in *Vita St. Columbani*, chap. lvi. For further references see Pertz, *Mon.*, I, 658, *s.v.* "Winedi." Considerable Wendish groups are still to be found in the Spreewald between Lübben and Kottbus, in Ober and Nieder Lausitz, and around Dresden. The latter still call themselves Sorben or Soraben. Altogether they now number about 170,000, scattered in over 700 villages, mere islets of people surrounded by German waters, remnants of the Slavs of the Elbe and the Oder valleys—Polabs, Ljutizi, Abodrites, Sorben, etc., who once played a great and sometimes formidable part in medieval German history from the eighth to the end of the thirteenth century (see Tetzner, *Die Slawen in Deutschland* [Braunschweig, 1902]).

[1] The Slav origin of many German place-names is manifest to the historian under mutilated or translated current form. Zerbst recalls the Sorben, whose prowess once taxed the arms of Charlemagne. Rostock in Mecklenburg bears a name which is found in six Czech localities. It is situated at the mouth of a river whose estuary is large enough to accommodate considerable shipping, and the name is derived from *roz*, a prefix implying "width or breadth of room," and the word *tek* or *tok*, meaning "to flow." Leipzig is simply "Linden-tree Place" (*Lipazig*) (Naebe, *Schriften d. Ver. f. d. Gesch. Leipzigs*, Band VII). Chemnitz in modern Saxony at first glance does not easily show a Slav derivation. But the primitive form was Kamenica, from *Kamen* ("rock," "stone"), a word reminding one of the mineral resources of the region. The name appears in no less than twenty-two places in Bohemia and Moravia. Torgau in Silesia is derived from the Slav root *terg* or *torg*, and corresponds to the German *Markt* ("market"). Pomerania is a pure Slav word, from *po* ("along" or "by the side of") and the word *morze*, meaning "the sea."

It is to be borne in mind that the persistence of Slavonic place-names is not necessarily an evidence of survival of a Slavonic stock in the locality. The Germans adopted local native names in the course of their eastward expansion precisely as the American pioneer adopted Indian names. See the cautious pronouncement of

The monarchical institutions of the Baltic Slavs were not highly developed.[1] The tribes were not compact entities, nor did they exhibit that capacity for union manifested among the early Germans. Evidences of a closer union appear about 800, when the pressure of Charlemagne's conquests began to be felt, and a tendency is noticeable toward hereditary succession in the chieftainship.[2] But no ruling dynasty was ever established among the Baltic Slavs as in the case of the Poles and Bohemians, who early developed a strong ducal power, which with the former even grew into a kingship. Political tendencies among them were centrifugal, and there seem to have been many small chieftains.[3]

As to social structure: There was a landed nobility,[4] a

Guttmann, "Die Germanisierung der Slawen in der Mark," *Forschungen zur Brandenburgischen und Preussischen Geschichte*, IX (1897), 431–32. In general, place-names with suffixes in *-itz*, *-in*, *-zig*, etc., are Slavonic endings, and many other places which appear to have German names are actually Slavonic, for example, Stettin, Wollin, Küstrin, Kamin, Danzig, Leipzig, Chemnitz, Lausitz, etc. Brandenburg is Germanized Brunabor; Merseburg is Germanized Mesibor, i.e., "the place in the woods," from Sorab, *mes* meaning "in" (Pol. *miedzy;* Bohem. *mezy*) and *bor* meaning "forest" (Schafarik, *Slav. Altherthümer*, II, 620). Schkeitbar, between Lützen and Zwenkau, commemorates a sacred wood of the Slavs, from Pol. *Swiety* ("sacred"), *Bor* ("wood"); Belgern, a castle near Torgau, means "White Hill" from Pol. *bielo* ("white") and *gora* ("hill"); the Bober River comes from Pol. and Bohem. *bobr* meaning "beaver." In Starigard, near Stettin, which Helmold (I, 12) explains, "Hoc est antiqua civitas," and in Belgrad, the suffix is akin to the *grad* ("a walled inclosure"), which is seen in Petrograd, Belgrade, Gratz, etc. Mecklenburg in Slavonic was called Wiligrad, or "Great City." Adam of Bremen (III, 19, 50) and Helmold (I, 88, 108) repeatedly call it Magnopolis. In Mecklenburg, Brisan signifies a locality planted with birch trees; Cowale, the place of a forge; Krukowe, a crow's roost. Königgrätz is Bohem. *Hradec* (pronounced *Hradets*); Kralove is "Queen's Castle," so named because it was given in 1363 by Charles IV to his wife, Elizabeth of Pomerania. To be consistent the Germans should have called the place Königinburg. The literature pertaining to Slavonic *Ortsnamen* is enormous: see Alfred Hennig, "Zur Entstehung der ländlichen Ortsformen," *Königreich Sachsen-Deutsche Erde*, XI (1912), 74–81, with an excellent map; Kühnel, *Die slavischen Ortsnamen in Mecklenburg-Strelitz* (2 vols., 1881–83); Hay, *Die slav. Siedelungen im Kgr. Sachsen* (1893); R. Virchow, "Wie lange waren Slaven in diesem Lande?" *Korrespondenzenblatt der deutschen Gesellschaft f. Anthropologie*, Band XXVIII (Munich, 1890); Bronisch, *Die slavischen Ortsnamen in Holstein und im Fürstentum Lübeck-Sonderburg* (1901); Müller, *Frankenkolonisation auf dem Eichfelde* (Halle, 1911),

[Continued on next page]

[1] Lippert, *Sozial-Gesch. Böhmens*, I, 121, 227.

[2] Einhard, *Annales*, p. 823; Guttmann, *op. cit.*, p. 398, **n. 2.**

[3] Guttmann, p. 399, nn. 3, 4.

[4] *Ibid.*, n. 1.

large free class composed of rude farmers,[1] cattle-raisers, and bee-keepers; fishing, perhaps, was the main source of livelihood, as was natural with a people living in so wet a country as Lower Germany was in the Middle Ages; slaves were numerous and were employed as field hands and artisans;[2] tribe enthralled tribe, and for centuries the slave marts of the Slavonic peoples supplied both Byzantium and the Germans of the West.

The westward drift of the Slavs was first acutely felt by the Thuringians, who were driven from their homes in the land between the Elbe, the Saale, and the Mulde rivers into the Thüringerwald and the Harz by the fifth century. There-

pp. 53–58; Stechele, *Ztschft. d. Ver. f. Thür. Gesch. und Altertumsk.* (N.F.), Band I (1879); Schulze, *Mitt. f. Anhaltische Gesch.*, Band VI (1884); Witte, "Wendische Bevölkerungsreste in Mecklenburg," *Forschungen zur d. Landes- und Volkskunde*, Band XVI, Heft 1 (1905); Witte, "Wendische-und Familienamen aus Mecklenburgisch. Urkunden," *Verein f. Meckl. Gesch.*, Band LXXI (1906); Kühnel, *Ztschft. d. histor. Verein f. Niedersachsen* (1902); Legowski, *Baltische Studien* (N.F.), Band III (1899); Vieth *et al.*, "Beiträge zur Ethnographie der hannoverischen Elbslawen," *Archiv. f. slav. Philologie*, XXII (1900), 107–43; Kühnel, *Finden sich noch Spuren der Slawen im mittleren und westlichen Hannover?* (Hannover, 1907). Bronisch, *Die slawischen Ortsnamen in Holstein und im Fürstentum Lübeck* (1901); Hilferding, "Die Ueberreste der Slawen auf der Südküste des baltischen Meeres," *Ztschft. f. slawische Literatur*, I (Bautzen, 1864), 81–97, 230–39; II, 85–111. For Slav place-names in the Moseltal see Lamprecht, *DWL*, I, 1, 152, nn. 3–4.

Several European princes still bear titles which are reminiscent of the history of German eastward expansion in the twelfth and thirteenth centuries. The late German Emperor and King of Prussia was also "duke of the Wends"; the grand duke of Mecklenburg is *Fürst zu Wenden;* even the king of Denmark yet bears the title "king of the Wends," though Danish power in Germany ceased with the battle of Bornhoeved in 1227. The question of how far the Slavs in Germany were dispossessed, and how far they were conquered and absorbed by the Germans instead, is a matter of controversy among historical scholars, unfortunately accentuated by too much race prejudice, for Russian and Polish students have entered the lists. See

[Continued on next page]

[1] Meitzen is of opinion that it is very difficult to say with certainty what the agrarian system of the primitive Slavs was. The transition from fishing and hunting with them to agriculture cannot be studied with any accuracy. The oldest sources which we have must be used with great caution since they deal with Poland, Moravia, Bohemia, Silesia, countries in which the Germans early got a foothold. But no part of Slav history indicates that they were ever nomads.

[2] Hauck, III, 86–87; Wendt, II, 9. For Wendish glass-making in Thuringia see Heim, *Correspondenzblatt der deutschen Gesellschaft für Anthropologie und Urgeschichte* (1885). The common boat was short, and made of alder wood, so light that two men could carry it. It was not rowed with oars but poled like a punt (see Herbordus, III, 17).

by the Saale River became the boundary between the two races. The Frankish conquest of the Thuringians in 531 drew the frontier sharp and clear, and the historic conflict between the Slav and the German peoples united under the rule of the Franks began.[1] During the reign of Dagobert (629–39) there were incessant Slav attacks on the eastern frontier.[2] In 630 the Slav fortress of Wogastisburg (today Wüstenburg, between Bamberg and Bayreuth)[3] was captured by the Franks. Between 674 and 687 the Franks were involved in bitter civil war and could not push an aggressive border policy. Fortunately for the German world at this perilous time, the racial unity of the Slavonic world did not

---

Pawinski, *The Slavs of the Elbe* (1871); J. A. Lebedev, *The Last Conflict of the Slavs of the Elbe against Germanization* (2 vols.; Moscow, 1878); Majewski, *Traces of the Wends in Franconia* (Warsaw, 1900). The earliest serious study of the subject dates back to 1789, when L. A. Gebhardi published at Halle his *Allgemeine Geschichte d. Wenden und Slaven und der Wenden in nördl. Teutschlande.* The controversy was given a new impulse in 1907 by an article by Kühnel in the *Forschungen zur Geschichte Niedersachsens* to which a reply was made by W. Ohnesorge (*Ausbreitung und Ende der Slawen zwischen Nieder-Elbe und Oder* [Leipzig, 1911]). Ohnesorge contends that the Slavs were not driven out, but were gradually absorbed. F. Tetzner, *Die Slawen in Deutschland. Beitr. z. Volkskunde d. Preuss., Litauer u. Letten, der Masuren u. Philipponen, der Tschechen, Mähren u. Sorben, Polacken u. Slowinzen, Kaschuben u. Polen. M. 215 Abbildgn., Krtn. u. Plänen, Sprachproben u. 15 Melod.* (Brschwg., 1902), contains the fullest information, with maps, for the Wends, Masurians, Cassubians, and Prussian Lithuanians. A Russian scholar, D. N. Iergorov ("Slaviano-Guermanskia Otnochenia v. Srednia Veka," *Colonisatzia Meklenbourga v. XIII Veke* [2 vols.; Moscow, 1915]), has learnedly endeavored to show that the nobility of Mecklenburg was not Germanized until the sixteenth century, and that German influence did not wholly displace that of the Slav until the Thirty Years' War. I do no profess to know this Russian literature at first hand, but only from German book reviews.

[1] For the Slav pressure upon Thuringia and the historical significance of the year 531 see Schafarik, II, 607–9; Schulze, *Kolonisierung*, p. 2; Posse, *Die Markgrafen von Meissen* (1881), p. 3; Lamprecht, III, 343; Meitzen, *Siedelung und Agrarwesen*, II, 149–51; Leo, *Untersuchungen zur Besiedelungs-und Wirtschaftsgesch. des Thüringischen Osterlandes in der Zeit des früheren Mittelalters* (Leipzig, 1880); Schottin, *Die Slawen in Thüringen;* Schlueter, *Die Siedelung im nordöstlichen Thüringen;* cf. *Hist. Vierteljahrschrift*, IX, No. 2.

[2] Schafarik, II, 419, 514. In the *Jahresschrift. f. d. Vorgesch. der Sächsisch-Thüringischen Länder*, Band III, is an archaeological article by O. Foertsch on remains found in ancient Slav tombs in Thuringia.

[3] Ernest, Baron von Aufsess, *Archiv f. Gesch. . . . . von Oberfranken*, Band XIX, Heft 1 (1893). For Slav place-names in Lorraine see Lamprecht, *DWL*, I, 1, 154, nn. 3–4.

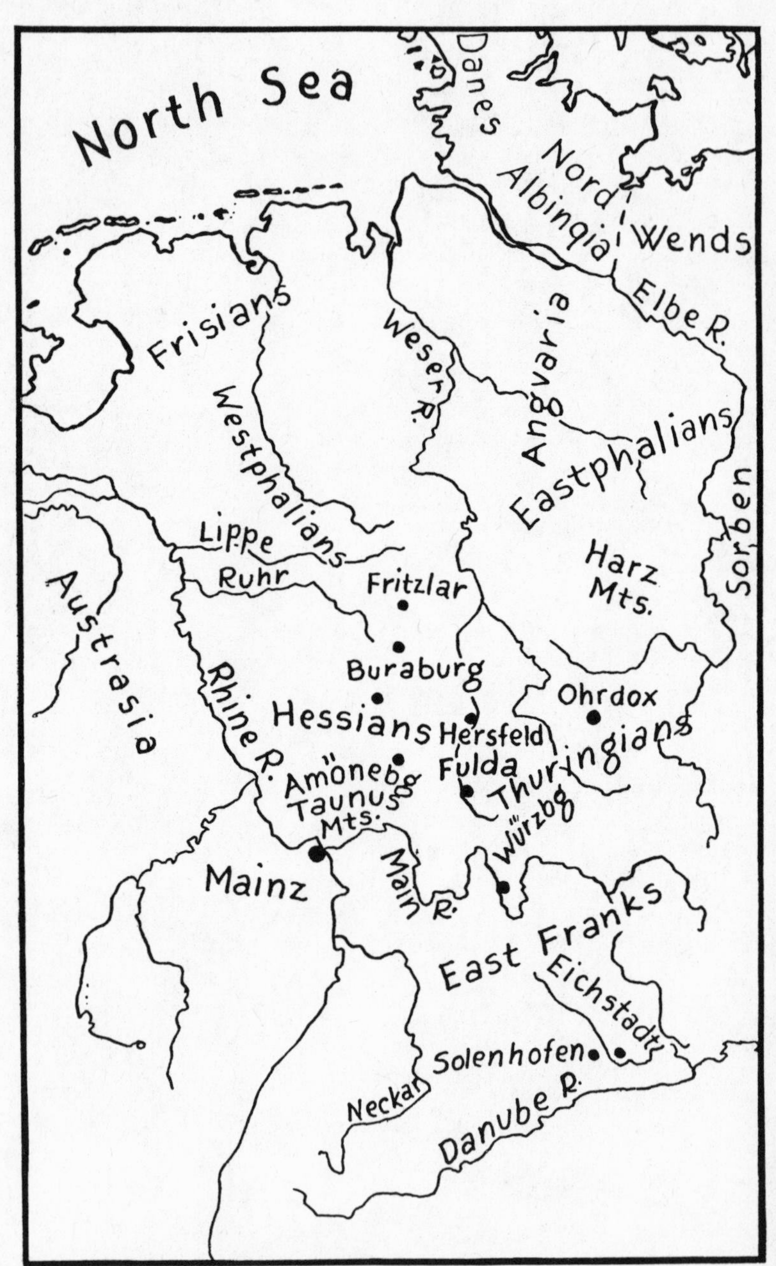

Bonifacian Mission Stations in Hesse

imply political unity as well, so that the Slav pressure was spasmodic and intermittent.

We can fix the time of the change in the relation of the two races with some precision. The real German anti-Slav offensive began with the founding of the mission posts of Boniface. Regensburg (739), Würzburg (741), and Eichstädt (743)[1] were half houses of God, half border fortresses designed for the conversion of the Slavs, buttressed by the genuine forts of Bremburg and Wogastisburg in the Bavarian Nordgau and Castle Salzburg (near Neustadt) in Franconia.[2]

In addition to these episcopal seats which lay echeloned along the eastern border of the Frank realm from the Danube to the mouth of the Rhine, a cluster of monasteries garrisoned Thuringia, Hesse, and the Nordgau: Disibodenburg (675), Amönaburg (722), Fritzlar (732), Buraburg (741), Fulda (744), Heidenheim (750), Hersfeld (759). With the eye of a military commander contemplating a frontal attack upon the enemy, Boniface unerringly perceived the strategical position of Thuringia as a *point d'appui*.[3]

The Thuringia of the eighth century (including Hesse) was far larger than the territory of the same name later. It was a tributary duchy of the Austrasian power which extended over the whole of Central Germany. Charles Martel had administratively included within its sphere a part of Austrasia and the Bavarian Plateau. It comprehended the valleys of the Lahn, the Main, and the Neckar. Southward and eastward the Thuringian frontier reached as far as the Raab. On the north it sloped through the valleys of the Werra and the Fulda toward the plain of Saxony. Militarily, politically, ecclesiastically, control of Thuringia carried with it the domination over Central Germany, and it was the natural base of operations for any forward movement, whether to the north, the east, or the southeast.

The social texture of Thuringia also was as firm and solid as the hills themselves. The admixture of Frankish blood, the

[1] Kretschmer, *Hist. Geog.*, p. 417.

[2] On this last place see Reiniger *Archiv d. hist. Ver. von Unterfranken und Aschaffenburg*, Band XXV (1879).

[3] See Willibald, *Vita Bonifatii*, chap. v, sec. 15.

Saxon ingredient introduced from the north and east, acted as an alloy to gold to harden the rugged native Thuringian stock. By the side of the Thuringian nobility, among whom land monopoly had nothing like the enormous influence possessed by the same class in the Frankland, there was a numerous class of free peasant farmers. Serfdom prevailed but again not so widely or hardly as elsewhere. A few traders and artisans made up the residue of the population exclusive of the clergy.[1]

With the completion of the Frank conquest of the Saxons in 804 the *Drang nach Osten*, or, as it has been more accurately called, *Die Besiedelung von Ostdeutschland durch die zweite germanische Völkerwanderung*,[2] got in full swing. The history of the gradual dispossession and almost complete extermination of the Wends is a long and terrible one, and extends from the time of Charlemagne to the middle of the thirteenth century. Lamprecht's words have become a classic utterance: "Weit mehr als die Eroberung der Slawenländer im zwölften und dreizehnten Jahrhundert erscheint deren Germanisation als ein wahrhaft erstaunlicher Vorgang: es ist die Grosstat unseres Volkes während des Mittelalters."[3]

In 789 Charlemagne began the long and relentless war between the races which was to endure for centuries by attacking the Wilzi. In 806 he fixed the official frontier along the Elbe and Saale rivers, which was protected by a line of posts.[4]

[1] The evidence for this paragraph may be found in Willibald, chaps vi, vii, and viii; *Acta*, SS. XI, Octobris die xxvi, 950; but the fullest light is cast by Boniface's own sermons, which are of great value for evidence as to the social texture in Thuringia. See Migne, *Patrol. Lat.*, LXXXIX, 843 f., sermo III, 849, A, B; V, 853, A, C, D; IX, 861, A, C, D; XI, 864, B; cf. Kylie, "The Condition of the German Provinces as Illustrating the Methods of Boniface," *Cambridge Journal of Theolog. Studies*, VII, 32.

[2] Beheim-Schwarzbach, *Sammlung . . . . Vorträge* (Berlin, 1882), p. xvii.

[3] *Deutsche Gesch.* (5th ed.), III, 363; cf. Nitzsch, II, 215.

[4] Einhard, *Annales* (*anno* 806); *MGH, Leg.*, III, 133; Lippert, I, 137. There is an excellent map by Peisker in *Camb. Med. Hist.*, Vol. II. For traces of Charlemagne's Saxon limes see Adam of Bremen, II, 18; F. Bangert, "Spuren der Franken am nordalbingischen Limes Saxoniae," *Ztschft. d. hist. Ver. f. Niedersachsen* (1904), pp. 1–62; Schuchhardt, "Ausgrabungen am Limes Saxoniae," *Ztschft. d. Ver. f. Lübeck. Gesch.*, XV, 1–26. The posts were Bardowick, Magdeburg, Erfurt, Halstadt, Schesel, Pfreimt, Regensburg, and Lorch. Intermediate fortified points connected

But though actual Frank sovereignty was not extended farther, it was to the interest of the Frankish monarchy to keep the border peoples in a state of intimidation.[1] The expedition was a military demonstration. The Wilzi were beaten but not intimidated. In 810 they stormed the Frankish border fort at Hobucki on the Elbe near Gartow,[2] and in 812 three Frankish armies had to be sent against them.[3] Then it was that Charlemagne was compelled to reorganize the east border on firmer lines and the scattered Marches were all linked together in a chain stretching from the North Sea to the head of the Adriatic.

It was an irrepressible conflict in which race supremacy, religion, language, trade, customs, and land to live in were the issues.[4] On the part of the Germanic people the struggle became a gigantic series of missionary campaigns and colonizing conquests protracted through centuries. Monk missionaries penetrated the Slavonic wilderness bent on peaceable or compulsory conversion of the Wends, and the sword of a semi-theocratic kingship was stretched out to protect or

---

these. One of these lesser fortresses has been identified, the Chat near Bamberg, so called from the medieval Latin word *catus* (see Klieber, *Bamberger Historischer Verein* [1882], Bericht 45). The Carolingian Limes has been thoroughly studied by Beyer, *Der Limes Saxoniae Karls des Grossen* (1878) (cf. *Jenaer Literaturzeitung* [Feb. 15, 1879] and *Hist. Ztschft.* [N.F.], V, 1879); and two articles by Handelman in *Archiv d. Vereins f. deutschen Gesch. des Herzogtums Lauenburg*, Band II, Heft 3 (1879); Band III, Heft 1 (1880); Lipp, "Das fränkische Grenzsystem unter Karl dem Grossen," *Untersuchungen z. deutsch. Staats- und Rechtsgesch.* (1892); Blochwitz, *Die Verhältnisse an der deutschen Ostgrenze zwischen Elbe und Donau zur Zeit der ersten Karolinger* (1872). Henigsheim, "Limes Sorabicus," *Ztschft. d. Ver. f. Thür. Gesch.*, XVI, No. 2 (1906), thinks that the Limes was not a fortified line, but merely a border patrol between fortified posts. The Karlschanze near Willebadessen in Westphalia was a Saxon castle destroyed by Charlemagne (Schneider, *Festschrift f. d. Gesch. Westdeutschlands.*, Band VIII (1888).

[1] Guttmann, *op. cit.*, p. 408, compares Charlemagne's expedition in 789 across the Elbe to Caesar's crossing of the Rhine.

[2] Dehio, *Gesch. des Erzbistums Hamburg-Bremen*, I, 38, n. 5.

[3] Einhard, *Annales* (812); *Chron. Moissac* (812); Schafarik, II, 319 f., 423–25, 456 f., 517–21. The most recent history of the conflict between the Germans and the Slavs before the time of Henry I is Merbach, *Slawenkriege d. deutschen Volkes*, Part I (1914).

[4] Hauck, III, 89–91. His ferocious characterization is not exaggerated.

avenge the priests whom the Wends slew or expelled.[1] But back of the enmity of race and religion was the fierce land-hunger of both peoples fighting for fields to till in order to feed millions of mouths whose hunger it was hard to satisfy in the primitive conditions under which agriculture was then practiced.[2]

The eastward drift of the German peoples, intimations of which are observable in the sixth century, and which by 800 had become a definite trend,[3] was powerfully influenced by the slow economic, especially agrarian, revolution which took place in Frankish Gaul and the Rhinelands in the seventh and eighth centuries. The increase of the benefice system, the extension of the manorial régime, the adoption of more

[1] "Eroberung und Missionierung Hand in Hand," *ibid.*, III, 79.

[2] For detail see Joh. Müller, *Frankenkolonisation auf dem Eichfelde*, pp. 12–13; cf. *Hist. Ztschft.*, CXIV, No. 3; Meitzen, *Siedelung und Agrarwesen*, II, 401–6; Lamprecht, III, 311–65. Absolute statistics are, of course, impossible as to population in the Middle Ages. But modern scholars have made some relative determinations. In Carolingian times, favorable regions like the valley of the Moselle, seem to have had a fairly dense population. Indeed, along rivers which were important highways of trade the place-names seem to have been more numerous than now, particularly along the Meuse. In late Merovingian times and down to the invasions of the Northmen, between the Seine and the Rhine the density of population is estimated to have been as much as 300 per square mile. The population of the East Frank kingdom, i.e., Germany, in late Carolingian times is estimated to have been two and one-half to three millions. It certainly increased under the Saxon rule and probably was between three and three and one-half millions; the Franconian period (1024–1125), in spite of the civil war in the reign of Henry IV, was one of great economic prosperity for Germany, and the population may have been five to six millions by the beginning of the twelfth century. In the Moselle region the population doubled between 900 and 1100, and by 1200 was quadrupled (Lamprecht, *DWL*, I, 1509; 1235–36). In Frederick Barbarossa's time it probably was between seven and eight millions. At the accession of the Saxon house in 919 there were not over 30 towns in Germany; at the end of the Franconian period (1125) there were above 150. In the ninth and tenth century not over 1 to 2 per cent dwelt in towns; in late Franconian times (1075–1125) from 3 to 5 per cent were town people. Consult R. Kötzschke, *Deutsche Wirtschaftsgesch. bis zum 17. Jahrhundert* (1908), pp. 50–52; Beloch, "Die Bevölkerung Europas im Mittelalter," *Zeitschrift f. Soz. u. Wirtschaftsgesch.*, III, 417 f.; G. Caro, "Zur Bevölkerungsstatistik der Karolingerzeit," in his *Beiträge*, pp. 38 f.; Lamprecht, *DWL*, I, 181 f.; Inama Sternegg, *DWG*, I, 514 f.; II, 29 f.; Curschmann, *Hungersnöte im Mittelalter* (1900). The author of the *Descriptio Theutoniae*, written at the end of the thirteenth century derived "Germania" from the Latin *generare*. "Dicitur Germania, quia multos homines dicitur generare; nulla enim terrarum in tanto spatio dicitur tot homines continere" (*MGH*, SS. XVII, 238 [cf. Michael, *Gesch. d. deutsch. Volkes*, I, 128, n. 2]).

[3] Kötzschke, pp. 47 and 110.

intensive agricultural methods,[1] in particular on the manors of the fisc and of the church, slowly tended to depress the small free farmer into the condition of a tenant or a serf upon his own lands, the proprietorship of which passed from him to some adjacent noble or high cleric; or else the changing order of things ejected him from his ancestral holding and made him a homeless wanderer—a *homo migrans*. The small land owner could not compete with the grand proprietor in the economic and social transformation which was in process in these years.[2]

As a result the dispossessed and evicted turned to the forests for refuge, there to carve out a clearing in the wilderness and to establish a new home.[3] The forest was the poor man's home.

But the coil of private ownership gradually wound itself around the forests, too. Traces of the intrusion of private proprietorship upon the forests appear in the Burgundian and the Visigothic codes. The forests of the Vosges began to be appropriated in the time of Gregory of Tours (*ca.* 600), those of the Ardennes by the early seventh century.[4] In Charlemagne's time the upper Mosel, the Sieg, and the lower

[1] There are signs of soil exhaustion in the oldest parts of Germany as early as the ninth and tenth centuries (Lamprecht, *op. cit.*, I, 1, 113).

[2] E. Dobbert, *Ueber das Wesen und den Geschäftskreis der Missi Dominici* (Heidelberg, 1861) (at end). This reference and the extracts from the capitularies are cited by Hodgkin, *Italy and Her Invaders: The Frankish Empire*, VIII, 297–99. The *Paroenesis ad judices* ("Exhortation to Judges") of Theodulph graphically shows the temptations to official corruption which beset the *missi dominici*. See the long extract in Guizot, *Civilization in France*, Lect. XXIII, pp. 60–64.

[3] "Freilich spielte daneben der Wildbruch im Walde bereits eine immer grössere Rolle; in den Vordergrund aber trat er erst nach voller Sesshaftmachung des Volkes, seit etwa dem 5. bis 6. Jahrhundert. Seitdem ziehen Generationen auf Generationen nachgeborener Söhne in den Urwald und sengen und roden. Das 7. bis 9. Jahrhundert sah einen ersten grossen Ausbau des Landes hinein in die unerschöpflichen Bestände der Bergwälder. . . . . Im 6. bis 8. Jahrhundert war vor allem der gemeinfreie Träger der Waldsiedelung gewesen; im genossenschaftlichen Verbande hatten die jungen Männer des Volkes ein neues Heim in den Tiefen der Waldtäler gesucht" (Lamprecht, *DG*, III, 53). Cf. Kotzschke, p. 47, the last paragraph. For detailed exposition of the economic transformation set forth in this paragraph see von der Goltz, *Gesch. der deutschen Landwirtschaft*, I, 93–98; Inama Sternegg, *Deutsche Wirtschaftsgesch.*, I, 246 ff.; Arnold, *Deutsche Gesch.*, II, 2, 44, 100–109.

[4] Lamprecht, *DWL*, I, 1, 469–70.

Main began to be penetrated by private claims. The early years of the reign of Louis the Pious witnessed such wholesale seizure of forest tracts by private proprietors that the Emperor canceled the titles to all forest holdings of a private nature established without express authorization.[1]

In order to escape from the pressure imposed upon him by the increase in the number and the extent of these great landed estates, both lay and clerical, west of the Rhine and in the Middle Rhinelands, the small landowner and the dispossessed freeman tended to drift eastward into the upper Main and Bavaria, where land was freer and the population less dense along the border. The conquest of Saxony does not

[1] *Lex Visigoth.*, VIII, 3, 8; *Lex Burg.*, Art. XIII (*MGH*, *Leges*, III, 538), Art. LXVII (*ibid.*, p. 561). For the Vosges see Hillman, *Deutsche Finanzgeschichte des Mittelalters*, pp. 249–50; Petit du Taillis, "De la signification du mot 'forêt' à l'époque franque," *Bib. de l'École d. Chartes* (jan.-avril, 1915), pp. 118–19; for the Ardennes, Lamprecht, *Deutsches Wirtschaftsleben*, I, 93 ff.; II, 626; Petit du Taillis, *op. cit.*, pp. 112–17. In 648 Sigbert of Austrasia granted the monastery of Stablo a tract 12 miles square *in vasta Ardenna*, which Childerich II reduced to 6 miles in 667. Inama Sternegg, *op. cit.* (2 ed., 1909), I, 283, and n. 3. Karlmann in 774 gave Fulda a tract measuring 4,000 paces each way (*ibid.*, p. 284, n. 2); in 779 Hersfeld possessed a forest 2 miles in circumference (*ibid.*); in 811 and 813 two Frank nobles owned tracts 2 miles long and 2 miles broad in the Ardennes (*ibid.*, n. 6). Louis the Pious gave Benedict of Aniane's cloister of Cornelimünster a huge tract of the forest of the Ardennes (*Acta* SS. II [Feb. 12], 10). For interpretation of the terminology of the forest in the Middle Ages see Wiener, *Commentary to the Germanic Codes*, pp. 98 ff. In general see von der Goltz, *op. cit.*, I, 139–40; Roscher, *System der Volkswirtschaft; Nationaloekonomik des Ackerbaus und der verwandten Urproduction* (11th ed., 1885), sec. 191; Schröder, "Die Ausbreitung der Salischen Franken," *Forschungen zur deutschen Geschichte*, XIX, 139 f.; Maury, *Les forêts de la France* (1856), chap. vi. For Charlemagne's liberal legislation see *Cap. de Villis*, § 36 (with the notes of Gareis, *Die Landgüterordnung Kaiser Karls d. Gr.*, pp. 44–45); *Cap. Aquisgran*, § 18; cf. Dopsch *Wirtschaftsentwicklung der Karolingerzeit*, I, 175; Arnold, *Ansiedelungen und Wanderungen*, pp. 241 f. For the legislation of Louis the Pious see *Cap. 818–819*, § 7, in Boretius, I, 288; *Cap. missorum* (819), § 22 (*ibid.*, p. 291); cf. *Mélanges Bemont*, p. 63. Petit du Taillis, *op. cit.*, p. 134, makes the point: "La signification constante du mot 'forêt' dans les capitulaires permet d'affirmer que les forêts créés par des particuliers, dont parle Louis le Pieux, étaient des réserves de chasse, ou de pêche, et l'ordre d'abolir les forêts nouvellement instituées, en prouvant qu'il y avait d'autres forêts privées, de fondation ancienne, auxquelles Louis le Pieux ne voulait pas toucher, nous reporte au moins au viiie siècle."

We have no information on private forests at this early period. The increasing curtailment of the right to use the forest was a continuous grievance of the medieval peasantry. Jonas, bishop of Orleans in the ninth century, voiced their protest in a treatise entitled *De institutione laicali*, II, 23: "Deus in commune mortalibus ad utendum concessit, pauperes a potentioribus spoliantur, flagellantur, ergastulis detruduntur et multa alia patiuntur. Hoc ut justo libramine decernant utrum lex mundi legem evacuare Christi debeat, necne" (Migne, *Patrol. Lat.*, CVI, 215).

seem to have been followed immediately by any considerable immigration into the region from points farther west.

The mission of Boniface and the conquests of Charlemagne were the first important stage in the long and bloody struggle between the German and the Slav. In 822 a castle was built on the Delvenau, an affluent of the lower Elbe near Lauenburg, in order to protect Saxony from the inroads of the Abodrites.[1] Under Louis the Pious, Würzburg and Hamburg became advance posts of Christo-German *Kultur*. In 832 the former had fourteen mission churches among the Slavs of the Main.[2] In 834 Anskar founded Hamburg, henceforth the base for the conversion of the north, both Slav and Scandinavian, until the establishment of Bremen.[3]

In the early ninth century the *populi Sclavorum*[4] were as yet floating masses, without close tribal organization and without leaders. The east border was relatively undisturbed until 862 when Ludwig the German made an expedition against Dobomysl, the Abodrite duke. In 866 the Winidi gave trouble. In 869 the Bohemians and Moraven under Swatopluk invaded Bavaria, while the Sorben and Siusli, kindred to them and dwelling along the Mulde, crossed the Saale and penetrated into Thuringia whence they were expelled by a joint Thuringian and Saxon army. Ludwig the German's two sons, Charles (the Fat) and Karlmann, drove Swatopluk back. In 872, 874, 877, 880, 889, 892, 893, 898, there was heavy fighting along the border.[5]

Dopsch justly makes the point that in all likelihood the eastern colonization movement of the German people was

[1] *Ann. Lauresh.* (822); Giesebrecht, *Wend. Gesch.*, I, 108.

[2] Rusam, *Beiträge zur Bayerischen Kirchengesch.*, IX, 1.

[3] Adam of Bremen, I, 24, 27, 36 (= *Vita Rimberti*, chap. xvi). See Bril, "Les premiers temps du christianisme en Suède," *Revue d'hist. ecclés.*, XII (1911), 17–37, 231–41, 652–69. In 864 Nicholas I removed the seat of the diocese to Bremen. Cf. Joachim, *Mitth. d. Inst. f. oesterr. Gesch.*, XXXIII, No. 2 (1912); Reuter, *Hist. Ztschft.* (3d ser., 1910), IX, No. 2. The alleged diploma of Charlemagne for Bremen is false (Tangl, *Mitt. d. Inst. f. oesterr. Gesch.*, XVIII, No. 1).

[4] *Annales S. Bert.* (844).

[5] *Ruod. Fuld.* (for these years); the lineaments of the future Sorben Mark may be descried in these events (Schafarik, II, 460–61, 524; Lippert, I, 148). We know the names, preserved in *Ann. Fuld.*, of two of the margraves, *Ratolf* (873–80) and Poppo (880–92); cf. Dümmler, I, 714 f.; Riezler, *Gesch. Bayerns*, I, 217 f.

relatively as strong in the ninth century as later. It differed chiefly in direction, being toward the southeast instead of the northeast, and was more exclusively aristocratic and clerical in its nature than the colonization movement of the twelfth century, which was largely a popular wave. If the sources for the reigns of Ludwig the German and Arnulf were proportionately as full as those of the Salian and Hohenstaufen periods, there is little doubt that the continuity of the history of German eastward colonization would clearly appear from the time of Charlemagne onward.[1]

What Professor Turner has called "the common sequence of frontier types—fur trader, cattle raising, pioneer, small primitive farmer"[2] is true of the frontier of medieval Germany, although for lack of the abundant evidence which American history affords the differentiations cannot be so clearly established and the impression is not so definite. Yet the distinctions are perceptible. While the Rhine cities in the tenth century were obscurely building up a trade which blossomed into rich fruitage in the Salian era and the Rhinelands were intensively cultivating the grape, Mainzer merchants imported grain and cattle into the city from the estates of the Hessian monasteries of Fulda and Hersfeld or from the Slav-tilled fields of the upper Main, freighting the grain downstream to the Rhine.[3] Beyond the monastery

[1] Dopsch, *op. cit.*, I, 174–75; cf. Inama Sternegg, *op. cit.*, I, 280–81; Lamprecht, *DWG*, I, 245, 290–97. Even in spite of the poverty of information in the chronicles the documentary evidence is impressive. See the long list of Carolingian grants in Eggers, *Der königliche Grundbesitz im 10. und 11. Jh.*, pp. 28–32.

[2] "The First Official Frontier of Mass.," *Col. Soc. of Mass.*, XVII (1914), 254.

[3] *Translatio SS. Marcellini et Petri* (by Einhard); "Mercatores quidam de civitate Mogontiaco, qui frumentum in superioribus Germaniae partibus emere ac per fluvium Moinum ad urbem devehere solebant." Cf. Mathai, "Einhards Translatio, SS. Marcellini et Petri in kulturgeschichtlicher Beziehung," *Progr. d. Gymn. zu Laubach* (1883–84), p. 12. Mlle Bondois, *La translation des saints Marcellin et Pierre* (Paris, 1907), curiously ignores these economic data. In the eighth century wheat cultivation and spelt appear among the peoples bordering on the Franks, and, per contra, in the ninth century the cultivation of rye, the grain of the Slavs, makes its appearance in the German sources (Kretschmer, p. 201). On the economy of the Bonifacian monasteries see Sommerlad, *Die wirtschaftliche Tätigkeit der Kirche*, I, 278, 288; II, 152. Inama Sternegg, *DWG*, I, 8; Meitzen, "Der aelteste Anbau der Deutschen," *Jahrb. f. Nationaloek. und Statistik* (N.F., 1881), II, 1–46; Roscher, *Ansichten der Volkswirtschaft aus dem geschichtlichen Standpunkte* (3d ed.), I, 205–

ranches and great farms of Hesse and lower Franconia conditions became more primitive, and in their place appeared small farms, clearings in the forest, and patches of soil crudely tilled by a German peasantry in Thuringia and Saxony, and by Wendish folk in upper Franconia, along the higher reaches of the Main and the Regnitz. From this "back-land" zone things rapidly shaded off into the pure frontier marked by the Saale and the lower Elbe rivers.

The border warfare was a profitable source of serf and slave supply for the Bonifacian monasteries, which had great need of raw labor for the exploitation of their vast properties.[1] The greater portion of eastern Franconia, the upper Main around Bayreuth, Bamberg, Würzburg, and Nuremberg, was solidly Slav before the year 1000.[2] It was not until the twelfth century that the pagan Slavs in these regions were converted, although the districts had figured as *Gaue* on German maps since 889. When the bishopric of Bamberg was established in 1007 the synod of Frankfort decreed "ut paganismus Sclavorum inibi destrueretur."[3] Yet in the proceedings of the synod of Bamberg in 1058 one reads: "Erat enim

38; Waitz, *DVG*, I, 32–52; Seeck, "Die aelteste Kultur der Deutschen," *Preuss. Jahrb.*, LXXVI (1894), 32–58; Lamprecht, "Zur Sozialgesch. der deutschen Urzeit," *Festgabe f. Hanssen*, pp. 61–72; Riedel, *Mark Brand.*, II, 10–11 and notes. For the subject of cattle-raising in general see Langethal, *Gesch. der teutschen Landwirtschaft*, I (Jena, 1847), 46 f.; von der Goltz, *Landwirtschaft*, I (1902), 67–84, 98–116; Lamprecht, *DWL*, I, 532 f., 543 f.; and especially Lauffer, *Das Landschaftsbild im Zeitalter der Karolinger* (Göttingen diss., 1896), pp. 63–76. Regensburg was evidently a center of cattle-raising in the time of Otto I (Widukind, III, 36).

[1] Schafarik, *op. cit.*, II, 607. The registers of Fulda often mention clusters of Slavonic villages in the woody districts around the abbey (Zeuss, *op. cit.*, p. 646, quoting Schann, *Buchonia Vetus*, pp. 46–48). Of Slavs in the Lower Harz near Mansfeld we have mention in a deed of 973: "De possessionibus S. Bonifatii martyris [follows the names of 12 localities] . . . . villis villarumque partibus quas Slavuainicae familiae inhabitant" (Zeuss, *op. cit.*, p. 647, after Schann, *Tradit. Fuld.*, p. 241).

[2] Seyler, *Archiv f. Gesch. und Alterth. von Oberfranken*, Band XVII, Heft 3 (1889). The Council of Tribur in 895 (*Regino*, II, cap. 5, n. 43; Burchard Worm., Canon 69), and the *Poenitent. Merseburg.* imposed penance for the practice of pagan rites (Mannhardt, *Der Baumkultus*, p. 245, n. 3; p. 331, n. 1; Friedberg, *Bussbücher*, pp. 24, 61, 86). For Slav paganism in the vicinity of Bielefeld (*ca.* 940) see Giesebrecht, *Wendische Geschichten*, I, 83. For legislation of the Eastern church against the persistence of pagan practices among the southern Slavs see Mannhardt, *op. cit.*, pp. 470–71.

[3] Migne, CXL, 115.

plebs hujus episcopii utpote ex maxima parte Sclavonica." Half a century later, in 1111, Arnold, bishop of Halberstadt, still could write to Otto of Bamberg: "Totam illam terram paene silvam esse, Sclavos ibi habitare." Later deeds of Bamberg for many years make mention of Slavs, and the appearance and dialect of the people yet attest a large Slavonic admixture.[1]

Along the line of the Elbe from the Erzgebirge to Hamburg, German colonization annexed immense tracts of border territory, while in the interior dukes and margraves, bishops and abbots, vied with one another in clearing forests, reclaiming moors and swamps. In addition to these acquisitions thousands of acres of arable land in the form of farms were given to the church by the piety of nobles and the complacency of kings. These gifts were manors either of the noble donor or taken from the royal fisc. Moreover, the church extended its manorial machinery in the imposition of tithes and other economic obligations upon the free peasantry more and more so that in the end they were either compelled to evacuate their holdings all together, which the church promptly assimilated with its own lands, or else to accept the condition of serfdom upon their once free acres, which ceased longer to belong to them.

The stages in the eastward expansion of the German people are marked, though not so clearly, as the same phenomenon in the United States. In Charlemagne's reign the frontier of settlement (for we must distinguish between the military boundary and the edge of civilization) was barely beyond the Rhine. A line drawn through Frankfort and Soest, across the sources of the Ruhr and the Lippe, would perhaps mark it. For the chain of fortified trading posts along the course of the lower Elbe, the Saale, and the Nab rivers from Bardowick to Regensburg was far from the civilization of the Frankish empire.[2] Under the rule of the Saxon house (919–1024) the frontier of settlement and the military boundary became more nearly identical. The line of civilization was extended to the Saale in Thuringia, but in Saxony

[1] Schafarik, *op. cit.*, II, 609; Hauck, III, 418–19. [2] Hauck, III, 77–78.

proper stopped at the Aller and the Ocker rivers.[1] Along the middle Main civilization had also crept up as far as Würzburg, as a charter of Otto III shows, which granted special privileges to settlers who would come and reclaim the forests and drain the marshes.[2] By the eleventh century Bamberg, which Henry II founded in 1007, had succeeded Würzburg as the frontier outpost of the Main Valley.[3] The sources of the Saxon period show the large progress made in eastward colonization.[4] Along the eastern edge of the kingdom from the mouth of the Elbe to the mountains of Styria, German colonists annexed immense tracts of territory.[5] But the Elbe was not permanently crossed until the twelfth century.[6]

These pioneers were chiefly engaged in cattle-raising. Court judgments in this region were imposed in cattle fines under Otto I, and the legislation shows the prevalence of agrarian crime, especially cattle-stealing.[7]

At the opening of the tenth century, the beginning of the Saxon epoch, the population of Germany was very unevenly

[1] Gerdes, *Geschichte des deutschen Volkes*, I, 357; Schulze, *op. cit.*, pp. 50 f.: Schwarz, *Die Anfänge des Städtewesen in den Elb- und Saale-Gegenden* (1892).

[2] Gerdes, I, 371; Matthias, *Klosterpolitik Heinrichs II*, II, 74. In the time of Arnulf, a century earlier, the bishopric of Würzburg was solidly Slav (*Ep. Arnulfi*, in Jaffé, V, 477), and still must have been heavily so in the year 1000.

[3] Hauck, III, 418–19.

[4] For cattle-raising along the frontier see Sommerlad, II, 266; Wattenbach, *Deutschlands Geschichtsquellen im Mittelalter*, II, 33 f. The *Vita Meinwerci* is rich in economic data.

[5] Gerdes, I, 337 f.; Lamprecht, *Deutsche Geschichte*, III, 52 f.

[6] An exception, of course, is here inferred for Holstein and Ditmarsch. As we have already seen, in 804 Charlemagne deported the Nordalbingian Saxons, and permitted the Abodrites to settle in their room. At what subsequent period and under what circumstances the Saxons recrossed the river and acquired a permanent foothold again in Holstein and Ditmarsch is not known. History has left no record of this movement. *Holsati* simply means "settlers in the wood" (*Holz*). But the suffix *satas* or *settas* elsewhere usually indicates a "frontier," or at least a "settlement under wilderness conditions." Thus in Anglo-Saxon England we find along the western Marches the names Dorsaetas, Somersaetas. *Thiatmarsgoi* means "dwellers in the marshes of Thiatmars," hence Ditmarsch. In fine, we do not know how and when Holstein and Ditmarsch were repeopled with Saxons. Place-names are our sole historical evidence (see Hansen, *Ztschft. d. Gesellschaft f. Schleswig-Holstein. Gesch.*, Band XXXIII).

[7] Wid., II, 6; Roscher, *Polit. Economy* (Eng. trans.), I, p. 353, note.

distributed. In the Rhinelands, from the mouth of the Rhine to the Hochgebirge, the peopling seems to have been quite dense and there was a high degree[1] of material culture. In Lorraine, west Franconia, and Swabia the population must have been numerous and the material civilization considerable. But Saxony, Bavaria, and the Ostmark were still thinly peopled, and until the forays of the Magyars were arrested effective southeastward movement of the Germans was impossible. The upper Neckar was not penetrated by settlers until the verge of the eleventh century,[2] and the Frankenwald[3] and high valley of the Murg were not colonized before the twelfth.[4]

The Wends seem to have confronted fort with fort against the Saxons. We know from Einhard's *Annals*[5] that they had palisaded towns, or at least *castella*, along their western border, and modern archaeological research has discoverd the site and explored the ruins of a considerable number of ancient Slav fortifications. Ibrahim ibn Jakub, the Mohammedan traveler in Germany in 973, describes their town walls as high and made of hard-packed earth.[6]

[1] For the colonization of upper Swabia see Victor Ernst, "Zur Besiedelung Oberschwabens," *Festschrift Dietrich Schäfer* (1915).

[2] Weller, *Wuerttemb. Vierteljahrshefte f. Landesgesch.* (N.F., 1894), Band III.

[3] Meyer, *Alterthumsforschender Verein zu Holenhauben*, Band LII.

[4] Hartmann, *Wuerttemb. Jahrb. f. Statistik und Landeskunde* (1893) (with map).

[5] *Anno* 808: ". . . . captis aliquot Sclavorum castellis."

[6] Wigger, *Jahrb. f. Mecklenburgische Gesch.* (1880). See for this subject Saalborn, *Neues Lausitzisches Magazin*, Band LV (1879); Kasten, *Baltische Studien*, Band XXIX (1879), a study of the foundations of the castle of Winburg on the Pregel, which are of Wendish origin; Grupp, *Jahresbericht über den historischen Verein zu Brandenburg an der Havel* (1881), shows that the lower strata of the ancient walls of Potsdam and Rathenow are of Wendish construction; cf. Handelmann, *Ztschft. der Gesellschaft f. Schleswig-Holstein*, X, 4–24, on fortifications of the Polaben and Wagrians; Schildt, *Jahrb. d. Vereins f. Meckl. Gesch.*, Band LII (1887), *castrum* Wustrord on the Tollensee; Schumann, *Baltische Studien*, Band XXVII, Heft 1 (1887), Randow; Welter, *Ztschft. f. Kulturgesch.* (3d ser., 1893), Heft vi, (Lüchow in Hannover). Widukind, III, 45, 51, 62, mentions three Wendish fortresses, and apparently Merseburg before Saxon conversion of it into a *Burg* was another Slav stronghold, for Thietmar, I, 5, writing *ca.* 1000 calls it "an ancient city," and its name, despite its apparent German character, is Slavonic, i.e., *Mesibor*, or "Town in the Woods" (Schaferik, *Slav. Alterth.*, II, 620; Meitzen, *Siedelung und Agrarwesen*, II, 332).

The military prestige of Duke Otto the Illustrious (d. 912) acquired in warfare with the Wends, and which passed on to his son Henry the Fowler, was an important factor in securing the latter's election to the German kingship in 919.[1]

With the accession of Henry I to the German throne, the eastward pressure of the German race was actively pushed. The Sorben land between the Saale and the upper Elbe was the first territory wrung from the Slavs by the German sword and the first to be Germanized. But it is a mistake to regard the conquest and settlement of this land as a prototype of the colonization of the territory across the Elbe, i.e., Nordalbingia, Mecklenburg, and Brandenburg. The eastward expansion of the German people was not a uniform movement, nor was the process the same in every part. In Nordalbingia and the Billunger March the expansion was, as we shall see, a natural expansion and the settlement a true colonization. But in the Sorben "triangle" it was a conquest made by government and not by the people—a military occupation made for the purpose of strengthening and straightening the frontier against the Poles and the Bohemians. Over a century was to elapse before any real colonization or much exploitation of the soil began. Even the church had no part in the process until a considerable time had elapsed. The Thuringian March was a veritable *Reichsland*.

In the tenth century the eastward pressure of the German race, which was arrested during the ninth century, partly owing to the lesion of government and society within, and partly to a brief hardening of the Slavonic offensive, was aggressively resumed. This border policy was purely Saxon in initiative and interest[2] although it was destined in the ultimate to be of profound importance to the entire German people. Henry I committed Germany to a policy of a thousand

[1] Arnulf in 897 calls Otto "fidelis marchio noster" (Dronke, *Codex Fuld.*, No. 295).

[2] Hauck, III, 76: "Die wendischen Eroberungen sind die weltgeschichtliche Tat Heinrichs I. Durch sie hat er das deutsche Volk in das Gebiet geführt, in das sich nach fast einem Jahrtausend der Schwerpunkt der deutschen Macht verlegen sollte." Cf. Guttmann, "Die Germanisierung der Slawen in der Mark," *Forsch. zur Brand. u. Preuss. Gesch.*, IX, 411.

years. Yet purely Saxon as it was, Henry's border policy was in alignment with the Carolingian tradition. His aim was to make the trans-Elbean Wendish peoples tributary again to the German power, from which they had escaped in the ninth century. In pursuance of this course, in the winter of 928–29 Henry made a campaign across the frozen marshes of the Havel River and "by hunger, sword and cold," as Widukind[1] says, took Brunabor, the chief town of the Hevelli, and converted it into a *Burg* after the fashion of the fortified places he had established in Saxony and Thuringia. Such is the particular beginning of Brandenburg. Before the force of this drive was spent the Saxon arms had advanced up the Elbe clear to Meissen, conquered the Daleminzi in this region, and gained a vantage-point of great importance for the future.[2] The Saxon menace was so great that it inspired a coalition of the threatened tribes—Abodrites, Wilzi, Hevelli, Daleminzi, and Redarii—of whom the last were the warlike custodians of the shrine of Slavonic faith at Rethra and the leaders of the war for independence. A furious battle was fought at Lenzen on the right bank of the Elbe below Wittenberg, in September, 929, the issue of which left the Wends broken and shattered.[3] A Saxon expedition in 932, up the Elster, culminating in another engagement at Lebusa, completed the reduction of the Slavs between the upper Elbe and the Saale.[4] The German "sphere of influence" extended to the Oder and the Erzgebirge. Even Bohemia, with Bavarian assistance, was reduced to tribute.[5]

Of the importance of these achievements Henry the Fowl-

[1] I, 35: *fame, ferro, frigore* (Schafarik, II, 372). For the cruelty of Henry I see Hauck, III, 74–78; for the retaliation of the Wends see *ibid.*, p. 91.

[2] "Hic montem unum juxta Albim positum et arborum densitate tunc occupatum excoluit, ibi et urbem faciens, de rivo quodam, qui in septentrionali parte ejusdem fluit, nomen eidem Misni imposuit; quam ut hodie in usu habetur, presidiis et imposicionibus caeteris munit" (Thietmar, *Chron.*, I, 9).

[3] All the chroniclers notice this battle (Wid., I, 36; Thietmar, I, 10; *Annal. Corb* [929]; *Chron. Breve Brem.*, *MGH*, SS. VII, 391).

[4] *Annal. Hildesh.*, *Annal. Weissenb.* (932); Thietmar, I, 16. For nearly a century, until repeopled by Henry II in 1012, it was desolate (*ibid.*, VI, 59). The territory between the Mulde and the Saale was called Osterland.

[5] Lippert, I, 170.

Slavonic Tribes along Eastern Frontier in Tenth and Eleventh Centuries

Barred marking in Wagria = Half Germanized

er seems to have had a slight appreciation. He was content merely with the payment of tribute.[1] He had no constructive ideas to apply to the conquered territory for its pacification and civilization, such as Charlemagne had applied in Saxony. There was no thought of a March of Meissen under him, although nearly the whole line of the Elbe was under Saxon control.[2] He established no systematic defensive organization along the eastern frontier. He made no effort to promote colonization or Christianity in the region.[3] Henry I seems to have valued the Slavonic tribute chiefly as a means of defraying the cost of his military reforms in Saxony[4] and the warfare on the border principally as a training school for his soldiery against the Hungarians. He did not even attempt to extend the Burgward system, which he had so successfully instituted in Saxony and Thuringia, beyond the Elbe and the Saale rivers. Brandenburg and Meissen were isolated frontier posts with no chain of forts to sustain them. No effort was made to colonize the country. The land lay undeveloped, peopled by a cowed but sullen and hostile population. The real Germanization of Meissen begins with Wiprecht von Groitsch.[5]

Yet for his failure to promote German settlement in these regions Henry I is hardly to be blamed. The Saxons were still dwelling in an almost primitive culture. Their social structure was simple and without the firmer distinctions of privilege and property which were attached to the more complex feudal society of France and the Rhinelands as well as Swabia and Bavaria. Saxony was a whole century and more behind them in social and economic development. Land was still cheap and abundant. Saxon feudalism was still simple and elementary in its form. The Saxon people had yet to experience the stress of social transformations and the thrust of economic pressure, such as prevailed farther west. That change came to Saxony in the late eleventh and twelfth cen-

[1] Wid., II, 20 and 30; Waitz, *Heinrich I*, p. 95; Hauck, III, 77.

[2] Richter, *Annalen*, II, 14*b;* Gebhardt, *Handbuch*, Vol. I, p. 249.

[3] Guttmann, *Forschungen zur Brand. u. Preuss. Geschichte*, IX, 417–18.

[4] Wid., II, 30; Wendt, I, 21.

[5] Tetzner, *op. cit.*, p. 293.

turies, but in the tenth century there was neither a surplus population nor social and economic discontent in Saxony sufficient to induce the Saxon peasantry to migrate to the "New East" which was just being opened up by the sword.[1]

Henry I had contented himself with reducing the Sorben to tribute. Established political forms in the Thuringian March began with Otto I who divided the country into *pagi* which roughly followed the older Slav lines.[2] These distinctions, however, seem to have been chiefly for topographical convenience. Effective German occupation was insured by division of the territory into military *cadres*, each district having a military base (Burgward),[3] which seems usually to have been a former Slavonic village fortified and garrisoned by the conquerors. In the course of natural evolution, in time these became units in the civil and ecclesiastical administration of the country. But in the Saxon epoch the administration was a purely military one.

This practice on Otto's part was actually the extension to the Sorben land of the military measures which Henry I had instituted in southeastern Saxony and Thuringia.

It was his father's tested-and-tried military system which Otto I and his successors extended over the new Sorben *Reichsland*. Like a huge net a meshwork of Burgwärde was spread over the country.[4] A map of the region exhibits that "exceedingly neat and artificial scheme of political geography" presented by the English Midlands at the same time.[5] It is not possible to locate every Burgward that is mentioned in the documents; but enough can be identified to show the thoroughgoing nature of Otto I's practice. The

[1] See the remarks of Schulze, *Die Kolonisierung und Germanisierung der Gebiete zwischen Saale und Elbe* (Leipzig, 1896), pp. 78–80; Wendt, I, 43, n. 3.

[2] Guttmann, p. 417, n. 6.

[3] These Burgwärde were all built of timber, as were the churches too. Thietmar, II, 36, mentions with astonishment that Zeitz in 970 had a stone church.

[4] "Das ganze Land muss mit einem Netz von Burgen bedeckt gewesen sein" (Gerdes, *Gesch. d. deutschen Volkes*, I, 431). It is interesting to observe that in 1830 a French writer substantially recommended this same practice to the French government for the conquest of Algeria (*La féodalité comme moyen de conserver et de civiliser l'Algérie* [Paris, 1840]), published anonymously.

[5] Maitland, *Domesday Studies*, p. 187.

Principal German Burgwarde

Notice their density in the Sorben Land

Burgward system was based upon the rivers of the region, namely, the Saale, the Weisse Elster, the Mulde, and the Elbe, all of which flow north and roughly parallel. On the Saale lay Nienburg, Bernburg, Wettin, Giebichenstein, and Merseburg; on the Elster were Schkeuditz, Leipzig, Taucha, Zwenkau, Groitzsch, Döbilzschen, Teilzig, Zeitz; on the Mulde and its affluents, the Zwickauer Mulde and the Freiberger Mulde, lay Düben, Eilenburg, Püchau, Wurzen, Döben, Rochlitz, Kohren, Allenburg, Colditz, Leisnig, Döbeln, Lobnitz, Nerschav; on the Elbe, Wörlitz near Dessau, Torgau, Mühlburg, Belgern, Strehlen, Boritz, Zehren, Zadel, Meissen, Pesterwitz, Briesnitz; Dohna commanded the Nollendorf Pass over the Erzgebirge into Bohemia. The four rivers formed a quadruple line of occupation and defense. In order to connect them, transverse lines of Burgwärde were established so that the country was not unlike a vast gridiron. For example, between the upper Saale and the Elster were Hohen and Mölsen; between the Elster and the Mulde lay Altenburg; between the Mulde and the Elbe were Oschats, Jana, Lommatzsch, and Mügeln.[1]

[1] The paragraph above describes the system in result rather than in process. Many of the Burgwärde were founded in the time of Otto II, Otto III, and Henry II —or at least not mentioned in sources of Otto I's reign. For example, Merseburg and Meissen were founded by Henry I. Kühnau and Steene, near Dessau, appear in 945; Osmünde, Trotha, and Groitzsch appear in 952; Giebichenstein, Wettin, Löbejün, Rothenburg, and Bernburg in 961; Rosenburg and Grimschleben in 965; Brachstedt, Oppin, and Gutenberg in 966; Pratau, Torgau, Belgern, and Rädewell in 973; Nerschau and Zwenkau in 974; Norits in 979; Schkeuditz (though it probably was older), Tauscha, Wurzen, Püchau, Eilenburg, Düben, Lobnitz, and Geserzisca in 981; Mügeln in 983; Treben, Kreuschberg, and Schkölen in 993; Seusslitz in 997; Strehlen in 1003; Rochlitz in 1009; Leisnig in 1040; Colditz and Zschaetz in 1046, etc. Leipzig is mentioned as a Burgward first in 1050, but it must have been such before.

Interspersed between the Burgwärde were also many *castella* or *oppida*, especially in the north and middle. Thietmar mentions sixteen of these, and others are referred to in the *diplomata*. They may be described as finer meshes of the network which covered the country. These castles seem to have been intrusted to single captains having a mere handful of men, perhaps not over a dozen. Generally a few Wendish villages were attached to them. Smaller still than these and of less number, pointing to the fact, perhaps, that the manorial régime in Saxon times was yet young in the land, we find mention of *curtes* and *villae*—communities consisting of but one hamlet. Thietmar mentions seven of the former and eleven of the latter. The distinction between them is to be observed. The *curtis* was a fortified manor-house (*villa munita*). The *villa* an open, unfortified village (*vicus*). The relatively slight number of these communities, when compared with the large number of Burg-

Within this conquered triangular area, where peace was maintained by the sword, scattered between the lines of the Burgwärde and castles lay the hamlets of the Sorben people. In the vicinity of Zwenkau in the time of Otto I a Wendish chieftain of some eminence is found. To this day the well-watered and fertile country west of Dresden is predominantly occupied by a Wendish peasantry. Judging from the numerous localities of Slavonic name which Thietmar mentions, and the many Wendish place-names which still survive, the Sorben population must have been fairly dense for the time.

A paragraph from Schulze describes the actual state of the Sorben land at the end of Saxon times:

> [There was] an unfree, half-pagan Sorb population mixed with a few German serfs, ruled over by a great number of German lords and military *ministeriales*, who occupied the Burgorte and Burgsitze throughout the land, and lived upon the products of the acres which these (and the landless house-servants) cultivated for them, or from which they made various payments in kind. There was no Germanization, no penetration or permeation of the land with German customs and German life. It was a condition of affairs analogous to that in the Russian Baltic provinces, where a German sphere of domination grew up as a result of the settlement of German knightly families. The Germanization was neglected because the occupants failed to attract German peasants. The towns do not come into consideration because they were essentially but slightly connected with the land and found their centre of gravity and the focus of their interest in their relations with the west.[1]

The few Saxon settlers who came brought with them into the newly conquered country their own method of measuring

---

wärde and castles, shows how much of a conquered country the region was thought to be. For further details see Waitz, VIII, 192 f.; von Essenwein, *Kriegsbaukunst*, p. 6; Delbrück, *Kriegskunst*, III, 70 f.; Lipp, *Das Fränk. Grenzsystem;* Hellwig, *Städtewesen zur Zeit der Ottonen;* Köhler, *Kriegswesen*, III, 1, 343 f.; Schulze, *Kolonisierung*, pp. 63–69; Kaemmel, *Sächische Geschichte*, pp. 22–25; Wendt, I, 32–43; Gerdes, I, 459–61. In the Salian period the word Burgward became obsolete, the usual term being *castellum* (Waitz, VIII, 210). It is noteworthy that only in the cases of Meissen and Merseburg had the population grown to such proportion that the walls could not include it all, and a part of it was clustered outside *in suburbio* (Thietmar, VI, 55; VIII [VII], 23 [15]; Widukind, II, 3). With the development of town life and trade in the thirteenth century the Pfahlburg (=*faubourg*) became a characteristic of almost every German city. For a description of that around Worms see *Ann. Wormat.* Fontes, II, 190.

[1] Schulze, *Kolonisierung*, p. 120; cf. Hauck, III, 97; Hanstein, *Siedelung des sächs. Vogtlandes* (1904).

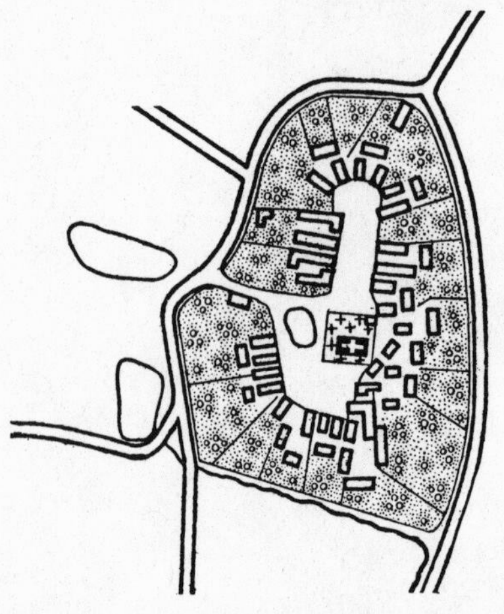

Ground-Plan of a Slavonic Runddorf or Round Village

the land and their own land unit.[1] The rudely cultivated fields of the Wends were too irregular and probably too scattered to admit of any other form of survey.[2] Consequently, the incoming Germans do not seem to have made any effort to preserve either the native method of survey or even native lines of division, but to have "dealt out" the conquered lands after the manner with which they were familiar. Such surveying was probably simple when confined as it was to the tilled acres of the Wends. Owing to their primitive rural economy,[3] the farms of the Wendish folk must have usually been of small extent, so that a considerable number of native villages with fields, pasture, and woods must often have been included in a single grant. The larger domains of the church must frequently have embraced within their complex hundreds of the small farms of the Wendish people. In these early days there was tillable land enough without the necessity of breaking new ground in forest and marsh as developed later. Resort was not made to this pioneer practice until the twelfth century when there was an enormous influx of immigrants into the trans-Elbean lands.

In the submissive Sorben land the courts of the margrave, the clergy, and the nobility were naturally German, although there are traces of a Wendish upper class, even a few of knightly rank.[4]

[1] The Germans, like the Norse, measured land by means of a rope (*funiculum*). Helmold, I, 83 (pp. 162–63), and II, 14 (p. 218), describes the method. For the same practice in Normandy see Freeman, *William Rufus*, I, 68 n.; II, 562–64. For France see Suger, *Vita Ludovici* (ed. Molinier), p. 48; *Cart. de l'abbaye de St. Bertin*, III, 344.

[2] Meitzen, *Ausbreitung der Deutschen*, p. 39; Inama Sternegg, I, 443.

[3] Oxen were scarce and horses even rarer among the Wends. Two oxen or one horse was reckoned to the "plowland," which implies that the Wendish farms were very small (Helmold, I, 12, 14, 89). Two hundred years later, in the twelfth century, the same condition of agriculture still prevailed (Helmold, I, 88; Heinrici, *Chron. Lyvoniae*, II, 7). The German plow was like that of the Romans. In the Slavonic plow the angle of beam and point was more acute. It had no share and no knife-edge. See on this subject Rau, *Gesch. des Pfluges* (Heidelberg, 1845); Anton, *Gesch. der deutschen Landwirtschaft*, I, 51, 96, 379; II, 256; Langethal, *op. cit.*, I, 551 f.; II, 344 f.; von der Goltz, *op. cit.*, pp. 29, 128 f.; Dopsch, *Wirtschaftsentwicklung der Karolingerzeit*, II, 136.

[4] Thietmar, II, 24: "Cuchovic senior Slavorum"; Lepsius, *Naumburg*, I, 203: "quidquid per beneficium Sememizl tenuit" (1040); *Codex diplom.*, A, I, 79–142:

The great mass of the population in the Sorben March was an unfree Wendish peasantry. For many years Meissen was the sole important German town.[1] Leipzig is first mentioned by Thietmar of Merseburg in 1015, but of trace of trade yet there is no evidence.[2] In 1104 the colony of Franken settled by Margrave Conrad of Wettin (1123–57) in his forest by Lausigk appears.[3]

The jealous eye with which Otto the Great regarded the Sorben land, the value of which both as a buffer and as a connecting link between Saxony and Bavaria he fully appreciated, is in sharp contrast to the relative indifference he displayed toward Brandenburg and Nordalbingia. In the north, Hermann Billung was made both duke and margrave.[4] But Gero, despite his long and loyal service in the Thuringian March, was always kept in a distinctly official capacity. No feudal dignity or rank was attached to his position. He was not even made a margrave,[5] although his deeds and daring found him a place as "marcgrâve Gêre" in that hall of fame—the *Nibelungenlied*. "Great was he and so was called," says Thietmar in eulogy of him.[6] Yet to the end of his days Gero's

"Liber homo Bor, natione Slavus," (1071); "Szwizla fidelis" (1031); "Moic miles" (1042); "Jarmir miles" (1045). See Winter, *Cistercienser*, I, 35–37; Wendt, II, 5 n. Meitzen, *Jahrb. f. Nationaloek. und Statistik*, XXXII, 879, gives special attention to the partition of the Wendish lands. He argues that the race mixture necessarily compelled a supreme military organization. For the church in the Sorben land see H. H. Grössler, "Die Begründung der christlichen Kirche in dem Lande zwischen Saale und Elbe," *Ztschft. d. Ver. f. Kirchengesch. in d. Prov. Sachsen*, Band IV (Eisleben, 1907).

[1] Lippert, *Geschichte Böhmens*, I, 11, 69, 70, 79, has collected the few data in regard to trade at Meissen.

[2] *Chronicon*, VIII, 25, 66; IX, 7.

[3] *Annales Pegav.*, SS. XVI, 247; cf. Posse, *Die Markgrafen von Meissen*, p. 297. For the growth of the church in the Sorben March at the end of the eleventh and in the early twelfth century see Hauck, IV, 555–63.

[4] Widukind, II, 4; Adam of Bremen, II, 7.

[5] Gero's title *marchio* was not an official one, and was not current during his lifetime. It grew up when legend began to gather around him, as it did early. "Gero . . . . olim licet multis gestis insigniis clarus haberetur" (Widukind, III, 54). Widukind only styles him *comes* or *praeses* (see Guttmann, p. 415, n. 2).

[6] III, 54 and 75; VI, 57. For a modern appreciation see Heinemann, *Markgraf Gero*, p. 117.

office was an inferior one, either because Otto I was determined to hold the newly conquered territory as a *Reichsland* and was jealous of even a delegation of authority,[1] or because he hesitated to promote to one of the highest of feudal dignities a man of low birth, whatever his capacities, whom the Saxon nobles hated.[2]

If now we turn to the territory bounded by the Baltic, the Oder, the marshes of the Havel and the lower Elbe—to Brandenburg and Nordalbingia, in a word—we find that here the border problem and its solution were very different. There was here no compact Slavonic mass like the Sorben, but detached and often mutually hostile Slav tribes, Abodrites, Wilzi (or Ljutizi), Redarians, Polabians, Hevellians, etc., whose division naturally weakened their power of resistance to German pressure.[3] In 936 Otto I erected this whole region from the Trave to the Peene rivers into a March and put it in the care of Hermann Billung,[4] who was given far larger liberty than Gero in the Sorben March. Otto's lack of vision was destined to throw future control of German colonization toward the northeast out of the hands of the German kings, who in their national office should have been the directors of it, and into the hands of the feudal princes.[5]

The loose and lavish nature of this grant is in sharp contrast with Otto's jealous retention of the Thuringian March

[1] "Der König als Eroberer betrachtete sich als Eigenthümer alles Bodens" (Guttmann, p. 416).

[2] Their hatred of Gero is creditable to Gero's sense of rectitude: "Cum milites ad manum Geronis presidis conscripti crebra expeditione attenuarentur et donativis vel tributariis premiis minus adjuvari possent, eo quod tributa passim negarentur, seditioso odio in Geronem exacuuntur" (Widukind, II, 30; cf. Schulze, p. 54; Nitzsch, I, 333, 342).

[3] Cf. Sommerfeld, *Geschichte d. Germanisierung des Herzogtums Pommern*, in Schmoller's *Forschungen*, XIII, No. 5 (1896), 7.

[4] *Annales Corb.* (934); Widukind, I, 40; Thietmar, I, 9; Adam of Bremen, I, 57, 59; Waitz, *Jahrbuch*, pp. 277 ff., Excursus 24. The account of the origin of the Billunger in Adam of Bremen, II, 9, is saga; cf. ed. Schmeider, p. 67, n. 2; Dümmler, *Otto I*, pp. 570–76.

[5] See the observations of Lamprecht, IV, 13–14, on the bearing of this course upon the future history of Germany and cf. Fisher, *Medieval Empire*, I, 263, 314–15. More foresighted than the crown the church made use of the tithe in the colonial lands from the very beginning (Lamprecht, *Deutsche Geschichte*, III, 116).

in his own hands. The original trans-Elbean policy of Otto I seems to have been to adhere to the Carolingian tradition of exacting tribute of the border tribes, partly as a guaranty of keeping the peace, partly as a means to defray the cost of policing the border. He never seems to have contemplated carving another crown land out in Nordalbingia, as he did between the Saale and the upper Elbe. Hermann Billung was far more independent than Gero.[1]

Hermann Billung, in his new and powerful capacity as "lord of the north," immediately set to work to make his office profitable to himself and his house. Avarice was a notorious Billunger attribute from generation unto generation.[2] The Saxons were proverbially land greedy.[3] The Slavonic tribute, by diligent manipulation, soon was made a lucrative source of revenue by the Billunger.

Unfortunately, we know nothing in detail of the degree of German colonization instituted at this time by Hermann Billung and the Saxon church across the lower Elbe. Judging from Helmold's observations made regarding it two hundred years later, there must have been a considerable pioneer movement into the Wendish lands. But the occupation was doomed to be of short duration. A generation of clerical and feudal tyranny was certain to bear bitter fruit.

Modern history both in Spanish America and in North America offers a melancholy example of the contact of a "higher" with a "lower" race.[4] The history of the long and harsh relations of the Germans with the Baltic Slavs in the

[1] "Interim Hirimannus dux Saxoniam *regebat*" (Thietmar, II, 28). Weiland, *Entwicklung des Sächsischen Herzogtums*, p. 1, has shown that officially the future Billunger duchy was not the old tribal duchy of Saxony, but a command of the Marches; cf. Sommerfeld, *op. cit.*, p. 10, n. 8. Otto I really kept Westphalia as crown land and gave the country between the Weser and the Elbe to Hermann. The test of ducal independence was exemption from the royal fisc. "So lange ein Land noch an den königlichen Fiscus steuert, ist es kein Herzogthum" (Giesebrecht, *Wendische Geschichten*, I, 186). Ekkehard, *Casus S. Galli*, IV, 83, is specific in this particular: "Nondum adhuc illo tempore Suevia in ducatum erat redacta, sed fisco regio peculiariter parebat sicut hodie et Francia."

[2] Adam of Bremen, II, 46; III, 22; Helmold, I, 16, 21.

[3] "Saxonibus vero pro gloria et pro terra adquirenda certantibus," says Widukind (I, 9).

[4] Cf. Bourne, *Spain in America*, p. 256.

Middle Ages is a medieval and relatively unfamiliar example of a "phenomenon of familiar occurrence in later history of the contact of nature peoples with a ruling race."[1] Considering the fact that the Baltic Slavs had no inheritance of civilization from Rome and the church to help them along as the Germans of the fifth century had possessed, their culture was quite as high as that of the early Germans and promised as much. The utter destruction of their material and moral culture between the tenth and the thirteenth centuries is a fact which every student of the history of civilization must deplore. Henry I, when he captured Jana, put the village to pillage and massacred the adult inhabitants.[2] After the battle of Lenzen all prisoners were put to the edge of the sword.[3] Otto I was no more humane. The victory of Racknitz was followed by a butchery which lasted until nightfall; several hundred prisoners were massacred before the eyes of the conquered Slav chief. Gero, the famous margrave, treacherously slew thirty Wendish chieftains whom he had lured to a banquet under pretense of peace.[4] Henry the Lion and the Teutonic Knights in the twelfth and thirteenth centuries were no whit less cruel.[5]

The reigns of Henry I and Otto the Great (936–73) constitute the heroic period of German eastward expansion. But only in the Thuringian March—the triangle between the Saale, the upper Elbe, and the Erzgebirge—was the result

[1] E. G. Bourne, *Spain in America*, p. 211, and n. 2. Widukind, II, 20, is interesting as the reaction of a tenth-century German's *Kultur* toward the culture of the Wends.

[2] Widukind, I, 35.

[3] *Ibid.*, 36.

[4] *Ibid.*, II, 20; III, 55. But Tetzner, p. 292, thinks this mere legend. Thietmar of Merseburg, IX, 2, approves of these cruelties. The events here alluded to completely conquered the Sorben, who henceforward were passive. Their further history does not enter into this chapter.

[5] See Hauck, III, 88–89. For German contempt of the Slav see Fredeg., *Chron.*, IV, 68; *Ann. Fuld.* (871); *Monk of St. Gall.*, II, 12; Thietmar, III, 17; VIII (VII), 59 (44); Adam of Bremen, II, 45 (schol.); Helmold, I, 16.

The comment of Cosmas of Prague (*ca.* 1045–1125), the first Slavonic historian of the western Slavs, is interesting in this particular: "Perpendit enim innatam Teutonicis superbiam, et quod semper tumido fastu habeant despectui Sclavos et eorum linguam" (*Chron.*, I, 40; *MGH*, SS. IX, 62; cf. *ibid.*, X, 84). For centuries *Wend* and "heathen" were synonymous terms to the Germans (Widukind, III, 68; *Annal. Hildesh.* [*anno* 1056]; *Dipl.* [*anno* 945], I, 146, No. 65; cf. Hauck, III, 84).

permanent. The death of Gero in 965 may be said to mark the term of this first period. Not until 1125 was the eastward movement of the German people resumed, when the great constructive work of Adolph of Holstein, Henry the Lion, and Albrecht the Bear began.

The Wends were not pliant subjects, and their tribal organization, their religion, their language, energetically resisted the assault of German militarism and ecclesiasticism. In 955 the Wends, presumably taking advantage of the great Magyar invasion of that summer, raided the Thuringian March so terribly that all Saxony trembled. Widukind,[1] who tells the story, interrupts the history of the Hungarian invasion to relate it, and reports a speech of Otto I which manifests the grave anxiety of the King.

In 983 the whirlwind came. The recoil of Otto II's crushing defeat in Calabria[2] was felt along the whole course of the middle Elbe, where a formidable Slavonic uprising and pagan reaction took place. Havelburg, Brandenburg, and Zeitz were desolated; Hamburg was plundered. The three margraves of the Nordmark, Meissen, and Lausitz, with contingents of troops furnished by the bishops of Halberstadt and Magdeburg, defeated the revolted Slav tribes at Belkesheim (near Stendhal), but the victory was without permanent effect.[3] Fortunately for Germany in this time of national reverse and peril the iron administrative system established by Otto I in the Sorben land held good, else the whole eastern border of Saxony would have been driven in. But Germany's trans-Elbean power, save in Nordalbingia and Holstein, went down like a house of cards.[4] Not until the twelfth century was the river crossed again. For more than a century and a half

[1] III, 45–47.

[2] Bruno, *Vita S. Adalb.*, chap. x (*MGH*, SS. IV, 598); Hauck, III, 251; Usinger, *Jahrb. Heinrichs II*, I, 478–86. For other sources and literature see Richter, *Annalen*, II, 135–38.

[3] Thietmar, III, 10–19; Bruno, *loc. cit.; Ann. Sangall. maj.*, 983; Giesebrecht, *Kaiserzeit*, I, 604 ff., 850, and his *Otto II*, pp. 91 ff.; L. Giesebrecht, *Wend. Gesch.*, I, 264 ff.

[4] "Die deutsche Herrschaft nach halbhundert jähriger Dauer einfach wegzublasen war" (Guttmann, *op. cit.*, p. 418).

the bishops east of the great river were in exile and only titular holders of sees which were *in partibus paganorum*.

The desolation was complete.[1] In the twelfth century, when Lower Germany, under the great leadership of Adolph of Holstein, Henry the Lion, and Albrecht the Bear, had recovered the "lost provinces," Helmold of Holstein, whose intelligent observation entitles him to no mean honor as an archaeologist, found a melancholy charm in surveying the ruins and churches and monasteries in Schleswig and Wagria and in "the land which is called Balsemerlande and Marscinerlande, where the Saxons are said once to have dwelt"[2]—crumbled memorials of German power there in the days of the Ottos. He says:

> There still remain many evidences of that former occupation, especially in the forest which extends from the city of Lütjenburg through the mighty [*longissimas*] tracts of Schleswig, in whose vast and almost impenetrable solitudes yet may be descried the furrows which once marked out the plowlands. Even the lines of former towns and villages may be traced in the ruins. Along the streams in many places mounds of earth and silt, formed by the tributary waters, yet testify that every such site was once inhabited by Saxons—when Saxon valor was formidable.

Helmold sighs over the spacious and fertile soil once radiant with the harvest, but now gone over to bramble and brier and scarce inhabited. It is the same even on the left bank of the Elbe between the great bend and the upper Aller (today the territory around Halberstadt, Stendhal, and Salzwedel), "where still may be seen the ruins of old levees which were constructed in the lowlands along the banks of the Elbe. When the Slavs overran the country the Saxons were cut off, and the land was possessed by them down to our own time."[3]

[1] When Henry II in 1017 crossed the Elbe in an expedition against Boleslav he came to a *curtis* of the Bishop of Magdeburg named Leitzkau, ruined and inhabited by wild animals. "Albim ad Liesca, curtem quondam Vigonis episcopi et tunc feris innumerabilibus inhabitatam venit" (Thietmar, VIII, 57).

[2] Helmold, I, 12 and 89.

[3] Balsamerland (Beleseim, Belesem, Belshem, Belsheim, Balsamia terra) answers to the later Altmark. The name was derived from the Slavic *Bielazemia*, or "White Land." It was a prolongation of the marshes on the eastern side of the Elbe (Schafarik, *op. cit.*, pp. 593–94). The difference in the way in which Helmold writes of the former occupations of the Saxons in Schleswig and Wagria, on the one

For years the conflict between the Germans and the Wends of the middle and lower Elbe was a series of border forays and grim reprisals.[1] Magdeburg stood like a rock in a flood, a single point of German Christendom in a welter of barbarism and paganism; half the ecclesiastical province, as it was, was lost.[2] There was danger lest even the heart of Saxony be pierced, so that Bishop Bernwald of Hildesheim built a Burgward at the confluence of the Ocker and the Aller.[3] The weakest feature of the weak reign of Otto III

hand, and of the marsh land of Balsemerlande and Marscinerlande, on the other, is to be noted. In the first case he speaks from personal observation; in the latter he is apparently writing from hearsay ("feruntur . . . . ut videri potest" [I, 89]). It is not always possible to distinguish between the direct and the indirect sources of Helmold's information. For example, in I, 18, where he relates the circumstances of the death of Benno of Hildesheim, he almost paraphrases the Bishop's epitaph in part of the account, which makes Lüntzel (*Gesch. der Diöcese u. Stadt Hildesheim*, I, 181, n. 3) and the latest editor of Helmold's *Chronica* (Schmeidler's ed., 1909), p. 39, nn. 1 and 3, believe that Helmold actually had visited Hildesheim. The history of dikes and dike-building in medieval Germany is a very interesting one. "Forces tending toward associational organization found here a fruitful field of action. The dikes along the sea-coast and in the lowlands of the greater rivers were originally constructed by voluntary colonizing associations [*Siedelungsgenossenschaften*] as a preliminary to the original settlement of marshy districts, and later by communes after the settlement of the diked land thus created, for the better security of their economic interests. From the end of the Carolingian period onward, particularly in the 1100's and 1200's, there appeared, in addition to the old communal dikes built by associations, others constructed by ecclesiastical and secular lords, churches, cloisters, and cities, usually in connection with great colonizing enterprises, and upon the basis of land grants given for enclosure. But dikes continued to be erected by individual 'dike lords,' or by free peasant communes, or by 'dike unions,' that had nothing to do with such colonial settlements" (Huebner, *History of Germanic Private Law*, p. 288, sec. 40). For literature on this subject see Anschütz, "Deichwesen," *HWB der Staatsw.* (3d ed., 1909), III, 462–81; Stengel-Fleischmann, *Wörterbuch* (2d ed., 1911), Band I, "Deichwesen"; Detlefsen, *Holsteiniche Elbmarschen*, I, 57, 89; Gierke, *Die Geschichte des deutschen Deichrechts* (cf. *Hist. Vierteljahrschrift*, Band XIV, Heft 2 [1903]); Eckermann, *Ztschft. d. Gesellschaft f. Schleswig-Holstein-Lauenb. Gesch.*, Band XXI (1891); Band XXIII (1893); Band XXV (1896); Hansen, *ibid.*, Band XXIV (1894). Koegel, "Beowulf," *Ztschft. f. deutsches Altertum*, Band, XXVII, Heft 3 (1893), thinks that Beowulf was the personification of agriculture, and the killing of Grendel, the sea monster, symbolically represents the construction of dikes along the North Sea Coast in order to protect the fields from inroads by the ocean.

[1] *Ann. Hildesh. Annal. Qued.* (985–87); Thietmar, IV, 7–10; *Ann. Hildesh.* (990).

[2] For the "appeal" of the bishops of the province of Magdeburg against the Wends see Tangl, *Neues Archiv*, Band XXX, Heft 1.

[3] *Vita Bernwardi*, chap. vii (*MGH*, SS. IV, 779). It was called Mundburg. *Origines Guelf.*, IV, 435. Bernward of Hildesheim was also compelled to erect two

was the defense of the eastern frontier. In 992 Brandenburg was won and lost again. By 994 all the Slav tribes of the middle and lower Elbe except the Sorben had thrown off the German yoke. In the year 1000 a part of Nordalbingia for the first time was devastated with fire and sword. A few years later, in 1018, the whole region was again overrun by the infuriated Ljutizi and Wagri. The churches were destroyed, the clergy slaughtered. Even Hamburg was stricken, for many of the priests and people there were carried off into captivity. Sixty priests of Oldenburg, with the sign of the cross derisively cut in bleeding characters upon their tonsured heads, with hands bound behind their backs, were dragged and beaten through the towns of the Slavs until they perished from exhaustion.[1]

For 142 years—from the great Wendish rebellion in 983 to the accession of Lothar II in 1125—the eastward expansion of the German people across the Elbe was stopped by the Slavs. After two hundred years of effort the Franconian period ended with pitiably insignificant results, so far as east German colonization was concerned. In 1125 the linguistic frontier was still where it had been in the reign of Charlemagne.[2] Yet within the term of the next generation,

---

Burgwärde in 995 against pirates of the coast who penetrated inland (*Vita*, *loc. cit.*; cf. Adam of Bremen, II, 33 and 69; III, 3). Bremen and Hamburg were walled by Archbishop Unwin (1013–29). Rietschel, *Markt und Stadt* (Leipzig, 1897), p. 82, contends that Adam's words, ". . . . ipsa Brema vallo muniri cepit fortissimo," do not mean the *Stadt*, but the cathedral. At any rate, Bremen seems to have had immunity from pirates henceforth (Thietmar, VII, 28 [VI, 53]). For Hamburg see Adam of Bremen, II, 60.

[1] Cf. Hirsch, *Jahrb.*, III, 93 ff.; Adam of Bremen, II, 40–46. Adam honestly recognizes the just grievances of the Wends and condemns the avaricious policy of both the Saxon dukes and the Saxon clergy as being responsible for this rebellion: "plures etiam propter odium Christianitatis. . . . . Bernardus enim dux, ... per avaritiam gentem Winulorum crudeliter opprimens, ad necessitatem paganismi coegit." He quotes Rom. 9:18; Ps. 7:12; Acts 13:19, not with the whining piety of so many medieval chroniclers, but with some of that lofty ethical sense and resignation which Lincoln manifests in his "Second Inaugural."

[2] Wendt, II, 5–7; cf. Lavisse, *La marche de Brandebourg*, p. 36. Hauck, IV, 555: "Man hat bemerkt, dass die wenigen Kirchen, die es gab, fast alle in Burgorten lagen. . . . . In den Burgorten sassen die deutschen Herren mit ihren Mannen und ihrem Gesinde. Ihnen dienten diese Kirchen. Sie waren weniger Missionposten als Gotteshäuser für eine kleine christliche Diaspora in einem heidnischen Lande"

in the middle of the twelfth century, the entire fabric of Slavonic tribal independence collapsed. Mecklenburg, Brandenburg, and Pomerania were conquered and settled by the German people; the native population was converted and reduced under German domination. The speed and effectiveness of this rapid change is to be ascribed partly to the breakdown of the capacity of resistance among the Wends; more, perhaps, to the accumulated pressure of things in Germany which bore down all barriers of opposition.

The economic and social transformation of Germany, especially Saxon or Lower Germany, during the Franconian epoch was enormous, and it is in these changes that the causes of the German people's eastward expansion in the twelfth century are to be found. The evidences of this important revolution are manifold. They are to be seen in the manifestations of peasant unrest, which can be discerned as early as the tenth century; in the slow depression of the Saxon freeman to the status of a serf; in the extension of manorial rights over mills, bake ovens, wine presses, breweries, and other activities of the economy of the German village; in the increase of "split" holdings, a tendency observable in France as far back as the reign of Charles the Bald, who forbade the practice in the Edict of Pîtres in 864;[1] in the transition from a freehold to a rent system; in the break-up of the ancient mark community and the dissolution of the *Allmend;* in the evolution of the *ministerialis* class; in the extension of the

---

(cf. Schulze, pp. 294, 316). Yet he cites instances of a few churches outside of the Burgorten (p. 141).

[1] B. Guérard, *Polypt. d'Irminon*, I, 494. Not only the fields but also the taxes in produce in course of time became divided into two, three, four, and even more portions, giving rise to social distinctions in the codes like *Halbbauern*, *Halbspaenner*, *Halbhufner*, etc. As early as 808 we find village plowlands divided into three parts (there is a case of six parts in 797); and no less than sixteen parts occur in 1141. The *Polyptique d'Irminon* (about 820) gives an instance of twelve peasants who shared one carucate between them, another of sixteen households having six carucates, a third of one hundred and eighty-one owning eighty-one carucates, etc. The tendency toward "split" holdings became so common that the charters make particular mention of the occurrence of undivided plowlands (*hoba integra*) (Roscher, *Ackerbau*, sec. 71). Lamprecht, *DWL*, I, 2, 705, cites 50 *Morgen* in the ninth century lying in three places: 25 in one place, 13 in another, 6 in the third, and 6 in the fourth; 17 *Hufen* scattered in two counties; 4 *Hufen* divided in thirteen different localities.

tithe from grain and wine (*der grosse Zehnt*) to include small produce like vegetables, fowls, eggs, honey, etc. (*der kleine Zehnt*); in the engrossing of the land by the nobles and the clergy, even the forests, so that lay and ecclesiastical estates ranging from eight thousand to sixty thousand *Morgen* were not uncommon; in the agricultural revolution, largely due to the superior methods of the French Cistercians who introduced new and more scientific practices of farming; in the rise of land values, which Lamprecht estimates to have been as much as 40 per cent in older provinces like Swabia, Franconia, and the Rhinelands between the tenth and the thirteenth century; in the extension of private ownership to the forests, hitherto ever the poor man's home (the Frankenwald was appropriated in Saxon times, the Harz by the middle of the twelfth century); in the changes in social texture from a simple to a complex composition; in the movements of the lower population into new localities, frequently forest and marsh, where in "clearings" or patches of soil laboriously drained the peasantry tried still to preserve their freer form of living; in the development of commerce and industry; in the rise of the towns, a social phenomenon which strikingly characterizes the reign of Henry IV.[1] The great rebellion of Saxony during the war of investiture which Henry IV so drastically suppressed left in its train large numbers of impoverished and broken freemen, who sought to begin life over again beyond the Elbe.[2]

Under these new and changed conditions it was natural that the "New East" beyond the Elbe beckoned to the Saxons of the twelfth century much as the "New West" beckoned to the American pioneer. In both cases the sparsely populated back lands tempted men from the more settled regions. The frontier of medieval Germany lay at "the hither

[1] This long paragraph merely makes "points." The reader is referred to Lamprecht, *DG*, III, Book 8, chaps. 1–2; *DWG*, I, 149, 163–64, 368–73, 603–22; 862–70, 1235–36; Schulze, *op. cit.*, pp. 122–27; Sybel, *Hist. Zeitschft.*, IX, 409; Inama Sternegg, III, 386 f., 407 f.; Nitzsch, II, 8 ff.; Below, "Zur Entstehung der deutschen Städte," *Hist. Zeitschft.*, LVIII, 193–244; Wendt, II, 7–8.

[2] *De unit. eccles. conserv.*, chap. xxviii; *Ann. Sax.* (*MGH*. SS. VI), p. 723; Ebbo, *Vita Ottonis, ep. Bab.*, I, 32; *Vita Bennonis*, chap. xix; cf. the remarks of Fisher, *op. cit.*, I, 137–38, 141.

edge of free land" as truly as did the American frontier. The increasing economic and soil pressure in the older parts of Saxony and elsewhere pushed the hardier and the braver spirits across the line. They "trekked" eastward to establish new homes for themselves in the wilderness, leaving the great manors of church and noble—in particular the former,[1] which had supplanted the Saxon free farmer—to be farmed more intensively by Flemish and Dutch settlers used to deep plowings in the heavy soils of the Low Countries, who were imported by Adolph of Holstein, Henry the Lion, and many of the bishops. "Hard times" and feudal oppression were powerful factors in the migration of peoples in the Middle Ages.[2] The Bavarian colonization of the Ostmark, the Frankish colonization of parts of Saxony and the Thüringer March, the settlement of Westphalian, Dutch, and Flemish colonists east of the Elbe, are examples.

The relation of these internal changes in Germany to the peopling of the border needs further investigation. The history of German eastward expansion has been studied more in the results than in the formative processes which produced the movement. A remarkable proclamation (probably of the

[1] Kötzschke, *Quellen*, p. 48; Pueschl, p. 8.

[2] A few references, from many which might be given, must suffice: "Hanc silvam incole propter diversas pauperum necessitates adgressi sunt cedere et facere novalia [*anno* 1101]" (*Mittelrhein. Urk.-B.*, I, 401).

". . . . Qui autem pauperiores erant, faciebant sibi novalia et villas in memoribus et forestis S. Bonifacii" (*Gesta Marcuardi abbat. Fuld.*, Boehmer, *Fontes*, III, 166; also in Dronke, *Trad. Fuld.*, p. 154). The date is between 1150 and 1165.

"Exactores—ad ultimam homines nostros pauperiem redegerunt et exire de patria et de hereditate sua mendicandi coegerunt causa [1102]" (Martène, *Coll.*, I, 595). "Dum quidam pauperum de familia ecclesie nostre [S. Pantaleon in Cologne] in curtes nostras Embe et Anhe pertinentes frequenti nos proclamatione merendo pulsarent, eo quod ad jus eorum, qui plenum debitum solvunt, compulsi tanta saepe violentia comprimerentur. ut nonnulli vacuas quas tenebant possessiunculas relinquentes patriis et sedibus migrare disponerent" (Lacomblet, *Urk.-B.* [*anno* 1141], I, 344): "Avaritia et rapina potentum pauperes et ruricolae opprimuntur et ad judicia injusta trahuntur. Haec lues peccati multos vendere patrimonia et ad peregrinas migrare terras compulit." This significant reference was first pointed out by Teutsch, *Zehntrecht*, p. 7; cf. Sybel, *Hist. Zeitschrift*, IX (1863), 409, and Schulze, *Kolonisierung*, p. 125, n. 4. It relates to the Sieburger region. The date is 1183. Cf. also I (1149), 367; *Mittelrhein. Urk.-B.*, II (1197), 171; Lacomblet (1099), p. 256; *Cod. Lauresh.*, I (1148), 153; Seibert, *Urk.-B.*, I (1166), 56, cited by Inama Sternegg, II, 19, n. 2; p. 24 n. In general see Curschmann, *Hungersnöte im Mittelalter* (Leipzig, 1900).

year 1108) cleverly calculated to promote settlement in the new land, and signed by the leading bishops and Fürsten of Saxony, clearly expresses the motives of the time:

> They [the Slavs] are an abominable people, but their land is very rich in flesh, honey, grain, birds, and abounding in all products of the fertility of the earth, when cultivated, so that none can be compared unto it. So they say who know. Wherefore, O Saxons, Franks, Lotharingians, men of Flanders most famous—here you can both save your souls, and if it please you, acquire the best of land to live in.[1]

Mixed with that negative ingredient to be found in every complex society, vaguely seeking a way out of its discontent by change, was a large element of the best blood and bone of the German race in this migration. A large proportion of the emigrants in the twelfth century were men of firm fiber actuated by a determination to better their condition, and ambitious to seize the opportunities offered in a new country. Many of these settlers came from Westphalia and eastern Franconia,[2] regions which had themselves been frontier districts in the tenth and eleventh centuries, what might be called the "Old East" in contrast with the "New East" just opening up.

The rival political ambitions of the Germans and the Danes for control of the Baltic strand in the first half of the twelfth century complicated the border question, and drew both the Count of Holstein and the Duke of Saxony into the vortex. The Danes hated the Saxon incomers,[3] and naturally

[1] This remarkable document is to be found in Kötzschke, *Quellen zur Gesch. der ostdeutschen Kolonisation im 12. bis 14. Jahrhundert* (Teubner: Leipzig, 1912), pp. 9–10. It may also be found in *Codex Diplom. Sax. Reg.*, II, i, No. 40; *Codex Diplom. Anhalt.*, I, No. 172; *Mecklenb. Urk.*, X, 457 ff.; *Neues Archiv.*, VII, 624; *Archiv für slavische Phil.*, VI, 216. For commentary see Hauck, *Kirchengesch. Deutschlands*, IV, 599, n. 4; Tangl, *Neues Archiv.*, XXX, 183; Meyer von Knonau, *Jahrb. d. deutschen Reiches unter Heinrich V*, VI, 79 ff.; Lubenecker, *Regesta Hist., Thur.*, I, No. 1048 (pp. 1039 ff.).

[2] F. Boll, "Mecklenburgs deutsche Kolonisation im 12. und 13. Jahrhundert," *Jahrb. f. Mecklenburg. Gesch.*, XIII (Schwerin, 1848), 57–112, with an Appendix by Lisch on the places whence these settlers came (pp. 112–15); H. Ernst, *Die Kolonisation Mecklenburgs im 12. und 13. Jahrhundert* (Schirrmacher's Beiträge), pp. 98–130; Ahlers, "Das bäuerliche Hufenwesen in Mecklenburg zur Zeit des Mittelalters," *Jahrb. f. Mecklenb. Gesch.*, LI (1886), 49–97; Michael, *Gesch. des deutschen Volkes*, I, 91–94.

[3] "Rex Danorum pluribus advenis Teutonicis terram suam incolentibus truncationes membrorum facit. Hac de causa imperator expeditionem super eum movere

the Abodrites became involved much as the Indian country in America was the bone of contention between the English and French.[1]

Schleswig, as a Danish duchy, was a *point d'appui* of Danish mainland aggrandizement. This Lothar II perceived, and he endeavored to take advantage of a conflict for the Danish succession to attach Schleswig to Germany again. In 1103 Eric I of Denmark died leaving a minor son Knut Laward[2] under the regency of the deceased King's brother Niels (or Nicholas). But the latter plotted to secure the succession for his own son Magnus, and accordingly sent his nephew into Schleswig in 1115, as duke of Schleswig. Here his pro-German affiliations became so evident that in 1125 Lothar II invested Knut Laward with the overlordship of Wagria to

intendit" (*Ann. Erphesf.* [*MGH*, SS. VI, 539]; Bernhardi, *Lothar II*, p. 538, n. 34). For the Germanization of Schleswig see Hansen, *Die Besiedelung der Marck zwischen Elbe- und Eidermündung;* Petermann, *Mittheil.* (1893), p. 177.

[1] In 810 Charlemagne, it will be remembered, wrested Schleswig from the pagan Danes and erected it into a German March. In 1027, after the conversion of the Danes, Conrad II ceded the tract which the Danes had ever struggled to recover to Denmark for Danish assistance against the Baltic Slavs. It was this dangerous policy on the part of the first Franconian king which whetted Danish ambition to acquire control of the Baltic strand by conquering Wagria and Pomerania, and compromised the political relations between the two crowns. Canute had Slav blood in him through his mother, who was a sister of Boleslav Chrobry of Poland (Larson, *Canute the Great*, pp. 15, 33). The famous Jomsburg Vikings played a striking part at this time in Pomerania.

[2]

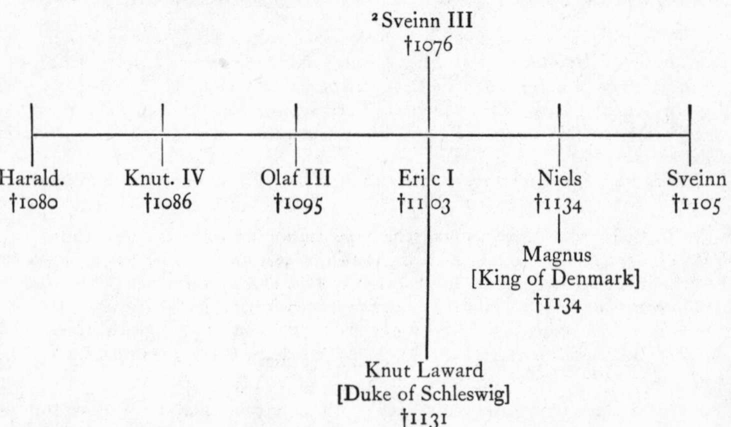

whom the Christian Abodrite chieftain Henry and his pagan people became vassal. Later (in 1128?) when Henry died, the Emperor judged the time to be opportune both to extinguish the quasi-independence of the Abodrite-Wagrian principality and at the same time to bind Knut Laward and Schleswig closer to Germany, and accordingly sold the *Regnum Abotritorum* to Knut Laward, who with a force of Holsteiners and Sturmarians, and in conjunction with Count Adolph of Holstein, invaded Wagria and captured Werle, but was soon recalled by a raid of the Rugian pirates upon the coast of Holstein. Niels of Denmark and his son Magnus regarded Knut Laward's course with intense animosity[1] and the Abodrites found national leaders of their cause in two new chieftains, a son of Butue, Pribislav, and his cousin, Niklot, the latter of whom was to prove the greatest leader the Baltic Slavs ever produced.

This triangular condition produced a state of things approaching anarchy along the border of Holstein and lower Saxony.[2] Knut Laward energetically set himself to establish law and order in this penumbral tract, and, after the ancient Danish fashion of punishment, nailed some of the worst offenders of the border to ships' spars in sight of all.[3] He then began to make good his claim to sway over Wagria, calling to his standard every pioneer German who hated the Wends and coveted the lands of the Abodrites, and began the erection of a castle on the site of an ancient Slavonic hill-fort which the Germans called Eilberch or Alberg. Pribislav and Niklot, the Abodrite chiefs, were dragged off in chains to Schleswig. Alt-Lübeck, the Slav capital, where the Christian Abodrite Duke had kept his court and maintained Christian worship in his private chapel, was captured. Apparently this warlike Danish Prince, by the accident of fortune become a

[1] Schafarik, II, 539.

[2] "Cepitque vir pacificus [Knut Laward] regionem compacare, auferens desertores de terra. Precipue vero Sleswicensibus beneficus erat. Contigit autem latrones forte comprehendi in mirica, quae interjacet Sliam et Egdorem, et perduci in faciem Kanuti" (Helm., I, 49).

[3] *Ibid.* On Knut's history in detail see H. Reich, "Knut Laward, Herzog von Schleswig," *Jahrbuch für Landeskunde der Herzogtümer Schleswig, Holstein und Lauenburg*, X, 203–54.

German vassal, promised to become the ruling prince in the north and the destined conqueror of the last of the independent Slavonic tribes along the Baltic. One wonders, had he lived, if he would have anticipated the career of Henry the Lion. But as it befell, Knut Laward was assassinated in 1131 at the instigation of his jealous cousin, Magnus. Intrigue and turmoil ensued in Denmark, which reminds one of Hamlet's time, and Danish enterprise upon the mainland was arrested, though for years border strife between Denmark and Holstein obtained.[1]

The death of Lothar II in 1137 precipitated a new storm against the Wends. The rebellion of Henry the Proud and the feud between Saxony and Brandenburg speedily involved the border. Pribislav destroyed the Saxon castle at Sigeberg and devastated the German settlements roundabout it. A new oratory and a new monastery there were burned. One of the monks was killed; the rest escaped to Neumünster. "In Slavia," writes Helmold, "affairs of the church lapsed."[2] A "Slavicus furor propter occupationes Saxonum"[3] swept over the border, and so many settlers quitted the country that in some places the land was reduced to a solitude. In retaliation, Henry the Proud in the winter of 1138–39 made a punitive expedition against the Abodrites and fearfully wasted the territory. Border strife became a chronic condition with no attempt on the part of the feudal nobles to restrain it.[4] In Nordalbingia the rivals were Adolph of Holstein and Henry the Lion. For a short time Albrecht the Bear fished in the troubled waters, seized the ancient commercial town of Bardowick and the castle of Sigeberg, and even extended his sway to Bremen and Hamburg, in the latter territory capturing a stone castle—a novelty in Lower Germany at this time—which the mother of Count Adolph had erected as a protection against pirates penetrating up

[1] For all this see Helm., I, 49–51; W. Fricke, *Untersuchungen zur älteren Holsteinischen Gesch.* (Jena, 1907), pp. 42 ff.; A. F. H. Schaumann, *Gesch. d. niedersächsischen Völker von der ersten Hervortreten auf deutsch. Boden an bis 1180* (1839); *Neues Archiv*, XXXIII, 561 ff.; Bernhardi, *Lothar II*, pp. 396 ff.

[2] I, 54.

[3] I, 56.

[4] "Nemine obsistente principum Christianorum" (*ibid.*).

the estuary of the Elbe. However, he soon found more practicable compensation farther east in Pomerania and left the field of Nordalbingia to Adolph and Henry, who in 1143 divided it between them, the former taking Wagria with the castle of Sigeberg, the latter the Abodrite land (or Polabia) with Ratzeburg as its chief seat. Roughly, the Trave River was the boundary between.[1]

The result of the reduction of the Wagri and Abodrites by Adolph of Holstein and Henry the Lion in 1143 was a large influx of German immigrants into the trans-Elbean lands, which were thrown open to settlement.[2] Settlers thronged in "cum equis et bubus, cum aratris et plaustris et personis ad opus idoneis,"[3] to the exasperation of the Wends who could do nothing but sullenly submit.[4]

Nothing so much resembles it as the American "rush" after the War of 1812 into the Western Reserve and the Ohio Valley. In the older parts of Germany the exodus was so great that manorial proprietors were compelled to ameliorate the condition of their peasantry lest they run away to the new lands beyond the Elbe.[5] It requires no stretch of imagination for the American scholar, who is familiar from his birth, through family tradition and education, with the history of the "making" of the New West, to visualize the nature and importance of this emigration across the Elbe. Helmold's paragraphs have the vividness of a panorama to his eyes. This great movement almost seems to be a chapter of the history of his own forebears. He says:

> Because the land was without people Adolph sent messengers into all the regions roundabout, even into Flanders and Holland, the bishopric of Utrecht, into Westphalia and Frisia, to proclaim that all who were in want of land might come with their families and receive the best soil, a spacious

[1] Helm., I, 54, 56; Bernhardi, *Konrad III*, pp. 61, 318.

[2] For extended treatment of this subject see Detlefsen, *Geschichte des Holsteinischen Elb-Marschen* (2 vols., with map; 1891–92); Niemeyer, *Das Slavenland unter Herzog Heinrich dem Loewen.*

[3] *Sidonis Epist.* (ed. Schmeidler), p. 240.

[4] "Slavi . . . . terram suam a Christianis Teutonicis incoli, exarserunt" (*ibid.*, p. 241).

[5] Kovalevsky, *Die ökonomische Entwicklung Europas*, III, 321–22.

country, rich in crops, abounding with fish and flesh and exceeding good pasturage.[1]

Like a true land-promoter Adolph deftly advertised the region. He said unto the people of Holstein and Sturmaria:

> Do you not see that you have subjugated the land of the Slavs—that you have bought it by the death of your brothers and your fathers? Why, therefore, do you not at once enter in and possess it? Be the first, and come into this delectable land, and cultivate it, and have a share of its products. For you should have the best of that which you have wrested from the hands of your enemies.

The response was a "rush" of settlers from the older parts of Germany, notably Westphalia, and even of immigrants from Holland and Flanders. "An innumerable multitude of various nations," we are told, "responded to the invitation." The Holsteiners took the nearest and safest stretch of land along the Trave and Schwentine as far as the Plöner-See;[2] the Westphalians settled in the Gau Dargunensis;[3] the Hollanders around Eutin; the Frisians around Süssel.[4] "And Adolph gave Oldenburg and Lütjenburg and the rest of the lands along the sea to the Slavs to cultivate, and they were made tributary to him."[5] They were driven, like the Indians of the Everglades, into the swamps and forests, where they eked out a wretched living on fish and game[5] or took to piracy among the Danish islands.[6]

[1] Helmold, I, 57.

[2] There is today a village named Holstendorf in this region between Ahrensboeck and Eutin.

[3] This location cannot be ascertained. Wendt (*Germanisierung*, etc., II, 15) thinks it near Lübeck; Schmeidler (ed. Helm.), p. 112, n. 3, fixes it near Ahrensboeck. Von Schröder and Biernatzki (*Topographie der Herzogtümer Holstein und Lauenburg* [Oldenburg, 1855], p. 6) incline to the vicinity of Rostock.

[4] All historians of medieval Germany touch upon this subject but add little to Helmold, I, 57. The most recent study is A. Gloy, *Der Gang der Germanisation in Ostholstein* (Kiel, 1884), esp. pp. 17 ff.; cf. Meitzen, *op. cit.*, II, 354 ff.; Wendt, II, 14–17.

[5] Helm., I, 69, 83; II, 13; Ebbo, *Vita Ottonis episc. Babenberg*, III, 4.

[6] Helm., I, 102. In II, 13, Helmold gives a graphic picture of their fugitive, predatory life. The island of Rügen, the last stronghold of independence of the Baltic Slavs, was the seat of these forays, which were not ended until the Danish capture of the island in 1168 and the complete destruction of the great temple of Arkona there. The Saxon princes, who hated the Danes, connived at these forays and even per-

Adolph of Holstein, if he had not been molested in his plans by his feudal neighbors, might have worked out some accommodation in the strained relations between the two races. He understood the Slavonic tongue and the Slavonic character as no other German of his time, save possibly Albrecht the Bear; without recourse to force he persuaded the Abodrite nobles to do him homage and induced them to open their lands to German settlers.[1] But Adolph's policy of peaceful colonization and benevolent intercourse between the two races was frustrated by the Wendish Crusade in 1147, by the enmity of Henry the Lion, by the land-greed of the Saxon baronage, by the eagerness of the inrushing settlers, who clamored for the expulsion of the Wends as loudly as the American settlers for the removal of the Indians. The middle of the twelfth century was no moment to advocate moderation. The Crusades, at once a fanatical religious war and a colonizing movement, were in full swing.

When the bloody strife was over, Nordalbingia was again a smoking wilderness.[2] Once more the work of colonization and settlement was resumed, and a veritable invasion of monks into the land of Wagria (East Holstein) followed as a matter of course,[3] along with a wave of new colonists who introduced the superior methods of German tillage.[4] The Germans brought both a higher form of economic life and a higher capacity for exploitation of the soil.

The end of I, 84, in Helmold's *Chronica* is an epilogue:

---

mitted captive Danes to be sold into slavery in the market places of German cities. Helmold, II, 13, says that he had heard from eyewitnesses of the exposure of 700 Danish prisoners for sale in Mecklenburg.

[1] Helm., I, 57 (end); cf. Hauck, IV, 603–4.

[2] "Omnis igitur terra Obotritorum et finitimas regiones quae pertinent ad regem Obotritorum, assiduis bellis, maxime vero hoc novissimo bello tota in solitudinem redacta est" (Helm., II, 5).

[3] *Sidonis Epist.*, p. 244; Kötzschke, *op. cit.*, p. 112. In *Meckl. U.B.*, I, No. 52, is a privilege of colonization granted by Conrad III to the Bishop of Havelberg in 1150.

[4] "[Henricus] precepit Slavorum populo, ut coleret vir agrum suum et exercerent laborem utilem et commodum" (Helm., I, 84).

"The Slavs little by little failed in the land, and the Saxons came in and dwelt there."[1]

Yet we must be cautious lest we take Helmold too literally. The German conquest of Mecklenburg and Pomerania was not completed until the thirteenth century, and until then the German settlers were quite certainly a minority of the population.[2] Indeed, the peasantry continued to speak the Slavonic idiom until the seventeenth century. It was the Thirty Years' War which exterminated the last vestiges of Slav culture in ancient Wagria and Pomerania, and completed the Germanization of the country.[3]

Says Schulze:

> Up to the twelfth century conditions in Germany had not developed to a point which necessitated an overflow of the excess population into distant border territory. The homeland still furnished sufficient land even for the younger sons, and the settling and exploitation of regions within the kingdom, the clearing of the extensive forests and wild land at home yet absorbed the energy of the peasant. Only as the available area grew narrower and narrower, when the land in many cases had been subjected to cultivation beyond the limits of productivity, and recourse had to be made to division of the Hufen, did the call of the princes and the nobles from

[1] *Mecklenb. Urkundenbuch*, I, 56: "Slavis ejectis"; *Codex Anhalt.*, I, 347, 414. Heinemann, *op. cit.*, p. 466; Guttmann, *Forsch. z. brand. u. preuss. Gesch.*, IX, 427–28.

[2] A MS book of tithe registers of Ratzeburg for the years 1229–30, preserved in the archives at Neu-Strelitz, shows that as late as that date not all the Slavs had been converted. In the property registers of the parishes one not infrequently finds opposite the name of this or that locality: "Sclavi sunt, nullum beneficium." See Koetzschke, *Quellen*, No. 44, from *Meckl. U.B.*, I, No. 375.

[3] Besides the literature already cited on the subject of the German colonization east of the Elbe, the following monographs or articles are important; Kuehnel, *Jahrb. und Jahresbericht d. Ver. f. Meck. Gesch.* (1881) (on Slav place-names in Mecklenburg); Malchow, *Gesch. des Klosters Doberan* (1881); Prümers, *Pommersche Urkundenbuch* (1254–78), and cf. *Hist. Ztschft.* (N.F., 1882), Band XII; Kuehlmann, *Neue Mitth. aus dem Gebiete historisch.-antiquarisch. Forschungen*, Band XV, Heft 2 (1882), important for the Germanization of the district of Plonim. Eichhorn, *Schriften d. Ver. f. Sachsen-Meiningische Gesch.*, Heft 20 (1895); Curschmann, *Die deutschen Ortsnamen im nordostdeutschen Kolonialgebiet.* Pyl, *Beiträge zur Gesch. der Stadt Greifswald* (1892), shows the existence of many Westphalian and Rhenish family names in Pomerania and Rügen; Fabricius, *Hans. Geschichtsblätter* (1894), a study of the municipal law in Schwerin, shows that it was introduced by German colonists in the twelfth century. On the *Bede* in Mecklenburg, see Techen, *Mecklenburg Jahrb. d. Ver. f. Meckl. Gesch.*, Band LXVII (1902). Witte, *Wendische Bevölkerungsreste in Mecklenburg* (1905), argues for the Germanization, not the expulsion of the Wends.

the Wendish lands meet with response. Thousands then emigrated, full of fresh courage and cheerful hope, into the east, where land in plenty and freedom and independent living upon their own acres awaited them.

Nor did they come with empty hands. Just as to-day the greater portion of rural emigrants is made up of the most efficient and energetic elements, who as a whole are not utterly without means, men to whom their home has grown too narrow, and which has ceased to provide sufficient play either for their economic or for their social energies, so it was then—that enterprise, energy, and rich experience which they had gained in farming the home acres these settlers brought with them. They could not have afforded to have been wholly without some material means. The hard labor of clearing the wilderness promised success and reward to their arduous endeavors only after years of toil. At the very outset the conditions of border life demanded the application of all their strength and skill, the expenditure of a not inconsiderable capital in the form of implements and tools, equipment and supplies, and at times also of ready cash.[1]

The Saxon population along the border (*Marcomanni*, or "Marchmen," they were called)[2] had need, as Helmold says, to be of strong endurance, and to be ready to risk their blood. These medieval German frontiersmen were resolute and hardy, hard working, and given to a rough hospitality toward strangers provided they were Germans and lived Saxon law like themselves, but hated the Wend, and detested foreign incomers like the Dutch and Flemings.[3] Both their culture and their Christianity were rude and crude when compared with the more refined German life of the cities in old Franconia and the valley of the Rhine.[4] In Helmold's *Chronica*

[1] Schulze, *Kolonisierung*, p. 79.

[2] Helm., I, 66, 67, 87. A map showing a multitude of Slav *Ortsnamen* in present Saxony may be examined in *Deutsche Erde*, XI, 92.

[3] For evidence of the contempt of the Germans for the Wends see Fredegar, *Chron.*, IV, 68; Monk of St. Gall, II, 12; Thietmar, III, 17; Adam of Bremen, II, 43 (schol.); Helm., I, 13 and 16: Cosmas of Prague, I, 40 (*MGH*, SS. IX, 42); *ibid.* X, 84. For Saxon hatred of Flemish *advenae* see Helm., I, 63–64.

[4] "Tres autem sunt Nordalbingorum populi: Sturmari, Holzati, Thetmarki, nec habitu nec lingua multum discrepantes, tenentes Saxonum jura [cf. *Sachsenspiegel*, Book III, art. 64, § 3] et Christianum nomen, nisi quod propter barbarorum viciniam furtis et latrociniis operam dare consueverunt. Hospitalitatis gratiam sectantur. Nam furari et largiri apud Holzatos ostentacio est. . . . . Habitudinem loci campumque vasta et sterili mirica perorridum, preterea accolarum genus agreste et incultum, nichil de religione nisi nomen tantum Christianitatis habentes" (Helm., I, 47). Helmhold frequently uses the word "uncouth" (*agrestis*) to describe border conditions, e.g., I, 13; in I, 67, the Holsteiners are "gens libera et cervicosa, gens agrestis et indomita."

There are two paragraphs in the *Dialogus* of Herbordus (II, 2, pp. 60–61;

Slavorum we get authentic glimpses of German frontier life, of new settlers pressing into the region, chiefly Flemings and Dutch, who redeemed the fenlands around Bremen and in the Havelland.[1] As in America in the seventeenth and eighteenth centuries the blockhouse guarded the frontier settlements against Indian foray, so in the debated land between the Saxon and the Slav timbered castles (*munitiones*, *oppida*, *castra*, *castella*) protected the sparse and scattered pioneer German population. "Around them," says Helmold, "the settlers clustered, but in great fear of attacks."[2] One sees the barbarian side of the picture, too: the gradual dispossession of the Wends and the seizure of their lands by German colonists, whose hunger for land and faculty for establishing settlements roused the ire of the Slavs.[3]

In all this energy and violence upon the border the part which the Saxon people played in it, and not merely nobles and bishops, is to be observed. German eastward expansion had ceased to be only the covetous land-grabbing aspiration of the great, and had become a deep and strong national movement. "Die Grosstat unseres Volkes während des Mittelalters," as Lamprecht has styled it—the conquest of two-fifths of modern Germany was beginning its historic work.

Henry the Lion's seizure of Lübeck in 1158 from Adolph of Holstein made the position of Niklot and his people more precarious than ever.[4] By that time the very sight of any Slavs along the Baltic between him and the sea had grown intolerable to Henry. In 1160 he invaded the Abodrite territory "with fire and sword." Niklot, in desperation, after

---

30, p. 143), which interestingly depict the impression the cultivated clerical society of Michelsberg, in Bamberg, had of German wilderness life.

[1] I, 57, 88–89.

[2] "Jam enim circumjacentia oppida incolebantur paulatim a Christicolis, sed cum grandi pavore propter insidias latronum. Castrum enim Plunense necdum reedificatum fuerat" (Helm., I, 75). So it was in America: "A log hut, a little clearing edged by the primeval forest, with the palisaded fort near by—this was the type of home they made" (Turner, *American Historical Review*, I, 73).

[3] "Slavicus furor propter occupationes Saxonum" (Helm., I, 56).

[4] Hauck, IV, 620.

an unsuccessful attack upon Lübeck, burned his towns—Mecklenburg, Schwerin, Dubin, Ilow (near Wismar)—and fled to the marshy tract around Wurle in the valley of the Warnow.[1] From this place he carried on a guerilla warfare. Henry's practices were merciless, for he hanged every Wend who fell into his hands. Niklot himself was finally killed and his head brought into the Saxon camp. His sons burned Wurle, too, and fled into the deep forests near the coast. Henry offered them and the broken fragments of the Abodrites the territory around Wurle, the ancient land of the Kissini and Circipani. But they refused it, and the bitter strife went on for some years. In 1163 Wertislav, one of the brothers, was captured and carried in chains to Brunswick. The elder, Pribislav, in retaliation, in the dead of winter, surprised the garrison of the castle of Mecklenburg while the commandant was away, and put the whole garrison together with all the refugees within it to the edge of the sword. The capture of Ilow followed and a terrible devastation of the province.[2]

Again the border was in a panic. It was the last flurry of the Baltic Slavs. The call to arms went wide and far—to all Saxony, to Waldemar of Denmark, to Adolph of Holstein, though the Christian Slav soldiery of the last, intermingled with his Holsteiners and Sturmari, were looked upon askance. Pribislav's base was at Dimmin where he had massed all his horse and foot forces. A bloody battle was fought near the Kummerower-See in July, 1164, in which twenty-five hundred Wends were slain. On the German side the most conspicuous who fell was Adolph of Holstein. The shattered remnant of Pribislav's forces fled to Pomerania. In 1177 the end came, when Henry the Lion destroyed Dimmin and Lauenburg and Niklot became a fugitive.[3]

But Pomerania offered no asylum. In the winter of 1124–25 Lothar of Saxony, as we have seen, had made a victorious expedition against the Rugians, destroyed their temple at

[1] Today Wyck between Schwaan and Bützow-Lisch (*Mecklenb. Jahrb.*, VI, 88).

[2] Helm., I, 93, 97, 98.

[3] Arnold of Lübeck, II, 4; III, 4.

Rethra, and broken their power.[1] The missionary labors of Otto of Bamberg in Pomerania at the same time completed the German conquest. The *terra Rugianorum*, too, was coveted and conquered by the Germans. For the land was boasted to be "ferax frugum, piscium atque ferarum."[2] The Pomeranian duke, Kazimir, even if he had dared, would have been unable to sympathize with the cause of the Abodrites, girdled as Pomerania was by Brandenburg and Poland. The survivors of the tribe were sold by people of their own blood into slavery among the Poles, the Bohemians, and the Sorben. The last independent group of the Baltic Slavs upon the mainland was obliterated.[3]

The conquered country was secured by garrisoned castles and thrown open to settlement, the best tracts being apportioned like military bounty lands, among Henry's vassals and the Saxon clergy.[4] The nature of these settlers' holdings varied.[5] Many of them were not large—a circumstance which points to a considerable influx of peasantry. What the extent of the peasant grants was is left to conjecture. But the minimum area must have been at least three *Hufen*, for, according to the *Sachsenspiegel*, the possession of three *Hufen* was a qualification of a *Schoffenbarfreimann*.[6]

[1] Helmold fails to give us this information, but the fact is recorded by Ebbo, *Vita Ottonis episc. Babenberg.*, III, 5; cf. Wendt, I, 85, n. 1.

[2] Helm., II, 12.

[3] *Ibid.*, II, 4–5; Arnold of Lübeck, III, 4, 7.

[4] "Porro terram Obotritorum divisit militibus suis possidendum . . . confluerent de terris suis homines Teutonici ad incolendam terram spaciosam, fertilem frumento, commodam pascuarum ubertate, abundantem pisce et carne et omnibus bonis" (Helm., I, 88). "Slavi usquequaque protriti atque propulsi sunt, et venerunt . . . populi fortes et innumerabiles et obtinuerunt terminos Slavorum et edificaverunt civitates et ecclesias et increverunt divisiis super omnem estimacionem" (*ibid.*, I, 89; cf. I, 102).

[5] We find a variety of terms as *praedium*, *allodium*, *villa*, *curtis*, etc. The distinctions are more legal than economic. See Kretschmer, *op. cit.*, p. 198, and bibliography.

[6] Schulze, p. 117. The *Hufe* was not invariable in area. Its size was fixed by regional custom and varied greatly, from 15, 20, 36, 45, 60, 120, 160 *Morgen* (Lamprecht, *DWL*, I, pp. 366–70; Kovalevsky, *Oekonomische Entwicklung Europas*, III [1905], 217). But a *Hufenmass* of less than 30 *Morgen* was rare. An *aratrum theutonicale* was equal to $2\frac{2}{3}$ *mansi* or *Hufen* (Michael, I, 116, n. 4). The same variableness is attached to the term *Morgen*. Defined as "ein Landstück für welches die

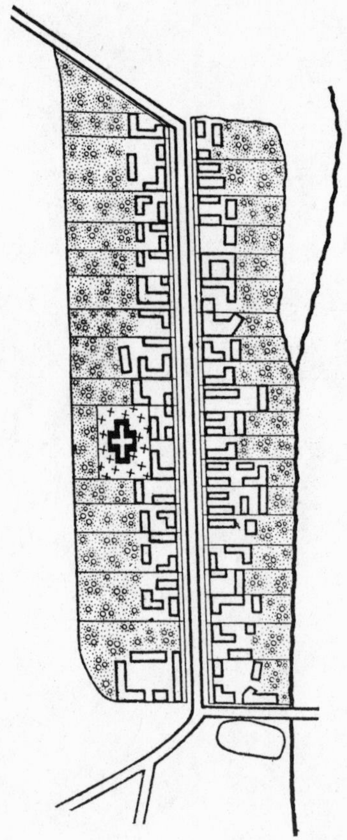

Ground-Plan of a Typical German "Street" Village

In general, in the method of surveying the land there was a manifest tendency to discard the traditions and practices of the familiar manorial system, with its demesne, its strips of glebe land and dividing "balks." Instead, the land was marked out in rectangular or oblong blocks—the *mansus regalis* (720 rods long, 30 rods broad) of the Carolingian fisc.[1] Meitzen has shown that this division of allotments into rectangular or oblong blocks obtained in Frisia as early as the time of the Frank mayors, although it was originally foreign to the Frisians. The first obscure traces of the granting of *Hufen* of this form do not, in Frisian lands, antedate Karl Martel. The extension of the system along the whole Frisian Coast and to the *Waldhufen* of the royal domain is ascribed to the Carolingian administration. In Holland, Zealand, and Frisia the cultivation of the moorlands began very early. These marsh and moor *Hufen* were surveyed almost without exception in straight strips, a practice which also soon came to obtain in forest clearings, or *Waldhufen*. In the level moor-

---

Pflugarbeit eines Morgens, von Sonnenaufgang bis Mittag, erfahrungsgemäss in Anspruch genommen wurde" (Kötzschke, p. 68), the measurement was naturally conditioned by the nature of the soil, the size of the team, and the length of the working day. A *Morgen* in one place was not the same in area as a *Morgen* in another place. But it was a definite unit for the manor, or the region, concerned. Thirteen *Morgen* usually equaled *ca.* 10½ *hectares* (Lamprecht, *DWL*, I, 346; Langethal, *Landwirtschaft*, II, 362, 373; Hanssen, "Die Ackerflur der Dörfer," *Abhandl.*, II, 179 f.). See, further, Schmidt, *Zur Agrargeschichte Lübecks und Ostholsteins;* Kovalevsky, *op. cit.*, III, 193 f. The Dutch colonists in the region preserved their own ancestral law for centuries (*Hollensch. Recht*), for in 1438 the Holsteiner towns Zarneckau and Gumale went over to *Holsten Recht* (Wendt, II, 15).

[1] The earliest mention of the *mansus regalis* in legislation is in *Cap.* 801–813 (*MGH*, LL, p. 189). The rod was approximately 16 feet, varying by a few inches in different regions, except in Lorraine, where it was only 10 feet. The "royal rod" was 5 feet longer. If 16 feet be taken as the normal German rod this would make the royal rod measure 21 feet, which would nearly agree with the English "perch of the king" (20 ft.), the "lawful perch of the vill" being 16½ feet. Inama Sternegg, I, 439, n. 3; II, 25, following Meitzen, says that the customary German rod was 10 feet and the royal rod 15 feet. But Lamprecht, I, 343, has shown that the short 10-foot rod was customary only in Lorraine. If, therefore, the royal rod was 5 feet longer than the customary rod it was probably 21 feet, or even 21½ feet. Meitzen has estimated that the *mansus regalis* included from 48 to 50 *hectares* of land, (one *hectare* equals 2.47 acres) nearly 125 acres. But on the assumption that the royal rod was 21 feet the *mansus regalis* would be proportionally larger than this estimate. The Bremen tract must have been at least a mile and a half square. See next page, and also chapter xiv.

lands there was no difficulty in following this simple plan. The axis of both kinds of *Hufen* was a main road along which the homesteads were in a row, the houses being situated either at the end or in the middle of the strip.[1]

This rectangular system of survey was imported into the German borderlands by Frisian and Dutch settlers from the Low Countries. A charter of Albrecht the Bear specifically mentions these "manors of Dutch measurement."[2] The earliest recorded example of this form of settlement in Germany is that of a colony of Hollanders settled by the Archbishop of Bremen in 1106 in the marshes of the Weser near Bremen.[3]

These villages established in the German colonial lands were very different in appearance from the older, manorial type of village. They formed a long street, with dwellings on either hand, each set in the midst of a separate rectangular subdivision, with the kitchen-garden or orchard around the house near the road, then the farm acres, then the pasture, and last the wood lot. Of course, the order would be subject to natural features, but this was the preferred arrangement if possible. Holstein, Mecklenburg, and Brandenburg were largely colonized in this way. The system in time was widely extended, however, as the restless population of Germany in the twelfth and thirteenth centuries searched out for themselves new homes in the wilderness or in less-frequented localities. Parts of the Black Forest and the Odenwald, of Upper Bavaria, of the upper reaches of the Mulde and the Pleisse, of the region between the Lippe and Luneburg, were so settled. The same is true of nearly one-quarter of Silesia and

[1] Meitzen, *Siedelung und Agrarwesen*, II, 47–53, 343–44; Inama Sternegg, *DWG*, I, 439–43. Since Meitzen wrote, Blanchard (*La Flandre* [Lille, 1906]) has thrown new light upon this subject. See esp. pp. 151–57, 423–27. On p. 424 is a map of one of these "street" villages in East Flanders. A lucid, untechnical account of these villages east of the Elbe (based on Meitzen) is by Schmid-Kunz, *Nord und Süd*, No. 257 (June, 1899).

[2] *Mansos Hollandriensis dimensionis* (Riedel, *Die Marck Brand.*, II, 51; *Codex Diplom.*, I, 338; Lavisse, *op. cit.*, p. 187).

[3] See the document in Kötzschke, *Quellen zur Geschichte der ostdeutschen Kolonisation im 12. bis 14. Jahrhundert* (Leipzig, 1912), pp. 1–2; also in *Bremisches U.-B.*, I, No. 27; Altmann-Bernheim, *Urkb. z. Verf. Gesch. Deutschlands*, I, No. 80; Inama Sternegg, *DWG*, II, 13. There is an English translation of the charter in Thatcher-MacNeal, *Source-Book for Mediaeval History*, No. 298.

the marsh land in the basins of the Oder, the Wartha, and the Netze. But the whole practice goes back to the original colony of Hollanders who settled in the Weser marshes in 1106.[1]

In Brandenburg the administrative machinery for the encouragement of settlement was better organized than in other parts of Germany. The immediate instrument in the promotion of colonization was a contractor (*locator*), which may be appropriately translated "promoter" in American parlance. These agents would contract with a large landed proprietor—bishop or baron, abbot or noble—to bring settlers in and establish them upon the grants which they had acquired from the margrave. For this purpose the tract was rectangularly subdivided after the manner which has been described. One "section" in every such rural community (*Landgemeinde*) was set aside for the parish priest. But the rights of the priest were strictly defined. There was no room in Brandenburg for the intrusion of priestly authority. One-tenth went to the *locator* as his fee. The balance of the land was apportioned among the incomers by lot, who lived under German law and worked the farms on the three-field system.[2]

[1] Meitzen, *op. cit.*, III, 264–68, and cf. the map illustrating "Die Holländer-Kolonien in den Marschen um Bremen," *ibid* (Atlas), No. 86.

[2] The influence of the practice of the Carolingian fisc was a factor in promoting the extension of the *Dreifeldersystem*. It seems to me that it is a defect of Meitzen's and Hanssen's treatment of the subject of the history of medieval German agriculture that both ignore too much this influence. Meitzen (I, 33–36, 67, 169) and Hanssen (*Agrarhistorische Abhandlungen*, I, 171) have focused their attention too exclusively upon the important three-field region east and south of the Weser and overemphasized the influence of the system there upon other localities. It should be added, however, that in Brandenburg and Austria, owing to the large proportion of Wendish peasantry there, the agricultural régime shows admixture of Slavonic land survivals. Kovalevsky, *Oekonomische Entwicklung Europas*, III (1905), 191, 215. On the institution of the *locator* see Riedel, *Die Marck Brandenburg*, I, 196; Wohlbrück, *Gesch. des ehemaligen Bistums Lebus*, I, 200 ff.; Lavisse, *La marche de Brandebourg*, pp. 201–2; and esp. Schulze, *Kolonisierung*, pp. 154–66. The following excerpts illustrate the form: "Nos Henricus, Dei gratis episcopus . . . . volumus esse notum quod nos . . . . perspeximus, quod de Suscoutz villa nostra episcopali . . . . nobis et nostrae ecclesiae modicum utilitatis et commodi perveniret, praedictam villam . . . . fideli nostro . . . . ad locandum *iure teutonico* tradimus" (Wohlbrück, I, 201; cf. Heinemann, *Albrecht der Bär*, Nos. 39–41). On p. 204 Wohlbrück cites the sale by the prior of a women's convent situated at Czarnovans, in Upper Silesia, of 21 manors to a *locator* named Siegfried, who formed a new town in the way described, which was called Frauendorf. Riedel, *loc. cit.*, instances a large number of places terminating

The land which was to be settled was divided into equal strips of land,[1] the rent for each of which amounted on the average to a quarter of a mark.[2] Besides this rent which was paid to the margrave, they had to pay a "malter" of three kinds of grain in the form of a tithe to the parish church. The owner, lay or clerical, would call to himself a colonization agent (called *advocatus*, or more commonly *Vogt*) and would enter into a contract with him for the colonization of his unoccupied lands. These lands were surveyed and partitioned into equal strips (*Lehen*, *lanens*, *mansi*, or *Hufen*), and each colonist received one of these *Lehen*. When the colonist had made the purchase, he gave a deposit on the first payment (*arrha*, *anleit*), which generally ranged from one to ten pieces of silver, according to the grade of the land, and then he obligated himself to pay interest from the remaining sum. But besides these stipulated payments, the colonist generally bound himself to pay the lord certain commodities, such as a few measures of the three kinds of grain, a few head of poultry, some dozens of eggs, etc. The settler became a hereditary renter of the fields and of the house he lived in. For the uncleared ground the rent generally was not paid until the eighth year after clearing.

The reward of the *Vogt* who colonized a particular locality consisted of a free and hereditary holding, for which neither he nor his posterity paid any payment whatever. Besides, the *Vogt* held the office of the *Dorfmeister*, which office (the *justicium*) combined the administrative with the judicial functions. The proceeds of the legal suits determined before him were divided into thirds, two of which went to the lord, and one was his own. Furthermore, the occupant of the *justicium* was given the free use of the village mill, the management of the village inn, and other similar privileges. Both he and his parents had the privilege of free fishing and the permission to cut the wood in the forest for their use. An

---

in the suffix *dorf*, as Mertinstorf, Cunradstorf, Michelstorf, Gerhardstorf, Wilkendorp, etc. Schultze, *Rechtsgeschichte* (5th ed., 1881), § 148, 5, claims that the German system of title-deed and land registration goes back to this form of grant.

[1] *Hufen*, *sortes*, *mansi*.

[2] "Also etwa fünf Mark unseres Geldes" (Grünhagen, p. 39).

energetic *Vogt* often colonized more than one village, and thus attained the *justicium* with its incomes and privileges in all the places he had colonized.

The settlements thus founded received their names either after the "lay" of the land or other such local circumstances, or after the *Vogt* or the colonists themselves. The most common endings of such names are: *-berg* ("hill"), *-au* ("meadow"), *-bühel* ("hill"), *-hart* ("woods"), *-bach* ("brook"), *-dorf* ("village"), *-schlag*, *-reut*, or *-rote* ("a clearing in the woods").[1]

Helmold, though with some exaggeration, described Nordalbingia as a great Saxon colony by 1171:

> The whole land of the Slavs, beginning at the Eyder [River], which is the boundary of the Kingdom of Denmark and lies between the Baltic Sea and the Elbe, and extends through a vast tract of country clear to Schwerin —a country which was once vexed with war and almost without population—now, through the grace of God, has all been conquered and, as it were, formed into a single colony of the Saxons. Towns and castles are being builded there, and the churches and ministers of Christ are increasing.

The last paragraph of this most original narrative of German medieval frontier history tells how Pribislav, the Abodrite duke (the only one of his family left, for Henry the Lion had hanged his brother), "sate quiet and content with the portion of territory allotted him 'by the rope' [i.e., surveyed], and rebuilt the towns of Mecklenburg, Ilow, and Rostock, and collected his people therein."[2]

Thus was the German feudal system extended over the Slavonic lands. Helmold says:

> But because some of the Slavs were prone to robbery and molested the Germans who were settled in Schwerin and roundabout, Gunzel, commandant of the castle, a brave man and vassal of the duke, ordained that whoever of the Slavs thereafter was found travelling, not on the mainroads, but in the bye-ways, unless the reason was evident, should be hanged at once.[3]

[1] For a typical example of this nature see Kötzschke, *Quellen*, No. 8.

[2] Helm., II, 14 (end); cf. I, 84. This method of surveying with a rope also obtained in France: "... mansiones et funiculos possessionum colonis distribuit" (*Cart. de l'abbaye de St. Bertin*, III, 344; Suger, *Vie de Louis le Gros* [ed. Molinier], p. 48). It was the ancient Hebrew system of allotment (II Kings 8:2; Amos 7:17).

[3] Chap. cx. Cf. Arnold of Lübeck, III, 4.

Pribislav became an avowed if not a sincere convert to Christianity, and personally participated in the foundation of the Cistercian monastery at Doberan near Rostock, by Bishop Berno in the year 1170, providing the new foundation with lands. But in spite of this there was for the present no extensive settling of German colonists. Pribislav sought to collect the remnants of his own people and to accustom them to a peaceable manner of life. After his death, however, the suppressed hatred of his subjects toward the German incomers once more asserted itself in a wild deed of revenge. The monastery of Doberan was destroyed in 1179 by the surrounding population, every one of its inmates, seventy-eight in number, suffering violent death. But the son and nephew of Pribislav, Henry Borwin and Niklot, who succeeded him in the government of Mecklenburg, were both friendly to the Germans at the outset, and found ways and means to give new life to colonization very soon. At the court of Niklot, whose residence was at Rostock, we already, in the year 1189, meet with several German nobles. With the help of Berno he also refounded the monastery at Doberan, which a few years later already possessed four German and twelve Slavonic villages. Henry Borwin, as early as 1179, is said to have turned over to the German knight Heinrich von Bützow half of the district of Marlow in northeastern Mecklenburg, immediately contiguous to the northwestern boundary of Pomerania, for the purpose of colonization. At any rate, we find here eight places with German names as early as 1210.

Thus, at the end of two centuries and a half of effort, after three severe reverses to their arms and years of wasting war and border strife, at last the combined strength of the feudal princes of Saxon Germany and of the no less warlike feudal bishops of the German church—men like the fierce Burckhard of Halberstadt, for example—united with the material assistance of thousands of nameless colonists who occupied the conquered lands, wore down the opposition of the Baltic Slavs.[1]

[1] In 1221 Wizlaw of Rügen said: "Gott möge es verhüten dass das Land jemals wieder in seinen früheren Zustand zurückfalle, dass die Slawen die deutschen Ansiedler vertreiben und wieder anfangen, das Land zu bebauen" (*Meckl. U.B.*, I. No. 278); quoted by Pueschl, pp. 4–5 and n. 1).

Henry the Lion was undeniably one of the greatest, perhaps the greatest, and most constructive statesmen, whom Germany possessed in the Middle Ages except Henry IV. He was a true empire-builder endowed with imagination, daring, will, and like almost all such statesmen was not averse to the use of blood and iron in achieving his imperious purposes.

Arnold of Lübeck, recognizing the continuity of history as recorded by Adam of Bremen and Helmold, and aspiring to be their continuator into the thirteenth century, appropriately pays tribute to the genius of Henry the Lion in the Prologue to his *Chronica Slavorum:*

> Et quia usque ad tempora Heinrici ducis Saxoniae atque Bavarie series decurrit, ipsum in fronte ponamus; qui super omnes, qui ante ipsum fuerunt, duritiam Sclavicam perdomui et non solum ad tributa solvenda coegit, sed etiam erga veri Dei cultum, relictis superstitionibus idololatrie, humiliatis cervicibus promptissimos fecit. Pacem etiam maximam in omni terra Sclavorum firmavit, et omnes provincie aquilonares Wagirorum, Holzatorum, Polaborum, Obotritorum ocio et quieti vacabant, et prohibita sunt furta et latrocinia terra marique, et fruebantur mutuis mercationibus et negotiationibus.

And yet, how strongly the need of German colonists was felt is indicated by a contract made in 1210 between Bishop Dietrich of Lübeck, and Heinrich Borwin, a half-Slav noble. The latter, according to the contents of the document in question, had settled German colonists on the little island of Poel, near Wismar (which politically belonged to Mecklenburg, ecclesiastically to Lübeck), "because of the poverty and small number of Slavs in that neighborhood, who were insufficient for the cultivation of the land." He insisted, as the Bishop says, that these settlers should not be held to the payment of all the church tithes, which the peasants always felt to be a very oppressive burden. The Bishop finally, though seemingly not without demur, contented himself with one-half the tithe, rendering the other half to Heinrich Borwin as a fief, an arrangement which with greater or less variation is found repeated in many of the other colonized regions.[1]

[1] Hauck, IV, 589, n. 2; 620–25. For fuller comment see Sommerfeld, pp. 136 ff.; Guttmann, *Forsch. zur Preuss. und Brand. Gesch.*, IX, 429; Wendt, II, 20 n. Many of the Slav serfs were yet pagan (Michael, I, 94–97; Kötzschke, *Unternehmerthum*, pp. 24–36).

The district of Schwerin (the region west and south of the Schweriner-See) as well as the neighboring localities, Ratzeburg and east Holstein, in the course of a short time were heavily colonized with Germans. In the diocese of Ratzeburg two generations later, among 277 settlements only 8 are mentioned as having Wendish inhabitants.

There still is one region of Transalbingia—namely, Brandenburg—whose colonization remains to be briefly considered. The two German nobles of the twelfth century who exhibited a keen yet sympathetic understanding of the problem involved in the relation of the Germans and the Slavs along the Elbe frontier were Adolph of Holstein and Albrecht the Bear of Brandenburg. The moderate and statesman-like policy of Adolph, as we have seen, was ruined by the Saxon princes, especially Henry the Lion. But Albrecht was strong enough to hold his own against the pressure and to carry out his own ideas within his territories without molestation or inhibition. In Tuttle's words:

> Albert was a statesman as well as a soldier, and by a politic liberality insinuated first his religion and then his authority upon many of the most influential Wends. Arms and diplomacy thus composed a hostile and refractory people into a body of sympathetic subjects. At the same time he fixed the conditions of his social policy on such a firm yet prudent basis that even before his death the prosperity of the Mark had begun to excite the envy of his neighbors.[1]

While yet Albrecht von Ballenstedt, before Brandenburg fell to him by the favor of fortune, Albrecht had followed Otto of Bamberg's pacific labors in Pomerania with interest, if we may believe the biographers of the bishop.[2] Certainly after 1134, in which year he acquired the Nordmark, an opportunity to study the effects of Otto of Bamberg's course in Pomerania was afforded, for the lines of the Nordmark were vague and Albrecht, in denial of the claims of Poland to

[1] Tuttle, *History of Prussia*, I, 13–14. For a fuller discussion see Guttmann, *op. cit.*, IX, 444–50; Passew, *ibid.*, Band XIV, Heft 1 (1901); Schillmann, *Grundsteinlegung zum Brand.-Preuss. Staat um die Mitte des 12. J.* (1883); Krabbo, "Albrecht der Bär," *Forsch. zur Brand.-Preuss. Gesch.*, XIX, 253.

[2] Ebbo, III, 10; Herbordus, III, 8.

Pomerania, claimed jurisdiction clear to the Oder River.[1] This Mark, in Prussian history known as the Alt-Mark, lay along the left bank of the Elbe in the bend below Magdeburg and was roughly included in the quadrangle made by the Ohre, the Aland, and the upper Aller. The eastern part formed the *pagus* Belinesheim and ecclesiastically was attached to the bishopric of Halberstadt; the western part, the *pagus* Osterwolde, belonged to the diocese of Verden.[2] In the eastern part the ancient fortresses of Werben, Tangermünde, and Arneburg guarded the Elbe; the most important place in the western half, which less needed protection, was Salzwedel. At the time of Albrecht's acquisition of the Alt-Mark the population was thin. Most of the places mentioned in documents of the tenth century as pertaining to the churches of Havelberg or Magdeburg had disappeared in the eleventh in the various wars of Slavonic reaction, or in the struggle for supremacy, in Saxony, between Albrecht and Henry the Lion.[3]

What little population there was in Brandenburg at Albrecht's accession was mixed German and Slav, a forecast of the future social composition of the country.[4] Albrecht had

[1] *Codex diplom. Pom.*, I, 33; Rachfahl, *Forsch. z. Brand. Gesch.*, Band V, Heft 2 (1892); L. Giesebrecht, *Wend. Gesch.*, II, 363; Heinemann, *Albrecht der Bär*, p. 344.

[2] Kretschmer, p. 337.

[3] "Siquidem has terras Saxones olim inhabitasse feruntur, tempore scilicet Ottonum, ut videri potest in antiquis aggeribus qui congesti fuerant super ripas Albiae in terra palustri Balsamorum, sed praevalentibus postmodum Sclavis, Saxones occisi et terra a Sclavis usque ad nostra tempora possessa" (Helm., I, 88). A charter of Conrad III to the church of Havelberg in confirmation of its possessions and privileges is unusually vivid for an official document in describing the deserted state of the Alt-Mark: ". . . . Et quoniam praenominatae civitates et villae saepe irruentibus paganis vastatae sunt ac depopulatae, adeo ut vel nullo, vel raro habitore incolantur, volumus atque praecipimus ut idem episcopus liberam absque contradictione habeat facultatem ibidem ponendi et locandi colonos, de quacumque gente voluerit vel habere potuerit" (Riedel, *Die Marck Brand.*, II, 40).

[4] "Gens illa saxonica slavica" (Riedel, *Codex diplom. Brand.*, IV, 2); "gens permixta Slavonica et Saxonica" (cited by Wendt, II, 21 n.). Both allusions are from the *Pulcavae Chronica*, which is of the fourteenth century. This, of course, would normally vitiate its evidence for the twelfth century. But Riedel (*Codex diplom. Brand.*, IV, 1; Introd., pp. ix–xvi), Heinemann (*op. cit.*, pp. 421–22, and Schillman, *op. cit.* [1882]) have shown that this chronicle embodies extracts derived from an earlier and lost Brandenburger chronicle. They have attempted to restore it. Cf. Lavisse, p. 61, n. 1; p. 71, n. 2. Of course the statement in the paragraph involves the

wisely held aloof as much as he could from participation in the Wendish Crusade of 1147, so that the broken fragments of the pagan Slavs looked upon him with a not unfriendly eye, and in 1150, when the Christian Wendish chieftain in Brandenburg died without heirs and left his territory by bequest to Albrecht, a German extension over Brandenburg was made possible without friction.[1]

Albrecht the Bear's firm yet tactful policy reconciled the Wends in his domains to German domination, while a liberal land policy induced heavy immigration by settlers from regions farther west. Brandenburg and Pomerania, where the ministry of Otto of Bamberg (1124–25, 1128–29) peacefully paved the way for the extension of German rule, are the only two Wendish lands not acquired at the price of bloodshed in the twelfth century.[2] Before Albrecht died this region, so uninviting and sparsely peopled by a mixed Wendish and German population, had become so prosperous that Brandenburg excited the envy of the Margrave's neighbors.

It is worth observing that in Brandenburg there is a striking absence of those meticulous rights, services, and obligations in this new country such as were familiar to the emigrants in their former homes. The multitude of trivial and exasperating obligations imposed upon the peasantry of older Europe at this time, and from which they had fled, is

---

burning question of whether, and how far, the population of modern Brandenburg is mixed German and Slav. For literature on this subject, in addition to that already cited, see Lavisse, *La Marche de Brandebourg*, pp. 188–94, esp. p. 192, n. 2; Guttmann, *op. cit.*, IX, 395–514, and Wendt, *Die Nationalität der Bevölkerung der deutschen Ostmarken vor dem Beginne der Germanisierung* (Göttingen, 1878). Mielke, in a remarkable study of house architecture in Brandenburg, finds Slav, Saxon, Flemish, and French types surviving, interesting evidence for the mixed ingredients of colonization in Brandenburg. See *Archiv der Gesellschaft f. Heimatskunde der Provinz Brandenburg*, Band I (1894).

[1] For an analysis of the evidence concerning this remarkable measure see Lavisse, p. 61, n. 1; Wendt, II, 21. For Albrecht's policy see Hauck, IV, 608–20.

[2] Brückner, *Die slavische Ansiedelung in der Altmark* (Leipzig, 1879); Ernst, *Forschungen zur Brand. und Preuss. Gesch.*, Band XXIII (1910); von Flans, *Ztschft. d. hist. Ver. f. Marienwerder* (1897), No. 35. For the missionary work of the Norbertiner and Cistercians (Danish) in Pomerania in the twelfth century see Hauck, IV, 588–90.

not found in Brandenburg.[1] Law and government in the early centuries of Germany's New East were simpler and more wholesome than in Western and Central Germany. The social spirit and temper of the people who settled the border provinces of Germany in the twelfth and thirteenth centuries were freer and more democratic (I use this word in a relative sense only, of course), less permeated by that class feeling which accentuated social relations in older and more feudal Germany, for the reason that the social texture of German frontier society was less complex, less closely knit. Albrecht was the freest and most untrammeled prince in Europe in the twelfth century. He was like William the Conqueror in 1066. There were few "traditional" rights and no antiquated feudal interests burdening the soil of Brandenburg when he acquired it. He could build a state and establish a society almost *de novo*. His political authority was simple and complete. Every person from peasant to baron and bishop was a subject of the Margrave.[2]

[1] Conrad III (*anno* 1150) for Havelberg: "ea videlicet libertate, ut nullus dux, nullus marchio, nullus comes, seu vicecomes, nullus advocatus seu subadvocatus aliquam exactionem exinde extorquere audeat, nullus aliquod dominium sibi usurpare presumat, nullas petitiones publicas ibi faciat, nullus eos ad ligna portanda vel secanda vel faciendas fossas cogat." Riedel, *Die Marck Brandenb.*, II, 40. The same was true of the colonists around Bremen. *Henric. Wolteri Chron. Brem.* (*ca.* 1142): "Item voluit idem archiepiscopus, quod omnes villici et cultores agrorum ejusdem ecclesiae liberi esse deberent ab omni censu civitatis vel villae et quod essent liberi ab omni advocatia" (cited by Inama Sternegg, *DWG*, II, 29, nn. 1 and 2). "Just as it was earlier customary to make leases of freshly cleared woodlands in return for a heritable rent, in order to have them cleared (*Waldhufen*, *assart*, *virgate*) so a free tenancy of inheritance known as *Gründerleihe* ("colonial tenure") was the favored form in which the colonization of Eastern Germany was realized. The German colonists were granted heritable holdings as freemen by the founders of marks, or villages, and, aside from a nominal rent paid to the owner of the land (i.e., to the territorial princes or to ecclesiastical or secular magnates) in recognition of their title, were subject only to public taxes and services which left entirely unaffected their personal status. The favorable situation of these colonists in Eastern Germany reacted in turn upon the position of the peasant population in the older parts of Germany, and caused a recedence of manorial types of tenancy. To this end the decay of the manorial organization also contributed" (Huebner, *Germanic Private Law*, sec. 45, p. 325).

[2] It must be admitted that this state of things changed with the decline of the Ascanian house in the fourteenth century and that Brandenburg in time was assimilated to the condition of the other and older principalities of Germany. But this history is later than the period with which this chapter is dealing. G. F. Knapp (*Grundherrschaft und Rittergut* [Leipzig, 1897] and *Die Bauernbefreiung und der*

The colonizing genius of the Ascanian house showed unimpaired vitality down through the thirteenth century, and then only began to decay. The progress of the margraves across the Oder after 1242 brought them into conflict with Poland. The founding of towns in the Neumark began with Frankfort on the Oder in 1253 and ended with Falkenberg in 1337. Yet great as was the importance of towns for the development of new Germany, their influence was less than that of the towns in Western Germany. On the other hand, if the burgher population was stronger in the west than in the east, the condition of the peasant population in the east was better than in the west.[1]

The peasants of Brandenburg as well as knight, baron, and bishop were all alike indebted to the Margrave for their titles to the land. If they paid established taxes, which were few and simple when compared to what obtained elsewhere in Germany, they were free.[2] No wonder, as Lavisse, writing in 1875 well said, "the German emigrant in the Middle Ages went beyond the Elbe in order to find free land as today he is crossing the Atlantic."[3]

The speed and effectiveness of this transformation of

Ursprung der Landarbeiter in den aelteren Teilen Preussens) has demonstrated that the great oppression of the peasantry does not date from the Middle Ages, and that the manorial régime in medieval Germany was not abusive, however onerous, of the rural classes. The real sufferings of the German peasantry date from the reception of the Roman law in the fifteenth century, and more still from the horrors of the Thirty Years' War. The height of oppression was in the eighteenth century, after the Seven Years' War. Cf. S. B. Fay, "The Roman Law and the German Peasant," *American Hist. Review*, XVI, 234.

[1] Niessen, *Forschungen zur Brand. und Preuss. Gesch.*, Band IV (1891); Band XVI (1903).

[2] Cf. Tuttle, *History of Prussia*, p. 29. A gloss of the *Sachsenspiegel*, which dates from the early fourteenth century, emphasizes this relation between a free soil and a freeman in Brandenburg. The peasants were free because they were the first to clear the land. "Mit uns aber, das ist in der Marck, haben die gebawer auch Erb am zinfsgut, und mögen es lassen, wenn sie wollen, welches daher kommen ist, dass unser landt also sindt besatzt worden. Denn do solches gesehen, hat man den bawern die huffen erst wildt und unangebawet ausgethan, welche, nachdem sie nochmals durch der leute arbeit sindt gebessert worden. Darumb mögen sie dieselbingen auch ihres gefallens verkeuffen" (cited in Riedel, *Die Marck Brand.*, II, 281 n.; also Lavisse, *op. cit.*, p. 204, n. 1).

[3] *Loc. cit.*

provinces and peoples which had so long resisted German sway cannot be wholly ascribed to the colonizing genius of Henry the Lion and Albrecht the Bear. Things are stronger than men. The push of two centuries of endeavor and experience was behind the movement. It does not rob them of the laurel to say that they were fortunate in their day and generation, or that they were the unconscious instruments of potential forces in the Saxon nation operating for expression and solution.

Saxon Germany had been partially transformed in economic conditions and in social texture under the rule of the Ottos. But the Salian period was a melting-pot, a vast crucible, out of which North Germany emerged with tremendous and unguessed forces pent up within her and struggling for expression. Within the two centuries represented by the rule of the Saxon and Salian houses, Germany—especially North Germany—was radically transformed, in economic and social condition. Population had become denser; competition keener; life more complex.[1] In a word, old Germany had become feudalized.

Colonization and reclaiming of land entirely changed the condition of the rural population between the tenth and thirteenth centuries. In the time of the Carolingians wood and land had still been regarded as inexhaustible goods of the nation, like the sun, air and water. But now the limitations of the geographical basis of national life appeared more and more clearly. There had been an immense range of land to grow food upon; but now the supply became limited, chiefly and first on the Rhine, in Swabia and Franconia, afterwards in Saxony, and finally in Bavaria, the Tyrol and Styria. The people had to shift on a limited area. The soil became more than before an object of economic value. Its price kept continually increasing. In the twelfth century in some prosperous districts, land seems to have attained twelve times the value it had in the ninth and afterwards even down to the second half of the thirteenth century an increase of about 50 per cent is to be observed. Taking into consideration that land was still regarded, especially by the ruling classes as the only basis of social and political influence (though already other sources of large

[1] In 1222 Caesar of Prüm wrote of the advancement of agriculture and the agrarian civilization of Germany since 893 as follows: "In tempore tam diuturno constat multas silvas esse extirpatas, villas edificatas, decimas auctas, multa molendina sunt in praefato tempore edificata ac multe vinee plantate, terre infinite culte" (*Mittelrheinisches Urkundenbuch*, I, 201; cf. Lamprecht, *DWL*, II, 50).

incomes were gradually arising), we may understand how intense the struggle for the possession of the soil must have been at this period.[1] On the other hand, we also find that increase of population induced emigration from the older parts of Germany into the New East.[2]

A knowledge of American history is not without value for an understanding of this movement. A young nation discovers the marks and *indicia* of its growth which are undiscernible in the early history of an old nation, whose tree trunk is covered with the lichen and moss of centuries. The newer, fresher, nearer history of America embodies principles of social development and the play of economic forces which have been foreign to Europe for six hundred years. It still holds in solution, as it were, institutions which have been crystallized for generations across the sea. Friedrich List, the German economist, when he visited America early in the nineteenth century, clearly perceived the sequence of frontiers in our history. Indeed, he is the first who formulated the fact historically. In his *National System* he wrote:

> There one may see wildernesses grow into rich and mighty states; and progress which requires centuries in Europe goes on there before one's eyes, viz.: that from the condition of the mere hunter to the rearing of cattle, from that to agriculture, and from the latter to manufactures and commerce.

More than thirty years ago the Italian economist Loria said that "America has the key to the historical enigma which Europe has sought for centuries."

Every student of American history knows the effect of the westward movement upon New England in the depletion of the population, the increase of the number of abandoned farms, the gradual degeneration of the "stay-at-homes" owing to the fact that the strongest and sturdiest blood had

[1] Lamprecht, *DG*, III, 56–57. See also G. von Buchwald, *Zur deutschen Wirtschaftsgesch. in endenden Mittelalter* (1885) and an article by Schaeffler and Brandl in *Archivalische Ztschrift.* (1880).

[2] "Multa milia puerorum a sex annis et supra usque ad virilem aetatem .... quidam aratra vel currus quos minabant, alii pecora, que pascebant, vel si qua alia habebant pre manibus relinquunt" (Lamprecht, *DWL*, I, 1,463 and n. 1, from *Chron. Reg.* [1213], p. 191). The exodus was so great that there is complaint of abandoned farms and even whole villages in Hohenstaufen times.

emigrated, empty houses and grass-grown streets in the towns, etc. But it comes with something like a shock to discover these same phenomena and identical complaints with reference to the older parts of Germany in the late Middle Ages.[1]

The frontier between the German and the Slav in the twelfth century interestingly exhibits characteristics which are familiar to every student of the history of American westward expansion. That "return to primitive conditions in a continually advancing frontier line, and a new development of that area," which Professor Turner has pointed out as so significant in the history of the formation of the West is true of the east border of Germany in the twelfth century. Border ruffians and robbers infested the Marches.[2] One is reminded of Morris Birkbeck's observation touching the condition of southern Indiana in 1817:

> The inhabitants of Indiana . . . . are lawless, semibarbarous vagabonds, dangerous to live among. . . . . An unsettled country, lying contiguous to one that is settled, is always a place of retreat for rude and even abandoned characters, who find the regulations of society intolerable.

By the beginning of the twelfth century Germany had become historically conscious of the worth of its frontier and as eager to occupy it as our forefathers here in America were. What the trans-Allegheny country was to the United States in 1800 that the trans-Elbean country was to Germany in 1200. The hardy rustics who tilled their little farms redeemed from marsh and swamp and forest in Ditmarsch and Holstein, in Mecklenburg and Brandenburg, were men like unto our own ancestors in conditions of livelihood, in courage, in hope, in perseverance. Life on the East German border then was rude and crude and impinged as sharply upon the feelings of the cultured and refined society of older Germany as the Kentucky of Boone grated upon the sensibilities of staid tidewater communities like Baltimore or Philadelphia. The frontier as it advanced geographically reflected the reactions

[1] See Lamprecht, *DWL*, I, 2, 871, for citations.

[2] Helm., I, 49, 66, 67, 87.

between the physiography and the society settling it by modifying inherited institutions to meet new conditions.[1]

An analogy between the two frontiers, though so far removed in time and place from each other, is not a fanciful one. The greed of the Americans for the lands of the Indians, and the intolerance of the rifleman toward the Red Man, has a parallel in the conduct of the Saxons toward the Wends. The history of the Cherokees has its prototype in medieval Germany. The protest of the nameless Abodrite chief in Helmold, I, 53, against the erection of the *castellum* of Sigeberg reminds one of the harangue of that Delaware chief recorded by Heckewelder. Niklot's reply to Adolph of Holstein

[1] By far the most important difference between East-Elbean and West-Elbean Germany was in the character of the agrarian system prevailing. The researches of G. von Below, *Territorium und Stadt;* of T. Knapp, *Gesammelte Beiträge zur Rechts- und Wirtschaftsgeschichte;* of Fuchs (translated in Carver's *Readings in Rural Economics*, pp. 223–53, under the title "The Epochs of German Agrarian History and Policy"), have done much to modify or supplement the earlier work of Meitzen and Hanssen. The country east of the Elbe was, and still is, pre-eminently the region of great patrimonial landed estates (*Gutsherrschaften*). In the words of Fuchs: "It was a threefold landed proprietorship, that of the reigning prince, of the German cloisters, which received as gifts vast tracts of land for colonization with German peasants, and of the great vassals constituting the high German and native nobility. . . . . The large manorial estates in the East were from the very beginning geographically closed domains." For excellent general accounts of the contrast between these great produce-yielding estates of the cultivating lords to the east of the Elbe (*Gutsherrschaften*) and the rent-yielding estates of landlords in the south and west of Germany (*Grundherrschaften*) see G. v. Below, *op. cit.* (Leipzig, 1900), pp. 1–96, and T. Knapp, *Gesammelte Beiträge zur Rechts- und Wirtschaftsgeschichte* (Tübingen, 1902), pp. 348–88 (reprinted from *Zeitschrift d. Savigny-Stiftung*, XIX [1898], 16–51). Monographs on special regions are noted in Dahlmann-Waitz, *Quellenkunde der deutschen Geschichte* (8th ed.; Leipzig, 1912), Nos. 2173–2275. The ground plans of these new towns in the East, the structure of villages, and the history which may be read in different forms of house- and barn-building types which moved with the German colonists across the whole of North Germany from the Low Countries to the Vistula, may be mentioned here as subjects which have yielded rich results to German scholarship. See Fritz, *Deutsche Stadtanlagen* (Strassburg, 1894), with ground plans of German "colonial" towns; Heil, *Die deutschen Städte und Bürger im Mittelalter* (Leipzig, 1912); Meilke, *Das deutsche Dorf* (Leipzig, 1913), and especially Püschel, *Das Anwachsen der deutschen Städte in der Zeit der mittelalterlichen Kolonialbewegung* (Berlin, 1910), which shows the relation between German eastward expansion and agricultural prosperity and urban growth. He has studied the topography of fifteen towns. There is an admirable map in *Deutsche Erde*, VIII, 256, illustrating East German colonization by the spread of types of German house architecture. It interestingly confirms the historical facts set forth in this chapter. In the same volume, p. 80, may be seen ground plans of these various house types.

Lübeck (center)

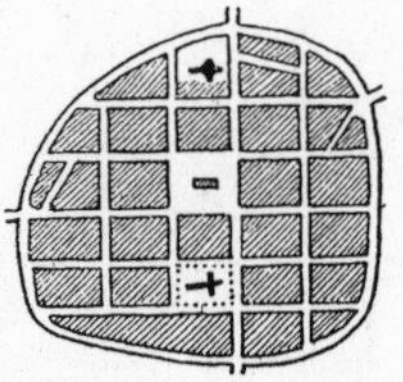

New Brandenburg in Mecklenburg-Strelitz

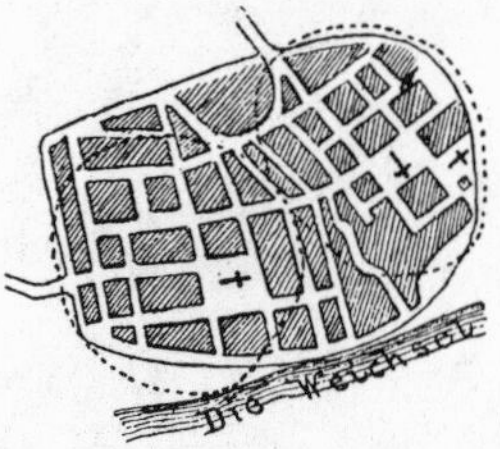

Thorn

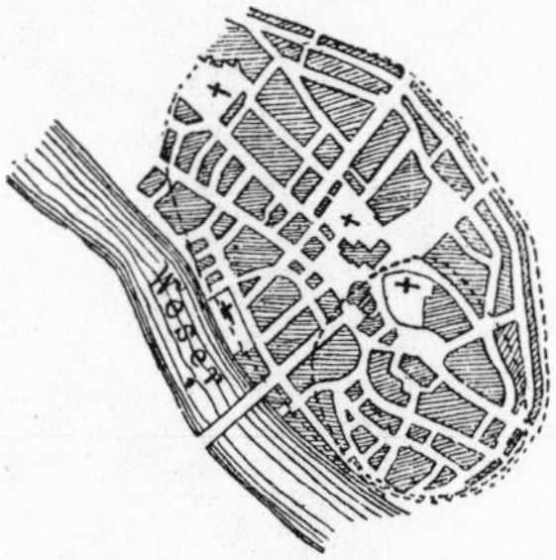

Bremen

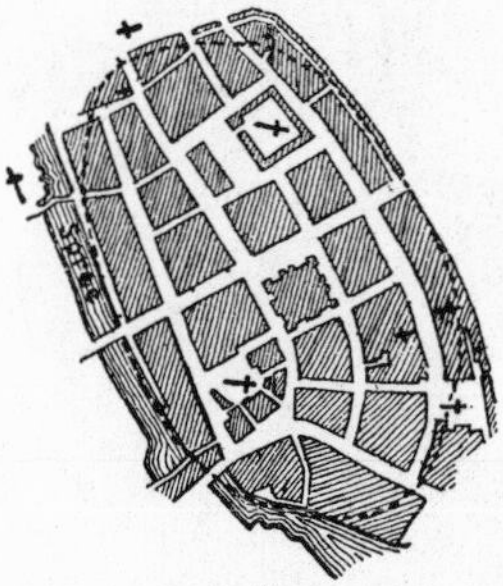

Berlin

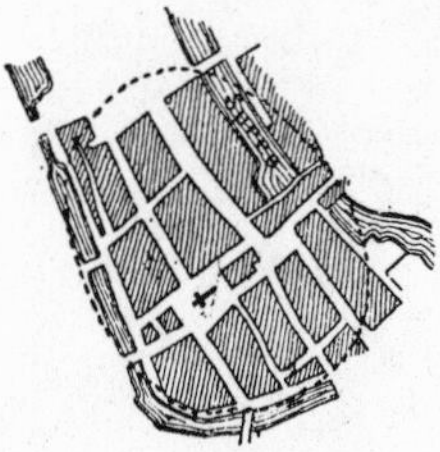

Çölln

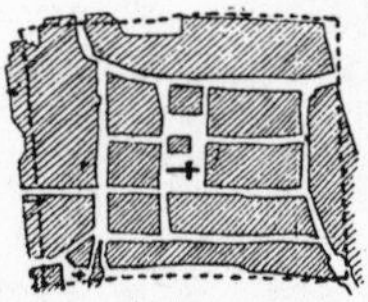

Hildesheim (Neustadt *ca.* 1230)

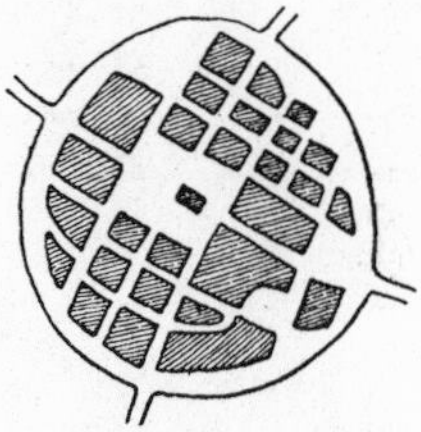

Reichenbach in Silesia

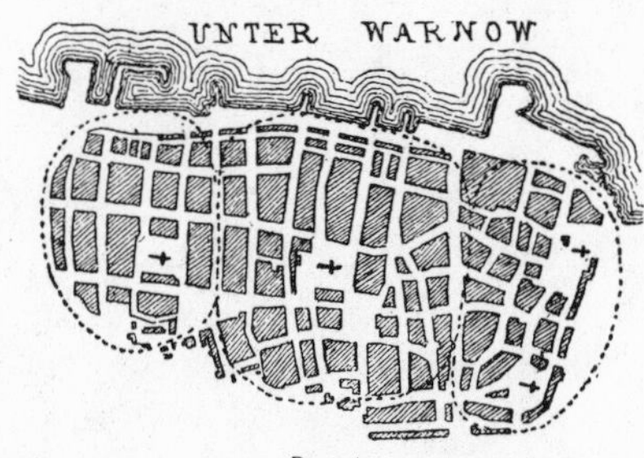

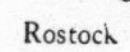

Rostock

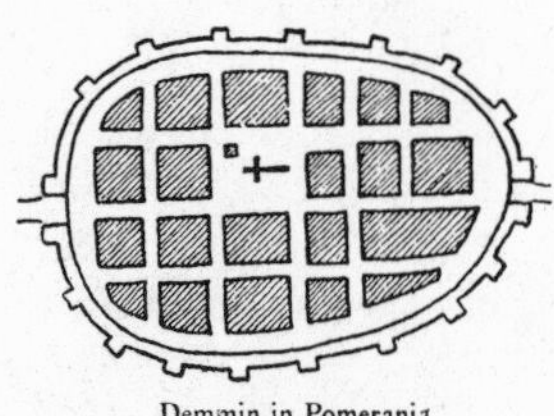

Demmin in Pomerania

GROUND PLANS OF "NEW TOWNS" IN EAST GERMANY

is like that of a friendly Indian chief whose friendship has been betrayed.[1]

Every great nation, however old, has gone through a long, formative stage of development. If we could clear away the mold of ages of history around the roots of the nations, we not only would know more of their history but we probably would also perceive that there are certain primary characteristics which are roughly common to the formative period of every people. There is a parallel, not absolute, of course, but relative between the border history of medieval Germany and that of America. The German pioneer faced the wolf and the Wend; he endured the isolation and sometimes the desolation of his settlements; he felled the forests; he drained the swamps; he built up a civilization—often, it is true, with crude instruments and with unskilled hands. But for his own time, for his own country, for his own people, he accomplished a work as large and as lasting as the formation of our own Ohio and Mississippi commonwealths has been for the United States.

The endeavor has been made in this chapter to trace the history of German eastward expansion from its inception down to the time when the Elbe became a German river. Perhaps one might take as culminating dates of the movement the year 1134, when Albrecht the Bear acquired Brandenburg, and 1158, the year in which Henry the Lion became possessed of Lübeck. Effective, permanent German life across the great river practically began with these two events. It is to be noticed, however, that these dates terminate only the first period of the history of German colonization.

While the rulers of Brandenburg, Mecklenburg, and Pomerania were slowly building the superstructure of a great Germanic civilization in North Germany, which was to reach brilliant culmination in the cities of the Hanseatic League, the forward movement still drove on eastward over Pomerellia and Livland, and clear around the bight of the Baltic into Kurland and Esthonia.[2] When once the Baltic Slavs were crushed, the tribes east of them, long since de-

[1] Helm., I, 62.

[2] Cf. Hauck, IV, 627–57.

serted by Christianized Poland and Bohemia, fell an easy conquest to the German sword. Once the Elbe was permanently crossed, the other rivers were slight barriers to German advance. One after the other, in rapid succession, the Slav towns at the mouths of the Baltic rivers—Danzig, Riga, Reval—fell into German hands.

It is with a sensation akin to astonishment that the historian reads the record of this continued eastward expansion. For over three hundred years the fecund *Mutterland* sent her children forth from the Old West into the New East, to build roads, to bridge rivers, to clear forests, to drain swamps, to establish towns, to found a civilization in the wilderness. As a story of a great people, as the history of empire-building, the making of the German Northeast in the Middle Ages is matched only by the formation of our own great Northwest. What Burke said of the American colonists when he made the rafters of St. Stephens ring with his oratory in that masterful speech on conciliation with the colonies, "We cannot, we cannot falsify the pedigree of this fierce people," may be as well applied to the German settlers of Mecklenburg, Brandenburg, Pomerania, Livonia, as to the New England colonists.

> In the year of the incarnation of the Word, 1186, the episcopal see in Livonia was founded in the place called Riga. And because that region abounded in many good things owing to the beneficence of the soil, Christian settlers never failed there, and planters of the new church. For the land was one of fertile fields, of abundant pasture, well watered by rivers full of fish, and well covered with trees. . . . . Moved by the impassioned preaching of the lord abbot Berthold of Loccum not a few well to do and gentry, for to break the strength of the heathen and to establish the religion of Christ took the road of migration. . . . . A vast number of them came from all Saxony, from Westphalia, from Frisia, prelates and priests, soldiers, merchants, rich and poor, unto Lübeck where were vessels laden with arms and foodstuffs, whence they went to Livonia.[1]

These words were written by Arnold of Lübeck concerning the colonization of Livland between 1186 and 1196. The spirit of these settlers in the Slavonic wilderness beyond the Vistula is not far from that which actuated those who came to America in the seventeenth century.

[1] Arnold of Lübeck, *Chron. Slav.*, V, 30.

It is a long tale, this history of German eastward expansion and colonization, to which I now bring a term. It is a history of blood and iron, of strong men and women, of lusty strife, of daring adventure, of hard work. As the dust cloud of the arena sometimes obscures the figures of the racing horses, so in the thick turmoil of this strenuous expansion of a great people we may sometimes lose sight of the greater process which worked itself out.

For there was a great process in the movement and an increasing purpose striving for realization. The colonization of the New Northeast was the product of a great faith and great works. It had in it that elemental energy which all discovery and new conquest possess.

It was the great deed of the common people of medieval Germany,[1] just as the making of the American West has been the achievement of the common people of America, from whose loins, "new birth of a new soil," sprang the first American. What the "Old Northwest" has been to the United States, that, in much the same degree and similar way, was the Northeast—the trans-Elbean-Oder country—to medieval Germany.

Nor were the conditions which these German colonists encountered in the new land so different from those endured by the settlers of New England. With change of time and place, this extract from Peter von Dusburg's *Chronicon terrae Prussiae*[2] would fit into Winthrop's *Journal*, or Bradford's *Plymouth Plantation:*

> For they had left the sweet soil of their native country and entered into an alien land, in which their future was to be, where for many years they were destined to endure hardships without hope of return homeward even unto the fourth or sixth generation of them. They came from a fertile homeland, peaceful and quiet, and penetrated a country of horror and

[1] "In den Landen deutscher Zunge, in denen die traditionelle Macht des Adels heute noch am besten erhalten ist, ist er fast völlig frei von allem Blute der altfreien Edelgeschlechter. An der Kolonisation des deutschen Ostens hat der altdeutsche Adel keinen anderen Anteil gehabt, als ihn die wenigen Dynastenhäuser dieser Gebiete und einige wenige Prälaten und Ordensritter nahmen. Schon Hermann von Salza war ein Dienstmann" (Aloys Schulte, *Der Adel und die deutsche Kirche*, p. 300).

[2] *SS. rerum Prussicarum*, quoted in Kötzschke, *Quellen*, No. 39; cf. Hauck, IV, 642–52.

vast solitude and filled with baneful war. In a word, putting behind their backs an abundance of everything in this world, liberty, home, honor, they accepted hunger and thirst, endured infinite poverty, endless discomfort, failures and perils.

For about seventy-five years the Vistula River remained the boundary between the expanding German and the shrinking Slavonic world. Then, early in the thirteenth century, the Teutonic Knights, having no longer a field in the Holy Land, and driven out of Hungary, found a new field of conquest, in 1231, in Prussia.

By 1346 their rule extended clear to the Gulf of Finland. Prussia, Courland, Livonia, and Esthonia were conquered in succession. As each region was conquered a fortress was built to enforce obedience and to serve as a base for further operations; that of Marienburg is a conspicuous example of such a castle. German settlers were introduced to colonize and redeem the devastated lands. The energy of the Knights in building towns was remarkable. By 1400 they had ninety-three cities, the most important of which were Riga and Reval.

CHAPTER XIV

EARLY TRADE RELATIONS BETWEEN THE GERMANS AND THE ELBEAN AND BALTIC SLAVS

THE HISTORY of German eastward expansion in the Middle Ages is the *Vorgeschichte* of the Hanseatic League. Unfortunately few Hanseatic historical writers go back to the founding of Lübeck in 1143, and none farther than Lothar II's diploma of 1134. It is true that effective commercial life did not begin in North Germany until the rise of Lübeck. But the founding of Lübeck was as much the term of one epoch as it was the point of departure for a new period. Bächtold in his excellent *Der norddeutsche Handel im 12. und beginnenden 13. Jahrhundert*[1] perceived that the history of the genesis of the Hansa had not received its due proportion of treatment; but the limitations of his subject prevented him from going farther back than the twelfth century. It is this neglected aspect of the history of medieval German commerce which I have tried to relate in this chapter.

In spite of the immemorial antagonism between the two races, from early times a certain amount of border trade seems always to have existed between the Germans and the Slavs. Desire for commercial aggrandizement was a not unimportant motive of German eastward expansion and subjugation of the Slavs.[2] As far back as the first half of the

[1] Rothschild (Berlin and Leipzig, 1910).

[2] "Kaufleute, Krieger und Priester," Wendt, *Die Germanisierung der Länder östlich der Elbe*, I, 10. (Liegnitz, 1884). Bugge, "Die nordeuropäischen Verkehrswege im frühen Mittelalter," *Vierteljahrschrift f. Soz. und Wirtschaftsgesch.*, IV, 237, has written: "Die grösste Bedeutung der nördlichen Völker für die Handelsgeschichte liegt doch darin, dass sie überall im Auslande, wo sie im 9., 10. und 11. Jahrhundert als Eroberer hinkamen, Städte und Handelsniederlassungen gründeten. Dadurch wurde dem ganzen Verkehrsleben des nördlichen Europas neues Leben eingehaucht und der Welthandel in neue Bahnen gelenkt."

seventh century there is mention of adventurous Frankish traders penetrating into the Slavonic wilderness, bartering for slaves, amber, and beaver and marten skins.

In the reign of Dagobert I (629–39) an alleged renegade Frankish trader named Samo established commercial relations with the pagan Bohemians, Moraven, and Carinthians, and is said finally to have abjured Christianity and to have established a short-lived barbarian state which extended from the Drave and Silesia[1] to the frontier of Thuringia, and which was powerful enough to defeat the Frankish arms and important enough to have its alliance sought by the Byzantine emperor Heraclius.[2]

That a brisk commercial intercourse between the Frankish state and Samo's kingdom existed in the seventh century is

[1] Grünhagen, *Gesch. Schlesiens*, p. 4.

[2] Fredegar, *Chronicon*, IV, 48, "ex pago Senonago" (cf. 68 and 75). Usually this reading has been accepted as meaning Sens or Soignies. If so this would make Samo a Frank. But there is room for doubt. Apart from the dubious geographical reading and translation thereof, the name Samo does not sound like a German name, but a Slav. Certain it is that Czech tradition has connected Samo with the Bohemian national house of Przemysel-Schreuer, *Vierteljahrschrift f. Soz. und Wirtschaftsgesch.*, V, No. 2 (1907), 197–213; Goldmann, *Mitteil. d. Inst. für oesterr. Gesch.*, XXX, No. 2 (1909); Schafarik, *Slawische Alterthümer*, II, 416–20. For the extension of Samo's rule to Thuringia see Peisker, *Cambridge Med. Hist.*, II, 451 and note; for Samo and the Slavs in Carinthia, J. Goll, "Samo und die Karantischen Slawen," *Mitteil. d. Inst. für oesterr. Gesch.*, XI (1890), 443–46. Inama Sternegg, *DWG*, I, 234; Schulze, *Die Kolonisierung und Germanisierung der Gebiete zwischen Saale und Elbe*, pp. 5–7; Meitzen, *Siedelung und Agrarwesen*, II, 150, 405–6; Lippert, *Sozial-Gesch. Böhmens*, I, 219, all notice the trade importance of this item.

Peisker, in his article on the expansion of the Slavs in the *Cambridge Mediaeval History*, II, 451, argues that the chronology of Samo's reign must be corrected, for his overthrow of the Avars must have taken place some time between 602 and 605, most probably in 603. He points out that the revolt of the Croats and the Serbs, and finally the Bulgar Khan's revolt, followed in the years between 635 and 641. However, other dates also in Peisker's article differ from those commonly accepted, and no explanation is offered for this change of chronology. It is interesting to note in this connection, however, that another circumstance seems to favor Peisker's contention. According to his chronology, Samo died about the year 637–40. Duke Radulf (Fredegarius, *Chronicon*, IV, 75, 77) was put in command of Thuringia, to protect that territory from the inroads of the Slavs. He, however, became involved in some difficulties with Sigibert, the son of Dagobert, and finally rebelled against him. In order to strengthen his position, he sought alliance with the neighboring peoples, and most probably with the Bohemian Slavs also. This was in 641 (*ibid.*, IV, 77, 87), and it is noteworthy that the name of Samo—who certainly was an outstanding character and was well known to the chronicler—is not mentioned. This would indicate that he may have been dead by that time.

evident from the incident that some Frankish merchants were killed in Bohemia in 631, and when King Dagobert sent an ambassador to Samo, this untactful messenger insulted him and Samo had him literally thrown out of the country.[1] After that Dagobert invaded the country with an army composed of Allemanni, Bavarians, and even of Longobards from Italy, but was decisively defeated at Wogastiburc. As a positive result of this victory of Samo's, the Sorben chieftain Drevan fell away from his allegiance to the Frankish state and joined Samo's kingdom. Samo became thoroughly domesticated in the country of his adoption, and is said to have married at least twelve wives; if we may believe Fredegar, he had twenty-two sons and fifteen daughters. He ruled thirty-five years; when he died, the great territory which he had consolidated seems to have fallen back into its component parts again.

In the next century the *Life of Sturmi*, Boniface's disciple, and abbot of Fulda, who died in 779, shows that a regular trade route ran from the Saale River to Mainz through the Thuringian Forest.[2] In 805 (probably, the date is not certain) Charlemagne for the first time legislated in regulation of this border traffic, and established a chain of fortified trading posts along the Slavonic frontier from the mouth of the Elbe to the middle Danube. These posts were Bardowick and Schesel (near later Hamburg), Erfurt[3] in Saxony, Magdeburg on the great bend of the Elbe, Halstat (near later Bamberg), Pfreimt (in the later Ober Pfalz), at the confluence of the Wald Nab and the Pfreimt to form the Nab, Forchheim, Lorch, and Regensburg on the Danube at the mouth of the Nab.[4]

[1] *Ibid.*, "aejectus est Sicharius de conspectu Samonis."

[2] "Tunc quadam die . . . . pervenit ad viam a Turingorum regione mercandi causa ad Mogontiam pergentes ducit . . . . ibi magnam Sclavorum multitudinem reperit" (*MGH*, SS. II, 369, chap. vii). Cf. Rettberg, *Kirchengesch. Deutschlands*, I, 372; Dopsch, *Wirtschaftsentwicklung der Karolingerzeit*, II, 191.

[3] A letter of Pope Zacharias in 742 mentions Erfurt as "jam olim urbs paganorum rusticorum."

[4] Cap. Miss. in Theodonis Villa, chap. vii (*MGH*, SS. XI, 1, p. 133); ed. Boretius, 123, No. 44. For discussion of this legislation see Schulze, *op. cit.*, pp. 13–14; Dopsch, *Wirtschaftsentwicklung der Karolingerzeit*, II, 190; Waitz, *Deutsche Verfassungsgesch.*

Although the Frankish sources are silent as to the nature of this border trade, except the mention of arms, the exportation of which Charlemagne forbade, we know from other evidence what its character must have been. This evidence has to do with the economy of the Baltic Slavs.

They were a lowland people by nature, and the western or Baltic Slavs in the course of their expansion found a natural habitat in the vast marsh and lake region of modern Mecklenburg, Brandenburg, and Pomerania. Even at the present time these regions abound with lakes. There are 329 in Mecklenburg, the largest of which is the Schweriner-See; and more than 450 in East Prussia. Geologists estimate that in the twelfth century there were over 2,000 lakes in East Prussia alone. Medieval chroniclers show, and modern geology confirms their statements, that the whole territory in the valleys of the Elbe, the Oder, and the Vistula in the Middle Ages was dotted with lakes and ponds and covered with swamps.

The alluvial soil was fertile. Fish and game abounded. Communication was much by means of boats made of alder wood, so light as to be easily carried. They were poled or punted instead of rowed. Horses were used for war, but not for farming. The nobles estimated their wealth in terms of possession of horses. In the Wendish towns a market was held twice a week.[1]

In such a country only the dry islets were capable of cultivation, so that the agriculture of the Baltic Slavs was never as highly developed as that of the Germans. Cattle were scarce and horses even rarer. Two oxen were reckoned to the "plowland," which shows that the farms of the Slavs were small. Their plow was a tree, the trunk being the beam and the lopped-off projection of a strong limb the plowshare. It had no share and no edge.[2]

(2d ed.), IV, 51; Mühlbacher, *Deutsche Gesch.*, p. 285; Wendt, I, 21–22; Püschl, pp. 107–8. For the location of these posts see Maps 26A, 26B, in *Cambridge Mediaeval History*, Vol. II.

[1] Herbordus, *Dialogus*, II, 1, 21, 23, 26, 41; III, 17.

[2] For contemporary comment see Helmold, *Chronica Slavorum*, I, 12, 14, 88; Heinrici, *Chron. Lyvoniae*, II, 7; *Monumenta Lubensia* (ed. Wattenbach), p. 15.

Frontier Trading Posts with Slavs in Time of Charlemagne (Underlined)

Bee-keeping with all Slavonic peoples almost amounts to a passion, and the Baltic Slavs plied a brisk trade with the Germans in honey and wax for church candles and the sealing of documents.[1] Flax was much grown in the lowlands, and linen cloth or canvas an article of export.[2] Herbordus, the biographer of Otto of Bamberg, the apostle to the Pomeranians in the first quarter of the twelfth century, says that the Pomeranians wore shirts and trousers made of linen in summer.[3] Before this time, when German coin began to circulate among them,[4] strips of linen passed as currency like wampum among the American Indians in early colonial times. Weaving, pottery-making, and wood-carving were the principal industrial occupations.[5] Fishing, both fresh- and salt-water fishing, was a universal means of livelihood. Like the Norse, the Slavs of the Baltic coast were pirates and slave traders.[6]

We know nothing about the trade intercourse between the Germans and the Slavs in the ninth century, and it may be doubted if, in those tumultuous days of the break-up of the Frankish Empire, there was much. On the other hand,

---

For modern commentary see Langethal, *Gesch. der deutschen Landwirtschaft*, I, 51, 96, 379; II, 246; von der Goltz, *Gesch. der deutschen Landwirtschaft*, I, 128–29; Dopsch, II, 136; Michael, *Gesch. des deutschen Volkes*, p. 100.

[1] The church in Otto I's reign collected the Slav tithe in honey (*MGH*, Dip. I, 418, 603; II, 40). Payments in wax, furs, hemp, and flax are also recorded. Silver is first heard of along the Wendish border in 965 (Guttmann, *Forschungen zur brand. und preuss. Gesch.*, IX, 416).

[2] Adam of Bremen, II, 19; IV, 18; Helmold, I, 12, 14, 88. The merchants in Wagria in the time of Vicelin (1127) must have been buyers of Slav linen and furs.

[3] Herbordus, *ibid.*, II, 28. These linens were sometimes embroidered (*picturata*).

[4] Helmold, I, 38 (ed. Schmeidler, pp. 76–77). "Porro apud Ranos [Rugians] non habetur moneta, nec est in comparandis rebus nummorum consuetudo, sed quicquid in foro mercari volueris, panno lineo comparabis. Aurum et argentum quod forte per rapinas et captiones hominum vel undecumque adepti sunt, aut uxorum suarum cultibus impendunt, aut in erarium dei conferunt." Saxo Grammaticus describes at length the great Slav temple at Arcona sacred to the god Svantovit, with the tributes brought thither from all Slavonia. See English translation by O. Elton, pp. 393–95.

[5] Herbordus, II, 32.

[6] L. Giesebrecht, *Wendische Geschichten*, I, 205 f.

the Danes, with whom piracy and trade went hand in hand,[1] established commercial relations with the Slavs of the Baltic early in the period of their expansion. The little port of Reric (near later Wismar[2] which was not founded until 1237), where the Danes had got a foothold on the mainland, is mentioned in the *Annals* of Einhard (*anno* 808) as being frequented by Danish merchants.[3] These traders were chiefly men of Schleswig, from the port of Hadeby.[4] Fish and fur were the principal articles of trade, the importance of the former appearing as early as the ninth century;[5] as for fur, a yearly gift of marten skins was exacted by the Danish king of the Schleswiger merchants as late as the middle of the twelfth century.[6]

At the end of the tenth century, the piracy of the Danes, while not yet wholly abandoned,[7] had passed through the stage of foray. Their expeditions in the time of Harold Bluetooth (935–85), Sweyn (985–1014), and Knut (1014–35) took the form of territorial conquest and commercial expansion beyond sea. The Baltic policy of Denmark was to get a foothold at the mouths of the rivers, and so control the Wendish trade. The most important of such possessions was Jomsburg, on the island of Wollin at the mouth of the Oder, the seat of the famous brotherhood of pirates known as the Jomsvikings, which seems to have been established in the time of Harold Bluetooth.[8]

[1] See my article, "The Commerce of France in Ninth Century," *Journal of Political Economy* (November, 1915), pp. 865–67; Bugge, *loc. cit.;* Dopsch, II, 183–86.

[2] "In portu qui Wissemer dicitur" (*Codex Pomer. Diplom.*, No. 31).

[3] Bugge, *op. cit.*, p. 237, n. 243; Biereye, *Beiträge zur Gesch. Nordalbingiens im 10. Jahrhundert* (Berlin diss., 1909), p. 15. In Herbordus, III, 2, is an account of a Pomeranian of Stettin who traded with Denmark, and had six vessels.

[4] Biereye, *op. cit.*, p. 9 and n. 2; Bugge, *op. cit.*, pp. 232–33. Schwerin is first mentioned in 1018 by Thietmar, *Chronicon*, IX, 5.

[5] Herbordus, II, 1, p. 51; Vogel, *Hansische Geschichtsblätter* (1907), Heft 1, p. 56. Marten skins were much imported from Birka in Sweden (Adam of Bremen, II, 62).

[6] Biereye, *op. cit.*, p. 9, n. 3.

[7] For a mass of evidence see Richter, *Annalen der deutschen Gesch.*, III, 154–55; Haskins, *Normans in Europe*, p. 43.

[8] Wollin—or at least the Slav tribe Vuloini, whence the name came—is first mentioned by Widukind, *Rerum gestarum Saxonicarum*, III (*anno* 967), 69. Cf.

Wollin, at the mouth of the Oder, which must have been the chief point of connection between the Danish-Baltic trade and that of Eastern and Southeastern Europe,[1] reached its height in the first half of the eleventh century.[2] While Rurik and the Swedes in the ninth century had opened the famous Varangian Route from the Baltic to the Black Sea and Constantinople via Lake Ladoga, Novgorod, and the Dnieper, yet the shortest route between the two seas was across the isthmus via the Oder or the Vistula to Cracow and thence down the Pruth or Dniester.[3]

Adam of Bremen, *Gesta Hammaburg, eccl. pontif.*, II, 19; Herbordus, *Dialogus*, II, 24 and 34. Ebbo, *Vita Ottonis*, II, 7, severally describes it under the name of Jumna or Jumneta in the eleventh and twelfth centuries. It was the seat of the famous Jomsburg vikings, on which see Ersch and Gruber, *Encyclopädie*, XXII, 370–78; Bugge, *op. cit.*, pp. 242–43; Larsen, *The King's Household in England before the Norman Conquest*, pp. 154–57. Giesebrecht, *op. cit.*, I, 205, thinks Wollin was the present Swinemünde. But all other historians and philologists like Schafarik, *Slawische Alterthümer*, II, 576; Kemplin, *Baltische Studien*, XIII, 1, are agreed that Jomsburg, Wollin, Jumna, Jumneta, Vineta, were one and the same place. For latest information on this obscure question see C. Niebuhr, "Die Nachrichten von der Stadt Jumne," *Hans. Geschichtsbl.*, XXIII (1917); J. F. Leutz-Spitta, "Neues Material zur Vinetafrage," *Ztschft. Mannus*, VIII (1917). Another port, Truso, now Drausen, near the mouth of the Vistula, is mentioned in the travels of Wulfston by Alfred the Great (see Sweet's ed. of *A-. S. Orosius*, p. 19). Whether the Danes were trading there as early as the tenth century is not known (Bugge, *op. cit.*, p. 238).

[1] ". . . . apud Sliaswig, quae et Heidaba dicitur. . . . . Ex eo portu naves emitti solent in Sclavaniam vel Suediam vel ad Semlant usque in Graciam" (Adam of Bremen, *Descriptio insularum Aquilonis*, 1).

[2] See the long description of it in Adam of Bremen, *Gesta*, etc., II, 19. For the magnitude and extent of Danish trade at this time, in addition to the article by Bugge already cited, see *Baltische Studien von der Gesellschaft für Pommersche Geschichte und Alterthumskunde* (Stettin, 1885–92), Nos. 7, 13, 25.

[3] There is a very extensive literature upon the subject of early Balto-Slavonic-Byzantine commerce. See Peisker, *Vierteljahrschrift f. Soz- und Wirtschaftsgesch.*, III, Nos. 2, 3, 4 (1905); Heyd, *Histoire du commerce du Levant*, I, 68–86; Wilken, "Die Verhältnisse der Russen zum byzant. Reich im 9.–12. Jahrh.," *Abhandl. der Berl. Akad.* (1829), pp. 75 ff.; Lelewel, "Tableau historique du commerce des Slavons," *Numismatique du moyen-âge*, Part III, pp. 98 ff.; Jacob, *Der nordisch-baltische Handel der Araber im Mittelalter* (Leipzig, 1887) (with bib., pp. 126–27); Bugge, "Der Untergang der norwegischen Schiffahrt," *Vierteljahrschrift für Soz. und Wirtschaftsgesch.*, XII, 1, 245–50; Bury, *History of the Eastern Roman Empire* (802–67), pp. 402 f.; Guttmann, *Forschungen zur brand. und preuss. Gesch.*, IX, 399–400; Lamprecht, *Deutsche Geschichte*, III, 346–51; Fisher, *Mediaeval Empire*, II, 4–5; Wendt, *Germanisierung der Länder östlich d. Elbe*, I, 14–15; Schumann, *Baltische Studien* (N.F., 1902), VI; Fiddichow, *Monatsbl. v. d. Gesellschaft für pom. Gesch.* (1896);

But independently of this Wendish-Byzantine commerce, the nearer commerce of the Baltic Slavs was worth striving for by Denmark. Stettin, at the mouth of the Peene, Danzig at the mouth of the Vistula, Colberg, were rivals of Wollin, while inland the Slav towns of Wiligrad (Mecklenburg), Stargard (Oldenburg), Demmin, Cammin, and Schwerin, which have preserved their original Wendish name, were important places long before Bremen and Hamburg and Lübeck, the last of which was not founded until 1143.[1]

The long and bloody warfare waged against the Baltic Slavs by the Saxon Germans was partly motivated by religious bigotry, partly by land-hunger, and partly by a wish to acquire possession of the mouths of the rivers flowing into the Baltic, in order to control the Wendish[2] trade. The conquest was not completed until the Wendish Crusade (1147) finally subdued Mecklenburg and Brandenburg beyond all

---

Beltz, *Jahrb. f. Mecklenb. Gesch.*, LVIII (1893); Fischer, *Ztschft. f. Harz Ver. f. Gesch.*, XXIX, Heft 2 (1896); Bender, *Ztschft. f. d. Gesch. und Alterthumskunde Ermlands*, VI (1878).

[1] Herbordus, II, 25, in the middle of the twelfth century calls Stettin "civitatem antiquissimam et nobilissimam in terra Pomeranorum matremque civitatum." For other mention of it commercially see II, 40. Stettin is first mentioned under the name Schinesge in 995 (*Codex Pomer. Diplom.*, No. 503, p. 1026). Danzig appears as Gyddanizc in 997 (*Vita S. Adalberti-SS. rerum Pruss.*, I, 228.) Colberg, on the coast between Wollin and Danzig, traded especially with the "outer islands" (Herbordus, II, 39; cf. Martin Polonus, II, 28). It is interesting to observe that though the center of trade shifted from the island of Wollin, whose period of greatest prosperity was during the Danish occupation of the Baltic seaboard, to the mainland at Stettin and Danzig after the German conquest of Mecklenburg and Pomerania in the twelfth century, yet the configuration of the coast has not changed since the Middle Ages. For Adam of Bremen, II, 19, describes the three mouths of the Oder in terms which would hold today. Adam of Bremen, III, 19, describes the Abodrite city of Wiligrad (Mecklenburg) as "Magnopolis . . . civitas inclita Obodritorum," and mentions Ratzeburg and Stargard (Alt-Lübeck or Oldenburg), the latter of which Helmold I, 12, characterizes as "antiqua civitas." There is an excellent history of Danzig by Hirsch, and one of Stettin by Wehrmann. Stargard has found a historian in F. Boll.

[2] The word "Wend" was used (and still is) by North Germans to describe the Slavs of the Elbe and the Baltic coast, without distinction of tribe. The name was derived from the Wenidi or Winidi, a formidable Slavonic tribe in the time of Charlemagne, and came to be used to indicate the Slavs much as the word *waelsch* (English Welsh) was employed to indicate foreigners in general, e.g., French and Italians. A modern parallel is the Boer word *Uitlander* ("Outlander") in South Africa, to describe the English and Portuguese there.

hope of Slav recovery, and German domination was firmly fixed in the country by the vigorous rule of Henry the Lion and Albrecht the Bear.

But the Germans fought for the mouths of the Baltic rivers not only in order to capture the Wendish trade in the Baltic, but also to find an exit for their own inland commerce. The natural exits for products of the German Hinterland were the Elbe, the Trave, the Peene, and the Oder rivers. The Germans always controlled the mouth of the Elbe, but its middle course was not permanently secure until after 1147, when it became a German river from Meissen to the sea. Nor was full control of the other rivers acquired until after the Wendish Crusade. Leipzig appears by the year 1000 but was insignificant until the twelfth century.[1]

Heinemann thinks[2] that even as early as the Saxon period (919–1024) the border traffic between the Germans and the Wends was of sufficient importance to be taxed; but Guttmann believes this to be *ganz unwahrscheinlich*.[3] However, the growth of German trans-Elbean trade can be obscurely traced even in Saxon times. In 975 Otto II, at the prayer of Adalbert, archbishop of Magdeburg, granted protection "to merchants dwelling in Magdeburg" and freedom "everywhere in our realm, in Christian and in barbarous lands, to go and come unmolested."[4] In 1025 Conrad II reaffirmed this decree, and specific mention is made of the trade of Magdeburger merchants on the Havel and the Spree, i.e., in Brandenburg.[5] Intermediate between these two dates we have the statement of Bishop Thietmar of Merseburg (d. 1018), whose youth was spent in Magdeburg, that he had seen guards in the churches watching the goods of merchants

[1] Thietmar, VIII, 25, 66. Even in Martin Polonus, II, 39; III, 1, it is not yet important. In his *Proem* he writes: "Sed quia regio Polonorum ab itineribus peregrinorum est remota, et nisi transeuntibus in Rusiam pro mercimonio paucis nota . . . ." Cf. L. Giesebrecht, *op. cit.*, I, 23.

[2] *Markgraf Gero*, p. 42.

[3] *Forschungen zur brand. und preuss. Gesch.*, IX, 417, n. 5.

[4] *Hansisches Urkundenbuch*, I, No. 1.

[5] Boehmer, *Regesta*, No. 1272; Stumpf, *Regesta*, No. 1871.

deposited there for safekeeping.[1] These merchants were both Germans and Jews, chiefly engaged in the slave trade.[2]

The Slavonic reaction of 1018 must have given this frontier trade a setback. Yet by the middle of the century it is evident from Adam of Bremen that adventurous German merchants were again penetrating into the Wendish lands, going as far as Wollin, which was eight days' journey from Hamburg. They seem to have been unmolested provided they did not parade their faith. Apparently these merchants, or others like them, also went on to the Swedish coast and to Ostrogard-Novgorod, which was eighteen days' journey farther.[3]

When we reach the twelfth century evidence accumulates in regard to this trans-Elbean and Baltic trade. In the Abodrite country (it did not become the Duchy of Mecklenburg until after the conquest in 1147), at Stargard, later Germanized into Oldenburg, which was the capital of the Abodrite

[1] Thietmar, *Chronicon*, I, 12.

[2] *Ibid.*, III, 1; IV, 12; VI, 16. *MGH*, Dip. I, p. 416, associates German and Jew merchants together. These slaves were recruited from the border warfare between the German and the Slav peoples, and also from the internecine strife between the Slav tribes (Adam of Bremen, *Descriptio*, 18). The strife also between the Danes and the Germans furnished slaves. Helmold, II, 13, relates that 700 Danish captives were exposed for sale in the market at Mecklenburg in 1168. Thietmar of Merseburg deplored the barbarity of the Saxons in dividing up the families of prisoners when sold as slaves (Giesebrecht, *op. cit.*, I, 35). The Jews controlled the border slave trade upon which they paid a tax (Thietmar, VI, 12; Gerdes, *Gesch. d. d. Volkes*, I, 357, and n. 3, 359). Würzburg was an important base of slave supply in 1006. The better public opinion reprobated the practice, yet it flourished for centuries. Margrave Gunzelin was criticized for selling Wendish captives to Jew merchants (Thietmar, VI, 36); the Bohemians were reckoned "bad Christians" because they disposed of captives in war to the Jews (*Vita S. Adalberti*, chap. xii; cf. *Vita Johan. Gorz.*, chap. cxxi); Henry II in 1012 endeavored to restrain the traffic (*Ann. Qued.*, *MGH*, SS. III, 81). Slaves are mentioned as articles of commerce in a Bavarian tariff list on the Danube in 904 (Dümmler, *Ostfränk. Reich*, III, 533). Slaves are often mentioned with transfers of land (see Gerdes, I, 418–20, and Waitz, V, 207–8, for references). In 914, 23 slaves and 27 *Hufen* of land were exchanged for 30 slaves and 19 *Hufen*, which shows that a slave was valued about at the price of a *Hufe*.

[3] Adam of Bremen, *Gesta*, II, 19; *Descriptio*, 18, 21; Helmold, I, 6. The Gothland merchants had reached Novgorod long before the twelfth century (Bächtold, *op. cit.*, p. 256; Bugge, *op. cit.*, p. 251). A charter of 1023 mentions an "international" bridge where the German merchants changed wares with the Russians. A Russian chronicle mentions St. Peter's Church in 1184. First mention of the factory at Novgorod is made in 1199 (Bächtold, *op. cit.*, p. 256).

duke Pribislav, there was a considerable colony of German merchants settled in 1129.[1] German trading operations extended clear to the island of Rügen, whose inhabitants were still fiercely pagan, and where the famous Slavonic fane of Arcona was located,[2] and before the storming and capture of this sanctuary by a joint German and Danish expedition in 1168, it was necessary for the merchants not only to avoid parading their Christianity, but also to offer substantial presents to the god in order to be permitted to buy and to sell.[3]

Among the Rani, or Rugians, conditions of trade were so primitive that strips of linen cloth served for currency, like wampum among the Indians of America.[4]

Every year, in November, at the time of the "big wind" a fleet of western craft came for dried fish and furs.[5]

This Alt-Lübecker merchant group even penetrated into the Baltic and sought to capture the ancient Swedish-Russian trade of Novgorod and the Varangian route and had a "factory" or trading post on the island of Gothland. For in 1124 the emperor Lothar II took them under imperial protection.[6]

[1] Helmold, I, 48: "a mercatoribus quorum non parvam coloniam."

[2] *Ibid.*, 38.

[3] *Ibid.*, 6 (p. 17); cf. Breska, *Forschungen zur deutschen Gesch.*, XXII, 585–87.

[4] "Porro apud Ranos non habetur moneta, nec est in comparandis rebus nummorum consuetudo, sed quicquid in foro mercari volueris, panno lineo comparabis. Aurum et argentum, quod forte per rapinos et captiones hominum vel undecumque adepti sunt, aut uxorum suarum cultibus impendunt, aut in erarium dei sui conferunt" (Helmold, I, 38; cf. 36). This cloth currency was also once current among the Bohemians. In Czech the word for "linen" and the word "to number" come from the same root (Lippert, *Sozial Gesch. Böhmens*, I, 84).

[5] Helmold, I, 48, and II, 12; *Ann. Erphesf.*, 1135 (*MGH*, SS. VI, 540), supply other details as to the nature of this commerce. There is still a little village, now a watering-place, near Stettin named Heringsdorf. For the importance of the Baltic herring trade see Bächtold, *Der norddeutsche Handel im 12. und beginnenden 13. Jahrhundert* (Berlin, 1910), p. 261, and especially K. Jagow, "Die Heringsfischerei an den deutschen Ostseeküsten im M. A.," *Archiv f. Fischereigesch.*, Band V (1915). In Herbordus, *Dialogus*, III, 30, and Ebonis, *Vita Ottonis*, III, 23, is a curious account of how the conversion of the peoples of the mainland of Pomerania interrupted for some time the trade with the Rugians, who would have nothing to do with the converted Slavs.

[6] The original charter of Lothar is lost. But it is referred to by Henry the Lion in a privilege dated October 18, 1163, granted to the merchants of Lübeck (*Lübecker Urkb.*, I, 4, n. 3. Cf. Richter, *op. cit.*, III, 690 nn.; Jaffé, I, 155).

We know little more about this farther commerce until the formation of the Hanseatic League and the incorporation of the Wisby group with it in 1298.

Of the trade of the Pomeranian mainland in the first half of the twelfth century we have interesting information in Ebbo's *Life of Otto of Bamberg*, who twice visited Pomerania (in 1124 and again in 1128), and also in the *Dialogus* of Herbordus.[1] With the fall of the Jomsburg vikings[2] Wollin had begun to decline, though when Adam of Bremen wrote in the middle of the eleventh century it was still the most important port on the Pomeranian coast.[3]

By the next century, however, Stettin appears as the *totius Pomeraniae metropolis*, although it could not possibly have had a population of from six to seven thousand, as said.[4] Its chief rival was Camin. The spongy, marshy soil, upon which both towns were built was a serious drawback. Stettin was girded with swamps,[5] and the streets in Camin were so miry that bridges, which seem to have been nothing but planks, were everywhere. Otto himself fell off one of these planks and was pitched into the mud.[6] The people were hospitable, though rude and crude in manners.[7] Each town had a *forum* where business was done, and a certain degree of money economy obtained.[8] There were warehouses, chiefly, one imagines, for the curing and storing of fish. Fishing was the main activity of the inhabitants, though furs[9] and slaves were also articles of commerce.[10] The herring ran in

[1] *Vita*, II, 41; *Dialogus*, I, 36; II, 7, 12, 28; III, 1.

[2] Ersch and Grüber, *Encyc.*, XXII, 370–78; L. Giesebrecht, *Wendische Geschichten*, I, 205 f.; *Baltische Studien*, No. 13; Bugge, "Die nordeuropäischen Verkehrswege, etc.," *Vierteljahrschrift f. Soz. und Wirtschaftsgesch.*, XII, 92 f.; Sommerfeld, *Gesch. d. Germanisierung Pommern* [Schmoller's *Forschungen*, Band XIII, Heft 5, p. 15]; Lamprecht, *Deutsche Gesch.*, II, 267–69; III, 345; Barthold, *Gesch. von Pommern*, I, 360 f.; S. A. Krijn, *De Jomsvikingsaga* (Leiden, 1914).

[3] *Gesta*, II, 19.

[4] Herbordus, II, 5, 25, 34; Sommerfeld, *Gesch. d. Germanisierung des Herzogtums Pommern*, p. 54 n.

[5] Herbordus, II, 5.

[6] *Ibid.*, 24.

[7] *Ibid.*, 41.

[8] *Ibid.*, 9 and 26.

[9] *Ibid.*, 28.

[10] *Ibid.*, III, 2.

shoals in the Baltic; but there was a brisk trade in fresh-water fish, too.[1] The coastwise trade must have been considerable, for Otto easily traveled by water from port to port of the river mouths.[2]

By 1125 it is evident that there was a through route from the eastern parts of "New" Germany to the farther Baltic coast. Halle, on the Saale River, was the clearing house and emporium of all this eastern German commerce. Both times when Otto of Bamberg made his trips to Pomerania he "stocked up" at the fair (*nundinae*) in Halle, and thence traveled by boat down the Saale to the Elbe, down the Elbe to Werben at the mouth of the Havel, and up the Havel and down the Peene to Uzedom.[3]

If one were not already convinced of the activity of Lower Germany in the Baltic trade, the founding of Lübeck in 1143 by Adolph of Holstein ought to resolve his doubt, for its establishment was a turning-point in the history of North Germany. The site was not unknown before. In days gone by Kruto, the powerful Wendish chieftain who broke the German domination east of the Elbe by the great rebellion in 1066, had erected a castle surrounded by a wooden palisade on the large island where the Trave and the Wochnitz flowed together. Adolph's clear eye saw the advantage of the location in spite of its swampy nature. The new place, which was called New Lübeck, to distinguish it from

[1] *Ibid.*, II, 41; III, 21.

[2] *Ibid.*, II, 37; III, 14, 15.

[3] *Ibid.*, I, 36; III, 1. For further information on this trade see Giesebrecht, *Wend. Gesch.*, I, 16–35; Herzberg, *Gesch. d. Stadt Halle im Mittelalter* (1889); Sommerfeld, *op. cit.*, pp. 62–66; K. F. Klöden, *Beiträge zur Geschichte des Oderhandels* (Berlin, 1847–52), in eight parts. It seems to me that Wendt, *op. cit.*, II, 6, underestimates this commerce. For routes by road and water in Germany in this time see Kretschmer, *Historische Geographie von Mitteleuropa*, pp. 212–13; Gasner, *Zum deutschen Strassenwesen von der ältesten Zeit bis zur Mitte des XVII. Jahrhundert* (Leipzig, 1889), pp. 31–58; Lauffer, *op. cit.*, pp. 53 f.; Knull, *Historische Geographie Deutschlands im Mittelalter* (Breslau, 1903). The Baltic trade to South Germany was mainly up the Mulde and down the Nab to Regensburg, the former taking the place of the Saale when that stream was made the eastern edge of the German world in Charlemagne's time. In Bohemia a trade route ran from Prague up the Moldau and over the divide to Linz on the Danube. Another road was up the Eger—or through the Nollendorf Pass—and down the Nab to Regensburg.

Alt-Lübeck (the Wendish Stargard, now Oldenburg), and later merely Lübeck, soon became an important port.[1]

The rapid growth of Lübeck[2] aroused the resentment of Henry the Lion, for it cut into the trade of Bardowick, Charlemagne's ancient trading post, which belonged to the Saxon duke, and in order to get a share of the Baltic trade Henry founded Löwenstadt, named after himself, on the Wochnitz between Lübeck and Ratzeburg.[3] But his new city did not prosper. Lübeck, as Helmold says, "was more prosperous and better located."[4] Henry the Lion was not the man to brook a successful rival. In 1158 he seized Lübeck by force, removed the markets of Bardowick and Löwenstadt there, and established a mint. It soon became the emporium of the whole Baltic trade. Merchant vessels from England, Denmark, Sweden, Norway, and even Russia crowded the port.[5] Stettin was Lübeck's closest rival.[6] The Low German speech became the language of trade throughout the whole north, and the *Elbslavische* speech, which hitherto had been necessary for the conduct of Baltic trade,[7] gradually died out. More than a hundred years later the records of the Hanseatic League began to be written in it. The destruction of Bardowick in 1189 by Henry the Lion, after his return from exile, further contributed to Lübeck's growth.[8]

[1] Helmold, I, 57 and 63; *Ep. Sidonis* (in Schmeidler's ed. Helmold, p. 245); Hoffman, *Gesch. der Stadt Lübeck* (1889).

[2] Helmold, I, 48, 57, 63, 71, 76, 85.

[3] *Ibid.*, I, 86; cf. Simonsfeld, *Jahrbuch*, I, 555–56.

[4] Helmold, I, 90.

[5] *Ibid.*, I, 86; Arnold of Lübeck, II, 5. Henry the Lion founded the monastery of St. Mary and St. John in Lübeck (1177) and because of slenderness of episcopal revenues there endowed it with half of the villa Renseveld (*Urkundenbuch der Stadt Lübeck*, I, n. 5), a second "villula" across the river called Cleve, but in the same parish, and a third of the tithes in Greater and Lesser Gladenbrugge (parish of Sigeberg) and in Stubbendorf. Certain property within the city of Lübeck (*curtes*) bringing eight marks rent annually and fields around Lübeck were also donated. The Duke's liberality, we are assured, stirred the envy of others.

[6] Wehrmann, *Gesch. von Pommern*, I (1904), 95, 112; Bächtold, p. 246: record of a citizen of Bamberg who had lived for years in Stettin as a merchant, and at his death left his property to the church in Stettin.

[7] Guttmann, *op. cit.*, IX, 408; Bugge, *op. cit.*, p. 240, n. 3; Iken, *Bremisches Jahrbuch*, XVII (1895).

[8] Helmold, I, 73; Arnold of Lübeck, V, 2. Cf. Hüllmann, *Ztschft. f. Geschichtswiss.*, IV, 1–9. Rostock is first mentioned in 1160 by Saxo Gram., SS. XXIX, 108.

A similar progress of German commerce, although not in the same degree, is observable at this time also farther inland.

In Brandenburg, when Albrecht the Bear fixed his capital upon the Spree, where Berlin now is situated, there were already there two Slavonic villages, Kollin (Ger., Kölln) on the island and Berlin on the right bank. Both names are of Slavonic origin. The German incomers settled on the river edge, while Kölln was chiefly inhabited by Wendish fisher folk. It is not without significance that the first Christian church erected on the island was dedicated to St. Peter, the fisherman, and that the German settlers in Berlin built their first church to St. Nicholas, the patron saint of merchants. The fact is typical of the difference between the two communities. In Berlin today the island part of the city is known as Alt-Kölln, where the fish market even yet is hard by the ancient church of St. Peter's. The two communities each received a separate charter and were not united into a single city until the fourteenth century, when Berlin became a member of the Hanseatic League.[1]

Ably seconded by the energetic archbishop of Magdeburg, Wichmann, the Margrave furthered the immigration of settlers, among them many Dutch and Flemish colonists, planted towns and granted town charters and commercial privileges which were models of their kind; on the rivers of the Mark plied the barges of merchants, whose goods were protected from brigands and predatory attacks of the hostile Wends by armed guards.[2] Warehouse privileges and toll stations were established at convenient points, such as Werben and Wittenberg on the Elbe, Potsdam and Heiligensee on the Havel.[3] The number of mints shows that a money economy prevailed by this time.[4] The traffic must have been

---

In 1189 a market was established there for the benefit of the monks at Dobberan. In 1218 Duke Heinrich Borwin of Mecklenburg granted the inhabitants *Zollfreiheit* and Lübecker law (Pueschl, *op. cit.*, p. 22). But Soesten law still continued inland away from the coast, and east of the Elbe Magdeburger law (*ibid.*, p. 7).

[1] Lavisse, *La marche de Brandenbourg*, pp. 134–35 and notes.

[2] Riedel, *Die Marck Brandenburg*, II, 99.

[3] *Ibid.*, II, p. 103; Lavisse, p. 128.

[4] Riedel, II, 97, n. 1.

almost exclusively in raw products, especially furs,[1] though the German colonists must have drawn some supplies, particularly domestic utensils and farm tools, from farther west, and the church and the Margrave's court created some demand for the luxuries of older Germany. There is no doubt that the towns of the margraviate commercially prospered under the enlightened régime and efficient protection given them by Albrecht the Bear.[2]

But one must not exaggerate the size or prosperity of these towns. In the twelfth century they were much behind the older cities of Central and Western Germany both in wealth and population, and, indeed, not until well down in modern times did Berlin and Frankfort-on-the-Oder come to rival Cologne or Nürnberg, or Frankfort or Lübeck. Brandenburg was located on the outer edge of the great commercial zone created in Northern Germany by the later formation of the Hanseatic League.

The conquest of Mecklenburg and Pomerania from the Slavs in the twelfth century had given the Germans control of the mouths of the German rivers, and Lübeck at the mouth of the Trave, Stettin at the mouth of the Peene, Wollin at the mouth of the Oder, and Danzig at the mouth of the Vistula, became not only outlets for the interior trade of Germany, but *points d'appui* whence German trade dominion was extended.

Beyond Danzig and the Oder mouth German commercial enterprise had expanded into Livonia before the end of the twelfth century (1186).[3] In Prague, in the reign of Wratislav (1061–92), there is mention of a group of Bavarian merchants, but of none from the north.[4] In Poland there is scarcely a trace of German commerce before 1175.[5]

[1] Lavisse, *op. cit.*, pp. 231–32.

[2] Tuttle, *History of Prussia*, Vol. I, chap. i.

[3] Heinrici, *Chron.*, I, 2, 11.

[4] Wendt, II, 6.

[5] *Ibid.* A papal privilege of 1155 for Breslau contains only one German name in a long list. In the thirteenth century a market was established before the church of St. Adalbert (Pueschl, 47).

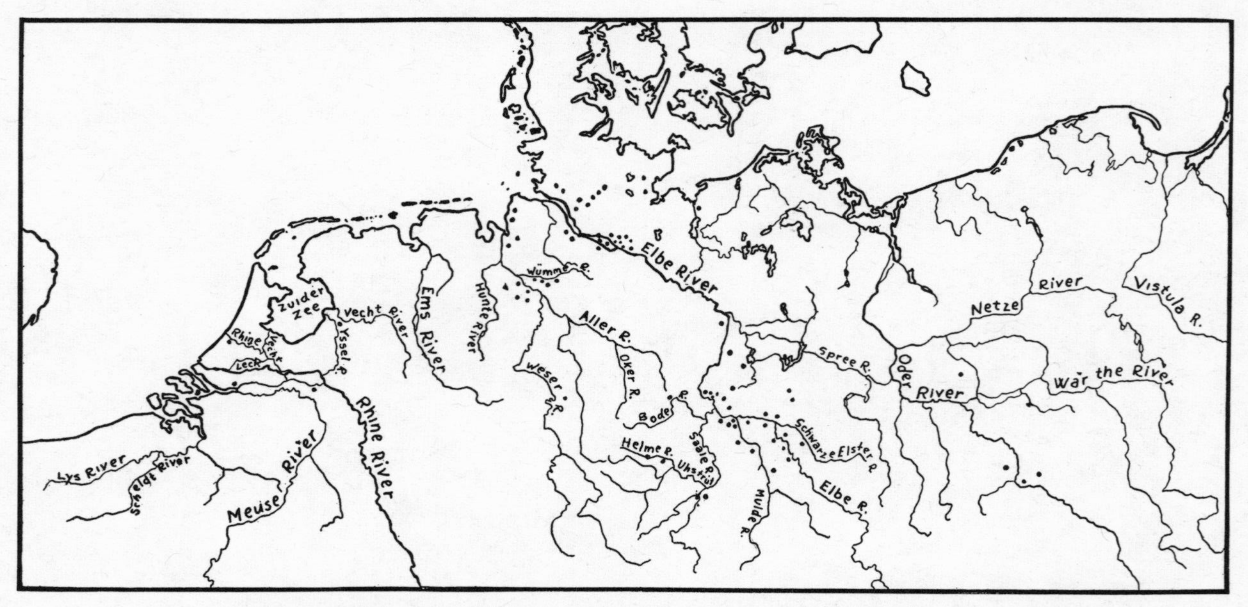

Distribution of Marshland Settlements Made by Dutch and Flemish Colonists

CHAPTER XV

DUTCH AND FLEMISH COLONIZATION IN MEDIEVAL GERMANY[1]

THE progress made in recent years in economic and social history has changed both the axis and the orbit of historical interpretation. Political, dynastic, and military history, the history of governments, laws, and institutions, has ceased to interest many students of history in these days. The Aristotelian mind of Western Europe and America has discovered new sources of information and new subjects of investigation. No one of these questions is more important to the medievalist than that of demography.

Among the discoveries which the modern study of medieval history has made is the profoundly organic and heterogeneous nature of medieval society—the complexity of its composition, the variety of its texture. The sharp cleavage once supposed to have existed between the three classes of medieval society, we now know, was not a hard-and-narrow line of separation, but a series of social gradations, some of them so slight that their parallax, so to speak, has not yet been accurately determined.

[1] The literature upon this subject is very large. It is cited fully in Kretschmer, *Historische Geographie von Mitteleuropa* (Berlin, 1904), pp. 371–72; in Schulze, *Die Kolonisierung und Germanisierung der Gebiete zwischen Saale und Elbe* (Leipzig, 1896), p. 129; in Kötzschke, *Deutsche Wirtschaftsgeschichte*, p. 109. The earliest important study of the subject was done by E. Borchgrave, in "Mém. de l'Acad. roy. de Belgique," Vols. XXVII, XXXII, XXXVI. Grünhagen has an article on the Walloon colonies in Silesia in the same series, Vol. XXXIII. Lamprecht, *Deutsche Geschichte* (3d ed., 1906), III, 309–42, has a great amount of suggestive material packed into a small compass. R. Kötzschke's *Quellen zur Geschichte der ostdeutschen Kolonisation im 12. bis 14. Jahrhundert* (Leipzig: Teubner, 1912), Nos. 9–20, is an indispensable collection of the charters. Helmold's *Chronica Slavorum* (ed. Schmeidler; Leipzig: Hahn, 1909), is the best narrative source. There are isolated examples of Flemish settlements in Germany before the twelfth century, but they have no continuity with the history of Flemish colonization in the high feudal age. Thus, for example, as far back as the sixth century a colony of Flemings seem to have settled at *Belgesheim* near Altmark. Some Flemings followed St. Adalhard and settled around New Corvey between 822 and 827, and others followed Anskar into the diocese of Hamburg.

The light cast upon the condition of the medieval peasantry in the course of these social and economic researches has been enormous. One of the most interesting of these findings is the startling discovery that the rural population of Europe in the Middle Ages was probably more nomadic and less sedentary than the lower classes of society today.[1] These displacements of population were not upon the gigantic scale of the German migrations in the fifth century or the Norse and Hungarian invasions of the ninth and tenth centuries. Nevertheless they were mass movements of large dimension —waves of popular migration sometimes succeeding one another through a series of years, which were primarily motivated by desire for improvement of material condition and powerfully affected by economic distress and the pressure of social forces. The Frankish colonization of the Spanish March in the time of Charlemagne and Louis the Pious is an example of such a movement.[2] More important and more typical is the history of the eastward expansion of the German people under the Saxon, Salian, and Hohenstaufen rulers, and their colonization of Mecklenburg, Brandenburg, Pomerania, and Silesia.

In this pioneer labor Dutch and Flemish immigrants from the Low Countries played no unimportant part. The emigration of the peasantry of modern Holland and Belgium in the twelfth and thirteenth centuries and their settlement in numerous scattered colonies in Lower Germany was due to the simultaneous operation of expulsive forces at home and the attraction which a new land presented. In the Middle Ages Belgium shared with Lombardy the honor of being the most densely populated region of Western Europe. The heart of the Frankish monarchy had been there, and the inti-

[1] This the late Achille Luchaire, *Social France at the Time of Philip Augustus* (Eng. trans.), pp. 404–6, clearly demonstrated. Cf. Powicke's review of the French original in *English Historical Review*, XXV, 565. The conclusion amply confirmed the previous researches of Lamprecht, *Études sur l'état économique de la France* (Fr. trans., Marignan), pp. 138–39, 222–23; Flach, *Les origines de l'ancienne France*, II, livre iii, prem. partie. For Germany the last half of Lamprecht, *Deutsche Gesch.*, Vol. III, to mention no other work, shows the same thing.

[2] See Imbart de la Tour, "Les Colonies agricoles et l'occupation des terres désertes à l'époque carolingienne," *Questions d'Histoire*, pp. 31–68.

mate association between the Merovingian and the Carolingian sovereigns and the church had resulted in the founding of many monasteries in the land. Nowhere else in Europe perhaps were they more thickly clustered, with their ample lands and their thousands of serfs exploiting the rich glebe farms. Here were the great historic abbeys of St. Vaast in Arras, St. Bavon in Ghent, St. Martin in Utrecht, St. Géry and St. Sepulchre in Cambrai, St. Laurence and St. Lambert in Liège, St. Omer, St. Quentin, St. Bertin, and St. Riquier, with their clustered communities of artisans, craftsmen, and petty tradesmen dwelling in separate "quarters" around the monastery walls, with the scattered villages of servile husbandmen on the abbey lands stretching roundabout,[1] and in the eleventh and twelfth centuries grown into more or less independent towns. Besides these great abbeys there were many others, Corvey, Lobbes, St. Trond, Nivelles, Andennes, Calmont, St. Hubert, Stavelot, Fosses, Alden-Eyck, Brogne, etc.

What these great monasteries did on a large scale in clearing forests and draining moor and swamp lands[2] those among the peasantry who were free did in less degree. For, as lay and ecclesiastical feudalism expanded, throwing its coils over the persons and lands of the free peasantry, rather than submit to servile conditions and bondage to the glebe they found refuge in remoter parts of the wide waste of moor and fen,[3] exactly as the population of the uplands fled to the forest, and there established their tiny villages, and by ditching and diking and draining redeemed a few acres of soil from the reluctant grasp of the sluggish waters. Cubes of turf served for building blocks for their cottages, and peat was their fuel.[4]

But in the course of time, as in the uplands the feudality appropriated the forests and reduced the free forest villages to serfdom, so in the Low Countries the feudal nobles gradually penetrated into the remote fen regions and extended

[1] See Flach, *op. cit.*, chap. vii; Blanchard, *La Flandre*, pp. 153–69; and my article in *Journal of Political Economy* (November, 1915), pp. 872–73.

[2] Blanchard, pp. 170–201.

[3] *Ann. Fuld.* (885): "Frisones . . . . pravissimis [parvissimis?], ut eis consuetudo, naviculis vecti. . . . ."

[4] Lamprecht, *Deutsche Geschichte* (4th ed.), III, 336.

their seigniorial sway over the free marsh villages.[1] With the spread of the feudal and manorial régime came the evils of private war, which neither the Truce of God nor the civil power (for the civil power was that of the lords themselves) was able to suppress, in addition to which the burden of heavy and vexatious manorial exactions was imposed upon the peasantry. From this condition of things emigration was the readiest form of relief.

Furthermore, the lot of the peasantry was made worse by the vicious commercial policy of some of the nobles, whose heavy taxation upon production, distribution, and consumption in the form of numberless *tonlieux*, *péages*, and *maltôtes* impoverished the peasants and discouraged or even ruined enterprise. The Bishop of Münster, for example, closed to the Frisians their market of the Ems, whither they had been accustomed to bring their cattle for barter. No other market was open to them because the Danes and the merchants of Bremen and Hamburg demanded money, a commodity which was very scarce in Friesland. As a consequence the Frisian cattle, practically the sole resource of the country, became diseased from inbreeding, and starvation ensued.[2]

Industrial coercion, again, was a factor in provoking emigration, for nowhere in North Europe in the eleventh and twelfth centuries was the development of industry and town population greater than in Belgium. If the burghers secured freedom of work and measurable political rights they stayed; if coercion succeeded they sought to migrate. What development had industry attained and in how far was it emancipated from the influence of agriculture and a rural environment and become urban? Levasseur has shown that a change had supervened in the relations between agriculture and industry by the beginning of the twelfth century.[3] It

[1] The history of this swamp reclamation and forest clearing in medieval Belgium has been the subject of various studies: Blanchard, chaps. xi–xiii; Duvivier, "Hospites: défrichements en Europe et spécialement dans nos contrées aux XIe, XIIe, et XIIIe siècles," *Révue d'histoire et d'archéologie*, Vol. I; Van de Putte, "Esquisse sur la mise en culture de la Flandre occidentale," *Ann. de la soc. d'émulation de Bruges*, Vol. III.

[2] Curschmann, *Hungersnöte im Mittelalter* (Leipzig, 1900), p. 23.

[3] *Histoire des classes ouvrières* (1st ed.), I, 173 f.; cf. pp. 320–21, and Lamprecht, *L'état économique de France*, pp. 241–47.

goes without saying that this change was intimately connected with the emancipation of the servile classes and the birth of the burgher class in the towns. There is no need to enter here into consideration of this complex and thorny question. But the tendency to freedom of industry and the formation of industrial combinations like the gilds, as everyone knows, were bitterly resented by the nobility, who tried to maintain the serfdom of industry quite as much as the serfdom of agriculture.[1]

An additional factor which induced migration in the Middle Ages, perhaps the most general of all influences, was famine. The occurrence of famine was not always due to adverse weather conditions. It is true that a hard winter which killed the peasant's seed corn in the pits, or a drought, or a prolonged wet season was often terribly destructive of the crops. But aside from these physical phenomena famine was often engendered, at least locally, by other causes, such as feudal war, exhaustive taxation both of production and distribution, in addition to which the rudimentary system of agriculture prevailing, with crude farming implements and ignorance of the use of fertilizers, must be taken into account.

Since Lamprecht deplored the absence of any monograph upon the history of medieval famine, the gap has been filled, at least for Germany and the Low Countries, by Curschmann's admirable book.[2] He has shown that in Belgium famine occurred four times in the eleventh century, nine times in the twelfth, and twice in the thirteenth. There is most certainly a connection between these hunger conditions—there was a three years' famine in 1144–47—and the huge emigration which took place from Belgium in the twelfth century.[3]

[1] Levasseur, I, 167; Guérard, *Polyptique d'Irminon*, I, 471 f., 717 f., 729 f.

[2] See n. 2, on previous page.

[3] Curschmann, pp. 40 and 140–41. He compares it (p. 8) with the great drought in Europe in 1847 and its effect upon emigration, particularly from Germany and Ireland. In the latter country the potato crop had also failed the year before. The effect of these "hard times" in provoking popular discontent and so promoting the revolution of 1848 has not yet been studied. Overpopulation and underproduction are sometimes the positive and the negative way of saying the same thing, and overpopulation in the Middle Ages was a very prevalent cause of migration. See for Belgium: Blanchard, pp. 485–88; Curschmann, p. 199; Pirenne, *Histoire de Belgique*, I, 135–40; for Germany: Püschel, *Anwachsen der deutschen Städte in der Zeit der*

Under stress of such privation no feudal lord could have been able to retain his tenantry. "Propter caristiam colono fugiente, plurimi vici deserti remansere," reads a chronicle. The cattle were slaughtered for lack of fodder and to furnish food. When they were consumed nothing but flight remained as a recourse. It is impossible to avoid this conclusion, even if one is not always able to establish a direct nexus between any given famine and any given migration. The simultaneousness of the two events was not accidental.

When the Frisian and Flemish peasant betook himself to the refuge of the marshes in order to escape from feudal oppression he found only a precarious freedom even there. For he lived ever in peril of the sea. The low coast, the many deep tidal estuaries, the flat plains across which the Rhine, the Vaal, the Meuse, the Scheldt, and their affluents meandered, and which often overflowed their low banks in time of freshet, the salt marshes, the swamps—all these conditions exposed the population to floods which were sometimes terrible in their devastation.[1] Inundation was a powerful incen-

---

mittelalterlichen Kolonialbewegung, pp. 13–15; Wendt, *Die Germanisierung der Länder ostlich der Elbe*, II, 17–18.

[1] In the middle of the first century A.D. Pliny the Elder, who had seen service in the Roman province of Lower Germany, described the condition of the Frisians in terms which are applicable to them a thousand years later. He says: "In this region the wretched natives, occupying either the tops of hills or artificial mounds of turf raised out of the reach of the highest tides, build their small huts, which look like sailing vessels when the water covers the land, and like wrecks when it has retired. For fuel they use a kind of turf [i.e., peat] dug by hand and dried rather in the wind than in the sun, and with this earth they cook their food and warm their bodies. Their only drink is rain-water collected in ditches under the eaves." Cf. Elton, *Origins of English History*, p. 49. Nearly a thousand years later, the *Anonymous* of Utrecht early in the ninth century described the Frisians as "living almost like fishes amid the waters which hemmed them in on all sides, so that they rarely had access to outside countries unless in ships." There is an ancient study of inundations in Flanders in the *Séances de l'Académie ... de Belgique*, I (1777), 63 f. Blanchard, chaps. ix-xi, is very interesting, as is also Curschmann, who gives extracts from the sources. See also Klopp, *Ostfriesland* (Hanover, 1854), pp. 98–100, 139–44; Wiarda, *Die geschichtliche Entwicklung des wirtschaftlichen Ostfriesland* (Jena, 1880), pp. 13–14; Spruner-Menke, *Handatlas*, No. 39, carton 5. Montagu Burrows, *Cinque Ports*, chap. xi, deals with tidal and storm effects of the English Channel on the south coast of England. The year 1405–6 wrought terrible havoc along all the North Sea Coast. It was perhaps the greatest storm in history, for it practically raged, with brief intermissions, over the whole of Europe from November, 1405, to April, 1406. Bruges, the greatest commercial emporium of the north,

tive to emigration.[1] The peasant who saw his little farmstead destroyed in a day, the labor of years of tilling, draining, ditching, diking, go for worse than naught, his crops ruined, his cattle drowned or lost in the awful confusion of a great flood, had no heart left to begin the struggle all over again in such a land.[2]

---

was ruined by it, for the sea overwhelmed the great tide gates at the mouth of the Zwin, regarded even in Dante's time as an engineering wonder, and so filled the harbor of Bruges with sand that nothing but the lightest draft vessels could enter. At the same time this great storm cleared a huge island of sand out of the mouth of the Scheldt and opened Antwerp, which hitherto had been a mere fishing village, to trade, and so it succeeded Bruges in commercial history. Popular opinion associated this mighty storm with the death of Tamerlane, who died February 19, 1405, but the news was not known in Western Europe until March, 1406. Wylie, *History of the Reign of Henry IV*, II, 470–75, has gathered a mass of data regarding its effects in England. The winter of 1407–8 was the "Great Winter"—one of the most famous known.

[1] Püschel, *Das Anwaschen der deutschen Städte in der Zeit der mittelalterlichen Kolonialbewegung* (1910), p. 15.

[2] It is curious to note that the regions of Flanders most subject to inundation were least likely to suffer from famine. Curschmann (p. 21) suggests that the reason may be found perhaps in the fact that the peasants were often able to drive their cattle out of reach of the floods and so preserve them. When this chapter was first published in the *American Journal of Sociology* (September, 1918), Mr. Maurice B. Hexter, secretary of the United Jewish Charities of Cincinnati, wrote me: "I have a suggestion to make as to the reason that in the regions of Flanders most subject to inundation the individual was least likely to suffer famine. For some years I have been getting data from American life on the adaptation of people in geographical sections of American cities to sudden changes. In a certain portion of Newport, Kentucky, inundations occur with a specific periodicity. I have noticed that other portions of Newport, Kentucky, less likely to be inundated have fewer inhabitants than the portion most likely to be inundated. This led me to study the people most likely to be flooded. I find that amongst these people there is a series of social gradations, the parallax for which can be accurately determined. There is, first, the group of newcomers attracted to this locality by low rents. There is, second, a class of inhabitants who have lived in this section for years. The third class falls in between these two just delineated. The class which has lived in this section for years, as I have witnessed during five or six floods, have a certain calm and a definite precision and methodology in rescuing their stuff from the ravages of the flood. They have lived there for years, and have learned to forecast the height of the water to be expected with an uncanny precision, and even go so far as to look upon the labors of the newcomers with a certain naïveté and supercilious contempt. The newcomers, on the other hand, after going through one or two floods usually move out. I think that a similar explanation can be made with reference to your note about the apparent paradox concerning the fact that the regions most subject to inundation were least likely to suffer famine. I do not think that Curschmann's suggestion can be demonstrated. Curschmann's suggestion is based upon ability; whereas the suggestion I offer is based upon practice. I think there is a difference."

Constant warfare against the sea was required despite the partial protection of a strip of sand dunes on the coast.[1] In Holland and Friesland, to the east of the Scheldt, this barrier had been broken down by inundations early in the Christian Era, and as the land progressively sank, relative to the sea, district after district was turned from arable land to swamp or perhaps completely submerged. So the islands along the coast were reduced in size, cut to pieces, or washed away; so the inland Zuider Zee was made an arm of the ocean in the years following 1200; and so shortly afterward were the Dollart and the Jadebusen scooped out by the voracious sea, which took, along with the land, the villages that happened to stand upon it. A flood of November 18, 1421, at the mouth of the Vaal River, destroyed no less than seventy-two hamlets.[2]

To the Frisian and Flemish peasantry, which in the eleventh and twelfth centuries suffered under the combination of adverse conditions which I have endeavored to summarize, Lower Germany beckoned invitingly, and thousands of them trekked eastward filled with new energy and fresh hope, seeking to found new homes for themselves and to find new economic and political freedom in a land where the population was sparse, land cheap, and little or no capital necessary to begin with.

We catch the echo of this hope of the lowland emigrants of this time in the text of an old Flemish ballad which has been preserved:

Naer Oostland willen wy ryden,
Naer Oostland willen wy mêe,
Al over die groene heiden,
Frisch over die heiden.
Daer isser een betere stêe
Als wy binnen Oostland komen
Al onder dat hooge huis,
Daer worden wy binnen gelaten,
Frisch over die heiden;
Zy heeten ons willekom zyn.[3]

[1] Blanchard, chaps. ix and xi. An early mention of these dunes is in *Ann. St. Bert.* (839).

[2] Knüll, *Historische Geographie Deutschlands im Mittelalter*, pp. 5–7.

[3] Quoted in Schulze, *Die Kolonisierung und Germanisierung der Gebiete zwischen Saale und Elbe*, p. 79; Lamprecht, *op. cit.*, III, 342. Willems, *Oude Vlaemsche*

The *Drang nach Osten* of the German peoples had long since been under way when the first "rush" of settlers out of Friesland and Flanders into North Germany began early in the twelfth century. From the time of Henry the Fowler, under the lee of the battle line, the frontier of colonial settlement had advanced, conquering the stubborn soil and the no less stubborn resistance of the Wends, until by the term of the Salian epoch Mecklenburg, Brandenburg, Pomerania, and the Thuringian Reichsland were studded with German settlements; the initial stages of a permanent political and ecclesiastical system were firmly grounded; Magdeburg, Bardowick, and Lübeck had become important trade centers; and colonies of German settlers from farther west, tempted by cheap land and the easy terms under which titles might be acquired, were established.

But the Flemish and the Frisian pioneers did not come into these regions until the subjugation or expulsion of the former Wendish peoples there had been accomplished by the sword of the Saxons through two centuries of almost unremitting warfare against them, and the preliminary work of settlement made by German colonists. They were not men of the battle edge, but of the rear-guard.

For the land into which they came the Fleming and the Frisian were singularly adapted. In the high feudal age Lower Germany along the coast of the North Sea was an almost uninterrupted series of marshes and fens, which, owing to the sluggish flow of the rivers across the flat plain and the deep indentation of estuaries like the mouths of the Weser and the Elbe, sometimes extended a considerable distance inland. Mecklenburg and Pomerania were dotted with lakes. Even in the interior there was much bog land and some areas which were huge morasses.

The first German incomers into these regions had naturally avoided these places and appropriated for themselves the tilled soil of the conquered Wends. When almost all of this had been occupied, chiefly by the clergy and high feudality, the settlers, where possible, still clung to high ground and cleared the forests.

Liederen (Ghent, 1848), p. 53, has claimed that this ballad is not of the twelfth century, but later. He prints the complete text on p. 25.

Before the coming of the Dutch and Flemings into Germany in the twelfth century the swamps and marshes, if used at all, were used only for pasturage[1] and occasionally, if not too wet, for hay meadows. But the German peasantry before their immigration knew little or nothing of the process of making such bottom lands arable.[2] The German feudal princes and prelates who imported these lowlanders by hundreds knew their value for swamp reclamation.[3] They had an ancestral affinity for swamps and flats. Since Roman times dike-building and artificial drainage had been practiced in Flanders and Holland.[4]

It was the slow increase of population in Germany,[5] and especially the enormous land-hunger of the great proprietors, both lay and clerical, which gave a new value to these neglected spots and was the primary factor in inducing the bishops, abbots, and princes of Germany to bring in colonies of Dutch and Flemings. They were used to deep plowings in heavy soils. Moreover, the labor was without peril. It was a new country, but it was not exactly the frontier.

Intelligent nobles like Adolf of Holstein, Henry the Lion, and Albrecht the Bear vied with churchmen like the four great archbishops of Hamburg-Bremen, Adalbert, Adalbero, Frederick, and Hardwich, with Bernhard of Hildesheim and Wichmann of Magdeburg, in promoting the immigration of these Frisian and Flemish settlers. The Cistercian monasteries, however, were the most active promoters of lowland colonization. Having been but recently established, this order found little place for itself in older Germany, where

[1] Heinemann, *Albrecht der Bär*, p. 227; Meitzen, *Siedelung und Agarwesen*, II, 451.

[2] Vogel, *Ländliche Ansiedelungen der Niederländer*, p. x.

[3] Alpertus, *De div. temp.*, II, 20–21, has a remarkable tribute to the capacity of the Frisians to redeem swamp lands for cultivation. "[Frisi] . . . . praedones vero, eis postea subjugatis, singulis ad modum uniuscujusque culturae ad extirpanda novalia terram diviserunt eamque colere jusserunt et sibi vectigales fecerunt." For the skill of the Flemings in gardening see Michelin, *Der Mainzer Hof zu Erfurt* (Jena, 1853), pp. 3–6.

[4] Heinemann, p. 143.

[5] For information on this head see Kötzschke, *Deutsche Wirtschaftsgesch.*, pp. 50–52, where much literature is cited.

enormous areas of land had been for centuries in the hands of the Benedictines and Cluniacs. In consequence the Cistercians were compelled to found their houses in the unsettled parts of Germany, where land was still cheap, and, in the case of monks, could be acquired for nothing.

Within the space of a hundred years the lower Weser, the whole valley of the Elbe from Meissen to Hamburg, the marshes of the Havel, the bottom lands of the Mulde, the Black and the White Elster, the banks of the Oder below Breslau, together with its affluents like the Netze, were peopled with these Dutch and Flemish settlers. Place-names like Hollern, Hollen, Hollernweg, Hollernklink, Hollernstück, Hollanderhof, Hollerndick, Hollerwisch, Hollerwettern, Hollerbrock, and other names of localities of Flemish origin like Flemsdorf, Flemingsthal, Vlammingen, tell the tale, which is legible even today upon the map of Germany.[1]

Broadly speaking, these groups of Flemish settlers in Germany may be divided into two categories: Those founded by the church, by bishops and abbots, and those founded by German nobles upon their lands or within their provinces. Among the first group we find the colonies established around Bremen, in Holstein, at Wilster, Stoer, and Elmshorn in Thuringia, in the Goldene Aue, at Erfurt, Naumburg, near Meissen, in Anhalt, in the archbishopric of Magdeburg, in lower Lausitz and in Silesia. In the second group are included the Flemish settlements at Bitterfeld, Jüterbock, in Wagria, Brandenburg, Uckermark, Mecklenburg, Pomerania, the circle of Leubus, and in Austria and Hungary.

The methods of colonization varied between the extremes of the individual pioneer settler and the migration and settlement of groups of colonists, great or small in number. In the main, however, the latter was the practice. The day of the *homo migrans* of the Salic Code, and of the *hospes* of the annals and cartularies of the ninth, tenth, and even eleventh centuries,[2] had passed. While doubtless much forest land still

[1] Meitzen, III, 352–54; Kretschmer, *Historische Geographie*, sec. 227, where much local literature is referred to.

[2] See Du Cange, *Glossarium*, and cf. Lamprecht, *L'état économique de France*, pp. 230–41; Henri See, *Les Classes rurales et le régime domanial en France au moyen-âge*, pp. 212–38.

continued to be cleared by the lone pioneer, or bog land drained, or waste redeemed, the group idea was dominant. It was real colonization—the simultaneous co-operative migration of blocks of people, who took their cattle and household effects with them from the ancient homeland, and their settlement in a new country. This was the fashion in which the first important settlement of lowlanders was made in Germany, that of 1106 in the marshes of the Weser near Bremen.

The organized nature of these displacements of population in the twelfth and thirteenth centuries is one of the first things to strike the student. In another chapter I have endeavored to show this in the case of the history of the colonization of the trans-Elbean Hinterland by peoples of German stock who moved eastward from the older and more densely populated parts of Germany like Westphalia and Franconia. In the history of the influx of the lowland Fleming and Frisian, although the localities where they settled were different, we see the same purpose, the same motives, the same organization, and similar conditions of settlement.

One of the most interesting and most difficult questions in the history of these Flemish and Dutch colonies in Germany is that of ascertaining from what localities in Flanders or Holland these settlers emigrated. The sources in this particular are either silent or vexatiously indefinite, merely saying Flanders, Holland, the region of Utrecht, or more rarely Brabant. But the evidence of place-names enables us to make partial amend for this deficiency. Among localities in the Low Countries from which we may be sure some of these Flemish pioneers came may be mentioned Antwerp, Arras, Ghent, Lembeke, Bruges, Lille, Stockem, Daelhem, Velthem, Durstadt, Molhuysen, Herstal, and Liège.

But a word of caution is necessary. While some of them were initially formed of original settlers from Flanders and Frisia, which in course of time grew both from natural increase of the population and from agglomeration owing to the occasional arrival of new immigrants, on the other hand numbers of these Flemish and Frisian colonies in Germany evidently were not composed of *original* lowlanders,[1] but were offshoots of the mother-group. Confusion arises from the loose terminology of the sources, which do not always distinguish between Flemish and Dutch settlers, nor between original lowlander settlements and colonies derived from these. The lowland strain inclined to thin with each succeeding generation as the newcomers intermarried with their German neighbors, or with the local Wendish population which remained in its ancestral habitat. Finally, to confuse the investigator still more, the institutions of these lowlander colonies were sometimes copied by real German colonies, so that there are examples of the latter which bear the earmarks of Holland or Flanders, though they actually contained no inhabitant of that stock.[2]

The chief source of information for the history of these lowlander colonies is of a documentary nature.[3] Of the chronicles Helmold's *Chronica Slavorum* is far the most valuable. Philology has been an important auxiliary science in tracing the genesis of surnames and the names of places; and archaeology has thrown some light upon the subject.[4]

These Dutch and Flemish colonies in medieval Germany, as might be expected, were more numerous near the country whence the settlers came. The marsh lands of the lower Weser were the earliest place of settlement, then the lower and middle Elbe and its tributaries, then the Oder region. Traces of Netherlanders are to be found in Galicia, in Austria, and in the Carpathians. But little positive information is to be had concerning them.[5] The farther Baltic Coast

[1] For example, Lüntzel, *Gesch. der Diöcese und Stadt Hildesheim*, in mentioning the settlement established by Bishop Udo of Hildesheim calls it a "Flemish colony," whereas the names of the four men with whom the Bishop made the contract are obviously Frisian, i.e., Dutch, as Vogel, *op. cit.*, p. xi, has pointed out. Again, the fact that the Flemish form of landholding is found to obtain around Uebigau, Schweinitz, and Domnitzsch in the later Middle Ages does not prove that these places were settled by original Flemish colonists (Schulze, p. 127).

[2] Schulze, p. 126.

[3] Kötzschke, *Quellen zur Gesch. der ostdeutschen Kolonisation im 12. bis 14. Jahrhundert* (Leipzig, 1912).

[4] Meitzen, II, 358; Kretschmer, p. 374.

[5] Kaindl, *Gesch. der Deutschen in den Karpathenländern* (2 vols.; Gotha, 1907), II, 208; Knüll, pp. 94–95.

seems to have been settled chiefly by immigrants from Westphalia, although the dune and marsh topography might be presumed to have attracted the people from the Low Countries.[1] The high uplands of Germany and the mountainous region of the Erzgebirge and the Carpathians were usually avoided by them. They preferred cutting reed grass and digging turf to clearing timber and mining. The Flemish settlements near Waldheim and Altenburg (where even now there is a locality named Flemmingen) and the Dutch and Flemish (*qui et Flamingi*) colony near Koesen, which were certainly established there before 1140, that is, before the foundation of the Cistercian abbey of Pforta, are exceptional, for the reason that they found lodgment in a mountainous and forest country instead of a river plain.[2]

The earliest record of Netherlandish settlement in Germany is found in the *Bremisches Urkundenbuch* for the year 1062, when a small group of these immigrants was settled in the moors along the left bank of the Weser by the great archbishop Adalbert.[3] The fall of Adalbert and the plundering of the bishopric by the Billunger, coupled with the anarchy of Germany for so many years during the reign of Henry IV, probably deterred further immigration for a long time.

Things rapidly changed, however, soon after the century mark was turned. In 1106 Archbishop Frederick of Hamburg-Bremen energetically revived his predecessor's policy, and granted "certain lands which are uncultivated, swampy, and useless" to his own people to persons "who are called Hollanders," and who were apparently refugees, for the charter recites that they came to the Archbishop and "earnestly begged" for leave to settle on the moors.[4] The prelate, "considering that their settlement would be profitable," granted their request. The lands were divided into rectangular blocks measuring 720 "royal" rods in length and 30 in width. The settlers were to pay one penny (*denarius*) annu-

[1] Kretschmer, pp. 367–68; Lamprecht, III, 305.

[2] Schulze, p. 129 n.

[3] Lamprecht, III, 372.

[4] Kötzschke, *Quellen*, No. 1. There is an English translation in Thatcher-MacNeal, *Source Book for Mediaeval History*, No. 298. For commentary, see Meitzen, III, 264–68. Map 86 is a luminous exposition of the text.

ally for each hide or holding, to give every eleventh sheaf of grain, every tenth lamb, every tenth goat, every tenth goose, and a tenth of the honey and flax for tithes, besides a penny for each colt and a farthing (*obolus*) for each calf on St. Martin's Day. A tithe of these tithes was set aside by the Archbishop for the support of the parish churches, and each priest was to have one hide of land. They agreed to pay every year two marks for every one hundred hides for the privilege of retaining their own law and holding their own courts for the settlement of all their differences in secular matters. This they asked "because they feared they would suffer from the injustice of foreign judges." But the bishop's court was to be a court of appeal.

The success of the enterprise must have been soon manifest. For almost immediately afterward Bishop Udo of Hildesheim established a colony of Flemings at Eschershausen, west of the Harz,[1] and Dietrich of Halberstadt undertook the settlement of the lowlands between the Bode and the Ocker rivers.[2] Within two years after 1106 the promotion of Dutch and Flemish immigration for the redemption of swamp land became an organized effort of the clergy and lay nobles of Lower Germany. In 1108 the Archbishop of Magdeburg, the bishops of Merseburg, Naumburg, Meissen, Brandenburg, and three counts, Otto of . . . . , Wicbert of . . . . , Ludwig of . . . . , whose territories are not mentioned, "and all the greater and lesser lords of eastern Saxony" (*universi orientalis Saxonie majores et minores*) united in a joint circular petition to the Archbishop of Cologne, the bishops of Aachen and Liège, the Duke of Lower Lorraine, Robert, count of Flanders, and others, urging them to encourage the emigration of their surplus and hungry population into Lower Germany, which was represented, not unlike land-promotion schemes today, as a land flowing with milk and honey.[3]

[1] Kötzschke, *op. cit.*, No. 2. The original charter is lost. We know the fact from the confirmation of it by Udo's successor, Bernhard. For another such colony see Schulze, p. 158, n. 3.

[2] Vogel, *op. cit.*, p. vii.

[3] The text of this remarkable document is in Kötzschke, *op. cit.*, No. 3, where references are also given to a large amount of literature dealing with it.

We do not know what the immediate effect of this endeavor was. But by the middle of the century Flemish and Frisian immigration into North Germany was in full swing. Of the German nobles at this time Adolph of Holstein was the most active in this effort. Helmold says:

> In 1143, because the land was sparsely peopled, Count Adolph sent messengers into all the regions roundabout, even into Flanders and Holland, [the bishopric of] Utrecht, Westphalia, and Frisia, to proclaim that all who were in want of land might come with their families and receive the best of soil, a spacious country rich in crops, abounding in fish and flesh, and of exceeding good pasturage.[1]

The marsh lands of the lowest course of the Elbe at this time were the special region of colonization, where Eutin and Süssel were settled by Dutch and Frisian pioneers.[2]

The furious racial and religious war which broke out in 1147, known as the Wendish Crusade, devastated the whole eastern frontier of Saxon Germany from Magdeburg to Holstein. The new Flemish and Frisian settlements were imperiled at the moment when many of the men had returned to their old homes in the Low Countries to bring back the residue of their possessions which they had left there. When the infuriated Wagri burst into the region with fire and sword they found less than a hundred fighting men in the blockhouses which had been erected to protect the villages, instead of four hundred. Fortunately the Wends, while they hated the Saxons for their oppression of them, did not confound the Flemish and Dutch incomers with their German enemies. The frightened villagers, who could not have resisted if they had so dared, were spared, they and their herds and crops.[3] Alone the garrison in the blockhouse at Süssel, under the leadership of a priest named Gerlach, braved the foe.[4] What destruction did befall the colony, not without

[1] Helmold, *Chronica Slavorum*, Book I, chap. lvii.

[2] *Ibid.* Helmold confuses "Frisians" and "Flemings." For full information regarding these settlements see Gloy, *Der Gang der Germanisation in Ost-Holstein* (Kiel, 1894), pp. 17 f.; J. von Schröder and H. Biernatzki, *Topographie der Herzogtümer Holstein und Lauenburg*, I (Oldenburg, 1855), 6. The settlement of the Elbe marshes must, however, have been begun before 1144. For evidence see Wendt, *op. cit.*, II, 31.

[3] Helmold, Book I, chap. lxiii *ad fin.*

[4] *Ibid.*, Book I, chap. lxiv.

reason, was attributed to the violence of their Holsteiner neighbors, who were jealous of the industry of the settlers and hated them as "foreigners."[1]

The effect of the Wendish Crusade in 1147 was to open large tracts of border land to occupation which hitherto had been still precariously held by the Slavs, and a wave of Dutch and Flemish settlers followed hard upon a great influx of Westphalian colonists into the territory east of the Elbe, along both the lower and the middle course of the river.[2]

The promotion of this movement was participated in by all classes of landed proprietors—dukes, margraves, counts, bishops, abbots. The amount of lowlander blood infused with German in the middle of the twelfth century in the basin of the Havel River must have been considerable.[3] These tenacious lowlanders eagerly attacked the sodden soil. Thousands of acres of swamp land in course of time were redeemed by them. For example, documents of the year 1148 describe the region around Brettenburg on the river Stör as a huge morass. In the year 1340 the Dutch communities of Cronenmoor and Lütteringe are described as prosperous farming localities.[4] That the main body of settlers in Holstein was of Dutch origin Meitzen has shown from the fact that Christian I of Denmark in 1470 issued a decree canceling the jurisdiction of Dutch law in the Kremper and Wilster marshlands and substituting Danish law instead.[5]

No lord of North Germany was more active in promoting the colonization and settlement of these Dutch and Flemish

[1] The Holsteiners called these lowlander incomers "Rustri" (*ibid.*, p. 158 and n. 1). The term first appears in Schol. 3 in Adam of Bremen's *Gesta Hammaburgensis ecclesiae pontificum*, from whom Helmold, Book I, chap. lxxxiii, borrows it. See Pertz's edition of Adam of Bremen, the note to the scholium.

[2] This appears from a survey made by Bishop Anselm of Havelberg in 1150, after the Wendish Crusade was over, and is contained in the new *Fundationsprivileg* of Conrad III: ". . . . et cum praenominatae civitates et villae saepe irruentibus paganis vastatae sunt ac depopulatae adeo, ut vel nullo vel raro habitatore incolantur, volumus atque praecipimus, ut idem episcopus liberam absque contradictione habeat facultatem ibidem ponendi et locandi colonos de quacunque gente voluerit vel habere potuerit" (Riedel, *Codex Diplom. Brand.*, II, 438).

[3] Kötzschke, *Staat und Kultur im Zeitalter der ostdeutschen Kolonisation* (Leipzig, 1910), pp. 30–34.

[4] Meitzen, III, 354.

[5] Heinemann, *Albrecht der Bäer*, p. 222.

immigrants than Albrecht the Bear of Brandenburg. In this policy he was ably assisted by the bishops, especially Wichmann of Magdeburg. Except possibly Rainald of Dassel, Frederick Barbarossa's heroic archbishop of Cologne, and the versatile Christian of Mainz, who was for so long his viceroy in Italy, twelfth-century Germany had no abler prelate than Wichmann. On the paternal side he was descended from the Billunger dukes of Saxony, on his mother's from the margraves of Lausitz and Meissen.[1] After having completed his theological studies at Paris, Wichmann was successively prior of the chapter of Halberstadt, bishop of Naumburg (1148), and in the first year of Frederick I's reign was made archbishop of Magdeburg by him. He was a faithful adherent of the Emperor through all the long conflict with Alexander III and one of the chief negotiators of the Peace of Constance in 1183. He was an implacable adversary of Henry the Lion and a principal in the catastrophe which overcame the mighty Saxon Duke in 1181. In that year, with the aid of the Bishop of Halberstadt, he laid siege to Haldensleben. But the Count of Lippe, who defended the place, diverted the course of the Ohre River. Nothing daunted, Wichmann threw up dikes around the town so that the water overflowed the walls and drove the inhabitants to seek refuge in church towers and granaries. Wichmann then built a fleet of boats and with this little navy triumphantly sailed over the walls of Haldensleben and so captured it.[2]

Although Albrecht had received titular investiture of the margraviate of Brandenburg in 1134(?), the Slav element in the Mark was not wholly subdued until 1157,[3] an achievement materially aided by Wichmann. Already in the last year of his episcopacy at Naumburg, Wichmann had imported a colony of Flemings and settled them at Schul-

[1] Kechner, "Leben des Erzbischofs Wichmann von Magdeburg," *Forschungen zur deutschen Gesch.*, V, 417–562.

[2] *Chron. Montis Sereni* (*anno* 1181), in *MGH*, SS. XXIII, 158; Raumer, *Reg. historiae Brandenb.*, No. 1558.

[3] This information is contained in the fragments of the *Old Chronicle* of Brandenburg, to be found in Heinemann, p. 422; cf. Lavisse, *La Marche de Brandenbourg sous la dynastie Ascanienne*, pp. 71–72.

Pforta, where they long retained their own laws and gave their name—Flemmingen or Flaminghe—to the locality.[1] Six years after his transference to Magdeburg, when Albrecht's domination had been made complete in Brandenburg, Wichmann began the active importation of Flemish and Dutch settlers into the unoccupied marsh lands of the Havel. Wichmann, however, was not the original pioneer in thus settling these colonies along the upper Elbe, for already in 1154 Bishop Gerung of Meissen had established a group of them at Kühren near Wurzen.[2] But Wichmann was the greatest promoter of these enterprises, more so even than Albrecht the Bear himself.[3]

Of all the regions in North Germany in which these Flemish immigrants settled, perhaps the two most interesting colonies are those of Jüterbog and Bitterfeld. This is certainly true from the cultural point of view, for in these two places, as nowhere else, the descendants of the original settlers preserved for centuries the idiom of their ancestors. Jüterbog, a former Wendish village and the place where free and pagan Slavdom made its last stand in Brandenburg, fell into the hands of Albrecht the Bear in 1147. Perhaps this first margrave took the initiative in colonizing it. But the actual promoter was Wichmann, and the time of settlement between 1163 and 1167. The prosperity of the colony is evidenced by a charter of April 29, 1174, in which the Law of Magdeburg is granted to it,[4] and in the grant of which, to use the Archbishop's own words, he sought to "mitigate and to ameliorate" the condition of the inhabitants by exempting them from tolls and ordaining certain market privileges. Furthermore,

[1] Kötzschke, *Quellen*, No. 9; Wendt, II, 35. For a complete study see Rudolph, *Die niederländlichen Kolonien der Altmark im 12. Jahrhundert* (Berlin, 1889).

[2] Kötzschke, *Quellen*, No. 10; Vogel, p. vii; Schulze, p. 159.

[3] Kötzschke, *op. cit.*, Nos. 14, 15, 16, 18; Wendt, II, 30 f.; Heinemann, *Urkunden*, Nos. 38–41; Rudolph, *op. cit.* Hollanders were established at Krakau near Magdeburg, and at Kleutsch near Dessau; Flemings around Naundorf and Pechau near Magdeburg; Westphalians at Poppendorf, across the Elbe, opposite Magdeburg, *in pratis et paludibus*.

[4] Kötzschke, *op. cit.*, No. 31.

since the grace of God has followed our labor so that in Jüterbog where once pagan rites were carried on and frequent persecution of Christians practiced, now the Christian religion and the firm and guardian protection of Christianity obtains, on account of the devotion to the faith of all those who have migrated into this region or who may yet wish to come,

Wichmann grants the right of free pasturage to the people for their cattle "from Jüterbog to the farther hill of Zinna, and across the Bridge of the Flemings."

We know also from another source that these hard-working diggers and ditchers from the heavy soil of Flanders constructed a dike which first extended from Jüterbog to Nutritz and Dennewitz and later was prolonged to Schweinitz and Wittenberg. Around the point of intersection of the dike with the town grew up a *faubourg* called Damme. Was it so named from Damme in their homeland? In 1182 Wichmann, still liberal, established a mint at Jüterbog, the coins of which bore the superscription: *Moneta Nova Flamingorum Jutreboc.*

The details of the history of the settlement of these Dutch and Flemish colonies by Albrecht and Wichmann may be traced in the *Urkunden*. But Helmold's *Chronica Slavorum* has one chapter[1] descriptive of Albrecht's colonizing policy which is so excellent that it is here translated:

In that time [*ca.* 1157] the margrave Adalbert, surnamed the Bear, had possession of eastern Slavia, who by God's care over him very greatly prospered in his lot.[2] For he conquered [*misit sub jugum*] all the territory of the Brizani,[3] Stoderani,[4] and many other tribes dwelling along the Havel and the Elbe, and overcame those of them in rebellion.[5] Finally, as the Slavs gradually disappeared [*deficientibus sensim Slavis*], he sent to Utrecht and the regions of the [lower] Rhine, as well as to those peoples who live near the ocean and suffer the violence of the sea [*patiebantur vim maris*], namely, Hollanders, Zealanders, Flemings, and brought a great multitude of them and caused them to dwell in the towns and villages of

[1] Book I, chap. lxxxix.

[2] Helmold's phrase is *in funiculo sortis*. The figure is derived from the method of surveying land by measuring it off with a rope. Helmold several times mentions this form of mensuration, e.g., chaps. lxix, lxxi, lxxvii, lxxxiv.

[3] The Brizani were one of the small tribes belonging to the Baltic branch of the Slavs; they dwelt near Havelberg (Riedel, *Der Mark Brandenburg*, pp. 271 f.).

[4] A similar tribe in the same region (Riedel, pp. 306 f.).

[5] Albrecht the Bear recovered Brandenburg (the city) in 1157.

the Slavs. He greatly furthered the immigration of settlers [*advenae*] into the bishoprics of Brandenburg and Havelberg, wherefore the churches multiplied there and the value of the tithes greatly increased.

In this time Dutch settlers began to occupy the east bank of the Elbe. From the city of Salzwedel these Hollanders settled all the marsh and meadow land [*terram palustrem atque campestrem*] which is called Balsemerlande and Marscinerlande,[1] being very many towns and villages as far as the Bohemian frontier.[2] The Saxons are said formerly [*olim*] to have inhabited these lands in the time of the Ottos,[3] as can still be seen in the remains of old levees which had buttressed the banks of the Elbe in the swampy land of the Balsami. But afterward, when the Slavs prevailed[4] the Saxons were killed and the territory has been possessed by the Slavs until our time. But now, because God has generously given health and victory to our duke and the other princes, the Slavs everywhere have been worn down [*protriti*] and driven out, and peoples "strong and without number"[5] have been brought in from the borders of the sea, and have taken possession of the fields [*terminos*], and have built towns and churches and increased in wealth beyond all expectation.

Bitterfeld, between Wittenberg-on-the-Elbe and Leipzig, according to tradition, owes its foundation to a colony of Flemish refugees who were driven out of Flanders in 1153 by flood, and who were welcomed by Albrecht the Bear. Legend says that the original name was Beterveld (Besser Feld). Its history is a close repetition of that of Jüterbog.[6]

[1] Balsemerlande, Pagus Belxa, was the territory around Stendal in the diocese of Halberstadt. Marscinerlande is supposed to have been between Arnesburg and Werben, but Rudolph (*op. cit.*, p. 37) has questioned it.

[2] Helmold's words are *usque ad saltum Boemicum*. In chap. lxxx, p. 150, he uses the same phrase. Whether Helmold, who lived in Holstein, knew the difference between the Boehmerwald and the Erzgebirge may be doubted. Dehio (*Brem. Jahrb.*, VI, 85 f.) thinks the phrase refers to the Erzgebirge; Rudolph (*loc. cit.*), to the Boehmerwald. Schmeidler, the last editor of Helmold, is sure that the latter is not meant, and not certain that it applies to the former. I have translated the word *saltum* as "frontier," which, while not an exact rendering of the word, is sufficiently indefinite to express the hazy state of Helmold's mind.

[3] Cf. Helmold, Book I, chaps. xii and xviii.

[4] This refers to the great Slav rebellion in 1066.

[5] The words are quoted from Joel 1:6.

[6] There are several neighboring villages, as Puch and Muldestein, which are also of Flemish origin, and daughter-hamlets of Bitterfeld. In the latter are still the ruins of the castle and the chapel, today a church, which once belonged to the Bora family, to which Luther's wife, Catherine von Bora, pertained. An ancient lime tree near by long was called "Heinrich Flemming."

But the place in North Germany where either the Flemish colonization was densest, or the Flemish tradition longest preserved, is the region just east of Magdeburg, which is still known as the Fläming. It is the plateau which separates the Elbe from the Havel. All this district was peopled by the Flemings and became divided into Hohe Fläming and Nieder Fläming. Singularly enough, it was not the marshy nature of this locality, but its aridity that destined it for Flemish settlement. By reason of physical feature it was a waterless region and one never occupied by the Wends. But the Lowlanders were as expert in ditching as in diking, as skilled in making irrigation canals as in making fosses for drainage. Not all of the settlers here, however, were from Flanders; some were Hollanders. Upper Fläming was chiefly settled by Flemings; Lower Fläming by colonists from Holland. The place-names show it. We find Rohrbek, strikingly akin to Roosebeek in Flanders, Heinsdorf (from Henriksdorp), Markendorf (Marggravendorp), Woltersdorf (Wolterdorp), Gräfendorf (Grevendorp), Niemek, Genthin (from Ghent?), Kameryk (Cambrai), Brugge (Bruges), Aaken, Leeuweeden (Leuwarde), Eyper (Ypres) Lichtervelde. Significant, too, is the pronunciation of Mügeln, which is pronounced "Mecheln" in local idiom and reminds one of the medieval Flemish Mechelin (modern Malines). Among names of Dutch origin we find Stolzenhain (Stoltenhagen), Kaltenhausen, and Seehausen, all three in Nieder Fläming, Nimwegen, Gravenhage. It might be added also that family names in the Fläming even today bear out the double Flemish and Dutch lineage of the inhabitants.

Albrecht the Bear seems to have preferred the agency of others in promoting lowlander colonization of his territories to direct enterprise by himself. His favorite agencies were the Cistercians and the Praemonstratensians. In 1159 Abbot Arnold of Ballenstadt purchased two localities "formerly possessed by the Slavs" from the margrave, and sold holdings in them to "certain Flemings who had petitioned permission to occupy them and to preserve their own law."[1] In 1170 Otto of Brandenburg gave two villages, Dalchau and Druse-

[1] Kötzschke, *op. cit.*, No. 13A.

dow, to the Johannite Order, which had been settled by Hollanders during his father's lifetime.[1]

In the Weser region the initiative begun by Frederick of Bremen was continued by later archbishops. In 1158 Archbishop Hartwig I established a colony of Hollanders on the Ochtum, a small affluent of the Weser.[2] In 1170 Friedrich von Machenstedt, founder of the monastery of Heiligenrode, southwest of Bremen, received permission from his successor, Archbishop Baldwin, to settle the swamp lands between Brinkum and Machenstedt, west of the Ochtum, with Hollanders.[3] This example is interesting because Baldwin himself was a Hollander by birth, and in 1178 returned to his native land as bishop of Utrecht, over which he ruled until his death in 1196.

In Saxony the precedent of Dutch and Flemish colonization, which Adolph of Holstein was the earliest of the lay nobles of Germany to introduce, was followed by Henry the Lion, whose intelligent rule owes more to Adolph's example than his biographers have admitted. After all but the last remnants of the wretched Abodrite population were driven out of Mecklenburg in 1160, by a joint expedition of Henry and King Waldemar of Denmark, hundreds of lowlanders were imported into the bottom lands around Mecklenburg and Ratzeburg.[4]

As the end of the twelfth century approaches there is a noticeable falling off in Dutch and Flemish immigration into Lower Germany. How far this decline was due to the great revolution made in North Germany by the fall of Henry the Lion in 1181, or to the growing prosperity of the Low Countries, which, as every scholar knows, reached a high degree of economic development at this time, it does not seem possible to determine. One factor in "slowing down" this immigration perhaps may be found in this, that as the Weser and Elbe marshes increasingly became settled, the next available tracts, in the basin of the Oder, were so far away from the source of immigrant supply that it required unusual ac-

[1] *Ibid.*, No. 19. [2] Vogel, p. iv. [3] *Ibid.*

[4] Heinemann, p. 227; Henry the Lion founded a colony of Hollanders in 1164 around Erteneburg (Meitzen, III, 358).

tivity and unusually favorable terms to induce new settlers to go so far. Probably also the fact that the best marsh lands by 1200 had been taken up had its influence. What remained unoccupied was so huge and so hopelessly miry that simple peasants had neither the capital nor the engineering means to undertake its reclamation. Such enormous tracts of swamp as the Goldene Aue could be successfully drained only by corporate enterprise like that of the Cistercians.[1]

Almost without exception the Cistercian cloisters in medieval Germany were located in swamp or marsh regions, so that a system of drainage had to be worked out. The ruins of many of their foundations in North Germany still retain traces of these improvements. In the Harz and the hill country of Thuringia the tourist will come upon these remains. The swamps were drained, and the redeemed land (known as "polders" in Holland) was made fit for tillage and grazing. The water was impounded in reservoirs by dams and walls and used for both irrigation and milling purposes. The ditches were used as fishponds.[2]

As interesting as their use of engineering was the German Cistercians' effort to utilize the forests. Much of the face of the country was covered with dense forests. But instead of the former haphazard way of making clearings without reference to the value of the soil underneath, the Cistercians studied both the timber and the soil. They knew, or discovered, that where hardwoods grew there good land was to

[1] The standard work upon the German Cistercians is that of Franz Winter, *Die Cistercienser des nordöstlichen Deutschlands* (Gotha), Vol. I, 1868; Vol. II, 1871; Vol. III, 1871. For more recent literature see Werminghoff, *Verfassungsgesch. der deutschen Kirche im Mittelalter* (2d ed.; Leipzig: Teubner, 1913); Krüger, *Handbuch der Kirchengesch.* (Tübingen, 1911–12), Vol. I, Part 2, sec. 19, 5.

The economy of the German Cistercians has been made the object of a special study by E. Hoffmann, "Die Entwicklung der Wirtschaftsprinzipien im Zisterzienserorden während des 12. und 13. Jahrhunderts," *Historisches Jahrbuch der Görres-Gesellschaft*, Band XXXI (1910); Dolberg, "Zisterzienser-Mönche und Konversen als Landwirte und Arbeiter," *Studien und Mitteilungen aus dem Benediktiner- und Zisterzienser-Orden*, XIII (1892), 216–28, 360–67, 503–12. In general, for this colonization, see Winter, I, 137 f.; Hauck, *op. cit.*, IV, 326 f.; Lamprecht, *Deutsche Gesch.*, III, 386 f.; Michael, *Gesch. des deutschen Volkes*, pp. 91–120.

[2] Winter, II, 169. At Luttenbach, near Münster, water from the hills was conducted in underground conduits to freshen the orchard, to drive a mill, and to fill the fishpond.

be found. They never wholly denuded the forest but left patches of standing timber.[1] Moreover, they studied plant life for food purposes: seed germination, grafting of fruit trees, and mayhap even cross-fertilization. We know that in 1237 Doberan had a glass-roofed house for purposes of plant experimentation.[2]

When a brother went on his wanderings he always took with him plants and seeds and slips of trees and brought home whatever herbs and seeds he thought might flourish in the locality of his monastery. In this wise the culture of the grape was extended from the Rhinelands into Central Germany. The monks of Altencampen imported the prized vine slips of the vineyards of Basigny around Morimond to Cologne, whence other shoots were taken to Walkenried in Thuringia, and thence to Pforta and Leubus.[3]

The particular history of a few of the more notable Cistercian enterprises in medieval Germany may be of value as illustrative of the nature and extent of their labors. One of the most famous of their achievements was the creation of the Goldene Aue, or Golden Meadows.

The traveler who today traverses by railroad the fertile region from Naumburg to Artern, which passes through Memleben, with the ruins of the old Benedictine monastery there, where Otto the Great died, would not know that the broad tract, waving with corn in the summer wind, lying between Rosaleben and Artern, was once one of the most terrible swamp lands in all Northern Germany. For these Golden Meadows are in the very bottom of the Thuringian Basin.[4] Until the coming of the Cistercian monks hither in the middle of the twelfth century, this region was a wilderness of bog, morasses, and tree stumps.[5] In prehistoric times

[1] *Ibid.*, p. 171.

[2] *Ibid.*, p. 175. It was on the Baltic between Rostock and Wismar.

[3] *Ibid.*, pp. 173–74.

[4] For the geographical formation of the Thüringisches Becken see Kretschmer, *Historische Geographie von Mitteleuropa*, sec. 24.

[5] There is a valuable study on this subject, namely, R. Sebicht, *Die Cistercienser .... in der Goldenen Aue* (Halle, 1887); printed in *Ztschft. d. Harzvereins f. Gesch.*, Vol. XXI.

a lake had been here. The lake had now degenerated to a huge marsh whose sluggish waters found a partial exit through the little river Helme into the Unstrut and thence into the Saale. It was in the shape of a three-pointed star, one extension reaching from Sachsenburg to Meuthen, another, Untere Helmerieth, from Brücken to the Unstrut, and the third, Obere Helmerieth, from Brücken to Sundhausen.[1]

In 1144 Count Christian of Rothenburg a-d. Saale gave a portion of this boggy area near the village of Görsbach to the Cistercians of Walkenried, and later much enlarged the tract by subsequent grants. At the same time the Archbishop of Magdeburg exempted from payment of the tithe all the land which they might redeem. Within four years there was meadow where once there had been morass only. The monks then turned their attention to the lower Rieth. In the last years of his reign Frederick Barbarossa, who had learned to esteem those whom he had once persecuted, gave permission to Jordan, a monk of Walkenried, to drain the whole region of the lower Rieth. The Emperor gave Walkenried a *Hofstätte* (a manor court and farm buildings), with two hides of land, together with area sufficient for the erection of a mill, to which the water was carried by a canal. Not many years afterward the monks of the Goldene Aue[2] had mills in operation at Riethof, Bernigen, Görbsach, Windelhausen, and Kaldenhausen.[3]

Whatever the reasons, it is certain that there are proportionally fewer examples of the establishment of colonies of Dutch or Flemish in Lower Germany after 1180 than before that date. Hartwig II of Bremen in 1201 established a colony of Hollanders near Bremen, but it is noteworthy that exceedingly attractive terms were required to prevail upon them to come.[4]

[1] Winter, II, 190–93. For other literature on the Goldene Aue see Knüll, *Hist. Geogr. Deutschlands im Mittelalter* (Breslau, 1903), p. 93; Lamprecht, *Deutsche Gesch.*, III, 371–72; Schulze, *Koloniesierung*, p. 130.

[2] The term "Aue" first appears in the *Walkenried Urkundenbuch*, I, 10, 14 (Winter, II, 191).

[3] Winter, I, 193.

[4] Meitzen, II, 350–51; Kretschmer, p. 368; Knüll, pp. 7–8; Lamprecht, III, 326; Kötzschke, *Das Unternehmertum in der ostdeutschen Kolonisation des Mittelalters*

By the beginning of the thirteenth century the Hinterland of medieval Germany was not the valley of the Elbe, but the valley of the Oder. The "Far" East of earlier Germany had now become the "Middle" East,[1] and Breslau had taken the place of Magdeburg and Brandenburg as a frontier city. In the thirteenth century Silesia and the territory of Lebus in farther Brandenburg, where the March touched the Oder, not the bottom lands of the Weser and the Elbe, not lower Saxony and Mecklenburg, were the parts of Germany whither the tide of overflow population from the Low Countries directed itself. In Lebus, where the population still was heavily Slavonic (it was the ancient land of the Leubuzzi), the local house was very active in attracting colonists from Flanders and Eastphalia, from Hesse and Thuringia. In the thirty-five years between 1204–39 it is said that over 160,000 acres of waste or bottom land was redeemed by them.[2] In lower Silesia, where the people were Polish in blood, there was a great influx of German colonists in the time of Boleslav the Tall and his son Conrad, who seem chiefly to have come from Westphalia, and it may be surmised that most of the Flemish immigrants who entered Silesia came into the country in the wake of these. Zedlitz, west of the Oder near Steinau, seems to have been one of these settlements, and Pogel near Wohlau certainly was a Flemish colony.[3]

(Bautzen, 1894), pp. 5–8. It is unfortunate that Kötzschke has not included this record in his *Quellen*.

[1] Professor F. J. Turner has made this distinction classic for the history of the American frontier between the "Old West," the "New West," and the "Far West," and I have applied it here.

[2] Fisher, *Mediaeval Empire*, II, 16. I do not know upon what authority he depends for this statement.

[3] In the middle of the twelfth century the Augustinians of Breslau brought a colony of Walloons into the Altmark (Grünhagen, *Les colonies wallones de Silesie* [Brussels, 1867]), and later some serfs from Namur are found in Silesia. The Walloon immigration into Silesia preceded that of the Flemings, but they were never numerous. Their coming was rather an infiltration than a migration. Since Grünhagen's study, Levison ("Zur Gesch. des Bischofs Walter von Breslau, 1149–1169," *Zeitschrift des Vereins für Gesch. und Altertum Schlesiens*, XXV [1901], 353–57) has thrown new light upon this obscure Walloon population. Cf. Pirenne, *Histoire de Belgique*, I, 138, n. 3. Among these Flemings in Silesia it is of special interest to follow the career of two brothers, Everard and Simon, whose names appear in the charters for a space of thirty years. In 1261 they are merely mentioned as "Everard

In general, it may be said that east of the Elbe River the Cistercian monks and the Praemonstratensian canons were more active in furthering lowlander immigration than either the bishops or the feudal nobles, while as to Prussia, the whole exploitation of the land was in the hands of the Teutonic Order. But the activities of the great military order of the north territorially fall outside of Germany proper.

As to Dutch and Flemish immigration into Southwestern Germany, there is little to be written. Leopold VI of Austria in 1106 issued a charter bestowing certain rights and liberties upon "burgenses nostros qui apud nos Flandrenses nuncupatur in civitate nostra Wiena."[1] But the intensely mountainous nature of much of the Austrian and Hungarian lands repelled settlers who were used to a fen country. The Erzgebirge and the Carpathians had more attraction for Saxon miners from the Harz than for them. There is no evidence of organized or group colonization by Flemings or Dutch in Southeastern Europe. The few lowlanders found in Vienna or Hermannstadt probably percolated into the country individually or at the most in family groups.[2]

It was natural that the changes and new conditions here outlined should develop new institutions. Almost from the very inception of the movement it acquired an organized character. The joint proclamation issued in 1108 by Adolph of Holstein and other Saxon nobles is an indication of this. The mechanism of both feudal and ecclesiastical government was early used to promote and govern the movement of Dutch and Flemish colonization in medieval Germany. In the rivalry between the two forms that of the church was

---

et Symon fratres, Gallici [Walloon?]." In 1268 the latter is Burgrave of Steinau, two years later *castellanus* of Welun [from Walloon?], then *prepositus;* in 1274 the two brothers have become *comites*, and three years later Simon blossoms forth as a *palatinus*.

[1] This valuable charter is reprinted from Herrgott, *Monumenta domus Austriacae, etc.* (1750–72), in Reich, *Select Documents Illustrating Med. and Mod. History*, pp. 264–65. Kaindl, *op. cit.*, II, 206–10, has summarized the information to be found. For other special literature see Schwind-Dopsch, *Urkunden zur Verfassungsgesch. d. deutschoesterr. Erblande* (Innsbruck, 1895), p. 38.

[2] Kötzschke, No 53A; *Archiv f. Kunde d. Oesterr. Geschichtsq.*, X. 92; Huber, *Gesch. Oesterrich*, I, 488.

superior to that of the secular nobles; and of the two branches of the clergy the system of the Cistercian Order was superior to all.

One of the earliest and most influential institutions that developed was the office and profession of "promoter," or *locator*. Usually he was a bailiff or steward of the feudal domains of some prince or prelate, who as agent of the lord surveyed the tract intended for colonization, and then, armed with the terms of settlement, betook himself into the Low Countries and there organized a company of "homeseekers" whom he conducted into the new territory. His fee was commonly a preferred share in the enterprise in the form of an allotment of land. Naturally he often also became an important official in the new community and a medium between the settlers and the reigning noble. The first mention of a *locator* occurs in the year 1149.[1] But it is evident from the allusion that the office was already an established one. In fact, this sort of real estate agency became a profession.[2] Even cities were established in the same manner.[3]

There is much variation in detail in these settlements, but a striking general uniformity both in method of distribution of the allotments and in institutions. The model for almost all agreements seems to have been the charter of Archbishop Frederick of Bremen to the men of Utrecht whom he settled in the Weser marshes in 1106. Instead of the nucleated manorial village, with its peasant strips or plowlands in the spring and autumn "plantings" separated by dividing "balks" of turf, its demesne land, its group of huddled cottages in one corner of the manor, its array of irksome farm tasks and "boons," these colonial villages were laid out in rectangular blocks—an American would call them "sections" and "quarter-sections"—of 40, 60, 80, or more acres, so that each homesteader had a farm composed of contiguous land,

[1] Meitzen, II, 348.

[2] On the institution of the *locator* see Kötzschke's *Unternehmertum*, *etc.*, which is the most recent study of it.

[3] Poeschl, *op. cit.*, is full of evidence on this point. More briefly described in Heil, *Deutsche Städte und Bürger im Mittelalter* (Teubner's "Sammlung," Band XLIII).

and not, as under the manorial régime, an assembly of widely scattered holdings. We find these "manors of Dutch measurement" among both the Dutch and the Flemings and among new settlements of German colonists, who recognized the enormous advantage of the practice over the old system.[1]

The village, instead of being a huddled group of cottages, was a long street, every house situated at the near end of the holding facing the road. Behind it lay the farm acres, the meadow, the wood lot, in this order if the "lay" of the land so permitted. Somewhere, usually near the center of the village, were the church and the priest's house, the priest, besides the local tithe, having a holding of his own (called "Goddes peece" in England) which was worked either by parish serfs or by the peasantry of the village. If there were several villages close together, a number of them collectively were formed into a parish.[2] The priest's house and that of the *locator* were generally the most substantial and commodious structures in the community.[3]

These Flemish and Dutch settlers brought their own house architecture with them in many cases. While doubtless the original "shack" might have been rudely built of logs, the permanent edifice was often of homemade brick made out of the local clay, with timber travesses and, of course, timbered superstructure. The floors too were brick; peat, with which the lowlander was familiar, but which the German peasant had no knowledge of, was burned in the fireplace. Sometimes the front of the house was decorated with rude and curious carvings, or painted pictures of horse heads,

[1] These *mansus Hollandriensis dimensionis* are frequently mentioned in the charters, e g., Kötzschke, *Quellen*, No. 19; Riedel, *Der Mark Brandenburg*, p. 51; *Codex Diplom.*, I, 338. Elsewhere they are called "Flemish"—*mansos ad mensuram Flandrensium* (Kötzschke, *Quellen*, Nos. 13C and 50C). They were also known as *mansus regales* or *Königshufen* (Sommerfeld, "Gesch. der Germanisierung des Herzogtums Pommern" in Schmoller's *Forschungen*," XIII, Heft V, 140, 149). Meitzen has an exhaustive monograph, *Volkshufe und Königshufe* (Festgabe f. G. Hanssen, 1889), pp. 1–60, republished in Conrad's *Handwörterbuch*, IV, 496.

[2] On these Flemish "street" villages see Blanchard, *op. cit.*, pp. 423–27, who gives some interesting maps. Cf. Meitzen, II, 47–53, 343–44; Inama-Sternegg, *Deutsche Wirtschaftsgesch.*, I, 439–43.

[3] Lamprecht, III, 364–65.

swans, windmills, etc.[1] Of course these luxurious appointments obtained only among the more well-to-do settlers who possessed considerable land which was well diked and drained. Poorer settlers on small holdings frequently exposed to flood and freshet had no means to indulge in the blandishments of art.

One of the primary inducements always offered to these settlers was exemption from the exasperating and multiple manorial obligations which burdened them in the homeland to such a degree that these grievances were a real cause of emigration. The sources abound with evidence on this point. The charter clearly defined what should be the rights, duties, and obligations of both parties to the transaction, which, so to speak, became a written constitution for the government of the community. Sometimes, however, in order to make the colonists doubly assured, after reciting the duties and obligations the charter went on specifically to narrate from what the settlers should be exempt, so that their freedom was doubly defined.[2]

But in common with much that was new these settlers commingled some things that were old. They tenaciously clung to the preservation of their own native legal customs in the new land. The persistence of this characteristic trait of feudal particularism, which itself is traceable to the old Germanic legal theory of the personality of law,[3] in spite of the fluxing of the old order of things and the development of so many new institutions, is a striking example of the conservatism of things of the law.[4]

[1] See Hübbe, *Jahrb. und Jahresberichte d. Ver. f. Meck. Gesch.*, Band LXI (1896); Vigenes, *Bezeichnungen zum Volk und Land der Deutschen vom 10. bis zum 13. Jahrh.* (Heidelberg, 1901); Alfred Ronse and Theo. Raison, *Fermes-Types et constructions rurales en West-Flandre* (2 vols.; Bruges, 1919), I, 29 f. Meitzen, II, 359–60, has a detailed account.

[2] Item voluit idem archiepiscopus, quod omnes villici et cultores agrorum ejusdem ecclesiae liberi esse deberent *ab* omni censu civitatis vel villae et quod essent liberi *ab* omni advocatia, etc." (Henric. Wolteri, *Chron. Brem.* [*ca.* 1142], cited by Inama-Sternegg, II, 29 n.). For other examples see Schulze, p. 157, n. 1.

[3] Meitzen, II, 349.

[4] Even the *Stadtrecht* of Goslar (1256), although it was a mining-town where few lowlanders settled, shows traces of Flemish law, e.g., the *institutio que vulgar. Kura*

The charters abound with records of this privilege. It appears in the charter of Archbishop Frederick of Bremen (1106), in the earliest instance of Dutch colonization, where their traditional *judicia et placita* are guaranteed;[1] in that of Bishop Wichmann of Naumburg (1152) to the Hollander colony in Schul-Pforta;[2] in that of Bishop Gerung of Meissen (1154), where the provision is curiously worded: *in placitis que cum ipsis et apud ipsos;*[3] in 1159 in that of Abbot Arnold of Ballenstedt (*jure suo*); in that of Wichmann of Magdeburg in 1166 (*jure Hollandensium*); in the swamp colony established by Archbishop Baldwin in 1170 between Brinkum and Mackenstedt;[4] in the Kremper and Wilster marsh settlements.[5]

In the nature of things these imported judicial institutions were assimilated in course of time with those of the German population among whom these Dutch and Flemish incomers settled. But in some cases these special laws endured a long time. The Dutch colonies of Zarnekau and Gumale in Holstein preserved their "Hollensch Recht" and did not go over to "Holsten Recht" until 1438;[6] Christian I of Denmark in 1470 canceled the Dutch law of the Hollander settlement around Breitenburg in the marshes of the Stör;[7] the statutes of the Flemminger *Societät* in Bitterfeld were in vogue as late as the eighteenth century, and remains of them are still traceable in this locality.[8]

It is a noteworthy fact that these Dutch and Flemish

---

points to the Keuren of Flanders. The town coinage of Jüterbog and Bitterfeld for many years showed the Flemish origin of the places (Schulze, pp. 126–27, n. 2). The Belgian scholar Van Houtte has made a special study of the survival of Flemish law among these Flemish colonies in medieval Germany (*Le Droit flamand et hollandais dans les chartes de colonisation en Allemagne au XIIe et au XIIIe siecle* [Bruges, 1899]).

[1] Kötzschke, *Quellen*, No. 1.

[2] *Ibid.*, No. 9.

[3] *Ibid.*, No. 10.

[4] *Ibid*, Nos 13A, 14; Vogel, p. v.

[5] Kötzschke, *Quellen*, No. 6.

[6] Wendt, II, 16. The word *Strantorosen* in Hanseatic charters means "Frisians."

[7] Meitzen, II, 354.

[8] Schulze, p. 130.

immigrants, especially the latter, were almost wholly a rural peasantry and not a townspeople, although the Flemish towns by the twelfth century were already well developed. The attractions of commerce and industry dissuaded this latter class from emigrating. In consequence the history of German town life in the Middle Ages shows little evidence of Flemish influence.[1] Nor do Dutch or Flemings appear in the records as servile *ministeriales* and household servants. In the war of 1166 waged by Henry the Lion's rebellious vassals, Count Christian of Amerland seized Bremen with a body of "Frisian" troops,[2] but this is the only instance of the kind which I have met.

On the other hand, Flemish effect upon the material development of the open country, especially bottom lands, was very great. While the Wends were traditionally a marsh folk, their crude agriculture was incapable of the engineering necessary to drain the swamps. As for the German, he was a woodlander by ancestral association and by preference; even the Low German of the North German plain usually avoided the river bottoms, until the process of feudal inclosure of the Almend and the forests drove him to them.[3]

But the incoming Flemish and Dutch settlers had a natural aptitude for this kind of labor. They were used to bog and fen, to peat marshes and swamps, and by inclination preferred lowlands to uplands. The great landed proprietors of Germany who promoted their settlement had a clear perception of their economic worth; hence the large privileges accorded them. The charter of Bishop Gerung lauds the "strong men of Flanders" (*strenuos viros ex Flandrensi*) who will redeem the waste of swamps around Meissen. Besides ditching, diking, and draining these lowlander immigrants

[1] *Ibid.*, n. 3. Gilds of Flemish weavers are traceable in Nordhausen, Langensalza, and Görlitz.

[2] Helmold, Book I, chap. ciii: *Fresonum manu.*

[3] On this process of "inclosures" see Lamprecht, *op. cit.*, III, 53–58; von der Goltz, *Landwirtschaft*, pp. 93–98; Roscher, *Ackerbau, etc.* (11th ed., 1885), secs. 79–80.

materially helped the country by building roads.[1] Another service to which we find several allusions is the extermination of snakes by them.[2]

One might think that these humble laborers who settled where others would not go and hardly competed at all with the German would have been welcomed by him. But this was not the case. Helmold relates that the Holsteiners, not without reason, were suspected of firing the villages of Flemish and Dutch settlers during the Wendish Crusade "on account of hatred of these immigrants" (*advenae*).[3]

The resentment of the Wends toward them was more reasonable, for the Wends were a fen people who often were actually dispossessed by these settlers from the Low Countries. This was particularly the case in Brandenburg around Dressau, Wörlitz, and Pratau, where a ruthless expulsion of the Wends took place under Albrecht the Bear and Wichmann of Magdeburg.[4] In the really eloquent complaint of Pribislav, the Abodrite chieftain, relating the sufferings of his people, which is given at length by Helmold,[5] Flemings and Hollanders are mentioned along with Saxons and Westphalians as those by whom his people have been expelled from their homelands. "Worn down by the coming of these settlers," as honest Helmold says, "the Slavs forsook the country." It was the fate of the Red Man in America.

Lamprecht has said that the greatest deed of the German people in the Middle Ages was their eastward expansion over, and colonization of, the Slavonic lands between the Elbe and the Oder. Most of this long and important labor was done by

[1] Kötzschke, *Quellen*, p. 11 n.

[2] *Ibid.*, Nos. 2 (p. 7), 4 (p. 11).

[3] Helmold, Book I, chaps. lxiii–lxiv. *Ibid.*, chap. lxiv, quotes at length the harangue of a German priest named Gerlach against the Flemings, in which he said: "Nulla gens detestabilior Fresis. Sane fetet eis odor noster." Every anthropologist and ethnologist knows the importance of this phenomenon among primitive peoples. So the children of Israel in Egypt complained to Moses and Aaron: "Ye have made our savor to be abhorred in the eyes of Pharaoh" (Exod. 5:21). Even to this day in Germany, from the Weser to the Oder, the terms *Vlämsch*, *Vlämischer Kerl*, *Vlämisches Gesicht*, etc., signify "uncouth," "heavy," "rough," "having bad taste" (Schulze, p. 130, n. 3 at end).

[4] Schulze, p. 130.

[5] *Chron. Slav.*, Book I, chap xcviii.

the Germans themselves. But a not inconsiderable portion of this achievement was due to these nameless pioneers dwelling by the ocean and suffering the violence of the sea, who came to redeem the marshes of the Weser, the Elbe, and Havel, the Oder, and even the Vistula.[1]

[1] "Dieser Pionierdienst in der Kolonisation des deutschen Ostens ist unter den vielen Grosstaten unserer westlichen Brüder eine der grössten; er soll ihnen unvergessen bleiben in jeder deutschen Geschichte" (Lamprecht, *Deutsche Gesch.*, III, 342).

CHAPTER XVI

GERMAN SOUTHEASTWARD EXPANSION AND THE FORMATION OF AUSTRIA

NO ONE needs to be told that South Germany differs from North Germany in physical formation, in racial ingredients, in history. North Germany, save for the massif of the Harz, is a great plain. South Germany is a rugged, broken, mountainous country, the great trough of the Danube being the only physical feature giving unity to the region.

As are the physical differences, so are the racial differences. North Germany had but two peoples in contact or composition, Saxon and Slav. The history of South Germany was the achievement of two Teutonic peoples of equal importance, the Swabian and the Bavarian, each of whom occupied a different part of the country, each of whom made his own distinct history.

The history of South Germany, moreover, is more complex than that of North Germany for the reason that the South was included for centuries, first within the great Celtic empire of Central Europe, and then within the orbit of the Roman Empire (the Danube provinces of Rhaetia, Noricum, and the two Pannonias, which extended from the source to the great bend), so that, in spite of the Germanic dominant in this region, the history of South Germany is a palimpsest, for deep below, in the very fibers of the parchment, may be read the record of earlier Celtic and Roman occupation of the country. Finally, later, a considerable infusion of Slav blood entered into the composition of Southeastern Germany.[1]

[1] For a general ethnographic survey of the populations of the Danube see Van den Ghyn, *Polybiblion* (1888); for the Celts in Germany, A. Bachmann, "Die Kelten im Norden der Donau," *Ztschft. f. d. österr. Gymn.*, XXX (1879), 81–93. Kämmel, *Die Anfänge deutschen Lebens in Oesterreich* (Leipzig, 1879), pp. 313–14, gives interesting examples of the survival of old Celtic names in Pannonia. For

The making of Southeastern Germany was the work of the Bavarians, as the making of Northeastern Germany was the work of the Saxons. These are the two great pioneer Germanic peoples. An offshoot or a remnant of the formerly great Marcomanni, whose prowess had taxed the arms of Marcus Aurelius in the second century, the Bavarians seem originally to have been settled between the Saale and the Erzgebirge, whence they expanded up the Elster and down the Nab, across the Vogtland and Nordgau of later times, to and beyond the Danube. Once having reached the right bank of the Danube further expansion was easy, via the valleys of the Lech, the Isar, the Inn, the Enns, those Alpine affluents of the great river.

The time of this migration was for the Bavarians that epoch when their tribal sentiment and tribal institutions

---

Celtic survivals in Swabia see Buck, *Württemb. Jahrb. f. Statistik und Landeskunde* (1879); for Austria, R. Müller, *Blätter d. Ver. f. Landesk. v. Niederösterr.* (N.F., 1888), XXII, Nos. 1–2, a study based on place-names. Buck has also from a study of 45 charters of St. Gall pertaining to the ninth and tenth centuries demonstrated the persistence of Romanized Celtic blood in Rhenish Switzerland and the valley of the upper Inn (*Ztschft. f. roman. Philologie*, Band XI, Heft 1). Schulte, from an examination of the oldest lists of monks in the monasteries of Gengenbach, Ettenheim, Schuttern, and Schwarzbach in Baden, concludes that the ancient Roman population there preserved some traces until the ninth century. Krones, *Mitteil. d. hist. Ver. f. Steiermark*, Band XXVII (1879), thinks the Romanized Celtic population in Noricum did not disappear until the sixth century, when it was effaced by Slav immigration. The Bavarian penetration, which took place later, was accomplished without violence and not only absorbed the greater part of the Slavs there, but also assimilated Celto-Roman fragments which had escaped fusion with the Slavs. For Slav traces in Bavaria see Zapf, *Beiträge z. Anthrop. und Urgesch. Baierns*, Band IV (1881), and for Slav survivals in the Alps, Dopsch, *Die ältere Soziale und Wirtschaftsverfassung der Alpenslaven* (1912), a review of which may be read in the *Hist. Ztschft.*, CVIII, No. 2 (1912). In this long article Dopsch seeks to refute Peisker upon the economic and social institutions of the Slavs in Styria and Carinthia. Peisker has claimed that there existed among the Alpine Slavs two sharply differentiated classes: (1) the *zupani*, former nobles reduced by the conquering Germans, but living like their forefathers by cattle-raising; and (2) the peasants, who were serfs. Dopsch holds that these contentions are untenable; that the *zupani* were nothing more than manorial agents like the German *ministeriales*, and were not to be distinguished from the peasantry except by their function. Automatically the other contentions of Peisker fall to the ground. The original meaning of the word *zupan* seems to have been that of "clan chieftain," then official of the lord enjoying a servile benefice, later possibly, like the *ministerialis*, developing into a petty *dominus*. Usage of the word with a territorial application like *pagus* is modern (Lippert, *Soz. Gesch. Böhmens*, I, 120, n. 2, and his article in *Mitteil. d. Ver. f. d. Gesch. der Deutschen in Böhmen*, XXXI, No. 3).

seem to have acquired fixity of form and to have crystallized. The dissolution of the Ostrogothic kingdom in the sixth century indubitably facilitated the spread of the Bavarians in the middle Danube region. But, at the same time, that very decline of Ostrogothic power north of the Alps tempted the Frank to expand his power farther eastward down the Danube. Nominal subjugation of the Bavarians to Frankish sway was accomplished between 552 and 555. But it was not a conquest of violence. For the Bavarian needed the strong protection of the Frank in his new land owing to the formidable pressure of the Avars below him in the bend of the Danube.[1]

But if the Bavarian had need of Frank protection against the Avar, the need of the Danubian Slavs for protection against him was greater. Soon after 611 all the Slavs between the Alps and the middle Danube seem to have fallen under Avar sway, from which Samo (628–38?) had for a time released them. But with Samo's death the Avar peril returned, and in 745 Borut of Carinthia in return for Bavarian help recognized some sort of Bavarian control over Carinthia.

The early history of Bavaria before the rise of the Agilofinger ducal house is very obscure, and our information is wholly of an ecclesiastical nature. From the time of St. Severinus (d. 481?), whose *Vita* throws some light on conditions in Pannonia in the last half of the fifth century, until the seventh century, there is hardly a shred of information with reference to the history of Bavaria. Although remnants of Christianity from Roman times survived in the middle Danube lands, the Bavarians were and remained pagan until the coming of St. Eustasius (d. 625) among them from the Irish monastery of Luxeuil in the Vosges. Progress was slow, however, until the end of the seventh century, when the effect of St. Rupert's missionary work began to become evident. The first bishopric established was Salzburg in 696. Rupert, we are told, traveled by boat up and down the valley of the Danube as far as the border of lower Pannonia,

[1] Bachmann, "Die Einwanderung der Bayern," *Sitzungsb. der K.K. Akad. d. Wiss. in Wien*, Band XCI; Mehlis, "Beiträge z. Anthrop. und Urgesch.," *Münchner Gesellschft. f. Anthrop., Ethnol. und Urgesch.* (1877–78).

scattering the seed of life. He came to Walarius (Seekirchen am Wallersee), where he built a church in honor of St. Peter, and another at the place anciently called Civitas Juvavensis (Salzburg), where in former times there had been churches which were then fallen utterly to ruin and covered by forest.

This early Irish missionary endeavor soon began to experience the superior competition of a similar movement which emanated from Frankish Benedictinism. It was through the latter influence that the cult of St. Martin penetrated into Württemberg, where before the eighth century places named Kirchheim are to be found, and where there were five churches founded in Merovingian times dedicated to St. Martin. From Swabia these Frankish black-frocked missionaries passed over into Bavaria, where we find the first churches of the Latin faith under the protection of St. Michael and St. Stephen, to the prejudice of favorite Irish saints.

But effective organization of the church in Bavaria did not begin until the coming of Boniface, who founded the sees of Regensburg, Freising, and Passau, and refounded that of Salzburg on a Roman basis. At the same time a swarm of Benedictine cloisters began to be established in Bavaria. Neither the Bavarian Duke nor his people seem to have taken kindly to this monastic invasion. It savored too much of Frankish and Roman domination, and local sentiment in favor of the Irish form of Christianity was vivid. Nevertheless, the progress of Benedictinism was not slow in Bavaria. The Agilofinger dukes had to promote it for expediency's sake.[1] But their veiled conciliatory policy did not save the Bavarian dukes from complete Frankish conquest. The deposition of Tassilo, the last Agilofinger duke, in 788 by Charlemagne was the sequel of the alliance between the Frankish crown and the papacy, made in 751.

The progress of Frankish monastic colonization in Bavaria was given new impulse by this event, and ere long we find direct contact of Frankish secular and ecclesiastical power with the southeastern Slavs. These mission posts cleared the

[1] See Fastlinger, *Die wirtschaftliche Bedeutung der Bayerischen Klöster in der Zeit der Agilofinger* (Freiburg im B., 1903), for details.

forest and worked the salt springs found in the region and mark the beginnings of German colonization among the Danubian Slavs.[1]

The fall of Bavarian independence in 788 opened Southeastern Germany as never before to an influx of Frankish colonists and settlers, chiefly monks and nobles, who vied with each other in hunger for land and desire to exploit the native border population in the development thereof. The *monastic* and *aristocratic* nature of the colonization of the middle Danube lands is marked. It is evident that this mixed missionary and colonizing movement was directly inspired by the Frankish court, and far less a natural and spontaneous expansion of the people than was the case with the eastward spread of the Saxons. As early as Charlemagne's reign swarms of settlers from the more densely populated regions of the Moselle and the Rhine seem to have poured up the valley of the Main and so over into Bavaria and Carinthia. The bishopric of Würzburg, founded by Boniface in 741, was the Carolingian base for the evangelization and subjugation of the southeastern Slavs, and not Salzburg, as one might expect. For the Slavs of the Main, among whom Charles the Great established fourteen churches, were the connecting link between the Slavs of the Danube and the Frankland.

The heavy labor on these plantations of the church in the Bavarian Hinterland was done by the "converted" Slavs. Already as early as this the word "Slav" had become equivalent to "slave,"[2] and the systematic exploitation of them by the church through the imposition of the tithe an established and onerous practice.[3]

[1] In 770 the little stream of the Mühlbach seems to have formed the dividing line between Bavarian and Slav territory. We know that in the eighth century the village of Bischofshofen on the Pongau was neighbored "a vicinis Sclavis" (*Salz. Urkundenb. des Landes ob der Enns*, II, 2, 6, 13), and another document of 834 describes the territory around Kronsdorf on the Enns as "pars Sclavorum"; a third of 906 of St. Florian mentions "Bavari vel Slavi istius patriae" (*ibid.*, 55). Today this region on the right bank of the Danube is pure Bavarian, the trace of Slovenism once there having been absorbed (cf. Niederlé, *La Race Slav*, pp. 80–81).

[2] *Mon. boica*, XXVIII, 1, 45; XXXI, 1, 55. Schober, *Die Deutschen in Nieder- und Ober-Österreich, Steiermark, Kärnthen und Krain*, I (1881), 17–18.

[3] Already in the cartularies *labores* is the equivalent of *decimae*. For the brutality of the tithes imposed upon the "converted" Slavs see Zeissberg, "Arno, erster

In the still unappropriated lands the villages of the Slavs maintained a precarious existence, beset on every side both by newly established monasteries and settlements of German immigrants from farther west, who hewed out clearings for themselves in the forests. But most of these German incomers, as said, were not free, but serfs belonging to great Frankish proprietors and to the abbeys, who moved them *en masse* from their crowded domains in the Frankland into these new and sparsely peopled regions along the frontier. Commingled with these dependents, however, doubtless was a sprinkling of the lower grades of Carolingian society, the *hospites*, *peregrini et pauperes* of the great capitulary of 789 (art. 75), whom economic distress and social strain had detached from their old homesteads. Such people, without family or village ties, or deprived of them by misfortune and poverty, were only too glad to find refuge, even at the expense of privation, in the new lands of the southeast. The great famine of 791 must have increased this class of homeless and destitute, and so have promoted a drift of population into the region of the middle Danube. For Saxony was not yet subdued, and any strong northeastward drift of the Frankish population is not yet perceptible.[1]

But all this southeastward progress, which had extended the sphere of German occupation as far as the Enns before the end of the eighth century, was arrested, and much of it even destroyed, by the Avars. In 791, 793, 796, Charles the Great made campaigns against these formidable marauders. Two subsequent campaigns, in 803 and 811, completed their conquest. At the diet of Regensburg in 803 the Emperor formally organized the Ostmark, destined so many years later to grow into the duchy of Austria, and linked it up with the chain of Marches which guarded the eastern frontier of

Erzbischof von Salzburg," *Sitz. d. kaiserl. Akad.*, XLIII, 24; Dümmler, "Ueber die südöstlichen Marken des fränk. Reiches unter den Karolingern (795–907)," *Archiv f. Kunde österr. Geschichtsquellen*, X (1854), 21, and Schröder, "Arno v. Salzburg," *Neue Heidelb. Jahrb.*, II, No. 2.

[1] Of 119 place-names in the charters of Freising before 800, 24 per cent end in *inge*, which indicates settlements of Swabian origin (Sommerlad, *Die wirtschaftliche Tätigkeit der Kirche in Deutschland*, II, 214).

the Empire from the mouth of the Elbe to the head of the Adriatic. At the same time, as in Saxony, whose conquest was just completed, forcible conversion and the heavy weight of the tithe were imposed upon the Avars in order to complete their subjugation.

The destruction of the Avar power opened the door wide to colonization of the Danube lands both for German and southern Slav. For, while there is reason to believe the statement is exaggerated to the effect that the Avar land was left utterly uninhabited[1] after the conclusion of the conquest, yet there can be no doubt that the land within the new Ostmark was very much reduced in population.[2] The repopulation of this vast devastated territory, together with that of the similarly decimated Spanish March, was one of the keenest interests of Charlemagne during his last years. In both countries settlers began to flow in from the more densely peopled central provinces of the Frank Empire. But the border condition in the Ostmark (and the same is true of the Spanish March) was such that haphazard settlement was unthinkable. Both territories were regarded as *Reichsländer*, primarily occupied by the military, who strictly regulated the colonization. Allotments of land seem to have been systematically made to bishops, abbots, and great nobles, who imported settlers, many of whom were serfs, from Bavaria, the lower Main and middle Rhine regions into old Pannonia and the Riedmark.[3]

The German colonization, then, of the Ostmark was made by collective groups, chiefly of servile condition, under the direction of a feudal and ecclesiastical aristocracy, and not by individual free settlers.[4] In this particular, as well as in the

[1] Einhard, *Vita Karoli*, chap. vi.

[2] "Quos [Avaros] invictissimus Karolus ita in annis viii perdomuit ut de eis minimas quidem reliquias remanere permiserit" (*Monachus Sangall.* [written about 885], II, 1); Regino, *Chron.* (889), refers to the "Pannoniarum et Avarum solitudines."

[3] See the long list of Carolingian grants from the crown lands in what is now Austria, Steiermark, Carinthia, Carniola, and the Isar Valley, as given in Eggers, *Der königl. Grundbesitz im 10. und 11. Jh.*, pp. 26–28, in proof of this statement.

[4] Inama-Sternegg, II (1891), 7, fails to make the essential distinction between German northeast expansion and southeast expansion. "Die Rodung des kleinen

government supervision of the movement, the settlement of Southeast Germany differs greatly from the nature of the expansion toward the northeast, where a large proportion of the settlers were freemen and the expansion natural and uncontrolled (except in the Thuringian March between the Saale and upper Elbe) by government. Dopsch has made the point that the tide of German immigrants was probably as strong in the one direction as in the other, though, owing to the poverty of the sources, we cannot measure the depth and swiftness of the current setting toward the Danubian lands as we can that setting toward the trans-Elbean lands. But the new territory of the Ostmark was not to be undisputedly of Germanic settlement. For there is faint trace of the influx of Czech settlers also into this old Pannonian land, especially from Moravia.[1]

Now, for the first time, in the ninth century, the Adriatic Slavs became a factor in German history. The Frankish destruction of the Avar power had removed the bulwark which for years had hindered the expansion of the Bulgars. They now began to penetrate into the eastern part of the former Avar territory. By the middle of the ninth century their influence extended as far as the Theiss and the Timok rivers and brought the Bulgars and Serbs into conflict.[2] The effect of this pressure by the Bulgars was to drive some of the Slavonic peoples, notably the Slovenes, into Carinthia and later Styria.

---

freien Mannes" is largely true of the former provinces (except the land between Saale, Elbe, and Erzgebirge); it is not true of the Danubian lands. At p. 8, n. 2, he cites an exchange of a manor (*praedium*) in Bavaria with two serf families upon it for one in Carinthia with eight such families as an instance of voluntary settlement of simple freemen.

[1] *Conversio Bag. et. Car.*, chaps. vi, x, xi; cf. Niederlé, *op. cit.*, pp. 82–86.

[2] "Tunc vero Sclavi post Hunos inde expulsos coeperunt istis partibus Danubii diversas regiones habitare" (*Conversio Car.*, chap. vi); "In Slavoniam, in partes videlicet Quarantanas atque inferioris Pannoniae," etc. . . . . Coeperunt populi sive Sclavi vel Bagoarii inhabitare terram unde illi expulsi sunt Huni, et multiplicari" (*ibid.*, chap. vii). For this westward drift of the Slovenes see Dümmler, *op. cit.*, pp. 25–29, 33. Down to 828 the Drave formed not only the diocesan limit, but also a frontier between the counts of lower Pannonia and Friuli. The Count Odalric, mentioned in 860 and 869, administered upper not lower Pannonia (Pirchegger, *Mitteil. d. Inst. f. österr. Gesch.*, XXXIII [1912], No. 2).

What the relative proportions were of the mixed peoples which were gathered together here in the middle Danube lands it is, of course, impossible to say. But it will escape no one that the intricate and varied racial composition of old Austria dates back at least as far as the ninth century. The process of assimilation or fusion of these various ingredients was a slow and unsuccessful one, in spite of the influence of the church and the military organization which obtained. For that influence was political and administrative in its nature, not social, except in the matter of depressing the population to a condition of serfdom. It requires more than a mortar and a pestle to effect the fusion of peoples. It takes time to change a mechanical mixture into a chemical compound by transfusion of blood. From its inception down to its latest history, Austria always has been a state which grew *par agglomération*, instead of organically *par assimilation.*

Historians have endeavored, on the evidence of place-names, to determine which localities were German and which were Slav in the old Ostmark. But apart from the fact that much of the Carolingian régime was destroyed at the end of the ninth century by the inroads of the Magyars and the work of recolonization had to be begun anew after 955, the findings cannot be conclusive. For in any case the distinctions would hold good only of the free villages (and these were few), and not of the manors of the *Grundherrschaften*, on which German, Slav, and even Avar serfs toiled side by side.

The physical area of this colonization, however, is not a matter of dispute. By the end of the ninth century the German sphere of influence extended beyond the Enns, which had been the farthest east of German expansion in pre-Avar times, and had reached the Raab. The civilization in this land was lustily, even brutally, materialistic in its character. "Wer mit der einen Hand den Pflug fasst und die andere am Schwertgriff halten muss, der hat für die Feder keine frei." The social texture was that of a warlike feudal and ecclesiastical aristocracy imposed upon a servile peasantry. The three-field system of farming was practiced, at least upon the manors of the church, along with some grape-growing on the sunny slopes. Other activities were lumbering, beer-making, salt-making, and bee-keeping.

But, once more, as in the eighth century, again at the extreme end of the ninth and beginning of the tenth, most of this hard labor of colonization in the lands of the middle Danube was doomed to go for naught. The history of German southeastward expansion exhibits the same alternation of advance and retreat that characterizes the history of northeastward expansion. Just as the Slav reactions of 983, 1018, and 1066 undid the work of trans-Elbean colonization, and threw the Saxon pioneers back across the Elbe three several times, so in the Ostmark the labor of settlement was twice undone, first by the Avars and then by the Magyars.[1]

By 896 the Magyars were settled upon both banks of the Theiss, and thenceforward for years both Germany and Northern Italy were harried almost annually by their depredations. In 900, the margrave Liutpold built the Ennsburg out of the stones of Passau's old Roman wall. The military reforms of Henry the Fowler of Saxony, and his victory on the Unstrut in 933, partially abated the Magyar danger. But effective check to their inroads was not made until Otto I's smashing defeat of them near Augsburg in 955. After that date a steady stream of German colonists seems to have flowed into the twice-wasted land of the Ostmark. The body of these pioneers probably came from Bavaria. But there is reason to believe that with them was a considerable proportion of Franconian and Swabian immigrants from farther west.[2]

[1] The eastward drift of the Carolingian Pfalzen is marked in the middle of the ninth century (Schröder, pp. 20–21). Ludwig of Bavaria is found at Tuln in 864 in the Ostmark (Jaffé, 2758). Pertz, *Mon. Ger. Hist.*, SS. I, 378, n. 52, thinks that Tuln was Theben, in the defile at the confluence of the March with the Danube, which Dümmler, *Ostfränk. Gesch.*, I, 528, n. 37, holds to be impossible. In 884 Charles the Fat was at Tuln (*Annal. Fuld.*). Until the coming of the Magyars the Raab was the eastern boundary of the Ostmark (Pritz, *Gesch. des Landes ob d. Enns*, I, 317; *Mon. Boica*, XXVIII, 1, No. 72, a charter of Charles the Fat). The first Carolingian castle at Regensburg was built by Charlemagne.

[2] When Adalbert of Babenberg and his house were exiled from Franconia in 906, their lands there were confiscated to the fisc. From this circumstance it was long believed that the Babenbergers were natives of Franconia. But evidence has been found to indicate that they came originally from Swabia (Stein, *Forschungen z.*

The history of Austria in the first decade of the tenth century begins obscurely to revolve around the great house of Babenberg, as the vaporous rings of superheated gas in the cosmic world slowly congeal around some stellar sun to form a new world. But, unfortunately, no contemporary writer has left us an account of the early history of the Babenbergers in Austria, such as Widukind and Adam of Bremen wrote of the Billunger dukes in Saxony. But it admits of no doubt that effective and permanent political formation of the Ostmark really began with the Babenbergers.

But that the progress of German southeastward colonization, however, was slow and not without arrest and interruption may be inferred from the fact that the Magyar peril, while much allayed, was not wholly removed by the German victory on the Lechfeld. For as late as 1020 Vienna was taken by the Magyars, and in 1043 Henry III was compelled to make a complete reorganization of the Marks which buttressed the southeastern flank of the German kingdom.[1]

Nevertheless, after 955, in spite of obstacles and setbacks, the advance of German southeast colonization, if slow, was sure. The stages by which the great Böhmerwald region and the Riedmark were settled by German colonists are very obscure.[2] But it is certain that there was a rather steady in-

---

d. Gesch., XII, 113–36; Hüber, *Mitteil.*, II, 374–82), whence it has been inferred more than demonstrated that there was a considerable commingling of Swabians among the German settlers who flowed into the Ostmark after 955 (Budinger, *Österr. Gesch.*, p. 161; Kötzschke, *Deutsche Wirtschaftsgesch.*, p. 110). The truth is that the place of origin of these pioneers and the stages by which the territory beyond the Enns and between the Danube and the upper Drave was resettled in the last half of the tenth century are not clear. The most complete examination of the subject has been made by Hasenörhl, "Deutschlands südöstliche Marken im X., XI. und XII. Jahrhundert," *Archiv f. österr. Gesch.*, LXXXII, 419 f. The maps are valuable.

[1] The term "Terra Ostarrichi in regione vocabulo Ostarrichi . . . . dicto" first appears in 996 (Meiller, *Regesten*, I, p. 2, No. 2); the form "Austria" in 1074 (Hasenörhl, p. 452, nn. 1–2). For Henry III's reorganization of the Ostmark in 1043, when the Neumark is first mentioned, see Thausing, "Die Neumark Österreich und das Privileg. Heinrici," *Forschungen*, IV, 361 f. The earliest mention of the Riedmark is in 1155 (Hasenörhl, p. 450, n. 33).

[2] Since Hasenörhl's monograph and maps were published Julius Strandt has studied the history of the Riedmark anew ("Die freien Leute der alten Riedmark: Wenden und Bajuwarensiedelung" [with 2 maps], *Archiv f. österr. Gesch.* [1915]).

flux of settlers through the whole Saxon and Salian period, and that the process was pursued with little conflict. For the Bohemian forest was too dense for habitation hitherto, and clearings had to be painfully and laboriously made with the ax, which was far more useful than the sword as a weapon of expansion. As before, so now again, the work was done by big "operators," namely, the high clergy and great feudal nobles. Unfortunately there is no chronicle of the Babenbergers to tell us the tale of this recovery and renewed expansion like Helmold's *Chronica Slavorum* for the German northeast. The history has to be traced through detached and often widely separated pieces of evidence in Meiller's *Regesten der Babenberger* and the charters in the *Monumenta Boica*. Historical imagination, from later facts which have come to light, and from the analogous history of the northeastward expansion of the German people, often must visualize the nature of the movement by a process of inverse reasoning.

Important, positive facts are few and far between. By 994 we know that Leopold of Babenberg had carried the frontier of the Ostmark down to the Wienerwald. For in that year, in which he lost his life by an accident, he organized the Traungau on the right bank of the Danube,[1] and the Riedmark and the Machland upon the left bank.[2] These three military erections must have been made to cover the thin line of German pioneers pushing eastward. This forward movement seems to have been quite sudden and of considerable pressure. For as late as 985 much of the bishopric of Passau is described as a wilderness, so bereft of serfs that freemen had to do villein service on the church patrimonies.[3] Yet when Pilgrim of Passau died in 991, the land between the Wienerwald and the Enns seems to have been fairly well settled.[4]

[1] For the Traungau see Strandt, "Das Gebiet zwischen der Traun und der Enns," *ibid.*, XCIV, 466 and 662.

[2] For Machland see Strandt, "Das Land im Norden der Donau," *ibid.*, p. 282.

[3] Meiller, *Regesten*, Vol. I, No. 3: "Ut liberi cujuscunque conditionis sint qui destinantur coloni in locis pertinentibus ad sanctae patauiensis aecclesiae, etc."

[4] Huber, I, 177. For examples of settlements of free peasants and serfs here see *Mon. Boica*, XXVIII, A 216, 243; B 88; XXXI, A 223.

North of the Danube at the same time a similar colonization in the Böhmerwald was effected by Wolfgang of Regensburg (d. 994).[1] The explanation of this sudden bulge of the frontier toward the southeast is probably to be found in the successful rebellion of the Slavs of the Elbe in 982, which destroyed all the German settlements across that great river, and set back the eastward expansion of the Saxon people for nearly a generation.

Leopold's son and successor, Henry I of Babenberg, continued to promote his father's work of colonization, and at this time we find Franconian settlers among the Bavarian and Swabian incomers. The record is to be read in ecclesiastical grants, not all of which, however, are genuine. For the church, taking advantage of the obliteration of the earlier boundary lines in these localities, which had been run in times preceding the Magyar invasions, forged new deeds in the effort to enlarge its already enormous possessions. In particular, the forgeries made by Pilgrim of Passau were notorious. The devastated monasteries of St. Polten, Kremsmünster, and St. Florian made paper claims of vast extent.

The magnitude of the tracts which the church claimed was only exceeded by the brazen effrontery with which these forgeries were fabricated. According to the *Passauer Saalbuch*, some time between 985 and 994 Duke Henry of Bavaria held an inquest, at which the bishops and abbots and nobles of the March were present, in order to determine the nature and extent of the "rights and liberties" of the Bishop of Passau, and it found that Passau's claims stretched clear up to the Wienerwald! It is evident that the Bavarian Duke who was overlord of the Margrave himself, as well as others in the region, was becoming jealous and alarmed over the land-hunger of the Bishop of Passau.

The Wienerwald seems for several years to have retarded settlement. But more important than the resistance of the

[1] *Mon. Boica*, XXVIII, A 227. For the date see Ficker, *Urkundenlehre*, I, 197. In 1010 the Böhmerwald, sometimes known as the Nordwald, is described as "silva quae vocatur in comitatu Adalberonis in longitudine a fonte flumenis quod dicitur Ilzisa sursum usque ad terminum praedictae silvae qui separat duas terras Baioriam videlicet et Boemiam et ita usque ad fontem fluvii qui dicitur Rotala" (cited by Hasenörhl, p. 444).

forest was the hostility of the sparse but resolute population (principally Magyars, but with some settlers of Slavonic blood) living east of the forest. This territory was a sort of "No Man's Land" between the two competitive groups, where every man's hand was likely to be against another, and certainly against any encroaching pioneers out of Germany. Thietmar of Merseburg tells the story of an Irish pilgrim named Colomannus, who was captured and killed as a spy by these borderers. A tinge of legend already when he wrote (1017) had gathered around this incident. But there is no reason to doubt the essential accuracy of the tale, which so clearly illustrates the suspicious nature of the population in this *terra nullius*. The first positive evidence of German settlement east of the Wienerwald is found in 1002, when King Henry II granted to a certain noble of Bamberg named Pilgrim a tract of territory eighteen miles square, from which in after-days the endowments of the abbeys of Zell and Heiligenkreuz were to be derived.

At some unknown date in the career of Margrave Adalbert of Austria (1018–55) the site of Vienna had been occupied by him, probably as an advance post to cover the German settlements which by that time had succeeded in penetrating the Wienerwald.[1] The establishment of these soon led to border strife between Germans and Magyars, in which apparently the former were the aggressors, so that King Stephen of Hungary interfered to protect his subjects. The danger to the Ostmark arising from this intervention was great enough to call Conrad II into the Danube lands. But in spite of the strong forces with him (the panegyrist of King Stephen says that the imperial host was drawn from "all Germany") the difficult nature of the country, which abounded with forest and swamp, made successful military operation impossible.

[1] If the author of the *Gesta Friderici I*, chap. xxxiii, in his account of Henry of Bavaria's Danube campaign in 1146 meant Vienna by "vicinum oppidum Hyenis," then the place must have been very insignificant at that time. Much discussion has revolved around the question of the origin of the word Vienna. Grienberger, *Sitzungsb. k. Akad. d. Wiss. in Wien*, Band CXXXI (1894), concedes that Roman Vindobona is of Celtic origin, but thinks Vienna of Slav origin. Müller, *Blätter d. Ver. f. Landesk. v. Niederösterreich*, Band XXX (1896), denies that the word is either Roman or Slav, but admits that its origin is unexplained.

While not actually defeated, perhaps, in a pitched battle, Conrad II lost a large number of men and was compelled to retreat, leaving the honors of the campaign with the Hungarian King, who captured Vienna.

German recovery from this reverse was slow. The narrow strip of territory between the Fischa and the Leitha rivers had to be ceded to Hungary. This frontier area, like the Scottish Border, was the scene of a strife which left a picturesque and indelible mark upon medieval German literature in the greatest of German epics; but in spite of the fact that the region was perilous ground, German settlers, and even some adventurous traders, persisted in creeping in.

The chance for German retaliation and recovery came in the reign of Henry III. In 1038 a war of succession disrupted Hungary, and Henry III was not slow to profit by it. In 1042 the country east of the March was invaded, the Maygar army terribly slaughtered, and all captives, men and women alike, massacred in cold blood. With considerable strategy the Emperor had avoided the marshy region of the Raab, which had so discomfited his father, and invaded Hungary through the Bavarian Nordgau, falling upon that part of the kingdom which lay north of the Danube. The whole valley of the Waag as far as the Gran River was fearfully devastated by the Germans. Nine Hungarian towns were taken, and two in addition destroyed by the Magyars themselves when evacuation of them was made necessary. A submissive Magyar embassy came to Regensburg in 1043 to sue for peace. Henry III demanded the cession of the debated territory between the Fischa and the Leitha, the return of all German captives, and the payment of 400 talents of gold as reparation for damage done to the German border settlements.

The Austrian Mark thus extended (the new annexation was called Neumark) entered upon a new history. More compact, though larger than before, it lay on both sides of the Danube, the rivers Thaya and March protecting its front north of the Danube, the Leitha doing the same south of the Danube, while the flank of the Mark was covered by the Mark of Carinthia. During the war just closed the Emperor had destroyed the two Hungarian advance posts, Hainburg and Pressburg, now mentioned for the first time in 1042, which lay almost opposite to each other on either side of the Danube. By the terms of peace the Germans retained Hainburg, but Pressburg had to be returned to Hungary and was at once rebuilt. Commanding the famous defile known as Theben, which forms a natural gateway, Pressburg was of incalculable importance to Hungary.

The conversion of Hungary early in the eleventh century introduced a new factor in the racial and border rivalry of the Germans and the Magyars. As early as the second half of the tenth century Christian missionary monks from Bavaria had begun to penetrate into Hungary, while at the same time the trade with Byzantium brought in missionaries of the Greek church. These rival groups in turn competed with Italian and Slovene missionaries from the dioceses of Friuli and Aquileia.

The inclination of King Géza was toward the German form of Christianity, for he feared Byzantine menace more than German pressure. Political interest, not religious "conversion," was the primary motive which inspired the marriage of the King's son Stephen to Gisela, a daughter of Duke Henry of Bavaria, with the result that many German notables swarmed into Hungary and soon came to form an influential party at the Magyar court, to the resentment of the Magyar nobles who looked with distrust upon this alien racial and religious intrusion.

But in spite of this opposition Stephen, who became king in 995, was favorable to German immigration into his kingdom, as his father had been before him. His attitude is seen in the advice he gave his son: "Hold the 'guests' [*hospites*] in honor, for they bring foreign learning and arms into the country. They are an ornament and a protection to the throne. For a kingdom of one language and manner of life is weak and easily destroyed." The first Christian King of Hungary modeled his administrative system after that of feudal Germany, and, in spite of hostility between the two governments and the two races, promoted the settlement of German colonists not only on the crown lands, but also on the lands of the nobles and clergy.[1]

[1] K. Schünemann, *Die Deutschen in Ungarn bis zum 12. Jahrhundert* (1923).

Abstractly considered, one may applaud the intelligence and liberality of this policy of the Magyar King in thus endeavoring to elevate the condition of his country and people by borrowing from the higher German civilization. But the policy carried with it the possibility of political reduction of Hungary to German vassalage, and evidence of strong anti-German feeling soon became manifest in the kingdom.

After the death of King Stephen, Hungary became torn by a strife between two factions: the one a pagan, national party; the other a Christian and pro-German party—a struggle in which control of the crown was the objective of each. The former was led by a pretender named Aba; the latter was represented by King Peter. In the issue, while Christianity triumphed, fortunately the Magyar nation was too vigorous to succumb to German pressure, and was able to preserve its independence and the genius of its people.

The illusions which once were cherished as to the antiquity of the early chronicles of Hungary have been dissipated by modern criticism[1] so that one is compelled to rely for information upon the sources of peoples neighbor to them, Germans, Poles, and Byzantine Greeks. One of the oldest accounts of Hungary and the Hungarians is to be found in the *Vita major* and the *Vita minor* of King Stephen (d. 1038), which were written after the canonization of that King by Benedict IX (d. 1044). Of these two sources the *Vita major* is the older. An additional source is the *Monita*[2] or book of instructions which this first Christian king drew up for his son and intended successor, Emerich, who, however, died before his father.

All three of these works were written by German monks dwelling in German monasteries established in Hungary in the years following the official recognition of Christianity by King Stephen in the year 1000.[3] They reflect German his-

[1] For example, the "Anonymi Belae regis notarii Gesta Hungarorum" (ed. Endlicher), *Rerum Hungar. mon. Arpad.*, I, 15–54, is now known to be of twelfth-century authorship at least, and not improbably of thirteenth.

[2] Migne, *Pat. Lat.*, CLI, 1234 f. Stephen's laws are in the same volume, cols. 1243 f., or *MGH*. SS. XI, 229–38.

[3] See the long critical dissertations upon these sources by Kaindl, *Archiv f. österr. Gesch.* (1894–1902); Heinemann, *Neues Archiv*, XIII, 63 f.; Steinacker, *Mitteilungen*, XXIV, 135 f.

torical tradition, e.g., *Regino* and the *Annals of Altaich*, and German sentiment toward the Magyars.[1]

Nevertheless, if we penetrate below the gloss of German prejudice and contempt, we discover the lineaments of a constructive administrative system of both state and church in Hungary. The episcopal system contributed much to the firm administration of the country, while the new monasteries, largely of Cluniac foundation, aided greatly the material and moral culture of the land and people. Administratively the kingdom was divided into counties. The court was organized after the German model. A landed aristocracy soon began to be formed, serfdom was introduced, though there were still many free Magyars. The penal laws were severe, especially upon pagans and heretics, although quite curiously Jews enjoyed greater liberty in Hungary than in Western Europe.

The pro-German, Christian party naturally looked to Germany for support, and Henry III was not slow in giving it. German politics and the interest of the German church were so combined together that German intervention in Hungary or war with the Magyars became chronic, on one pretext or another. In 1042 the Emperor made a formidable expedition into Hungary. He crossed the river Raab with Bavarian and even Bohemian troops, gained a great victory on July 4, captured the golden lance of the pretender Aba, and recovered many German priests and other Germans who had fallen into Aba's hands. At Stuhlweissenburg, King Peter was formally invested with the crown and scepter of Hungary as a German vassal. His first act was to ordain Bavarian law in the country for those of German lineage—a fact which shows that most of the incomers into the kingdom must have been of Bavarian stock.[2]

[1] "Barbarica gens Hungarorum" (*Vita minor*, 1); "filii perdicionis et ignorancie, populus rudis et vagus, culturam Dei nesciens, Ungari videlicet et Pannonie patriam inhabitantes" (*Vita major*, 1).

[2] "Illis etiam petentibus concessit rex scita teutonica" (i.e., German law and institutions); cf. Steindorff, *Jahrb.*, I, 211, n. 2. Herim. Aug. (1044), says, "Ungarios petentes lege baioarica donavit," a statement denied by Magyar historians as contradictory to Hungarian sources. For discussion of this moot point see Steindorff, I, 211; II, 452 f.; Waitz, V, 143; Giesebrecht, II, 661; Riezler, *Gesch. Bayerns*, I, 458, n. 3; Fränkel, *Forschungen*, XXIII, 125. Possibly only Christianized Hungarians are meant.

A new native and pagan reaction followed soon upon the withdrawal of the German troops, and again, in 1045, a second German intervention in Hungary took place. This time German suzerainty over Hungary was more formally declared, a process facilitated by lavish distribution of German gold among Peter's following. Pressburg, too, was garrisoned by Bavarian soldiery. The effect of the changed political condition at once was manifested in a great influx of German settlers into the Neumark. Grants of land were also made to German nobles and clergy in Transleithania, notably the gift of a hundred manors around Neusiedler See (significant name!), a big salt lake belonging to the Bishop of Freising.

But the turbulence in Hungary continued for some years yet. In 1047 German relief had again to be sent to the Christian-German party in Hungary, where, owing to the death of King Peter, a new pagan and nationalistic reaction was begun. His successor, Andreas (1047–61), attempted to reconcile the two hostile factions, and to avoid the religious issue by uniting them together in a common opposition to the growth of German ascendancy in the country. In 1051 Pressburg was captured by the Magyars, after a heroic resistance by the Bavarian garrison. Accordingly, in that same summer, for the third time Henry III invaded Hungary with a larger army than ever before, in which were Bavarians, Swabians, Franconians, Saxons, Burgundians, and even Lombards from Italy, and Slavonic troops from beyond the Elbe. Bishop Gebhard of Regensburg and Duke Welf of Bavaria were conspicuous leaders of the expedition. Immense supplies were floated down the Danube for the maintenance of the army.

In spite of the difficult nature of the country and the fact that his supplies threatened to fail, the Emperor pressed on. Relief for Hungary, which seemed likely to be crushed by this formidable host, came from a new and unexpected quarter. At this juncture the papacy was just beginning to unveil its programme of ecclesiastical reform and church ascendancy over imperial authority, although the clerically minded Emperor failed to read the signs thereof. The identification of the papacy with the radical wing of the Cluniac party had lately been effected, and Rome, anticipating the coming struggle, in order to weaken the imperial power began that policy of relaxing the German grip upon the subjugated border nations. It was an adroit stroke. For it simultaneously curtailed the imperial power and bound the newly converted border peoples closely to Rome, which posed as the protector of Bohemian, Polish, and Magyar liberty against German domination. The enormous historical significance of this course is apparent, and in the case of the Poles and the Hungarians explains their intense Catholicism even to this day. Hungary was saved from terrible punishment, perhaps even from destruction by Germany, through the intervention of Leo IX.

The clement policy of Henry III at this time undoubtedly weakened the imperial prestige. The anger of the German feudality at being thus balked of what they regarded as theirs by right of might was great. For their hearts had been set upon the spoliation of Hungary. Duke Conrad of Bavaria and Welf III, duke of Carinthia, were furious. Indeed, Bavarian disaffection at this time is the root, perhaps, of Guelf hostility toward the Salian house from this time forth.[1]

One of the things which a modern historian must guard against in studying medieval history is the error—for it would be an error—of translating later national antagonisms back into the feudal age. It is doubtful whether the hostility of the Germans as a race was greater toward the un-German peoples along the border than was the internal animosity of Frank, Saxon, Swabian, Bavarian, toward one another. Race and national feeling played a much less important part in the high Middle Ages than is usually supposed. The German border abounded with renegades from their own country and kindred, whose desertion is treated with astonishing condonation by the chroniclers. The Saxon clerk, Widukind, has no

[1] *Annales Altahenses maj.* (1053); Herim. Aug. (1053). Nitzsch makes much of the importance of this event. The famine at this time prevailing in Bavaria led to the flight of whole villages of peasantry, many of whom must have flowed over the frontier, "Vini frugum maxima penuria in tota pene grassabatur Baioria. Quapropter colono fugiente plurimi vici deserti remansere." *MGH.*, SS. V, 133; Curschmann, *Hungersnöte im Mittelalter*, p. 119.

word of reproach for Wichmann, who, because Otto the Great preferred his brother, deserted to the Slavs and waged guerilla strife with his own countrymen.

In harmony with the good old German precedent of deserting to the enemy for revenge, Conrad, with a large number of fellow-malcontents, now joined Andreas of Hungary, who gave the renegades a warm welcome. United, a force of Magyars and Bavarians invaded the March of Carinthia (it had been detached from the duchy of that name in 1035 and became the later Steiermark or Styria, which by this time had become fairly well populated by German settlers, although we know little about the process of this colonization), devastated the new settlements and captured Hengstburg on the river Mur, a northern affluent of the Drave, which the Hungarian King at once fortified.

The folly of the enterprise became apparent within a year. The Hungarian garrison in Hengstburg, worn out by the incessant attacks of the German population, evacuated the stronghold and fled to Hungary. The Emperor, seizing upon the incident as a pretext, while he nominally placed his infant son in the duchy of Bavaria as duke, practically incorporated Bavaria with the royal domain. As for Carinthia, a new history began for it with the accession of the house of Eppenstein. Andreas of Hungary compounded in the end for the ravaging of Styria. But for several years the Austro-Hungarian border was infested with border ruffians, the leaders being the outlaw Conrad and Chuon, the luckless Hungarian commander in Hengstburg, whom King Andreas proscribed.

In 1058 an attempt to establish a firm peace between Germany and Hungary was made by the betrothal of the Magyar prince Salomon and Judith, daughter of Henry III. But the time was not yet ripe for so intimate a relation. The national party rose in opposition under the leadership of Andreas' brother Béla. A German commission composed of Eppo of Naumburg, Margrave William of Meissen, and Duke Ernest of Bavaria was sent into Hungary. The appearance of this embassy, instead of ameliorating the situation, poured oil upon the flames.

The events which immediately followed (1060) have an almost Homeric quality of action and of courage. Andreas, as the chronicler says, "feeling that he would be safer in foreign territory than in his own country," endeavored to escape into the Austrian March with his wife Anastasia, who was a daughter of the Russian Duke of Kiev, but was intercepted by forces of Béla in the narrow defile of Theben, the famous gateway into Hungary where the river March falls into the Danube, a river for centuries the boundary between Austria and Hungary. Andreas was taken alive, but was almost instantly killed in a charge of the Magyar horse. The Queen, with her son and the royal treasure, escaped, and found refuge in the monastery of Melk. But all three of the German ambassadors were captured.

Nevertheless, in spite of the rout, the honors of the day were with the Germans. For Margrave William of Meissen and a Bavarian count palatine named Poto put up such a fierce resistance that if feudal Germany at this time had been as sensitive to romance as was France, the memory of their feat of arms would have rung down the ages in a medieval German *chanson*. "For these two," run the *Annals of Altenheim*, "when the others were slain took their stand upon a knoll and laid about them with such slaughter that the deeds of the very bravest men of former times seem small in comparison. From evening until sunrise they fought, nor could they be overcome even by the thousands (?) against them. They would not surrender until king Béla's word of honour to spare them was given." Ever afterward Poto was known as "the Brave." The chronicler Ekkehard, forty years later, wrote of him: "Truly was he believed to be sprung from the race of the giants of old."[1] So impressed was King Béla with

[1] Ekkehard Uraugiensis, *Chron.* (1104), SS. VI, 225. The memory of this famous day lived long in German song. In *Vita Bennonis II, episcopi Osnabrugensis* (written between 1090 and 1100), there is a most interesting allusion to it: ". . . . adhuc notae fabulae attestari solent et cantilenae vulgares." Cf. Hauck, *Kirchengesch. Deutschlands*, IV, 486, and n. 1. That Germany in the twelfth century was feeling the lilt of song within her breast is evidenced by a collection of songs composed in the Rhinelands, and recently edited by Karl Breul under the misleading title: *The Cambridge Songs. A Goliard's Song Book of the XIth century* (University Press, 1915). For the collection is manifestly of German origin, and nothing but the circumstance that it reposes in the Cambridge University Library justifies the

the prowess of Margrave William that he offered him his daughter Sophia in marriage. But fate intervened. The Margrave returned to Thuringia and prepared to remove permanently to Hungary *cum magna opum suarum ostentatione*, when he was taken suddenly ill and died. The Princess married Udalric, margrave of Carinthia, instead.

The expulsion of all Germans in Hungary, including Princess Judith and her young husband, followed this reverse. The new Magyar king, Béla, tried to avert a German retaliatory expedition by alleging that they had fled voluntarily, and disavowing responsibility for the exile of German subjects in Hungary, who were represented as quitting the country of their own accord. War ensued in the summer of 1063. A large German army invaded Hungary. Béla suddenly died and his son Géza became a fugitive in Poland. The pro-German and pro-Christian party in Hungary triumphed. Young Salomon, now practically a protégé of the German crown, was carried to Stuhlweissenburg and crowned king.

For eleven years the Christian-German party ruled in Hungary. But in 1074 the exiled Géza returned, and the national party triumphed. Emperor Henry IV had just taken the government into his own hands after the disastrous regency of his early youth; the Saxons were on the point of rebellion, and already the papal policy, though masked, was apparent. Henry IV's expedition against Hungary accomplished nothing except to rescue his sister and her husband.

But if German ascendancy beyond the Leitha was checked by these events, nevertheless the Hungarian wars had strengthened the Babenberger house in Austria. Margrave

---

title. No. 12 is a song in honor of the three Ottos, and especially a laudation of the great Hunnenschlacht in 955; Nos. 13, 14, and 17 are complaints upon the death of Henry II and Conrad II; two are songs in honor of Henry III (Nos. 15 and 16); and, finally, Nos. 19 and 20 are songs in honor of Heribert, archbishop of Cologne (999–1021), and Poppo of Trier (1016–47). With these evidences we may associate the interesting statement in Widukind, I, 23, of how, in his day, the memory of a great fight around the Ehresburg between the Saxons and the Franks two hundred years before was still commemorated in song and story: "Adhuc sermo in ore ejus erat, et ecce Saxones ei occurrerunt miliario uno ab urbe, et inito certamine, tanta caede Francis multati sunt, ut a mimis declamaretur, etc." Indeed, "mimi, joculatores, histriones," are often mentioned in the sources of the ninth and tenth centuries (cf. *Epistola Ermenrici Augiensis*, SS. II, 101, n. 39).

Adalbert (d. 1055) and his son Ernest (1067–74) were lavishly rewarded by Henry III and Henry IV, who saw the means not only to guard the frontier but also to check the hostility of Bavaria in the formation of a powerful Austria. Adalbert had received enormous grants of land from Henry III; Henry IV described Ernest of Austria as "our true knight," and rewarded his fidelity by the gift of forty manors in the forest of the Raab.

The progress of German culture in the southeast during this period is no less important than the political development. By the time of Henry IV, under the able administration of Bishop Altmann of Passau (1065–91), this portion of the Danubian lands had begun to lose the shaggy frontier aspect of a border diocese, and to acquire some of the material amenities at least of that civilization which might be enjoyed in older Germany.

The *Vita* of the Bishop casts interesting light upon this change. A native of Westphalia and educated at Paderborn, in his time the most distinguished school in Saxony, Altmann had become chaplain of Henry III at the court in Goslar, *ad radicem montis Ramisberc de quo argentum tollitur*. In 1065, when the wave of pilgrimages to the Holy Land was at its height, Altmann joined the huge pilgrim host led by Gunther of Bamberg. In Syria he, with the whole body of travelers, narrowly escaped capture by the Turks. Shortly after his return from the East, the see of Passau became vacant and, through Bamberg influence (for it was the favorite bishopric of the Salian emperors), Altmann was made bishop of Passau.

He was an enthusiastic supporter of the Cluny reform, and thoroughly purged the monasteries in his diocese, notably St. Hippolytus and Kremsmünster, of licentious and simoniacal monks. His labors for the material improvement of the church in the Passauer bishopric were no less active. He found the churches made of wood, he left them stone; he found them devoid of decoration and without books, he left them embellished with pictures and ornaments and equipped with libraries. Apparently, judging from the relation of his enthusiastic biographer, Altmann must have imported marble columns, and possibly even expert Italian workmen, into Bavaria, for it is hardly conceivable that the elaborate decorative work he accomplished could have been done by native German artisans.

In the field of politics Altmann seems to have been no less efficient. His influence won over the Margrave Leopold (1075–96) from the imperial to the papal side during the war of investiture, and, although Henry IV made a foray into the March, ejected Altmann, and "made the see of Passau the see of Satan," the King was unable to extend his power over the Austrian March.

Of the influence of these vicissitudes, both the German-Hungarian wars and the war of investiture, upon the extension of German colonization farther down the Danube, it is difficult to say much that is particular. It would seem that the anarchy in Germany during the reign of Henry IV must have led to an exodus from the older provinces of the kingdom, where the conflict was most fiercely waged, into the newer lands of Austria. We know that this was the case in the northeast. Why not also in the southeast? It is not mere inference that colonization of the Austrian lands was stimulated by the events of Henry IV's reign. For in the next century one finds a surprising number of new German communities established there. In the narrow border strip between the Fischa and the Leitha, the territory of which had been so bitter a ground of feud between Germans and Magyars earlier in the century, we find German domination rooted and firm. The exiled Salomon here ruled like a king of Yvetot over a toy "kingdom," and was lavish in making grants to the Bavarian bishops, especially to Freising, out of his domains.

Further tangible evidence of German extension in the Mark is found in the charters of the monasteries. The colonizing activities of the bishops and abbots in Austria, in Styria, in Carinthia, in the late eleventh and through the twelfth century, were very great. The multiplication of German place-names shows it. This progress of German colonization was no less energetic north of the Danube. German and Bohemian backwoodsmen clashed in the great Böhmerwald, where their spheres of settlement met. This is the time when Melk, Klosterneuburg, Heiligenkreuz, Lilienfeld, St. Maria Zell, Zwettl, Seitenstetten, Geras, and other abbeys began to grow rich and fat on gifts of land. At the same time families of the high feudality like the Ebersberg, the Falkstein, the Schala-Burghausen, the Bogner, the Plaien-Peilstein, the Sulzbach, who naturally brought with them a crowd of colonists, free and serf, began to rise. Some of these families probably drifted into the middle Danube lands from old Germany as the result of German participation in the Second and Third Crusades.

Naturally, the Bavarian sees, Salzburg, Passau, and Regensburg, which formed the frontal line of the church in the southeast, played the largest part in this process of colonization. But the work of Bamberg in this field is a notable one. Bamberg was the favorite bishopric of the Salian dynasty, and had been originally founded by Henry II in 1007 as a mission station among the Slavs of the upper Main. The tradition thus attached to its origin soon made Bamberg a radiant point for the extension of German influence in all the border lands, both northeast and southeast. The bishops of Bamberg long regarded the promotion of missionary work among the Slavs as the peculiar duty of their see.

The history of the splendid labors of Otto of Bamberg in the conversion of Pomerania early in the twelfth century is one of the brightest pages of medieval ecclesiastical history. But in the eleventh century Bamberg's missionary zeal was especially directed toward the southeast.

Bamberg, however, did not attempt to compete with the Bavarian bishoprics in the Danube lands proper. She left these regions free to Salzburg, Passau, and Regensburg. Her special mission was to the Slavs, not to German settlers in the Austrian Mark and its dependencies. Bamberg missionaries lived and labored particularly among the Slavs of Carinthia. The effect was to bring numbers of German colonists from Franconia, and even the middle Rhinelands, down into this remote corner of Central Europe, like the Eppenstein, the Sponheim-Ortenburg, the Herren von Hennburg, the Karlsberg, the Anstein, etc.—almost all Frankish names. In a word, while the German basis of the population of Austria was Bavarian, that of Carinthia was of Frankish origin.

In like manner Freising, too, marked out a sphere of missionary activity among the Slavs of the southeast. For Freising, finding herself blocked of direct eastern extension by Salzburg and Passau, executed a flank movement, so to speak, around them and found an exit for her colonizing impulses down the Save River, in a field which she made peculiarly her own in Carniola (Krain). The detachment of Krain from Carinthia in 1040, and its erection into a separate Mark, was partly influenced by military consideration, and partly by the historical difference between the German colonization of the two regions.[1] Here, as elsewhere, the colonization was predominantly aristocratic, and made by noble Bavarian families like the Herren von Hoflein, Stein, Hertenberg, Reydeck, Rabensberg, etc., though the presence of a few families of Swabian origin is discernible, like the Auersperg, Osterberg, and Gallenberg.

A unique and puzzling German settlement in this province is the little German *enclave* of Gottschee in Carniola, southeast of Laibach. The place of origin of the original settlers of this community is unknown. It is first mentioned in 1347, when Bavarian colonists from the Ortenburgen pushed into the region, then described as a wilderness, and found there already an islet of German population in a lake of Slav blood. Some scholars have thought that possibly this strange, isolated German group in Gottschee may have been descended from original Germans of the *Völkerwanderung*, who by accident got caught in a "backwash" of the current of the German nations then drifting westward and south and down into the Roman Empire.

The Slav population found by these German incomers in Carinthia, Carniola, and Styria (Steiermark) was less driven out than depressed, as was the case also in the northeast, in

[1] See, on this, Krones, "Die Markgrafen von Steiermark: Ihre Anfänge, ihr Verwandtschaftskreis und ihre Kärntner Markgrafschaft vor 1122," *Archiv f. österr. Gesch.*, LXXXIV, 137 f.; Dopsch, "Die Kärnten-Krainer Frage und die Territorialpolitik der ersten Habsburger," *ibid.*, LXXXVII, 1 f.

the Thuringian Mark, in Brandenburg, Mecklenburg, and Pomerania. Unfortunately, such full and vivid chronicles as those of Thietmar of Merseburg, Adam of Bremen, and Helmold, which cast so much light upon the history of German colonization in the northeast, are wanting for the history of southeastward German expansion. In partial compensation, however, a considerable body of charters has been preserved, and in the codices and cartularies of the monasteries founded in these lands peopled by the southern Slavs, place-names and family names, both German and Slav, are of frequent occurrence, which often give us clues to larger information. The beginnings of the German colonization of Neumark in 1045, in especial, are clearly revealed in the charters of Henry III.[1]

To sum up: Everywhere in the Danube, Drave, and Save lands the political and social overstratum was German and aristocratic; but the understratum differed. In Austria it was chiefly a German servile peasantry of Bavarian blood. In Carinthia, Carniola, and Styria a German peasant stock of servile condition was settled down side by side with the native Slav peasantry, also of servile condition. The provenience of these settlers differed. Carinthia and Styria (which was separated from Carinthia in 1035) were mainly colonized by Franconians and Rhinelanders; Carniola mainly by Bavarians, but with some Swabians.

The colonial nature of the history of all these provinces of the southeast, in what may be termed the "Austrian complex," was stamped upon their physical appearance and upon their institutional organization. That organization was simple and hard. For generations the people in these regions had wrought their way through enormous forests; they had faced savage beasts and hostile foes; they had had to build blockhouses, to fortify islands, to clear the woods. The wilderness put its seal upon the people. Life was rude and crude.

The administrative development was in harmony with this stern environment. It was intensely military and more centralized than in the older parts of Germany. The land was

[1] See Steindorff, *Heinrich III*, I, 235 f.; Giesebrecht, *Kaiserzeit* (5th ed.), II, 653.

not divided into *Gaue*, that immemorial local administrative unit of the German folk. Nothing so civil as that obtained. It is true that the word *Gau* appears as an alternative to *pagus*, but the *pagi* in the Danubian provinces were primarily military *cadres*. The word had a military not a civil meaning; and all the other similar terms, as *regio* and *provincia*, have the same connotation. Again, the political authority of the high clergy, which played so large a part in the history of old, feudal Germany, was not nearly so powerful in these new lands. No bishop, no abbot, exercised a sway comparable to that possessed by the Rhenish bishops or the abbots of ancient monasteries like St. Gall, Fulda, and Hersfeld.

Technically, the tenure of the margraves was wholly at the will of the German kings. They were removable like counts. In this position their status differed from that of the dukes whom feudal traditions and tribal consciousness of Bavarians, Swabians, Franks, Saxons, girded around. But practically, at least in Austria, for two hundred years the Ostmark had descended from father to son in the Babenberger house, and what was lost of moral influence owing to the absence of any tribal self-consciousness was compensated for by the centripetal pressure arising from Austria's frontier location and formation.

In theory, all territory won from the Hungarians was held to be imperial land. In fact, it became the Margrave of Austria's own. He consolidated his power within and extended his sway without. The first mention of Vienna as a *civitas* is in 1130; but from the time when Henry Jasomirgott made it the capital of the ancient Ostmark in 1156,[1] Austria was actually a feudal state different in formation from the older feudal duchies of Germany, but quite as independent. But instead of being a political entity in itself like them, Austria was really the center of a system of which, so to speak, it was the sun. Styria, Carinthia, Carniola, and lesser territories like Riedmark, Mark Pettau, and Mark Saunien were a loose complex of which Austria was the core, vaguely

[1] Out of the recorded acts of Henry in Meiller between the years 1156 and his death in 1177, 37 are made in Vienna and 29 elsewhere, chiefly when Henry was in attendance at the diets, or in Italy with Frederick I.

adhering together more by agglomeration than by organic unity. It was adherence, not coherence, which gave the Austrian lands whatever loose unity they possessed. The most active force was external, not internal, and this emanated from Hungary.

The strip of territory between the Fischa and the Leitha, so long in dispute between the margraves and the kings of Hungary, by the end of the eleventh century had become definitely German, and formed a buffer region between the two states. But it was a weak bastion. As long as Pressburg and the Theben Pass were in Hungarian hands, the Ostmark and the Nordgau were insecure. In 1108, when the storm of the war of investiture had nearly spent its fury, Henry V beleaguered Pressburg, but retired discomfited by the prowess of the Magyars and the difficulty of the *terrain*. In 1119 the border warfare was especially fierce. In 1131 the Steiermark was invaded by Hungarian forces, a raid in which the settlements established by the bishops of Salzburg suffered severely. In 1138 an allusion of Otto of Freising shows that Hungarian expansion north of the Danube had spread so far that Poles and Magyars clashed *in silva quae Polonios et Ungarios sejungit*, as already we have seen Bohemians were in border strife with Bavarian pioneers in the Böhmerwald.[1]

A century before the Marchfeld, history had determined that the Leitha was to be and remain the "farthest east" of German expansion. At the time when Frederick I erected Austria into a duchy in 1156 Hungary had recovered from her internecine wars and developed into a strong national kingdom.

Early in the twelfth century a new impulse to German colonization was imparted by the Cistercians whom Leopold of Babenberg, father of the historian Otto of Freising, first introduced into the Austrian lands. It was he who founded the famous cloister of Heiligenkreuz, whose house yet exhibits a statue of the last Babenberger prince.

[1] Hasenörhl, *op. cit.*, LXXXII, 444. A *Zollverordnung* of Conrad III shows that by his time a trade route had been cut through the Böhmerwald between Bavaria and Bohemia: ". . . . licentiam . . . . mercandi habeant usque ad silvam Boemicam" (*Urkundenbuch des Landes ob der Enns*, II [1852], 54).

The middle of the twelfth century is the high-tide period of German eastward expansion. It is the time of the huge colonizing activities of Adolf of Schauenburg, Albrecht the Bear, and Henry the Lion, when Mecklenburg, Brandenburg, and Pomerania were won to German blood and German culture. The provinces of the middle Danube felt the same force, and part of the current of colonization must have flowed toward the southeast, although we know relatively little about the movement when compared with the information we have concerning the lands across the Elbe. The principal event of this time is the famous settlement of 1156 when Frederick Barbarossa erected the Austrian Mark, which Conrad III had separated from Bavarian dependency in 1142, into the duchy of Austria. This act is both the term of a long process of formation and the point of departure of a new epoch.

The history of the Babenberger house during the century after this date, until its extinction in 1254, is merely an epilogue. The formative period of Austrian history terminated in 1156; the rest was but accretion.

The chief labor of Leopold V (1177–94) was to extinguish the overlordship of the German King in Styria. Fortunately Ottokar IV of Styria was childless and related to the Babenberger house, and whatever chagrin Frederick Barbarossa may have felt had to be concealed. For at this time the Emperor was too deeply involved in Guelf and papal politics to risk arousing a new and formidable opposition north of the Alps. Even though Frederick I had won in the struggle in Saxony with Henry the Lion, he did not want that struggle to be repeated in Austria. Leopold V had the Emperor at the point of his sword, and he knew it. Nothing in feudal law could prevent the Styrian Margrave from willing his allodial lands, his ministerial rights, his advocacies, etc., to his relative; and with these in his possession the Austrian Duke was so intrenched in the Steiermark that he could have defied the imperial ban, if it had been issued. Like his father, Henry VI, too, deemed discretion the better part of valor, and in 1192 formally invested Leopold with the possession of Styria.

This acquisition carried with it an implied claim of the

Austria up to the Hapsburg Conquest

||||= Probable limits of the Bavarian Ostmark, about 976

\\\\= Lands annexed to Austria by Ottocar II of Bohemia

≡= Conquests of the Babenburg margraves and dukes

*= Cities serving as capitals of the Austrian state at various times

‡= Seats of bishoprics

Babenbergers upon Carinthia. For in 1122, when the Eppenstein house in Carinthia died out, their rich possessions had fallen to the margraves of Styria, which now in turn passed to the Duke of Austria. The new ducal house installed in Carinthia by Henry V, the Sponheimer, held the duchy as vassals of the Emperor, it is true; but the Babenbergers had a strong foothold in the territory. Yet they were never able wholly to realize their ambition there. The extinction of the Babenberger house in 1254, and of the Sponheimer family in 1269, left Carinthia open to appropriation by the first comer, and Ottokar of Bohemia temporarily acquired possession, by a bold policy, of Austria, Carinthia, and Carniola during the interregnum.

The accession of Rudolf of Habsburg, however, to the imperial throne in 1273 soon changed the political situation in Southeastern Germany. For when Ottokar fell in the battle of the Marchfeld in 1278, Austria, Styria, Carinthia, and Carniola became Habsburg possessions. Rudolf gave the last two to Meinhard, count of Görz and Tyrol in 1286, thus letting the Slav principalities of the southeastern complex go. It is a pity that the last Habsburgs did not adhere to his wise policy. The history of this angle of Europe would have been different and could not have been worse than it has been in recent years.

CHAPTER XVII

MEDIEVAL GERMAN EXPANSION IN BOHEMIA AND POLAND

THE BOHEMIANS, or Czecho-Slovaks, and the Poles were the only nations of the northern Slavs during the Middle Ages who successfully maintained their national integrity and their national self-consciousness in the face of the enormous German pressure imposed upon them. All the other northern Slavonic tribes of Central Europe, sometimes known as the Elbean or Baltic Slavs, went to ruin like a broken cloud, leaving merely the débris of themselves in the conquered country between the Elbe and the Oder.

But it was not in the nature of things that even the Bohemians and the Poles could retain their ancient racial institutions uninfluenced by contact with Germany. So it came about in the fateful centuries between 800 and 1200 that their religion, their political institutions, their culture, their very blood (that of the Czechs more than that of the Poles), were potently influenced by German attrition and penetration. This permeation of things German, however, was not everywhere either quantitatively or qualitatively in the same proportion. In Silesia, German influence was overwhelming after the twelfth century. In Bohemia, where the process was slower and sometimes not without check or arrest, the spread of German influence continued until the Hussite wars. In Poland the degree of Germanization was never nearly so great as in Silesia and Bohemia. In them all, German colonization was of varying density in different parts of the country. Before the advent of Christianity—that is to say, before the tenth century—the most active German influence was that of commerce and trade.[1]

[1] Cf. Waitz, *Deutsche Verfassungsgesch.*, IV, 70–73 and notes, which are very valuable.

In the feudal age, as today, wedged in between the northern and the southern Slavs, lay the Moravians, the Bohemians, and the Poles, whom we may collectively describe as the "central Slavs." Of these three peoples, the Bohemians and the Moravians became of historical importance in the ninth century. The Poles are not mentioned until the tenth. The Moravians were the first to attract the attention of Frankish historians, when their representatives are mentioned as appearing at the diet of Frankfurt in 822.[1]

The process of consolidation of their separate tribal groups seems to have preceded that of the Bohemians; for, when the Moravians first appear in history, they seem to have been a homogeneous people. Perhaps it was the first Moravian duke of whom we have record, Mojmír (830–46), who effected this union, or at least completed the process of fusion. In 831, we learn of *multae legationes Sclavorum* coming to the court of Louis the Pious at Diedenhofen, among whom Moravian chieftains must certainly have been the most prominent personages.[2]

In 855, Emperor Lothar I made a futile expedition against Rastislav, the Moravian duke.[3] Apparently at this season the whole eastern "Middle Border" was in a state of unrest. For two years later a Frankish punitive expedition was sent into Bohemia against Duke Slavitah, son of the former Duke Viztrach, and drove him to find refuge among the Moravians. But Rastislav evidently had no mind to become compromised with the Frank Emperor through giving asylum to the fugitive. In the issue, a brother of Slavitah, whom he had exiled among the Sorbs, was put up as duke in Bohemia by Frankish power.[4] That Rastislav had learned precaution is further evident by his support of Ludwig the German in 866, when the latter's son (Ludwig the Young) unsuccessfully rebelled against his father.

[1] "In quo conventu omnium orientalium Sclavorum [i.e., *Abodritorum*], Soraborum, Wiltzorum, Beheimorum, Moravanorum, etc." (*Annal. Lauriss* [822]).

[2] *Annal. S. Bertin.* (831); Thegan, *Vita Hlud.*, chap. xlvi.

[3] ". . . . . sine victoria rediit. . . . . Magnam tamen provinciae partem praedis et incendiis vastavit exercitus" (*Annal. Ruod. Fuld.* [855]).

[4] *Ibid.* (857). Cf. Dümmler, *Gesch. d. ostfränk. Reiches*, I, 397; Riezler, *Geschichte Bayerns*, I, 209.

In 869, the whole middle border of Germany seems to have been in insurrection. While the Sorbs and Siusli invaded Thuringia, the Bohemians and Moravians, under the first great Moravian leader, Svatopluk, raided the frontier of Bavaria. Three armies were at once put in the field against them: a Thuringian-Saxon army under Ludwig the Young against the Sorbs, a Bavarian army under Karlmann against Svatopluk, and a Frankish-Swabian army under Charles (the Fat) against Rastislav. The collapse of the whole rebellion followed. Rastislav was captured and immured in a monastery, and the territory of Moravia united with the East Frank kingdom by extension of German county (*Gau*) government over it.[1]

But German hold upon the annexed country was precarious. In 871 a new rising of the Moravians occurred, which spread to the Sorbs and other Slavs of the Elbe. A bloody battle was fought on the Waldaha (Vltava or Moldau), where the German army under command of Archbishop Liutbert of Mainz (by the ninth century the art of war had become an important episcopal accomplishment) won a signal victory. Submission and peace were finally made in 874, when legates of Svatopluk appeared at Forchheim. It is of interest to observe that the head of this mission sent by the Moravian Duke was a Venetian priest named John.

The vassalage of Moravia to the German kingdom was established by this settlement, the payment of annual tribute being required. At the same time the Bohemian duke Bořivoj recognized the overlordship of Svatopluk, whose domination now extended over Lusatia, the Sorb land between the upper Elbe and the Saale, Silesia, western Galicia, and lower Pannonia. This whole vast area was put under the ecclesiastical jurisdiction of the Archbishop of Velehrad (Moravia), with two suffragan bishops. "Greater Moravia" under Svatopluk extended along the eastern frontier of Germany, from the middle of the Elbe to the great plain between the Danube

[1] Dümmler, *Gesch. d. ostfränk. Reiches*, I, 734; "Ueber die südöstl. Marken unter den Karolingern," *Archiv. f. österr. Geschichtsquellen*, X (1854), 40. The first counts were two brothers, Wilhelm and Engelschalk, from the Ostmark (*Annal. Fuld.* [871]).

and the Theiss. But it was too brittle to endure, and fate was adverse to it. The death of the great Duke in 892, the partition of his territories between three rival sons, and the dread menace of the Magyars wrought its downfall in the last decade of the tenth century.

Yet the greatest factor in the fall of Moravia was not political, but religious, namely, the hostility of the Bavarian clergy. Legend ascribes the introduction of Christianity among the central Slavs—first among the Moravians, later among the Czechs—to the two brothers, Cyril and Methodius, but it is of slender foundation.[1] We have no precise information as to when Christian missionaries first began to labor among the Moravians, though it is almost certain that they came from Regensburg and Passau. But they were not alone and without rivals. For Italian and even Greek missionaries were also there.[2]

As late as 852, Christianity had but slight and insecure hold upon the people of Moravia. Duke Mojmír himself was not a Christian,[3] but did not oppose the missionary work being done in his territory. Privina, Mojmir's vassal duke, who held the territory of present Slovakia, although himself a pagan, aided Archbishop Adalram (821–36) of Salzburg in the erection of a Christian church in his capital city of Nitra, which was completed about 830. It may be believed, however, that this was done more for political than religious reasons.

Between the years 833 and 836, Privina was driven out of his territory by his overlord Mojmír, and took refuge with his neighbor Ratbod, who introduced him to Ludwig the German. Under the influence of the German court, Privina received baptism, and was rewarded later by the gift of a fief in lower Pannonia. Here he built a very strong castle, Moosburg, on the Platten See; and as settlers came in, this place became the oldest town in the region. Evidently, Privina's espousal of the Christian faith paid him well, for in 847, as a

[1] Lippert, *Socialgesch. Böhmens*, I, 131.

[2] Hauck, *Kirchengesch.*, II, 639.

[3] Novotný, *Česke Dějiny*, I, 291, n. 2; Lippert, I, 130 f.

reward for his zeal, Ludwig the German gave him the territory as his hereditary property. Privina's chaplain, Dominic, became famous for his missionary work. In 850, Archbishop Liutpram, in the presence of many Slav nobles, consecrated the first church built at Moosburg, and dedicated it to the honor of the Virgin.[1] Within fifteen years, we are told, lower Pannonia boasted of thirty-two churches, besides several monasteries, like that of Niederaltaich (later acquired by Bavaria), and the bishops of Freising and Salzburg received extensive lands in the region.[2]

Rastislav, who succeeded Mojmír in Moravia in 846, was already a Christian. He was a clear-headed and able man, who saw that if he was to neutralize the continual German penetration, his people must become Christian. He perceived that the German missionaries were tools for the extension of German domination. For these reasons—mainly political, be it observed—he sent (*ca.* 860–61) to Emperor Michael of Byzantium, asking him to dispatch into Moravia some missionaries who knew the Slavonic language.

In response to this invitation, the famous missionary brothers Cyril (his original name was Constantine) and Methodius were sent. Thus the labors of these two blood and spiritual brothers did not begin, but continued, the progress of Christianity, which had already a few years earlier been introduced among the central Slavs. Whether they were actual Greeks or Hellenized Slavs is not certain. They eagerly began the work of evangelization, preaching in the tongue of the people. Cyril, who is said to have invented the Slavonic alphabet, conceived the design of using the vernacular not only in liturgical parts of the service, but even in celebration of the mass.

The enterprise of Cyril and Methodius soon aroused deep resentment among the German clergy, especially that of the bishops of Regensburg and Passau, whose sees were the chief base of German propaganda among the central Slavs. Possibly because of the complaints of these, who regarded the brothers as intruders, if not worse, Cyril and Methodius were

[1] Hauck, II, 635.

[2] Novotný, I, 314.

summoned to Rome by Pope Nicholas I. But before they reached Rome the Pope was dead (867). His successor, Hadrian II, approved the Slavonic liturgy, and Cyril was elevated to episcopal dignity. He, however, preferred to remain in Rome, and there he died in a monastery in 869. Methodius was then consecrated in his brother's stead. On his way back, he stopped at the court of the Pannonian duke, Kocel, the son of Privina, to whom the Duke seems to have suggested the restoration of the ancient metropolitan see of Sirmium,[1] with himself as archbishop. Accordingly, Methodius returned to Rome with this request, which the Pope readily granted.

But the project aroused bitter opposition among the Bavarian bishops. The Archbishop of Salzburg might have consented to the erection of a Moravian bishopric in a suffragan capacity to his own authority. But an archbishopric in a region formerly under his ecclesiastical jurisdiction, and in which Salzburg possessed many lands, was certain to incur his enmity.[2] Upon his return, Methodius seems to have fallen into the hands of these opponents, who treated him shamefully, and one of whom went so far as to slap him in the face. Hermanrich of Passau would have flogged him with a horse-whip, had he not been restrained by his cooler colleagues.[3] Finally, Methodius was dragged away to Freising, where he spent two and a half years in prison. It was not until the pontificate of John VIII (872) that his case came before the *curia* and was decided in his favor. Adalwin of Salzburg was commanded to reinstate him in his diocese, while Hermanerich of Passau and Anno of Freising were suspended from their offices.

[1] *Ibid.*, I, p. 345.

[2] Hauck, II, 646: "Die Deutschen [Bischöfe] machten Method zum Vorwurf, dass er in ein fremdes Gebiet eingedrungen sei; sie gingen davon aus, dass Pannonien zweifellos einen Theil der Salzburger Diozöse bildete. Method leugnete nicht, dass das Eindringen in einen fremden Sprengel verwerflich sei, aber er leugnete, dass dieser Vorwurf ihn treffe; Pannonien gehöre nicht zur Diözese Salzburg: es hänge von Rom ab; nur aus Ehrgeiz hätten die Salzburger die alten Grenzen ihrer Diozöse überschritten."

[3] For the history of this rivalry between the Slavonic and the Latin liturgy see Lippert, I, 154–57.

The Pope again approved the usage of the Slavonic liturgy and declared Methodius' teaching to be orthodox. Apparently, Methodius had won his long and bitter struggle with the German bishops. But the death of John VIII in 882 ruined everything and secured the triumph of the German church in Moravia. A letter purporting to be from the new pope, Stephen V, but actually a forgery made by Wicking of Passau, and a declared foe of the Moravians, was circulated. This alleged bull forbade the use of the Slav liturgy.

Methodius died in 885, having lived long enough to see the German ruination of his work. The German ecclesiastical "steam-roller" was rapidly rolled over Moravia. Some two hundred priests and deacons were driven out of Moravia, Duke Svatopluk apparently complying or conniving with the suppression because the German clergy condoned his notorious marital irregularities. Most of the exiled priests found refuge among the Bulgarians. But some were sold as slaves to Venetian slave-dealers, and probably ended their career in Mohammedan Egypt.[1]

In 890, Stephen V invited Svatopluk to Rome, but the perilous condition of his country forbade.[2] John IX recreated the archbishopric of Moravia (901), in spite of the opposition of the Bavarian bishops. But the hostility of the German clergy and the act of the Pope were alike useless. For a greater power than either had arisen in the bend of the Danube and the lands of the Theiss. By 896 the Magyars were across the latter river. In 900 Moravia was attacked and compelled to implore German assistance. By 906 the Magyars had overrun the country and the Moravian state disappeared. Down to the end of the tenth century it remained a dependency of Hungary. In 1003 it was conquered by the Poles, and in 1030 acquired by Boleslav I of Bohemia.[3]

The passing of the first and earliest Slavonic state in Central Europe, however, was not without compensation; for, as Moravia declined, Bohemia rose.

The earliest mention of the Bohemians occurs in the seventh century, and has to do with the episodic career of

[1] Novotný, I, 392. [2] *Annal. Fuld.* (890).

[3] Bretholz, *Archiv f. öster. Gesch.*, Band LXXXI (1895).

Samo. But permanent contact with the Bohemians was not made by the Franks until 788, when Charles the Great erected the Nordgau or Bohemian Mark, with the old fortress of Wogastisburg, which Karl Martel had earlier constructed at the instance of Boniface, as the chief post. The Eger Valley, which nature indicated as the natural avenue of German penetration into Bohemia, was thereby assured to German control.

Frankish annals, however, make no allusion to border warfare at this time. In fact, Bohemia is not again mentioned until 791,[1] when Charles the Great's army touched the edge of the country while returning from the first expedition against the Avars.[2] It was not until 805 that a Frankish army of invasion entered Bohemia in order to "convert" the heathen Czechs. The Bohemian stronghold of Canburg (we do not know its Czech name) was then besieged, but there is no evidence of its capture. For fourteen days the Frankish army plundered and devastated in the thick and almost pathless Bohemian forest.[3] Then it was that Charles the Great founded the famous frontier post of Bremberg on the Nạb back of Wogastisburg, which was too exposed, and linked it with the long line of border posts which extended from the mouth of the Elbe to the Danube. Two years afterward, in 807, a capitulary made provision for military service *in partibus Beheim*, and there can be little doubt that Frank domination at this time was extended over Bohemia as far as the Mittelgebirge,[4] whose basaltic peaks rise above the serpentine course of the upper Elbe halfway between Dresden and Prague, where the Pfraumberger Pass afforded ingress into the heart of the country. It seems probable that the Bohemians were at this time reduced to tribute by Charles the Great,[5] and included in the famous partition of the Empire made in 817 by Louis the Pious.[6]

[1] Lippert, I, 129.

[2] Czech pressure upon the Avars at this time is noticed by Einhard, *Annales* (805); cf. Zeuss, p. 740.

[3] Invia et saltus penetrantes (*Ann. Einhardi* [805]).

[4] Lippert, I, 137–38.

[5] Einhard, *Vita Caroli*, 15. According to tradition this was 120 oxen and 500 pounds of silver, the same amount that Břetislav paid in 1040, Lippert, I, 138.

[6] *M. G. H. Leges*, III, 198, sec. 2.

The significant features of Czech history in the ninth century are, first, the establishment of the Bavarian Nordgau in 849, as a bulwark both to guard the German frontier and to confront the Czechs; and, second, the internal hardening of the political structure of Bohemia by the consolidation of the "hrady" into counties, and the development of a national Czech chieftain or duke by the elevation of a single ruler above the various clan leaders. In a word, Bohemia began to cease to be a loose agglomeration of various Czechs stems,[1] and slowly to form a more compact national entity.

The legendary first duke of Bohemia was Přemysl, who is actually no more of a historical personage than the legendary Duke Piast, who is alleged to have founded the earliest ruling dynasty of Poland.[2] We can discern the lineaments of this process of political consolidation long before the result was achieved. In the nature of things, as long as the Bohemians were vassal to the Moravian Duke, independent political formation was slow. "Duke" Bořivoj (*ca.* 880–85), because he is alleged to have been baptized and thus to have become an instrument of providence for the conversion of the Czechs, is almost as much a figment of pious edification as Přemysl is of later Czech patriotism.[3]

The earliest mention of the introduction of Christianity into Bohemia is that of fourteen Czech nobles, who, on January 13, 845, appeared at Regensburg before King Ludwig the German and requested baptism.[4] No great importance, however, can be attached to this incident, for Christianity hardly began to get a foothold among the Czechs before 895.

We get on firmer ground in this year, when the two sons of Bořivoj, Spytihněv and Vratislav, recognized the German

[1] The *Annal. Fuld.*, 872, give the names of five of these clan chieftains, *cf. Lippert*, I, 143–47.

[2] Lippert, I, 112–19, has critically analyzed this "Premsylsage."

[3] Lippert, I, 145–47. It is pure legend that Cyril and Methodius ever visited Bohemia; Bretholz, *Mitteil d. Inst. f. österr. Gesch.*, XVI, Heft 1, cf. *Revue Hist.* C. 39 (review of Brückner, *Legendy o Cyrylu Metodym*).

[4] *Annal. Ruod. Fuld.*, 845. It is not said that Regensburg was the place. But this may be inferred, for Bohemia was included within the diocese of Regensburg. It is certain that the earliest missionaries in Bohemia came from Regensburg. See Pandler's *Mitteil. d. nordböhmischen Excursions-Clubs*, XVIII, No. 2 (1895).

overlordship of Arnulf at Regensburg, and fell away from the already shattered and doomed Moravian state. When Bohemia thus became a vassal state of Germany, it also entered into the German ecclesiastical system and was incorporated with the diocese of Regensburg.[1] In this double way the door was opened for the entrance of German institutions, German culture, the German church into Bohemia. Spytihněv introduced German priests who used the Latin liturgy, although the older Slavonic liturgy did not become obsolete for nearly two hundred years. It was he who founded the church of St. Peter and St. Paul at Budeč, near Prague. His brother and successor, Vratislav, established the church of St. George at the castle of Prague.

Nevertheless, although professing Christianity and ecclesiastically subject to a German bishop, the Czechs were far from supinely accepting German ascendancy over their country. Arnulf's precaution was well taken in 895 when he reorganized the Bohemian Mark, incorporating the Bavarian Nordgau with it, and intrusting the office of margrave to his nephew Liutpold.[2]

For the next thirty-four years (895–929) the history of Bohemia is very obscure. In the time of Conrad I (911–19) there is evidence of a colonization wave which threw into the Eger region a great number of Germans from the valleys of the Lahn, the Wetter, and the lower Rhine.[3] At the same time a more aggressive German penetration was taking place from the Bavarian angle of approach. Even before the end of the tenth century Bishop Wolfgang of Regensburg had claimed ecclesiastical jurisdiction over this wilderness country as far as the Chub River, where the Bayerischer Wald shaded off into the greater Böhmer Wald. In this huge forest zone Bavarian pioneers, hardy woodsmen, and border farmers clashed with the advance line of Bohemian settlers where

[1] Lippert, I, p. 167; II, 8–9. This arrangement gave great offense to the Bishop of Würzburg, who laid claim to ecclesiastical jurisdiction over the Slavs of the Main, the Sorben, and the Bohemians on the ground of the foundation of his see in 741 as a missionary station among the Slavs (Schafarik, II, 432).

[2] *Annal. Fuld.* (895); Dümmler, II, 392; Riezler, I, 245.

[3] Gradl, *Mitth. d. Ver. f. Gesch. d. Deutschen in Böhmen*, Band XVIII (1880).

the two expanding movements fused their edges in frontier strife.

Church tradition relates that Vratislav's son Václav succeeded his father in 921, but owing to his minority the administration was in the hands of his pious grandmother, "Saint" Ludmila, during whose rule there was a great influx of monks and nuns, who brought in relics and relic worship, psalters, manuscripts, and the moral and material apparatus of the German church. Modern criticism, however, reduces this alleged large growth of Christianity in Bohemia at this time to low proportions.

Yet there is some evidence of development of German influence during these years, although it was not of that pious nature alleged. It was just at this time that Henry the Fowler's (919–36) military reforms in Saxony were being instituted, and his newfangled warriors whetted their teeth in conflict with the Slavs of the middle and upper Elbe as preliminary training for the King's telling campaign against the Magyars in 933. In 929 Henry and his Saxon forces crossed the Elbe and captured Brandenburg. Before the drive had spent its strength, the Saxons had carried their victorious arms up the river as far as Prague and compelled the Bohemians to pay them tribute.[1]

The victorious drive of the Saxons brought to a head in Bohemia the latent opposition which Václav's weak and pietistic policy had created. Feeling ran high against the "foreign" priests in the land. The national party found a leader in the Duke's able brother Boleslav, the first important Czech in history who, in collusion with his mother Drahomiř, it is said, compassed the assassination of Václav. In German annals this act is represented as a bloodthirsty pagan reaction. But it was really anti-German, not anti-Christian.

A German retaliatory expedition soon afterward invaded Bohemia under command of Count Asic of Merseburg. The army was composed of Saxons, Thuringians, Hessians, and some Slav Massubians compelled to military service, and divided into two columns. Boleslav routed the Thuringian ,

[1] Widukind, I, 35; Lippert, I, 170. Palacký, *Gesch. Böhmens*, I, 232, thinks this the earliest case of tribute.

but was defeated by the Saxons. He rallied his forces, though, and, while the victors were plundering the dead, fell upon them and put them to flight.

Fourteen years of intermittent war followed between the Germans and the Bohemians, under the pressure of which the union of the Czech stems took place and the dukedom became a solid authority.[1] Finally, in 950 Otto the Great came in person into the land and captured Nimburg at the junction of the Elbe and the Medlina, in which Boleslav's son of the same name had taken refuge. Again Bohemia recognized German overlordship and paid tribute.[2]

The long rule of Boleslav I (929–67) is the true period of the formation of Bohemia, but there is no evidence that any German colonization then took place. The most positive German activity in the country at this time seems to have been commercial. These traders, however, really were not Germans, but Jews, who dealt in furs, salt, and especially slaves.

In 971 the Pope authorized the first Bohemian bishopric, that of Prague, which Otto I two years later caused to be erected, not, however, under the jurisdiction of the Bishop of Regensburg, as that prelate had fondly hoped, but under the Archbishop of Mainz.[3] The Emperor was too cautious to permit any political power to pass from Northern to Southern Germany, especially into such a feudal storm center as Bavaria notoriously was.[4] The first bishop of Prague was a Saxon monk from the Benedictine monastery of St. John in Magdeburg, who had lived in Bohemia for a long time and spoke the Czech language. He was not installed until 975 and then the coronation took place at Brumpt in Alsace. At his installation later at Prague in the church of St. Vitus, we are

[1] Lippert, I, 169, 177. The process is evident in Widukind's terminology. He calls Boleslav *rex* and the other Bohemian chiefs *duces*.

[2] Thietmar, *Chronicon*, II, 1; Lippert, I, 173, n. 2.

[3] Spangenberg, "Die Gründung des Bistums Prag," *Hist. Jahrb.*, XXI (1900), 758–73; Schulte, *ibid.*, XXII (1901), 285–97.

[4] Kretschmar, *Hist. Georg.*, p. 433; Lippert, I, 178. This arrangement offended the Archbishop of Magdeburg, who held all the newly established sees in Brandenburg and the Thuringian *Reichsland* under his authority. Perhaps Otto I was afraid of making Magdeburg too powerful.

told that the nobles and the priests chanted in German: "Christe keinado . . . . und die hailigen alle helfuent unse . . . . ," while the common people merely shouted "Krleš."[1]

Twenty years after this event the first monastery was founded in Bohemia, that of Břevnov (993) near Prague. It was richly endowed by Boleslav II. The first monks, twelve in number, are said to have been brought from the mother-monastery of Benedictinism, Monte Cassino, by Bishop Adalbert of Prague, who himself had once been an inmate of it. In 999, just before his death, Boleslav II founded the second Benedictine house in Bohemia, that of St. John on the Ostrov, named from the circumstance that it was situated on an island (*ostrov*) in the Moldau near Davle, south of Prague. This one was filled with monks from Kloster Altaich in Bavaria. The earliest nunnery in Bohemia was that of St. George, established hard by the old chapel of St. George in Prague, the first abbess of which was Boleslav II's youngest daughter, Mlada-Marie.

German influence, with a little Italian admixture, now flowed deeply and rapidly into Bohemia. In addition to things ecclesiastical like relics, missals, manuscripts, etc., a great impulse seems to have been given to trade.[2] The household of the Duke was largely German; Emma, the wife of Boleslav II, was of German birth. The higher and court clergy were German born and German educated. The Duke's own brother, Strachkvas (Christian), was educated in the monastery of St. Emmeran in Regensburg. When Boleslav II was stricken with paralysis he was cared for by Thiddag, a medical monk from Corvey in Westphalia.[3]

It must not be assumed, however, that the political relations between Germany and Bohemia were amicable during these years. German civilization and Christianity were one

[1] See A. Sedláček's article on Bohemia in Otto's *Encyclopaedia*. Novotný explains it by saying that the German chant was used because there was as yet no hymn in the Czech tongue. The later consecration chant "Hospodine pomiluj ny" had not yet been written.

[2] See the documents cited by Lippert, I, 227, which list a long series of articles.

[3] In accordance with Boleslav's wish Thiddag was made the third bishop of Prague, but was so drunken that Boleslav III expelled him, and he sought refuge with Ekkehard of Meissen.

thing, German domination quite another. In 976–77 Otto II made campaigns against Bohemia,[1] and from 985 to 987 there was war between the two states, the rebellion of Bohemia perhaps having been encouraged by the death of Dietrich of the Nordmark and Margrave Rikdag of Thuringia in 985, which relaxed German control of the middle border.[2] The effect was to clamp German overlordship and imposition of the tribute upon Bohemia more heavily than before.[3]

Boleslav II died in 999, and was succeeded by Boleslav III. An insurrection, led by his brother Spytihněv, soon drove him out, together with his mother Judith. It is evident that this rising was motivated by both anti-Christian and anti-German sentiment,[4] combined with the resentment of some of the great families in Bohemia against the ducal house because of its rapidly growing political authority, and who leaned toward German ecclesiasticism as a counterbalance to its increase. One of the most influential of these clans was that of the Slavnik, which Boleslav disposed of by massacre in 995, save a single scion.

This sole survivor was Vojtěch, more famous in history as St. Adalbert (b. 956), the martyred saint of both the Bohemians and the Poles. Adalbert, as we may call him, had been intrusted by his family, who early embraced the Christian faith, to the care of Archbishop Adalbert of Magdeburg, whose name he adopted as his own. In 983 he received orders from Dithmar, bishop of Prague; and in the same year, when Dithmar died, the popular Christian voice in Prague chose Adalbert as the new bishop, in spite of his youth, and he was consecrated by the Archbishop of Mainz on June 29, 983. His asceticism, his intense religious emotionalism, his vigils, so early as this gave him a reputation for sanctity.

[1] K. Uhrlirz, *Die Kriegszüge Kaisers Otto II nach Böhmen* (Prague, 1902).

[2] *Annal. Hild.* (985–87); Thietmar, IV, 7–8; *Ann. Necrol. Fuld.* (985), SS. XIII, 205.

[3] Stumpf, No. 942, grant by Otto III, May 1, 990, to the Moritzkirche in Magdeburg of a third of all the tribute "de tota Boemia in qualicunque re sit, sive in auro, sive in argento, vel pecoribus."

[4] Thietmar, V, 23 (15); Loserth, *Mitteil. d. Inst. f. österr. Gesch.*, Band IV, Heft 2 (1883).

For six years, secretly opposed by the Bohemian Duke, Adalbert labored in a diocese still largely pagan. In 989 he went to Rome and asked for papal permission to resign his see and to enter the monastery of St. Boniface in Rome. John XV granted his request and he became a monk, together with his brother Gaudentius. But the German primate demanded Adalbert's return to Prague. Again, however, he quitted it for Rome, where he became the most intimate friend of Otto III. For the second time the Archbishop of Mainz demanded Adalbert's return to his abandoned diocese. Obedient to the command of Gregory V, he was preparing to go when news of the murder of his family by Boleslav arrested him. Instead he went to Poland, resolved to become a missionary among the wild pagan peoples bordering upon Poland. The Pope gave him an itinerant episcopal title (*episcopus regionarius*). No Christian priest had yet penetrated among the heathen Prussians, whose ferocity was notorious, and thither he and his brother went.[1]

Duke Boleslav the Brave of Poland gave him a boat and a guard of thirty soldiers, and Adalbert floated down the Vistula River to Danzig, whence he went by sea to Samland. At Romowe, now Fischhausen, near Königsberg, he was murdered (April 23, 997). His two companions, having been spared for the moment, made their escape to Poland. Boleslav the Brave recovered Adalbert's remains and removed them to the church of Our Lady in Posen. Thither in the year 1000 came Otto III to do reverence to the memory of his friend.[2]

In Bohemia the insurrection of Spytihněv and the expulsion of Boleslav III and his mother Judith coincided with this event, and an imputation of paganism, or at least of pagan sympathies, rested upon the Bohemian Duke. Moreover, the

[1] Thietmar, VII (VI), 58 (35). Thietmar had a relative and intimate friend named Bruno, son of Count Bruno of Querfurt, who perished as a missionary among the Prussians in 1009, together with eighteen companions.

[2] *Ann. Qued.* (1000); Thietmar, IV, 44 (28), 45; Gregorovius, *Rome in the Middle Ages*, III, 415–16; Zharski, *Die Slavenkriege zur Zeit Ottos III und dessen Pilgerfahrt nach Gnesen;* Zeissberg, "Über die Zusammenkunft Ottos III mit Herzog Boleslav von Polen zu Gnesen," *Ztschft. f. d. österr. Gymn.*, XVIII (1867), 313–48.

anti-German nature of the movement was unmistakable. The Emperor took prompt action. Upon his return from Italy in 1004 a great flotilla of boats was collected at Merseburg to carry munitions and supplies, and a mixed army of Saxons, East Franks, Bavarians, invaded Bohemia via the upper Elbe River, which gave entrance into the heart of the country. Saaz, Vyšehrad, and finally Prague were taken. The rebel Bohemian Duke fled into the wilds of the Erzgebirge and disappeared from history. On its return the German army, in spite of fatigue and hunger, reconquered upper Lusatia from Poland.

The next two dukes of Bohemia, Jaromír and Oldřich (1004–37), were mere puppets of the German crown. The Czech people still lacked sufficient coherence and compactness to resist German influence. In 1032 the Duke refused to come to Merseburg to do homage to Conrad II, but an expedition soon brought him to reason. Balked of expansion westward (for although Czechs and Bavarians clashed in the Boehmer Wald the German eastern frontier was too hard to be pierced), the Bohemian Duke turned instead upon Poland. Moravia, which Poland had seized from the Magyars, was his first conquest.[1]

The anarchy of Poland after the expulsion of Kasimir was taken advantage of by Břetislav I (1037–55) to seize Silesia and Chrobatia from Poland and to conquer Cracow. But in addition to territory the Bohemian Duke was endeavoring to rehabilitate the stain of having persecuted Adalbert of Prague and indirectly of having superinduced his death among the heathen Prussians. Accordingly, in 1039, the body of Adalbert was forcibly removed by the Bohemians from Gnesen to Prague, where it was interred with magnificent honors. On the strength of his new evidence of zeal, Břetislav asked the Pope to elevate the see of Prague to an archbishopric. But Benedict IX, who was incensed at this bold piece of body-snatching, not only refused to do so, but imposed a penance upon the Bohemian Duke.[2]

[1] Bretholz, *Archiv f. österr. Gesch.*, Band LXXX (1895).

[2] For years historians have had doubts in regard to the reality of this translation of Adalbert's remains, and upon the authenticity of his remains at Prague. The

Břetislav I is the first distinguished ruler of Bohemia. His conquest of Silesia and seizure of Chrobatia from Poland was the realization of that Greater Bohemia of which he and his people dreamed.[1] War always increases one-man power; and Břetislav I saw in successful war not only the means of gratifying Czech ambition, but also of suppressing the authority of those local leaders who inhibited his own power. On the other hand, the German kings looked with resentment and suspicion upon this enlargement of Bohemia, and it was their interest to prevent either the enlargement or the consolidation of the ducal power.

Probably it was this fear of Germany that led Břetislav I, in 1039, to make an alliance with King Peter of Hungary, for both states were apprehensive of the extension of German domination over them. But the experiment was a disastrous one. Emperor Henry III, who had just come to the German throne, was the last man to brook such an arrangement. The result was a formidable campaign against Bohemia and the humiliation of Břetislav I at the diet of Regensburg, where he was compelled to pay the huge sum of 8,000 marks as tribute,[2] to restore Chrobatia to Poland, to permit German garrisons in the military posts which he had built in the Böhmer Wald and the Erzgebirge, to repatriate the captive Poles whom he had taken, and to give hostages for future good behavior.

From this time forth the Bohemian court was thronged

---

life of the saint early became the object of pious legend, and moreover the national patriotism of the Bohemians and Poles has mutilated actual history. But all doubt as to the genuineness of the remains interred at Prague was removed in 1880 when Adalbert's tomb was discovered. See a long article in *Theologisch-praktische Quartal-Schrift*, XXXIII, Heft 3 (1880), 437–69. A copious abstract of this may be read in *RQH*, XXIX (1881), 533–52. The literature on Adalbert is enormous, e.g., H. G. Voigt, *Adalbert von Prag: ein Beitrag zur Gesch. der Kirche und des Mönchtums* (1898); and his "Der Missionversuch Adalberts von Prag," *Altpreuss. Monatsschrift*, XXXVIII (1901), 317–97; Lohmeyer, "St. Adalbert, Bischof von Prag," *Zur altpreuss. Gesch.* (Gotha, 1907), 134–79.

[1] "Die Boleslavischen Ideen, die auf die Gründung eines unabhängigen grossslavischen Reiches hinausliefen, hatten in ihm einen fruchtbaren Boden gefunden" (J. Kröger, *Gesch. Böhmens* [from 1041 to 1086]; Leipzig diss. [1880], p. 1).

[2] This tribute was commuted in 1041 to military service of 300 Bohemian knights.

with Germans.[1] The two margraves, Otto of Schweinfurt, of the Nordgau, and Ekkard of Meissen were the Duke's close friends. The former, indeed, was Břetislav's brother-in-law, for the Duke had spectacularly abducted Otto's sister, Judith, from the convent of Schweinfurt, where the lady was being educated. She belonged to one of the oldest and noblest families of Germany, the Babenbergers.

Henceforth, through all the wavering allegiance or hostility of Poland and Hungary in the middle of the eleventh century, Bohemia held fast to Germany. This loyalty must not, however, be wholly attributed to spontaneous wish or to fear of Germany's heavy hand coming down again. The territorial ambition of Poland on his north, and the aggressive policy of the Hungarian kings on his south, made it expedient for the Duke of Bohemia to court German favor. Břetislav's donations to the first Bohemian cloister, Břevnov, and also to St. John-on-the-Island, and the erection of a stone wall around Prague are examples of the influence which German ecclesiastical and secular culture had upon him.[2] When he came to die Břetislav manifested that political judgment which so characterized him. Instead of dividing Bohemia up among his sons and thus perpetuating her weakness, he willed old Bohemia to his eldest son, Spytihněv II (1055–61), the three younger sons holding lands only in appanage.

This settlement soon gave ground for a family feud, and Spytihněv II has been represented by Cosmas as a hater of the Germans, who alleges that he expelled all Germans within three days from Bohemia.[3] It is true that his mother, Judith,

[1] "Fidelibus regis ad se vocatis" (Herim. Aug., *Chronicon* [1041]).

[2] Cosmas, I, 12.

[3] *Ibid.*, II, 14. "Prima die, qua intronizatus est, hic magnum et mirabile ac omnibus seculis memorabile fecit hoc sibi memoriale; nam quotquot inventi sunt de gente Teutonica, sive dives sive pauper sive peregrinus, omnes simul in tribus diebus iussit de terra Boemia. . . . ." But this particular passage of Cosmas has for a long time been held in suspicion. Giesebrecht, II, 525, 679, accepts it conditionally, i.e., doubts only that it happened on the day of the coronation; Steindorff, *Heinrich III*, II, 347, accepts it with the reservation: ". . . . ja, wenn man dem Geschichtschreiber Cosmas unbedingt Glauben schenken dürfe. . . . ." Loserth and Bretholz contend that Cosmas cannot be credited here. Novotný, II, 84, also expresses strong doubt as to the accuracy of the passage, and thinks that in this instance Cosmas' strong wish was the father of the statement.

left the country; but the reason for her expulsion is to be found in political complications, not in any anti-German sentiment as such. Cosmas expressly mentions the German abbess of St. Gregory's nunnery as another who was exiled because she had violently protested when Spytihněv demolished a portion of the convent to make room for the palisade he began to erect around Prague. This reputed antagonist of the Germans in Bohemia also drove out Slav monks of Sázava into Hungary and settled the monastery (where the Slavonic liturgy had survived until then) with monks using the Latin liturgy, and under a German abbot. Furthermore, it is certain that numbers of Germans remained in Bohemia; for we find them among the clergy, the traders, and around the court. Spytihněv's wife, Hidda, was related to the powerful German family of Wettin.

The epoch of the war of investiture in Germany decisively fixed the friendly relations between Bohemia and the German kingdom. Henry IV adroitly played off the enmity of Bohemia against the Poles, whose Duke was a strong adherent of the papal cause. In 1080 Duke Břetislav, fighting under the banner of the Emperor, captured the golden lance of the papal counter-king, Rudolf of Swabia, at the battle of Flarchheim. Bohemia's reward for this loyalty came six years later, in 1086, when Henry IV elevated the Duke to the rank of king,[1] but the pope refused to recognize the change. When the Concordat of Worms (1122) concluded the struggle of emperor and pope, the King of Bohemia still retained the old-fashioned sort of control over clerical offices within his kingdom.

The profoundest change in Bohemian life since the introduction of Christianity began just at this time, in the middle of the eleventh century, namely, the influx of German colonists and traders in large numbers. The order and the stages of this movement may be distinguished: first, the trader; second, the monk; third, the farmer in search of cheap land;

[1] Cosmas, II, 37; Kröger, *Gesch. Böhmens*, p. 66. The popes refused to recognize this elevation, and Lothar II, partly owing to his conciliatory ecclesiastical policy, partly owing, one may think, to the notorious hatred of the Bohemians by the Saxons (Otto of Freising, *Gesta Frid.*, I, 22), adhered to the same policy. Full royal recognition of Bohemia came in 1158 (*ibid.*, III, 14).

fourth, the miner. This period coincides with the reign of Břetislav II (1061–92). Commerce was active and of increasing volume. Below the castle of Prague on the Hradčany and in the Vyšehrad Street, besides the rich Jew slave traders, there was gathered a medley of various merchants. This also was the place where the fairs were held. The Prague Fair shortly became famous and attracted merchants from Germany, France, Italy, Poland, Russia. Many of these remained and settled permanently in Prague, especially Italian and French traders. But the German group always predominated, and they formed a compact community near the church of St. Paul, on the Poříči. Břetislav II granted them important privileges, notably the right of self-government under magistrates of their own election, and the right of living under German law. In course of time this German community filled an entire quarter of Prague.

Vladislav I, who drove out his brother Bořivoj II in 1120, was a great promoter of monastic colonization in Bohemia. His most important foundation was the Benedictine abbey of Kladruby (Ger., *Kladrau*) west of Pilsen, in 1115. This monastery was richly endowed; for the original grant comprised no less than 25 manors and the lordship of Zbraslav, in addition to small parcels of land scattered far and wide. The abbey was at first organized with Bohemian monks and a Bohemian abbot. But in 1117, perhaps because of pressure from his German wife, Richenza of Berg, Vladislav I enlarged the house by the introduction of six monks and six lay brothers from the Swabian monastery of Zwifalten. These newcomers, who were deeply imbued with the ideas of monastic reform which the abbey of Hirsau espoused (it was the center for the dissemination of Cluniac ideas in Germany), were scandalized at the looser life which prevailed at Kladruby, and also objected against serving under a Bohemian abbot. Within a year, they left the cloister, telling the King that they would not return unless these objectionable conditions were removed.

The main cause of disaffection was soon made manifest. In 1120 a new colony, which now amounted to twenty members, appeared at Kladruby, and this time the monks brought along their own abbot, whose name was Wizmannus.[1] The Bohemian abbot had to give way, while the German monks contemptuously tolerated the native brothers. The feud between the factions endured for years. After Wizmann's death, in 1124, and that of King Vladislav in 1125, the German monks chose to leave rather than submit to the rule of a Bohemian abbot. In 1130, however, they returned, bringing with them another German abbot, Berthold, who had gained the favor of the new king. After Berthold's death there was no acute struggle over the election of his successor, for by this time the German members seem to have become more contented.

Although the establishment of the Benedictine monasteries in Bohemia was mostly of foreign (German) origin, yet in course of time the incomers seem to have become adapted to the new and strange environment, and gradually the native Czech element became predominant. The history of Kladruby probably illustrates what happened elsewhere—the antagonism between the two races[2] slowly lost the sharpness of its edge, and the native representation finally rose to be the controlling influence in the monastery.

The Premonstratensian canons and the Cistercian monks followed hard upon the Benedictines. The first Premonstratensian house was established in 1140 at Strahov, near the castle of Prague, and was called Mount Zion. In that year, Prior Eberwin of Steinfeld-am-Rhein arrived, and the next year Abbot Geza came with a colony of German brothers to occupy the new foundation. Within ten years four other houses were established.

The Cistercians founded richly endowed monasteries at Plass, north of Pilsen, Sedlec, Mnichovo Hradiště, and Svaté Pole. That of Plass was colonized by monks from Langheim near Bamberg; Sedlec was settled by Bavarian monks.

There is an episode related as to the way in which the monastery of Želivo was refounded by the Premonstratensians which illustrates the competition of the various

[1] Novotný, II, 694.

[2] Ortlieb, *Zwif. Chron.*, chap. i; "quod isdem locus et abbatem et monachos habere de eadem nacione dicebatur"; cf. Novotný, II, 741.

orders for political preferment and for generous donations of land. When Daniel of Prague was elected bishop in 1148 he promised the Premonstratensians of Steinfeld the foundation of Želivo, which was a Benedictine house, and by a trick succeeded in dispossessing the lawful occupants.[1]

Generally speaking, until the end of the twelfth century, German colonization did not penetrate into the mountainous parts of Bohemia.[2] When German occupation of the territory of the Elbean Slavs was at its height, after the Sorben land, Mecklenburg and Pomerania, had been Germanized, the overflow of German settlers from points farther west began to pour over in some volume into Bohemia. The valley of the Eger was the great gateway of ingress for these pioneers. This movement was much aided by the fact that the Sedlec region came into the possession of the margraves of Wohlburg and of Frederick I in the twelfth century; furthermore, the important monastery of Waldsassen, which owned lands in Bohemia, lay right in the heart of the Eger Valley. The first German villages known in Bohemia are those of Penerit and Neudorf (although it is possible that these are two different names for the same locality) and were settled in 1196.

The group identity and provenience of these German settlers in Bohemia may be discerned and their geographical distribution perceived by a careful examination of the map. Broadly speaking, it may be said that Bavarians and Austrians settled in the south, East Franks from the middle Rhine and Main lands in the west, Saxons—almost all of them miners—in the Erzgebirge. But one finds numbers of examples of scattered *enclaves* of Germanic population, like islets surrounded by a pure Czech people.[3]

[1] Novotný, II, p. 836.

[2] Loserth, *Mitth. d. Ver. f. die Deutschen in Böhmen*, Band XXI, Heft III (1883).

[3] See articles by Schmidt, *ibid.*, Band XXXVI, Heft 3; Klimesch, *ibid.*, Band XXVIII (1890); and especially Hauffen, *ibid.*, Band XXXIV (1895). Schmidt has studied the German islet of Stritschitz (*ibid.*), and Simboeck that of Iglau in *Ztschft. d. Ver. f. d. Gesch. Mährens und Schlesiens*, Band VII (1903). Other places lured the German settlers because of the newly discovered silver mines; thus Jihlava (Iglau) on the Moravian border, first named in the contemporary documents in 1227, grew with unexampled rapidity. Later on Kutná Hora (Kuttenberg) became the most

It is necessary, however, to notice that while German colonists penetrated the Bohemian Grenzwald[1] in their restless search for free land, fully as important an inner Slavonic colonization went on also at the same time, by which the Czechs themselves founded new villages, cleared forests, and drained swamps and moors.[2]

Unlike the cases of Brandenburg, Mecklenburg, Pomerania, and Silesia, the Germanization of Bohemia was not so heavy nor were the settlers so evenly distributed throughout the country. The native Czech population never so lost its identity nor was reduced to such subordination as was the case with the Slav population in the Thuringian Mark, in Brandenburg, Mecklenburg, and Pomerania. On the other hand, it is an exaggeration of the self-sufficiency of medieval Bohemia to say that all the usual trades were practiced in Bohemia before the colonial era began, and that the Germans only brought the German miner's skill and German craft guilds,[3] or to argue that medieval Bohemia owed little to German enterprise outside the great towns.

By the end of the twelfth century the economic development of Bohemia had reached such proportions and the population in the more favorable localities had become so dense that now, on account of the steady pressure from the interior of the country toward the frontiers, settlements of colonists who cleared the forest and wrested for themselves enough tillable land to suffice for their needs grew in numbers. Hitherto the great forests encircling the country on all sides and which screened the frontier had been untouched. This was especially true of such border forests as those separating regions inhabited by populations of the same nationality, as was the case with the southwestern frontiers. The region of the ancient Vitorazsko (Weitra), south of Gratzen, lay in Austria at a later date. This territory, at the time with which we are dealing, politically pertained to Bohemia and was

famous of the mining cities. Likewise the origin of the cities of Německý Brod (Deutsch Brod), Krucemburg, Humpolec, and Přibram is connected with the mining industry.

[1] Kötzschke, *Quellen*, etc., Nos. 22, 23, 24, 25, 26, 27, 37, D.

[2] Lippert, I, 107 f.; 273 f.

[3] Novotný, II, 836.

peopled by a Czech population. But because of its remoteness and isolation it was gradually colonized and Germanized by the Austrian house of Künring.

It fell to Soběslav II's lot to be the defender of the rights of this Czech population, which, penetrating from the Bohemian side, came into collision with the German settlers drifting in from Austria. Soběslav was not minded to allow himself to be robbed of a portion of his territory by these squatters and therefore in 1175 asked the Austrian Margrave to surrender the title to the lands thus alienated. The demand met with a refusal, and a protracted conflict ensued, so bitter and so bloody that both the Emperor and the Pope protested. In the end Soběslav lost his throne in Bohemia, and Emperor Frederick Barbarossa seized the opportunity at the diet of Eger to settle the controversy to the advantage of Austria.[1]

In such manner the Germans settled during the thirteenth century the southern, the western, and the eastern frontiers of Bohemia. As an example of a systematic colonization may be cited the case of the monastery of Břevnov, whose Abbot gave the forests of Politz (near the Silesian border) to two German *Vögte*, Pertold and Wickmann, to be cleared and settled.[2] The vicinity of Litoměřice (Leitmeritz) was the first to be settled; the next settlements were those of Ellbogen (near Karlsbad) and at Saaz (on the Eger).[3]

Sometimes a Bohemian village received so many German colonists that it was practically changed into a German settlement, and then even its ancient name was changed. Thus the counts of Bogen, who held much land in the vicinity of the Bohemian forest, colonized the Czech village of Sušice with so many Germans that its name was changed to Schuttenhofen. When the Teutonic Knights received in 1252 the village of Chomútov (near the Erzgebirge; Ger., *Komotau*) they soon Germanized it so completely that a proverb arose: "You

[1] *Ibid.*, II, p. 1054.

[2] For the history of Břevnov *in extenso* see Winter, *Studien und Mitth. aus dem Bened. und Cisterc. Ord.*, Band XVI, Heft 1 (1895), and Schramm's study of the registers of Břevnov, *ibid.*, Band III, Heft 1 (1882).

[3] Palacký, II, 93.

can find people everywhere except at Chomútov, where there are Germans." Many of these villages were known by two names: thus Teplice was also known as Weckelsdorf, Skalice as Langenau, etc. Some Czech village names were frightfully distorted by this process of Germanization—for instance, Modlibohov was distorted into the impossible appellation of Nudelbaum.

Sometimes a Czech village was compelled to change its ancient character and conform to German practices. The nobles began to re-survey and to partition anew the lands appertaining to these villages, and the Czech peasants were forced to pay rent and to assume all other obligations in the same fashion as the newer settlers. They were compelled to do this for fear of being ejected from their ancient holdings in favor of the German colonists. This process of readjustment went on throughout the fourteenth century, and was not completed until the beginning of the Hussite wars.

King Václav (Wenceslas) was a great friend of the German colonists, and during his reign Bohemia was started on a road which would have led to a complete Germanization of the land. He even went so far as to drive the Czech peasants —his own distant relatives—out of Stadice, from which the founder of the Přemyslid dynasty came, and to settle it with Germans. It is no wonder that with such an example before their eyes the nobles assiduously followed in his steps. Both the King and the nobility, when building or rebuilding a castle (and the land soon bristled with castles,[1] especially after the Tartar invasion of 1241), would give them such names as were in vogue in Bavaria and Swabia. Thus Přimda was changed to Pfrimberg, Zvikov to Klingenberg, Hrádek to Burglin, Hluboká to Froburg, and Loket to Ellbogen. As for the new castles, we find Plankenberg (1220), and soon after that appear Lewenberg, Sternberg, Rysenburg, Rosenberg, Winterberg, and Rosenthal (now Rožmitál), so that a castle with a Czech name soon became a great rarity. This custom of giving the castles German names continued down to the fifteenth century.

[1] Building in stone first appears in the twelfth century in Bohemia (Lippert, I, 229–30; 432–33).

The monasteries, those very active centers of Germanizing influence, also did their share in the work of colonization in the thirteenth century, both in Czecho-Slovak and Polish lands. The Premonstratensians had a monastery at Chotěšov (Choteschau, southwest of Pilsen), and the Benedictines a priory at Politz (near the Silesian Glatz), both of which were founded in 1213. A commandery of the Teutonic Knights was instituted at the church of St. Benedict at Prague, and the first Dominican preaching friars were housed at St. Clement's in Prague in 1226. In Moravia, Vladislav Heinrich founded the Cistercian monastery at Velehrad in 1201. That the first monks were Germans is evident from those of their names attached to the charter: the abbot's name was Ticelin, and the names of the monks are Walkun, Eberhard, Gerung, Hartmut, and Pertold—all Germans.[1] They came from the Plass monastery in Bohemia. To these monks the ancient Slavic liturgy and customs savored too much of heathenism, and therefore we find a studied neglect as far as concerns any mention of the ancient glory of Velehrad, where the body of Archbishop Methodius lay. In 1211 a nunnery of the Cistercian Order was founded at Doubravník, and in 1225 the pious Hedwig of Znojmo founded and richly endowed the nunnery at Oslavany (or Marienthal) near Brno. In 1232 the widowed Queen Constance established another cloister at Tišňov, which was called "The Door of Heaven"; in 1251 Boček, the lord of Kunštát and Poděbrady, founded the monastery at Ždár (Saar) on the Bohemian frontier. The Premonstratensians built a monastery at Zabřdovice (Obrowitz) and a nunnery at Nová Říše (Neu-Reisch).

As for the military orders, the Knights of St. John were permitted by Markgrave Vladislav to settle the German colonists anywhere on their lands, and these settlers were exempted from the local (*župan*) laws and permitted to be governed by their own written law. The main feature of this German right was the fact that the Germans were thus freed from the various local (*župan*) duties and obligations, such as the upkeep of the fortifications, bridges, and roads, and the

[1] Dudik, *Dějiny Moravy*, VI, 23.

transportation, accommodation, and the boarding of the traveling district or crown officials. Other military orders were introduced into the country in the reign of King Václav I (1230–53). The Templars came in 1232, and twenty years later built the church of St. Lawrence in the old part of Prague; the Hospitalers came to Prague in 1238, and occupied two churches, that of St. Francis on the bridge, and the old German church of St. Peter.

The Dominicans came to Moravia shortly after 1227, as is evident from two bulls of Pope Gregory IX sent to Bishop Robert of Olmütz, who—it is interesting to note in passing—was an Englishman. As early as 1230 there is record of a convent of the Dominicans in Olmütz, and in 1239 in Znojmo, and in 1241 in Brno. The Franciscans, who arrived within the lifetime of the founder of their order, established their first house at Doubravník. Among these begging friars were not only Germans, but also Italians, and we find that they held services in their own language. Both these orders soon became involved in commercial enterprises, and thus interfered with the native interests.

Town-planting also went on apace with colonization during these eventful years of the twelfth and thirteenth centuries. The German colony in Prague, as we have seen, was the oldest, the greatest, and the richest foreign group within the country. Prior to 1203 it was the only important German urban element. All other German settlements in the land were either in rural localities or in the mountainous mining regions. Soběslav II (1173–79) demands special attention because of his very favorable attitude toward the German merchant colony in Prague. It was in his time that this group overflowed its original street and spread over a whole quarter. He not only confirmed the old privileges granted by Břetislav II, but materially extended them.[1] It would be an error, however, to think that Soběslav II so favored the Germans in Prague because of sentiment or attachment. His motives were those of practical advantage, of commercial and econ-

[1] Kötzschke, *Quellen*, No. 32; Lippert, I, 98–99; Werunsky, *Mitth d. Ver. f. d. Deutschen in Böhmen* (1881).

omic expediency. Thus the Prague colony continued to grow apace. By the time of Otakar I (1198–1230) it occupied almost the whole area of the Old Town, was surrounded by its own wall and moat, and formed a veritable town apart.

The first town in Bohemia to receive Magdeburg law (the basis of most of the municipal law in the country) was Litoměřice, but it is not certain whether this took place in the time of Otakar I or not until the time of Václav I. Then follow Kadaň on the Eger, Hroznětín (1213), Hradec on the Elbe (1225), Kynšperk (1232), Roudnice (1237), etc. Many of these originally were German foundations, but in the course of time a Czech population settled in them and gradually changed the social texture of these towns into that of its own nationality.[1]

The Poles were the latest of the Slav race to emerge into the light of recorded history, their prehistoric history extending almost to the year 1000. Roman and Byzantine historians and geographers knew nothing of the so-called Lekhites. Our knowledge of them is of an archaeological character. The Poles claim a legendary dynast in Piast.[2] But historical Poland only begins dimly to emerge out of the age of myth-making late in the tenth century under the rule of Mieszko of Poznan' or Posen (963–92), when German subjugation of the Ljutizi and Milzini, with whom the Poles had affiliation if not affinity, began to fill the Poles with apprehension.[3] This conquest was the achievement of the heroic Margrave Gero, after whom the whole territory between the upper Elbe and the Bober rivers was first called Marca Geronis. Here, too, as in the Sorben Mark, the native Slavonic population was reduced to serfdom.[4] Already as early as 963 we find Mark Lausitz distinguished from the Ostmark, and even a vague

[1] Palacky, II, 93.

[2] Gajsler, *Przegl. Hist.*, Vol. VI (1900), detected an analogy between the legend of St. Germain d'Auxerre and that of Piast, and has shown that each is derived from the same source, which is still unknown. Cf. *Revue hist.*, C, 398.

[3] Widukind, *Rerum gest. Sax.*, III, 68; Thietmar, *Chronicon*, II, 14; Schafarik II, 392.

[4] Ermisch, *Archiv f. sächs. Gesch.*, V, 73 f.

cleavage between upper and lower Lausitz.[1] When the great[2] Margrave died in 865 the middle border was divided by Otto I into several marks, which remained separate or were combined in the years which followed according to the influence of events. But in the fluctuation the Mark Lausitz stands out more and more clearly as the German bulwark against the Poles.

The future German conquest of Silesia is also foreshadowed as early as the reign of Otto I. For German political ambition, German expansive energy, the German colonizing spirit already in the tenth century dreamed of possessing the big tract of Slav land inclosed between the Katzbach, the Glatzer Neisse, and the upper Oder, the most striking feature of whose physiography was Mount Zlenz or Mount Zobten, a rugged mountain twenty-three miles southwest of a still undreamed-of Breslau. At some unknown date in the reign of Otto I a German Burgward was built at Nimptsch on the little river Lohe. Probably the site was originally an important palisaded Slavonic runddorf, like so many other German places in this land.[3] We are ignorant of the German name of this remote Burgward, indeed it may never have had one, but may have been called Nemzi, as it was named by the Slavs.[4]

With a rashness bordering upon foolhardiness German imperialism even coveted possession of the land beyond the Oder. In 979 Margrave Hodo, with the design of compelling the Polish Duke to pay tribute to Germany for the territory between the Oder and the Warthe rivers, made a foolhardy expedition into this region and was badly defeated near

[1] Thietmar, *Chronicon*, II, 9.

[2] He is called *magnus* by Widukind, III, 54 and 75; Thietmar, VI, 57; *Annal. Qued.* (1013).

[3] Soehnel, *Schlesiens Vorzeit in Bild und Schrift*, Band VI, Heft 1 (1894).

[4] It must have been lost by the Germans in 979 though no chronicler records the fact. Thietmar, VIII, 59, is the only historian who records the foundation of Nimptsch, and he is indefinite: ". . . . ad urbem Nemzi eo quod a nostris olim sit condita." The Polish word *niemiec*, Bohemian *němec*, Sorab *nimz*, Russian *niemetz*, all signify one who does not understand the Slav language and hence a foreigner, primarily a German. The usage is exactly similar to German use of the terms *Wend* and *Wälsch*.

Zehden, a Polish village on the right bank of the Oder.[1] But while the Poles were able to resist German military pressure by force of arms, they nevertheless began to succumb to the penetrating influence of the German church. For in 966 Mieszko married Dobravka—*quod Teutonico sermone Bona interpretatur*—a sister of Duke Boleslav II of Bohemia, in whose train the first Christian priests entered Poland.[2] Two years later the bishopric of Poznan was established, whose first incumbent was Jordan, a German.[3]

The great uprising of the Slavs of the Elbe in 983 might have been more compromising than it was to Germany if it had not been for the fortunate fact that the dukes of Bohemia and Poland fell out in 990 in spite of the marriage alliance between them. The former sought the alliance of the recently subjugated Liutizi, whereupon Mieszko appealed to the Germans for assistance. The empress-mother, Theophano, played her hand adroitly. In the upshot Poland recognized German overlordship over the territory between the Oder and the Warthe, and Bohemia was subjected to greater tribute.[4] For the first time in history a Polish duke visited Germany. Mieszko was present at the Easter celebration at Quedlinburg on April 5, 991. Both the clever woman who had brought him to terms and he died soon afterward—the Empress on June 15, 991; Mieszko in the following year.

His successor was his son, Boleslav Chrobry, or "the Brave,"[5] who at first dissembled his conquering ambition, and when the Slavs of the Elbe rebelled in 994, all except the Sorben, he came to the support of Otto III with a joint Polish-Bohemian army,[6] and kept the Ljutizi overawed while

[1] Bruno, *Vita S Adalb.*, chap. x (SS. IV, 598); Thietmar, II, 29; Giesebrecht, *Otto II*, p. 147.

[2] Thietmar, IV, 55.

[3] Schafarik, II, 393.

[4] *Annal. Hildesh.* (990); Thietmar, IV, 9–10; Diploma of Otto III (May 1, 991), in Stumpf, *Regesta*, No. 942, endowing the church of St. Moritz in Magdeburg with a tithe "de tota Boemia in qualicunque re sit, sive in auro, sive in argento vel pecoribus."

[5] Thietmar, V, 23, explains the word literally to mean "potestas exercitus."

[6] "Cum magno exercitu necnon Boemani cum filio alterius Bolizlau" (*Annal. Qued.* [995]).

the Saxon army campaigned in Mecklenburg and the Havel land.[1] But while the young Emperor was away in Italy in the next year (996) the Slavs of the Havel and the irrepressible Ljutizi raided the German frontier settlements and again had to be drubbed into submission by the Westphalian heerban.[2] The Polish Duke shrewdly took advantage of these circumstances and seems coolly to have paid himself for his recent aid by extending his sway across the Oder as far as the Bober River, an extension to which Otto III seems to have acquiesced.[3] Perhaps the young Emperor was influenced by his projected sentimental journey to the tomb of his friend, Adalbert of Prague, who had been murdered while laboring as a missionary among the heathen Prussians, and whose remains had been recovered by Boleslav and were now interred in the cathedral church of Gnesen.

Boleslav Chrobry resolved to utilize the imperial pilgrimage for his own advantage, and persuaded the Emperor to permit the erection of Gnesen to an archbishopric, the Pope's sanction having been previously secured by a promise that Poland would pay Peter's pence to Rome.[4] Breslau, Cracow, and Kolberg (Polish, Kolobrzeg) were put under Gnesen's ecclesiastical jurisdiction.[5] Only the bishopric of Poznan remained still subject to the Archbishop of Magdeburg, to his vast indignation.

The sequel soon showed the cunning of Boleslav Chrobry. Emperor Otto III died in 1002, and in the same year Margrave Ekkehard of Meissen, whose prowess had made him the bulwark of the eastern border of Germany, also died.[6] While the new emperor, Henry II, was engaged in subduing the rebellious margrave Henry of the Bavarian Nordgau, he fell upon the Lausitzer and Milziener Marks—"omnem Gero-

[1] Otto III was at Wismar on Sept. 10, at Neustrelitz on Oct. 3, at Havelberg on Oct. 6.

[2] *Annal. Qued.* (997).

[3] Thietmar, IV, 45.

[4] Grünhagen, p. 7.

[5] Stumpf, No. 1213. The date is March 15, 1000.

[6] Thietmar, V, 7 (5), eulogizes him as "decus regni, solatium patriae, comes suis, terror inimicis et per omnia perfectissimus."

nis marcham comitis citra Albim jacentem," wails Thietmar of Merseburg,[1] including Bautzen, Strehla, and Meissen. The whole Thuringian Mark east of the Elbe was lost.[2] The booty was immense. The rugged Bishop of Merseburg whose father had been a soldier in these border lands vents his indignation in no measured words: "God forgive the Emperor," he exclaims, "for ever having elevated Boleslav of Poland after he had once been reduced to tribute."[3] Flushed with this victory the Duke then turned his arms on Moravia, in dispute between Poland and Bohemia, and conquered it.

The Poland of Boleslav Chrobry was a country of formidable but fragile power. It was a country without natural frontiers, whose borders were easy to expand but difficult to retain. The Poles were warlike and brave, but incapable of making solid conquests. Poland's expansion at this time was more due to the weakness or divided state of her neighbors than to Polish prowess and Polish discipline.

But for the time being the militant ambition of Boleslav Chrobry now became a formidable bar to German eastward expansion and a menace to the whole middle border. Moreover, the critical condition of German politics in Italy handicapped Henry II and prevented effective measures against him for years. Fortunately for Germany the Redarii and the Ljutizi remained quiet, although the Milzini joined the Poles. An expedition made in the midst of winter for the purpose of punishing the Milzini and destroying the strongholds which Boleslav Chrobry had erected failed on account of the severity of the weather.[4] But in the next year (1005) Henry II invaded Poland in a devastating raid almost as far as Posen. Yet it was a futile military gesture. For the Poles fell back into their forests and swamps, to emerge in 1007 when the Emperor was in Flanders and deluge the whole part of the Mark beyond the Elbe again with fire and sword.[5] The entire province east of the river was devastated *juxta Magadaburch*, the settlements destroyed, the settlers either slain or taken

[1] V, 9. [2] *Ibid.*, V, 18. [3] V, 10.

[4] *Annal. Qued.* (1003); Adalboldi, *Vita Heinr.*, chap. xxx (SS. IV, 691).

[5] Thietmar, VI, 33, 34; *Annal. Qued.* (1007).

captive. Only the brave Margrave Hermann of Bautzen held out until succor proved impossible. There was a rude sense of honor in the surrender. The Polish Duke permitted the Margrave, his garrison, and all others within the fortress to return with their possessions, sad but free, to Germany.[1]

For three years the Poles remained unmolested in the conquered territory. A new German campaign in the summer of 1010 was frustrated by heavy rains which inundated the rivers and drowned the land.[2] But Henry II was determined to bring the Poles to terms. In 1012 Lebusa near the confluence of the Warthe with the Oder was converted into a gigantic military base. The stockade was large enough to hold ten thousand men within it, had twelve gates, and was built in two weeks. The Bishop of Merseburg grows so enthusiastic about this camp that he compares it with the camp of Caesar near Dyrrhacium, which shows that the Bishop had read Lucan's *Pharsalia*.[3] How far the Emperor relied upon church contingents is shown by the interesting fact that the Archbishop of Magdeburg and the bishops of Meissen, Halberstadt, Paderborn, Havelberg, Hildesheim, and Zeitz were all called upon for military service. But misfortune befell. Tagino of Magdeburg died on June 9 and his successor Walthard on August 12. Thietmar of Merseburg, the historian, after starting for Lebusa, was forced to return owing to illness. Henry II had not yet joined the army and the host had not entirely gathered, when on August 20 Boleslav Chrobry suddenly stormed Lebusa, slew a thousand of the garrison, and captured more. The Poles gorged themselves with the food and wine found there, divided the plunder, fired the fortress, and retired victoriously.[4] It was the darkest day the middle border had ever seen.

Not content with this success, the ambitious and energetic Boleslav also hatched a design for extension of Polish power

[1] "Licentiam hinc exeundi cum omnibus quae habebant . . . . urbem ei reddiderunt tristesque patriam repedebant" (Thietmar, VI, 34).

[2] ". . . . Crebra imbrium inundatione nostri tardarentur" (*ibid.*, VI, 56).

[3] Thietmar, VI, 59.

[4] Thietmar, VII, 20; *Annal. Magdeb.* (SS. XVI, 164).

in Russia. Diplomacy and war were his two agents. By means of the first he had succeeded in betrothing his daughter to the son of Vladimir, grand duke of Kiev, and force of arms was soon to follow. At this moment (1013) the Russian Duke was involved in trouble with the Tartar Petchenegs in the south, with whom Boleslav connived.[1] Accordingly he feigned to desire peace with the Germans, and in February, 1013, sent his son Mieszko II to Magdeburg, *cum magnis muneribus*, with an overture of peace, and later in May himself came to Magdeburg for a conference with the Emperor. Henry II was on the eve of his second Italian campaign, and was only too ready to make terms with Poland,[2] and resigned upper and lower Lausitz to Poland on condition of Polish recognition of German overlordship over the territories. So eager was the Emperor for this diversion of Polish interest away from Germany that he even furnished a contingent of German troops to the Polish Duke.[3]

But the event was soon to prove that "the Poles lied according to their custom."[4] For in 1015 while Henry II, having returned from Italy, was occupied in the western part of his kingdom,[5] Boleslav overran the Thuringian Mark and stormed Meissen. For the time being the Emperor's hands were tied and he could merely send an embassy to protest against the act and demand the restoration of the territory, to which Boleslav haughtily replied that Lausitz pertained to Poland and that he would keep it.[6] A war of two years' duration followed in which Saxon and Bavarian troops, assisted by Bohemian forces, were poured into the east border.[7] Nothing was spared from fire or sword in all the territory between the Elbe and the Bober. The outstanding

[1] Thietmar, VII, 31. See also Röpell, *Gesch. Polens*, I, 145; Hirsch, *Jahrb.*, II, 392.

[2] ". . . .Cum benefitio diu desiderato" (Thietmar, *loc. cit.*).

[3] "Nostris ad hoc auxiliantibus" (*ibid.;* cf. Hirsch, *op. cit.*, II, 396).

[4] *Annal. Hild.* (*anno* 1013).

[5] Thietmar, VIII, 9.

[6] *Annal. Qued.* (1015): "Addidit etiam imperator hoc anno legationem mittere ad Boleslavum pro restituendis regionibus quas abstulerat. Ille, ut solebat, superbe respondit se non solum propria retinere velle, quin potius non sua diripere malle."

[7] It is related at length by Thietmar, VIII, 16–24.

event was the siege of Nimptsch by the German forces, which was unsuccessful owing to an outbreak of pestilence in the army. At Bautzen in January, 1018, peace between Germany and Poland was made by the terms of which Poland was to retain possession of Lausitz, as before, under German suzerainty. The impelling motive of this peace, however, was not the failure before Nimptsch, but the great Slav and pagan reaction at this time in Wagria and the Billunger Mark.[1] The bellicose Boleslav Chrobry now turned his arms against Russia and sacked Kiev, to the vast enrichment of Cracow.[2] But in 1025 Boleslav repudiated the terms of Bautzen, flouted German overlordship over Lausitz, and renewed the war, even having the hardihood of appeal to the Abodrites and Wilzi again to rebel.[3] Yet Polish enmity toward Germany was political, not religious.

For in Poland Boleslav Chrobry's policy was favorable to the church. He tried hard to rid the country of the last vestiges of paganism, and for this reason called foreign monks into the land. In 997 he brought in a few monks of the rule of St. Romuald (Camaldulians), whom he settled near Posen. But they were soon murdered by robbers. The Benedictines were brought into the country about the year 1006, and were settled at Sieciechowie in Radomsko, at Miedzyrzeczi, on the Lysa-Gora at Sandomierz, and at Tyniec upon the Vistula near Cracow.[4] He transferred the bishopric of Kolobrzeg in Pomerania to Kruszwice in Poland, erected another bishopric at Lubush (=Lebus), and finally incorporated the bishopric of Posen with the archbishopric of Gnesen, and thus consolidated all Polish dioceses under one Polish archbishopric.[5]

Boleslav Chrobry is the true founder of Poland. He en-

[1] See Thietmar, IX, 5; Adam of Bremen, II, 40–46; Hirsch, *Heinrich II*, III, 93 f.

[2] According to Thietmar, IX, 32, Kiev had eight markets, which if true attests its commercial importance as a mart between the Baltic and the Black seas and an intermediate between Europe and Constantinople and Baghdad. Cf. Röpell, *Gesch. Polens*, pp. 145 f.; Strahl, *Gesch. d. russischen Staates*, I, 155; Hirsch, *op. cit.*, III, 89.

[3] *Annal. Qued.* (1025); *Annal. Corb.* (1025); Wipo, *Vita Chuonradi*, chap. viii.

[4] Baczynski, *Dzieje Polski*, p. 51.

[5] Tatomir, *Polish History*, p. 16.

larged Poland's frontiers to the edge of the Baltic by overcoming the Pomeranians; he conquered Silesia, Chrobatia, and Moravia from the Czechs; he wrested Lausitz from the Germans; he was the first Polish ruler to war against the Russians. He established bishoprics and monasteries. He had no fixed capital, dwelling turn by turn at Posen, Cracow, Plock, and Breslau.

Boleslav Chrobry died in the year 1025 and was succeeded by his son Mieszko II (1025–34), whose wife Richenza was German.[1] The new Polish Prince, inspired by his father's achievements, was ambitious to do no less than conquer the March of Thuringia for Poland, and in 1028 fell upon the middle border.[2] At this critical juncture Conrad II was in central Saxony,[3] and lost no time in reaching the imperiled tract.[4] While a son of Bretislav of Bohemia invaded Moravia (which, as we have seen, Boleslav Chrobry had wrested from Bohemia in 1003), and successfully recovered it, a German army advanced through "pathless forests, swamps and deserted tracts of territory"[5] upon Bautzen, only to beleaguer it in vain. The German campaign was a dismal failure. The protection of the Saxon Ostmark that winter of 1029–30 was left to Margrave Thietmar and Count Dietrich of Wettin, while the Emperor was in the Rhinelands.[6] But unfortunately the Margarve died early in January, and, taking quick advantage of the event, Mieszko II in the depth of winter fell upon

[1] She was a daughter of the count palatine, Erenfrid (Grünhagen, p. 8), and a sister of Hermann, archbishop of Cologne (*Ann. Magdeb.* [1034]).

[2] *Annal. Hildesh.* (1028): ". . . . Orientales partes Saxoniae cum valido suorum exercitu violenter invasit et incendiis ac depraedationibus peractis . . . . etc."

[3] He was at Dortmund on May 24–26 (Stumpf, Nos. 1972–73); at Paderborn probably in June (*ibid.*, No. 1974); and in Magdeburg on July 1 (*ibid.*, No. 1975).

[4] The charters indicate his continued stay in the east Saxon *pfalzen:* Allstedt, Aug. 1; Wallhausen, Aug. 20, 23; Imbshausen, in Leinegau, Sept. 11; Pöhlde, Oct. 10 (Stumpf, Nos. 1976–80, 1982–83: Bresslau, *Jahrb.*, I, 254, n. 5). Early in 1029 we find him still there (*Vita Godeh.*, chap. xxxv; *Annal. Hildesh.* [1029]).

[5] . . . . silvis deviis, palustribus desertisque locis (*Annal. Hildesh.* [1029]).

[6] "Imp. nat. dom. Paderbrunnen celebravit [he was there on Dec. 31 (Stumpf, No. 1998)], peractisque diebus festis ultra Rhenum ire proposuit." He was in Basel, March 18, in Ingelheim the first week of April where he celebrated Easter (Wipo, *Vita Chuonradi*, chap. xxv; Bresslau, I, 286, n. 1).

the Middle Border with appalling devastation. A hundred towns and villages were fired and destroyed and ten thousand captives carried away.[1] The work of years of German expansion and colonization was undone by one fell stroke. It was not until the next century that the damage was fully repaired.[2]

But Conrad II was made of sterner stuff than his predecessor. Realizing that the situation on the Polish border was an acute one, and not comparable in importance to that in Austria, he made peace (1031) with the Hungarians by yielding the territory between the Fischa and the Leitha to King Stephen of Hungary in order to have a free hand against Poland.[3] In the autumn of the year he drove the Poles out of Nieder Lausitz, and followed up this stroke by a crushing campaign in the next summer. The cards were in the Emperor's hands, for Mieszko II and his brother Otto—the German name is interesting—were at odds, the latter apparently being opposed to the Polish Duke's hostility toward Germany. Driven from Poland into Russia, the fugitive Otto made his way into Germany, where the Emperor welcomed him. The Thuringian Mark and Lausitz were cleared of the invading Poles, and in his turn Mieszko II became a fugitive.

Then followed the first partition of Poland. Lower Lausitz was given to Conrad of Wettin, with whom the particular history of the future great Wettiner house begins; Upper Lausitz was attached to the Mark of Meissen, and the residue of the territory given to Otto as duke under German overlordship. Otto was soon murdered by an unknown assassin, and Mieszko II, whose spirit adversity had now broken, returned to Poland whence he despatched emissaries to Conrad II saying that he would abide by the condition of Polish vassalage to Germany.[4]

[1] *Annal. Magdeb.* (1030); Bresslau, I, 291.

[2] Hauck, IV, 558.

[3] Wipo, *Vita Chuonradi*, chap. xxvi; *Annal. Hildesh.* (1031); *Annal. Altah.* (1033); in error for 1031.

[4] Wipo, *op. cit.*, chap. xxix; *Herim. Aug.* (1032); *Annal. Ratisb.* (1032); Bresslau, II, 481 f.

In 1034 the Polish Duke died, and his son Casimir succeeded him. The event was followed by a simultaneous Polish national, anti-German, and pagan reaction against German ascendancy and influence.[1] The three motives were combined, or rather confused. If it had not been that Christianity in Poland was represented by the German element, the reaction might possibly have been avoided. Poland's policy was anti-German and anti-imperial, not anti-Christian and pagan. It was opposed to German political and ecclesiastical imperialism, but not hostile to Latin Christianity.[2] Richenza was driven out of the country by this faction, and either at the same time with her, or soon afterward, Casimir, who was too much under the influence of his German mother, was also forced to leave the country and sought protection in Saxony. Chaos prevailed in Poland for the next six years (1034–40).

At this time the hostility of all three of the states on the east border, Hungary, Bohemia, and Poland, was pronounced against the Germans. But fortunately for Germany they could not make common cause together, and both Hungary and Poland were torn with internal dissension. Henry III's policy was to let Hungary exhaust herself in internal distraction, crush Bohemia by force of arms, and watch his opportunity in Poland. Accordingly, in 1040, when the Emperor was waging victorious war against the Bohemians, Casimir, whose cause was sustained by the Polish bishops, slipped back again into his own country with German consent, apparently on the understanding that Germany would assist Poland to recover Crobatia from Bohemia in return for Polish recognition of Germany's claim upon Silesia.[3] For eighteen years Casimir managed to hold his own in Poland. But when

[1] *Annal. Magd.* (1034); *Annal. Hild.* (1034); *Chron. Polon.*, I, 19 (SS. IX, 437); Bresslau, II, 491 f.; Roepell, *Gesch. Polens*, I, 174 f.

[2] Zeissberg, "Die öffentliche Meinung im XI. Jahrhundert über Deutschlands Politik gegen Polen," *Ztschft. f. oesterr. Gymn.* XIX, 83–90.

[3] "Primates ergo nostri ejus miseriae compassi . . . . regi decenter dant consilium ut supplicem clementer susciperet et priorem dominatum illi redderet. Quem ubi recepit, jusjurandum regi fecit ut tam fidelis illi maneret, quam miles seniori esse deberet, omnibus amicis ejus fore se amicum, inimicis inimicum, et nihil plus Bolaniae vel ullius regalis provinciae sibimet submittere, nisi duas regiones quas ibi meruit suscipere" (Cosmas, II, 12; Steindorff, I, 112, n. 5).

Boleslav II succeeded in 1058 a situation in Poland adverse to German interest developed.

The precarious internal politics of the middle border in the reign of Henry IV emboldened the Polish policy. The middle border at this time was divided into four segments: the Saxon Ostmark, Mark Lausitz, Mark Meissen, and Mark Zeitz. In the tenth century the crown's control over the margraves in these four areas had been whole and complete. But with the development of feudalism the margraves evinced a disposition to make themselves as independent as possible, and, further, endeavored to establish the hereditability of the margraviates in their houses, as the German duchies were hereditary. Conrad II and Henry III were able to check this inclination, but during the minority of Henry IV it became strongly manifest. When William, Margrave of Meissen, the hero of the engagement in the Theben Pass in 1060, died in the following year, his brother Otto succeeded for a brief season. But when Otto died, the widow of Margrave, William married the ambitious and turbulent Dedi, Margrave of the Saxon Ostmark, who laid claim to Mark Meissen in right of his wife (!), in which he was sustained by that far-from-gentle dame—Lambert of Hersfeld describes her as *saevissima uxor*. The energy of Archbishop Adalbert of Bremen, regent for the young King and loyal to the interests of the crown, however, frustrated this design and the Mark Meissen was intrusted to Count William of Weimar,[1] who in turn was followed by his brother, Otto of Orlamünde. When he died in 1067, the last scion of the Weimar house, Mark Meissen passed to Ekbert of Brunswick (1067), and a year later to his son Ekbert II.

At this juncture Henry IV had reached his majority and assumed personal rule. He was far from being content with seeing the territories of the middle border slip from crown control and become hereditary fiefs, half-independent of the royal authority. The result was that when the great rebellion of Saxony broke out in 1075 and was speedily followed both by revolt on the part of the high feudality and conflict with Gregory VII, Margrave Ekbert II joined with the King's

[1] Lambert of Hersfeld (1062); *Annal. Sax.* (1062).

enemies. The Poles were dangerously near taking advantage of this situation but were foiled by the adroitness of Henry IV, who, as we have seen, played Bohemia against Poland, detached Upper Lausitz and gave it to Wratislav of Bohemia, and thereby accomplished the double result of foiling Poland's designs to attack the middle border once more and acquired Bohemian support as well.

The Pope retaliated by sending the first papal legate to Poland who crowned Boleslav II as king in 1076.[1] Such bold action on the part of the Polish Duke could not go without punishment. A joint German-Bohemian army, in spite of the fact that civil war raged within Germany, soon invaded Poland, and Boleslav II, like the "Winter King" of Bohemia centuries later in 1618, was compelled to fly ignominiously from his realm. He sought refuge in Hungary. His fate is unknown.

Yet contrary to what we might expect, in spite of Polish sympathy with the papal cause the Gregorian reforms had slight effect upon the development of the church in Poland. The Polish episcopate developed without any great dependence upon either Germany or the papacy. In fact, we find that the reforms of Gregory VII hardly penetrated into Poland. The Piast dynasty considered the church to be a political institution, and the bishops were used as the first officials of the crown. The limits of the dioceses were not well defined. Celibacy was unknown. The Polish secular clergy, up to the end of the eleventh century, was composed mostly of foreigners, and therefore could not exert much influence over the people.[2]

On the other hand, monasticism of French Cluniac or Ital-

[1] The strong adherence of Poland to Rome at this time is in contrast with the attitude of Bohemia, which advocated the imperial cause in the struggle of pope and emperor. This attitude of Poland may be attributed to the large influence which Italian monks had in the land (Grünhagen, p. 20). The "Galli" of the chronicles of this time were not all French and Walloons, as is frequently asserted. Some were Italians whose influx and influence have been studied by A. Ptásnik, *Italian Culture in Med. Poland* (in Polish), Warsaw, 1923. Cf. *Revue historique du Sud Est Européen*, I, 296.

[2] Tatomir, *Polish History*, p. 36. Even polygamy obtained among the Poles as late as the time of Cosmas (Lippert, *op. cit.*, I, 205).

ian nature exercised more than slight influence. The monks introduced improved methods of agriculture and brought with them the elements of higher culture. The first chronicler of Poland arrived in 1109 in the person of Martin Gallus, probably a monk from St. Gilles in Provence who entered the country via Italy and Hungary, having been invited by the Bishop of Posen who was a former inmate of the monastery at St. Gilles. The comminglement of foreign cultures—Italian, French, and Flemish—in Poland from now on is interesting. At the beginning of the twelfth century a daughter of a French count, Godfrey of Lyons, was married to a Polish nobleman; another Polish nobleman was the husband of a Flemish wife who in 1109 founded at Gorka a house of Flemish Augustinians who came from Artois. A colony of Walloons was settled in Silesia who introduced flax-raising and linen-making into the land. Russo-Byzantine influence also is observable in the Polish coinage and in the architecture of the church of St. Michael which was built in the first half of the twelfth century by Count Jaxo, a nephew of Count Peter Vlast, the same who founded a house of Flemish Augustinians.

The fall of Boleslav II in 1079 marks a significant development in Polish history. It was less due to German intervention by force of arms than to an uprising of the Polish nobility, the *szlachta*, against him. The fact that this word is not a Polish but a German word (*die Schlacht*) indicates the historical origin of the Polish nobility and points to the fact that there must have been an obscure but influential penetration of German nobles into the land. This class was less pro-German in its sympathies than pro-feudal in its interests. Its aim was similar to that of the great German dukes—to localize and intensify their own power and to make the King their creature. In Germany feudalism did not triumph over the crown until 1250. In Poland it was an ever present factor from now on. In 1093 the magnates, conniving with the discontent of the two sons of the weak Vladislav Hermann, compelled him to divide the kingdom—a second partition, but one due to domestic disaffection and not imposed by foreign force. Great Poland was given to Zbiegniev, Little Poland to

Boleslav, and the king retained Mazovia under his personal domination. The pretext or occasion for this manifestation of power by the nobles was the ineffectual resistance made by the King to Bretislav of Bohemia, who in 1093 invaded Silesia and plundered the whole left bank of the Oder from Castle Ritschen to Glogau, with the exception of Nimptsch, which resisted all attack.

But if selfish and unpatriotic at home, the Polish nobles were warlike and ambitious for conquest abroad. They warred with the Bohemians and Hungarians, conquered Pomerania, even checked Henry V in 1109 before Glogau,[1] and during the troubled reign of Borivoj III (1100–20) of Bohemia overran Silesia, which Poland retained until 1163. The pacific mission of Otto of Bamberg redeemed Pomerania from Polish possession, while the ambition of the Polish magnates continued to rend the kingdom within. Again Poland was partitioned, this time into five parts: Mazovia was retained by the King, but the provinces of Great Poland, Silesia, Sandomir, and Cracow were allotted to his four sons, the eldest of whom, Vladislav II (1138–46), received the territory around Cracow which was now raised to the rank of a grand duchy. His attempt in 1146 to oust his brothers was prevented by the nobles who drove him into exile. His successor was Boleslav IV (1146–73), who was to all intents and purposes a puppet of Frederick Barbarossa and the half-German magnates. His wife was a daughter of Albrecht the Bear of Brandenburg. The discomfiture of the Pope at this ascendancy of German political influence in Poland was so great that anathema was decreed against the Emperor, the Polish magnates, and the Polish bishops for their part in the change. But by this time many of the Polish high clergy were Germans who were more interested in advancing their own ecclesiastical sway in Poland than in promoting papal prerogative there.

Vladislav never regained his throne, but after his death

[1] The *Chron. Polon.*, III, chaps. iv–xiv, gives a long and detailed account of this campaign, not without flattery of the Poles. For it is alleged that the masterly tactics of Boleslav III elicited German praise of him—"cantilena Allemannorum in laudem Boleslavi" (chap. xi).

in 1163 Silesia was divided between his two sons, Boleslav the Tall and Mieszko. Boleslav received Glogau, Liegnitz, Breslau, and Oppeln, while Mieszko received only Ratibor and Teschen.[1] Both princes had spent seventeen years in Germany, and were Germans by education and spirit. Thus the year 1163 is an epoch-making one in the history of the relations between Germany and Poland.

Boleslav the Tall resolved to redeem the land by calling in German settlers. The colonization was conducted systematically by dividing the tracts to be settled into great blocks of a thousand *Hufen*, or about three German square miles in area, partitioning these blocks into farms and intrusting the whole matter of settlement to a contractor, lay or clerical. The rent for these equal areas averaged five German marks.[2] German Cistercians and Premonstratensians were very active in this kind of enterprise. The founding of the Cistercian house of Leubus in 1175 may be regarded as a turning-point in the history of Silesia.[3] Scattered bits of evidence show, however, that the land had been traversed occasionally by German missionaries, merchants, and warriors from as early as the tenth century, and it is logical to conjecture that some of these people took up residence, but no proof is forthcoming in documents that there was any permanent colonization of German stock in Silesia before 1175. An early written record dating back to 990 mentions the presence of German knights at Nimptsch in Upper Silesia, in the pay of Polish landowners of the region.[4] In the early part of the twelfth century we learn of Augustinian monks from the county of Artois, in France, penetrating into the country and establishing in 1109 a monastery on the summit of the Zobten Mountains.[5] These French monks, following the usual practice of the time, introduced Flemings and Walloons into the land, partly as mer-

[1] Grünhagen, p. 23.

[2] Grünhagen, p. 39. The Polish mark was worth less than one-fifth of the German mark.

[3] Charter in Kötzschke, *Quellen zur Geschichte der ostdeutschen Kolonisation*, No. 35; for the history of Leubus see Schulte, *Die Anfänge deutscher Kolonisation in Schlesien* (Festschrift f. Grünhagen, p. 35).

[4] Lamprecht, III, 400.

[5] Michael, I, 89–90, n. 3.

chants and artisans, partly as farmers.[1] Proof of this is found, according to Weinhold, in certain place names, such as *Walgasse* (i.e., *Walhengasse*) to the southeast of Breslau, which name survived as late as the fifteenth century. Jankau and Kreidel also exhibit positive evidence of Walloon habitation introduced by the Augustinians. But, on the whole, French influence as introduced by the Augustinians was never large, and was extinguished by the Germans toward the beginning of the thirteenth century, when they began coming into the country in great numbers.

Even before the establishment of Leubus, there seem to have been two other sources of German penetration and influence into Silesia. One of these had its origin in the war of Frederick I, Barbarossa, against Poland as a consequence of his adopting the cause of the dispossessed claimant to the Polish throne, Vladislav II. His march into Poland as far as Posen in 1157[2] undoubtedly brought in German ways and innovations into the country. This was followed by the importation of German knights by the first Duke of Silesia to help him against the Poles, and also by the invitation to Germans to come into the land and trade and settle there. The other possible source of German penetration anterior to the founding of Leubus is much more dubious. It is the theory of Weinhold that the route of the Rhinelanders who, in the middle of the twelfth century, came into Siebenbürgen upon the invitation of King Geisa II of Hungary, passed through Silesia and that many of them chose to remain there without proceeding farther.[3]

Thus one may distinguish two distinct waves of German immigration into Silesia: an earlier one made up of Low Germans mainly from the Lower Rhine and by people from Holland and Flanders, and a later and more important penetration of Middle Germans. This earlier, or Low German penetration, was part of the general eastern movement of these peoples, the majority of whom came by invitation of

[1] Weinhold, *Die Verbreitung und die Herkunft der Deutschen in Schlesien* (1887), p. 164.

[2] Lamprecht, III, 402; Roepell, pp. 358–60.

[3] Weinhold, p. 206.

monasteries, the secular clergy, and the feudal lords. Along with these lowlanders came some colonists from Hesse, the Lower Rhine, Westphalia, and other western and Rhine regions.[1] It is difficult to determine just what share the Low Germans had in the founding of German villages and cities in Silesia, but probably it was considerable. From linguistic evidence it would seem that the penetration by the Low Germans extended throughout the land. Weinhold cites lists of words and family names that are of Low German origin, pointing out that while the language of Silesia is undoubtedly of a Middle German dialect, the vocabulary reveals words of Low German origin which are clearly not of recent importation.

But, on the whole, this Netherlandish–Low German colonization was small and was followed almost immediately afterward by people of Middle German stock, which soon became the chief source of German settlers into the country and whose dialect became that spoken by the German Silesians today. In the early days these incomers came chiefly from Thuringia and the neighboring regions where Germans had already settled. In fact, there is little difference in the type and culture of the inhabitants who took up residence in Silesia from those that colonized the German regions of Bohemia, Moravia, or Upper Lausitz, Meissen, and the Pleisner country. To these can be added the Germans who came into Zips, and the Burzenland. The proof of this is found in the language, in the place and proper names, in the plan of house and farm, and in the national traditions, says Weinhold. Under Bishop Siroslav, between 1170 and 1189, Germans were settled in the district of Treibnitz; by 1202–3 they were found between Jauer, Schonau, and Bolkenhain; by 1206, around Goldberg; in 1207, around Striegau and Frankenstein; in 1210, in Kittlau near Nimptsch; in 1211 Goldberg adopted German law, as did Breslau in 1214, and all contained German inhabitants. The pattern for the German law and city constitutions seems to have been furnished by Magdeburg.[2]

All the German immigrants into Silesia were freemen and

[1] Michael, p. 102.

[2] Weinhold, p. 167; Michael, p. 102.

were protected by the dukes of Silesia in this status, whenever the Polish nobility or others sought to interfere with them. The Poles living in the German cities, or cities under the German law, enjoyed all the rights and freedom possessed by the German inhabitants. The lot of the German newcomer was vastly better than that of his Polish neighbor. For the first few years after his arrival in Silesia, the colonist that had been invited by the Cistercians was exempt from all dues. Later he had only to pay a moderate yearly rental and to work certain days of the year, especially during harvest time, for the monastery. This improved standard of living and greater liberty of the Germans from the feudal lord had the effect indirectly of improving the lot of the Polish peasant, which heretofore was an exceedingly miserable one.

The coming of the Germans into Silesia immediately benefited the land in the most material way. Heretofore, Silesia had been largely a waste land of sand and swamp and rock, sparsely populated, with no cities and only a few villages of a very rude order, such as Breslau; agriculture was exceedingly elementary, cultivation being performed by a rude wooden plow; the industries of a very primitive order. All this the German *Einwanderung* transformed. Cities and villages were made to flourish, the swamps were drained, the land forced to yield rich harvests, and German civilization brought in.

The contrast along the middle border between the lands peopled by thrifty German colonists and the territory inhabited solely by a Polish population was a striking one. A Cistercian poet, even as late as the fourteenth century, pictures the country of the Poles as a land of forest and fen inhabited by wretchedly poor and lazy Poles who used the forked trunk of a tree for a plow, drawn by a pair of scrawny oxen or cows. The people lived without salt or metal or shoes, and were pitiably clothed. Nowhere was a town to be found. Markets were held in the open air, where barter took the place of coin.[1]

[1] "Nam sine cultore tellus jacuit nemorosa,
Et genus Polonie pauper fuit, haut operosa,
Sulcans in sabulo lignis uncis sine ferro
Et vaccis bobus nisi scivit arare duobus.

The wonder of it is that all this settlement was accomplished peaceably, without bloodshed, and in this fact German colonization of Silesia is quite distinctive from its history in other Wendish lands.

They conquered the land not in war with the sword, but instead as peaceful incomers they occupied it, coming with plow and harrow as peasants, with the spindle, the loom and other hand-labor devices as Burgers, and occupied it entirely through agreements and arrangements. They did not oppress the natives or drive them out. In many parts of the country these two unlike peoples fused together through intermarriage. But the children of such marriages did not follow the servitude of the Poles; instead they followed freedom; they became German.[1]

Under Henry the Bearded (1202–38), whose capital was Breslau, Silesia became an independent and progressive duchy, by a curious reversal of history exercising sway over all the Piast princes. Monastic and lay colonization, commerce and trade and town life, rapidly increased. Neumarkt (formerly Szroda), Löwenburg, Goldberg, Naumburg, Steinau, Guhrau, Ohlau, and Ratibor received Magdeburg law. German colonization progressed so rapidly that along the left bank of the Oder from the river to the mountains, and in the territory between the Bober and the Neisse rivers, the population is estimated to have been between 150,000 and 180,000.[2] Even the old Polish towns of Cracow, Lwow (Lemberg), Poznan (Posen), and Plock received a great influx of German settlers and became German outposts of commerce and political influence. Magdeburg or Halle town law was widely spread; German silver money became the predominating currency; even the municipal records of these Polish towns in the fourteenth century were kept in the German language.

Civitas aut oppidum per terram non fuit ullum,
Sed prope castra fora campestria, broca, capella,
Non sal, non ferrum. numismata nonque metallum,
Non indumenta bona, sed neque calciamenta.
Plebs habuit ulla, pascebat sola jumenta."
—*Monumenta Lubensia* (ed. Wattenbach), p. 15.

[1] Michael, I, p. 104.

[2] Grünhagen, 62; Schmoller, *Forschungen*, XIII, 41, who cites Meitzen.

APPENDIX

TABLE OF POPES AND EMPERORS, 800–1273*

	Popes	Emperors	
795	Leo III	Deposition of Constantine VI by Irene	797
		Charles I (the Great)	800
		(*Following henceforth the new Western line*)	
		Louis I (the Pious)	814
816	Stephen IV		
817	Paschal I		
824	Eugenius II		
827	Valentinus		
827	Gregory IV		
		Lothar I	840
844	Sergius II		
847	Leo IV		
855	Benedict III	Louis II (in Italy)	855
855	(Anastasius, anti-pope)		
858	Nicholas I		
867	Hadrian II		
872	John VIII		
		Charles II, the Bald (W. Frankish)	875
882	Martin II	Charles III, the Fat (E. Frankish)	881
884	Hadrian III	*Interval from* 888	
885	Stephen V		
891	Formosus	Guido (in Italy)	891
		Lambert (in Italy)	894
896	Boniface VI	Arnulf (E. Frankish)	896
896	Stephen VI		
897	Romanus		
897	Theodore II		
898	John IX		
900	Benedict IV	Ludwig (*the Child*)[1]	899
903	Leo V	Louis III, king of Provence (in Italy)	901
903	Christopher		
904	Sergius III		

* The names in italics are those of German Kings who never made any claim to the imperial title.

	Popes	Emperors	
911	Anastasius III	*Conrad I*	911
913	Lando		
914	John X		
		Bérenger (in Italy)	915
		SAXON HOUSE.	
		Henry I the Fowler of Saxony	919
928	Leo VI		
929	Stephen VII		
931	John XI		
936	Leo VII	Otto I (the Great), crowned E.	
939	Stephen VIII	Frankish king at Aachen	936
941	Martin III		
946	Agapetus II		
955	John XII		
		Otto I, crowned emperor at	
963	Leo VIII	Rome	962
964	(Benedict V, anti-pope?)		
965	John XIII		
972	Benedict VI		
		Otto II	973
974	(Boniface VII, anti-pope?)		
974	Domnus II (?)		
974	Benedict VII		
983	John XIV	Otto III	983
985	John XV		
996	Gregory V		
996	(John XVI, anti-pope?)		
999	Sylvester II		
		Henry II (the Saint)	1002
1003	John XVII		
1003	John XVIII		
1009	Sergius IV		
1012	Benedict VIII		
		SALIAN HOUSE	
1024	John XIX	Conrad II (the Salic)	1024
1033	Benedict IX		
		Henry III (the Black)	1039
1044	(Sylvester, anti-pope)		
1045	Gregory VI		
1046	Clement II		
1048	Damasus II		
1048	Leo IX		
1054	Victor II		
		Henry IV	1056
1057	Stephen IX		
1058	Benedict X		

	Popes	Emperors	
1059	Nicholas II		
1061	Alexander II		
1073	Gregory VII (Hildebrand)		
		(Rudolf of Swabia, rival)	1077
1080	(Clement, anti-pope)		
1086	Victor III	(Hermann of Luxemburg, rival) (1081)	
1087	Urban II		
1099	Paschal II	(Conrad of Franconia, rival) (1093)	
1102	(Albert, anti-pope)		
1105	(Sylvester, anti-pope)		
		Henry V	1106
1118	Gelasius II		
1118	(Gregory, anti-pope)		
1119	Calixtus II		
1121	(Celestine, anti-pope)		
1124	Honorius II		
		Lothar II (of Saxony)	1125
1130	Innocent II		
		HOUSE OF SWABIA OR HOHENSTAUFEN	
	(Anacletus, anti-pope)	Conrad III†	1138
1138	(Victor, anti-pope)		
1143	Celestine II		
1144	Lucius II		
1145	Eugenius III		
		Frederick I (Barbarossa)	1152
1153	Anastasius IV		
1154	Hadrian IV		
1159	Alexander III		
1159	(Victor, anti-pope)		
1164	(Paschal, anti-pope)		
1168	(Calixtus, anti-pope)		
1181	Lucius III		
1185	Urban III		
1187	Gregory VIII		
1187	Clement III		
		Henry VI	1190
1191	Celestine III		
1198	Innocent III	Philip (of Swabia), Otto IV† (Guelf) (rivals 1197–1208)	
		Frederick II	1212
1216	Honorius III		
1227	Gregory IX		
1241	Celestine IV		
1241	Vacancy		

† Never actually crowned at Rome.

	Popes	Emperors	
1243	Innocent IV	(Henry Raspe, rival)	1246
		(William of Holland, rival)	1246–7
		Conrad IV†	1250
1254	Alexander IV	*Interregnum*	
		Richard† (earl of Cornwall), Alfonso† (king of Castile) (rivals)	1257
1261	Urban IV		
1265	Clement IV		
1269	Vacancy		
1271	Gregory X		
		Rudolf I† (of Hapsburg)	1273

† Never actually crowned at Rome.

THE WELF AND BILLUNGER FAMILIES

Descent of Lothar II and Otto of Nordheim*

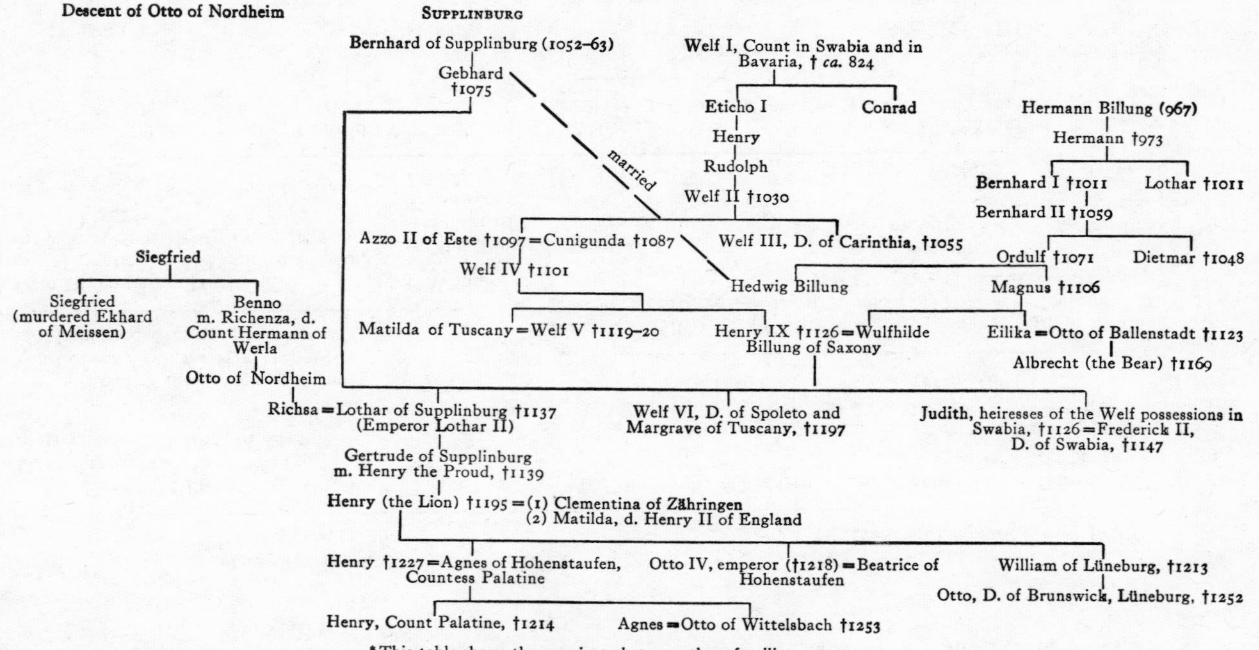

*This table shows the marriages between these families.

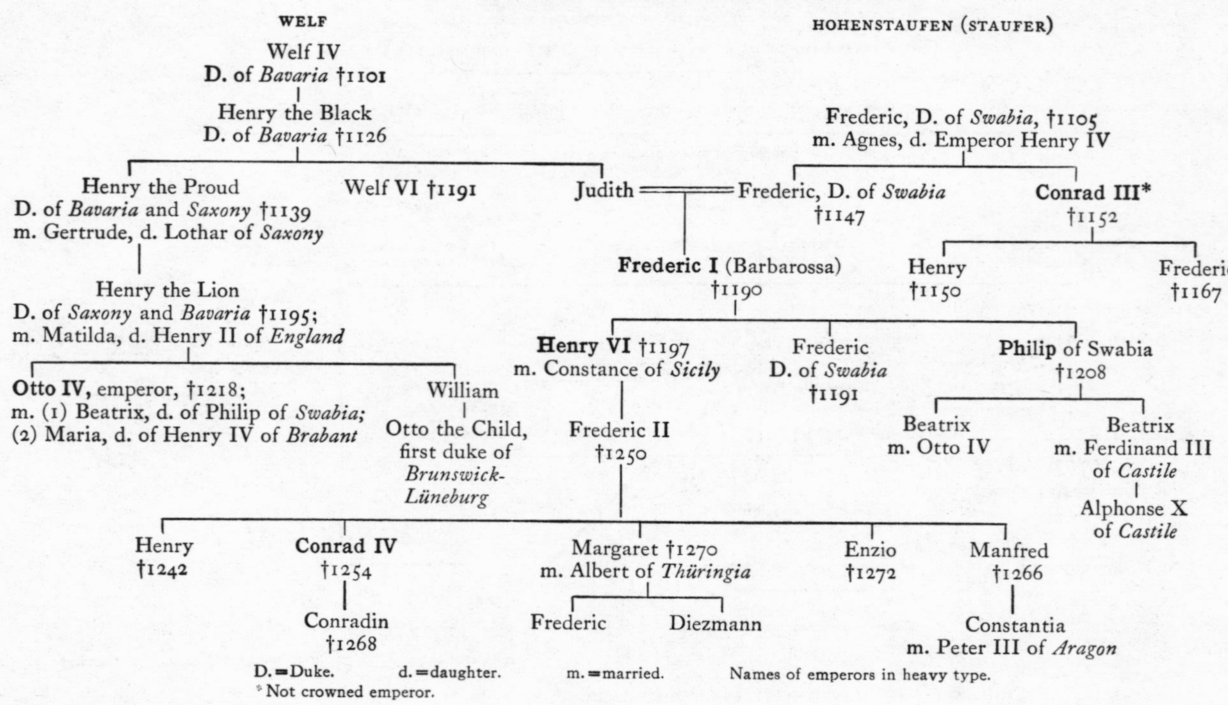
THE WELF AND HOHENSTAUFEN FAMILIES
WELF
Welf IV
D. of Bavaria †1101
Henry the Black
D. of Bavaria †1126
Henry the Proud
D. of Bavaria and Saxony †1139
m. Gertrude, d. Lothar of Saxony
Welf VI †1191
Judith
Henry the Lion
D. of Saxony and Bavaria †1195;
m. Matilda, d. Henry II of England
Otto IV, emperor, †1218;
m. (1) Beatrix, d. of Philip of Swabia;
(2) Maria, d. of Henry IV of Brabant
William
Otto the Child, first duke of Brunswick-Lüneburg
HOHENSTAUFEN (STAUFER)
Frederic, D. of Swabia, †1105
m. Agnes, d. Emperor Henry IV
Frederic, D. of Swabia
†1147
Conrad III*
†1152
Frederic I (Barbarossa)
†1190
Henry
†1150
Frederic
†1167
Henry VI †1197
m. Constance of Sicily
Frederic
D. of Swabia
†1191
Philip of Swabia
†1208
Frederic II
†1250
Beatrix
m. Otto IV
Beatrix
m. Ferdinand III
of Castile
Alphonse X
of Castile
Henry
†1242
Conrad IV
†1254
Conradin
†1268
Margaret †1270
m. Albert of Thüringia
Frederic
Diezmann
Enzio
†1272
Manfred
†1266
Constantia
m. Peter III of Aragon
D. = Duke.
d. = daughter.
m. = married.
Names of emperors in heavy type.
* Not crowned emperor.

THE ABODRITE AND WAGRIAN DUKES

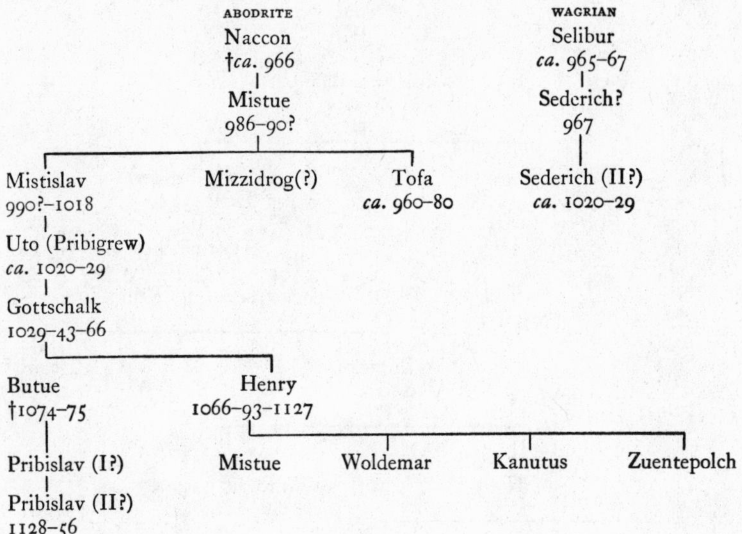
ABODRITE
Naccon
†ca. 966
Mistue
986–90?
Mistislav
990?–1018
Mizzidrog(?)
Tofa
ca. 960–80
Uto (Pribigrew)
ca. 1020–29
Gottschalk
1029–43–66
Butue
†1074–75
Henry
1066–93–1127
Pribislav (I?)
Mistue
Woldemar
Kanutus
Zuentepolch
Pribislav (II?)
1128–56
WAGRIAN
Selibur
ca. 965–67
Sederich?
967
Sederich (II?)
ca. 1020–29

THE SLAVONIC DUKES OF WAGRIA [LATER MECKLENBURG]

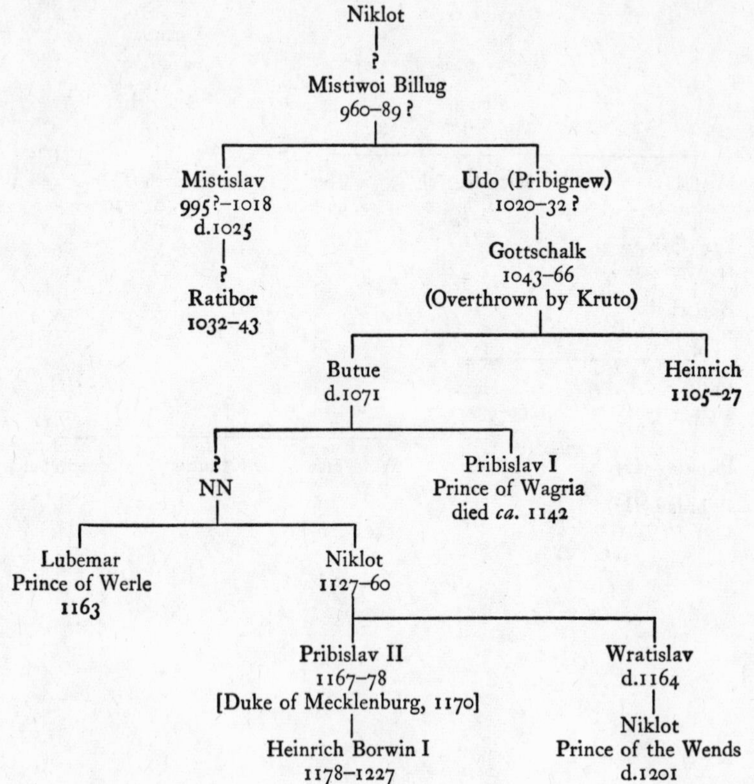

PRINCES OF MORAVIA, BOHEMIA, AND POLAND

Moravia	Bohemia	Poland
Mojmír, 830–46	Bořivoj I, —894	Mieszko I, 960–92
Rastislav, 846–70	Spytihněv, 894–905	Boleslav I (Chrobry), 992–1025
Svatopluk, 870–94	Vratislav I, 905–21	
Mojmír II, 894–906	Václav I, 921–29	Mieszko II, 1025–34
	Boleslav I, 929–67	Kazimir, 1034–58
	Boleslav II, 967–99	Boleslav II (Szczodry), 1058–79
	Boleslav III, 999–1003	
	Jaromír, 1003–12	Vladislav Herman, 1079–1102
	Oldřich, 1012–34	
	Břetislav I, 1034–55	Boleslav II (Krzywousty), 1102–38
	Spytihněv II, 1055–61	
	Vratislav II (king), 1061–92	Vladislav II, 1138–46
		Boleslav IV (Kedzierzawy), 1146–73
	Conrad (duke), 1092	
	Břetislav II, 1092–1100	Mieszko III the Old, 1173–77
	Bořivoj II, 1100–1120	
	Vladislav, 1120–25	Cazimir the Just, 1177–94
	Soběslav I, 1125–40	
	Vladislav II, as king, I, 1140–73	Leszek I the White and Mieszko III, 1194–1202
	Soběslav II, 1173–78	
	Bedřich, 1178–89	
	Conrad Otto, 1189–91	
	Václav II, 1191–92	
		Vladislav III (Laskonogi), 1202–06
	Přemysl Ottokar I, 1192–93	Leszek I the White, 1206–27
	Jindřich Bedřich, 1193–97	Henry I the Bearded, 1231–38
	Vladislav II, 1197	Henry II the Pious, 1238–41
	Přemysl Ottokar I, (again), 1197–1230	Boleslav V the Bashful, 1243–79
	Václav I, 1230–53	

INDEX

Abbreviations: abp.—archbishop; abpc.—archbishopric; abt.—abbot; bp.—bishop; bpc.—bishopric.